THE BOOK OF THE IRISH COUNTRYSIDE

THE BOOK OF THE IRISH COUNTRYSIDE

This book is supported by the ⛊ Kerry Group plc

THE
BLACKSTAFF
PRESS

TOWN HOUSE

First published in 1987 by
The Blackstaff Press Limited
3 Galway Park, Dundonald, Belfast BT16 0AN, Northern Ireland

© Text and illustrations, the contributors, 1987
Designed and produced by
Town House
2 Cambridge Villas, Rathmines, Dublin 6, Ireland
Printed in Northern Ireland by
Brough Cox & Dunn Limited

British Library Cataloguing in Publication Data
The Book of the Irish countryside.
    1. Natural history — Ireland
    508.415   QH143

Library of Congress Cataloging-in-Publication Data
The Book of the Irish countryside.
    Includes index.
    1. Natural history — Ireland.
QH143.B65   1987   508.415   87-18325

ISBN 0-85640-384-9

CONTENTS

INTRODUCTION

Ireland the Outpost is what Grenville Cole called it many years ago. 'Next parish America' is often heard in the west. And that is what Ireland is, an isolated low-lying rectangular blob, with a continental landmass stretching for thousands of miles to the east, and a temperate ocean stretching for thousands of miles to the west.

If sea-level were to rise by no more than 1000 metres, Ireland would be completely submerged. On several occasions in the geological past the area where Ireland now lies has been completely submerged, and sediments with remains of marine animals still cover much of the island. At other times it was an integral part of the European continent, and animals and plants could reach it freely, limited only by climatic conditions. When climate was warm dinosaurs could wander in the north of Ireland, and in a later warm interlude palms could flourish. In a late cold stage northern animals, ranging in size from large woolly mammoths to tiny lemmings wandered throughout Ireland.

Today Ireland is a small island washed by coastal currents which flow up the eastern margin of an ocean. The warmer waters of the North Atlantic Drift and the warm air-masses which they carry along with them lose heat as they move north-eastwards. The cooling air can no longer hold the content of water vapour that it acquired farther south. Its humidity rises, and large quantities of water are discharged as rain. The structure of the air-masses is in a constant state of flux, with the result that winds vary rapidly in direction and velocity, and rainfall comes and goes, while at all times the humidity remains relatively high. While summer temperatures are higher than those of winter, Ireland does not have any regular pattern of seasons. Instead there is an infinitely variable pattern of weather, which provides a never-ending topic of conversation.

If meteorology has provided Ireland with a wide range of weather types, geology is almost as varied. Size for size, few areas of the earth's crust can show such a variety of solid rocks as Ireland, or such a timescale of ages, which range back as far as 2500 million years ago. And the unconsolidated materials, the soils, which rest on the rocks, also show a great range of variety.

Over great areas of many parts of the world, such as central Africa, the climate has remained relatively stable for many millions of years, and weathering – the alteration of rock by atmospheric processes – has gone on undisturbed, penetrating to greater and greater depths. The local rivers were unable to carry off more than a fraction of the weathered debris, and a deep rather uniform mantle of soil has formed.

Until 2 million years ago, Ireland also had such a mantle of soil, but then the earth entered into a period of major climatic instability, which is probably not yet over. Great masses of ice formed in high latitudes, around the south pole as well as around the north, and lobes of ice advanced outwards from the poles. In western Europe the ice-sheets halted more or less along the line of the English Channel, failing to reach the northern coast of France. Though near the limit of the ice, the whole of Ireland was at one time probably covered by it.

This over-running of Ireland by ice had vast consequences for the countryside, its plants, animals and people. Instead of leaving the old soils where they were, the ice collected them up and carried them along. When it had cut down to the underlying still unaltered rock, it ripped off fragments of all sizes and transported them too. The ice moved along in a semi-plastic state, and the collected material – both soils and stones – became intimately commingled.

During these last 2 million years climate was unstable, and at times rises in temperature caused the ice-sheets to melt away. As the ice vanished the debris it had been carrying was deposited as overburden on the underlying rock. Before ice interfered, the soil had borne some relation to the rock below, because it had been derived from it. Now the overlying soil might derive from the debris of rocks totally different to the rock on which the ice deposited it. Sometimes when the ice melted, moving water had no opportunity to sort the released debris, and fine clay and coarse stones lay inextricably mixed together in the resultant deposit. If clay predominated, water found it hard to pass through the deposit, and a heavy, badly drained soil would result; such soils are all too common in Ireland. If stones prevailed, the soil would lose water rapidly and be liable to drought. Meltwater often flowed rapidly in channels under the ice, and gushed out when it reached the melting edge, distributing vast quantities of well-drained sands and gravels. As a result, the soils of Ireland are as varied as its weather and its rocks.

About 10,000 years ago climate in western Europe came back to approximately what we know today. Dramatic movements of plants and animals then set in, as life re-expanded into areas from which it had been driven out by ice and cold. In Ireland the vicissitudes through which the countryside had passed had left a wide variety of ecological niches available for colonisation. There was not a simple advance along a broad front, but a tortuous threading of the way between climatic variation, soil types, mountain ranges and water barriers. The long route to Ireland was heavily obstructed by physical barriers, and was effectively severed when the basin of the Irish Sea was flooded, perhaps as recently as 7500 years ago. The first men and women to reach Ireland, Stone Age people who lived by hunting and fishing, may have been able to enter the country on foot, but their successors, the neolithic (late Stone Age) farmers, must have used boats to bring their families and their domestic animals across the newly born Irish Sea.

Farmers everywhere at all times bring about change in the countryside in which they find themselves. This is inevitable as they substitute their domestic plants and animals for those indigenous in the landscape. What did the Irish countryside look like when the farmers made their first 'environmental impact'?

Except where it was interrupted by rivers, lakes and fens – all occupying areas much greater than they do today – woodlands covered the whole island. But in keeping with the underlying variation in weather, rock and soil, the woodland did not form a uniform carpet, but one of continuous variety. Hazel, one of the earliest trees to return to Ireland, was widely distributed, but was especially common in Tyrone and the surrounding counties. Pine, another early arrival, was very common on the western seaboard from Malin Head to Mizen Head, but was almost unknown in the midlands. Of the broad-leaved trees, rather later in arrival, oak was widely distributed; 'derry', derived from the Irish for oakwood, runs from one end of Ireland to the other as a place-name element. Elm was much more restricted in distribution; it was common on the east coast and especially so in inland Meath, but along the main coastline from Down right round to Wexford it was virtually unknown.

This original variation in tree distribution will have been repeated in the distribution of almost every plant and animal that succeeded in reaching Ireland. The countryside the first Irishmen saw was not a uniform carpet, but a rich and varied tapestry. Looking at the tapestry from a distance one could see major patterns, such as I have outlined for the woodlands, but looking more closely, smaller themes emerged, such as the transition from woodland edge through fen to open-water pond, and the richer ground vegetation where the woodlands opened up on mountain slopes. And smaller again the micro-habitats where the maidenhair fern found shade and humidity in deep cracks in limestone, and northern plants clung to north-facing mountain crags, protected against sun and sheep.

Human efforts at production, whether on the farm or on the factory floor, do not want variety; they want as far as possible a controlled environment in order to reduce the number of working procedures. For protection's sake, farmers want fences round their fields; industrial producers want wide flat floors for ease of operation. The first moment a neolithic farmer struck his sharp-edged polished stone axe against the trunk of an Irish tree, man's transformation of the Irish countryside began.

At first the impact was slight. Lack of metal tools and lack of mechanical devices were limiting factors, but these did not prevent the erection of massive structures such as Newgrange. Much of the landscape around the great Boyne tombs must have been turned into farmland to feed the labourers who carried out the construction.

The first impact was a mere trickle, but the attack swelled rapidly into today's torrent, which carries away vast areas of the environment and leaves behind fenceless tracts of cereals, sheets of coniferous trees, housing sprawls, drab industrial estates and twisting motorway interchanges.

The driving force behind this transformation was the endless search by man to give up or greatly reduce the production of energy by his own muscular effort, and replace it with energy produced by wind, water, fossil fuels or nuclear energy. In this search he has been all too successful. Having made so much energy available, man then sought to use it effectively, and here there are several limiting factors. Environment must be stable, human labour must be eliminated as far as possible, the operation must be on a large scale, and the necessary machinery must be cheap. All this is summed up in the words 'mass production'; and while such production may thrive where environment on a large scale is stable, in a small country like Ireland where environment is highly varied, the emphasis should rather be 'small is beautiful'.

Until forty years ago when the Marshall Plan revitalised industry and agriculture, Ireland had little industry, and agriculture drifted on traditional lines. But when we say 'traditional' we do not necessarily mean 'primitive'. Traditional agriculture had evolved in harmony with the environment through a prolonged period of trial and error. Irish weather is varied, Irish soils are varied, and so the farm carried a range of enterprises, dairy cows, bullocks, sheep, pigs, hens, cereals, potatoes. The summer might be a bad one, but not all the enterprises could fail.

The EEC has put the farmer into 'agribusiness'. He is now over-producing milk, which nobody wants (not even his wife, who gets hers in cartons from the supermarket), and is still constantly at risk from a devastating outbreak of tuberculosis in his crowded herd. To get still more grass he overdoses the soil with nitrogen which leaks down into the groundwater, with poisonous consequences which cannot yet be estimated. Another enterprise is cereals, which he lavishly sprays to remove diseases and pests, which are encouraged to flourish by the crowded conditions under which his monocrop grows. But one windy summer rainstorm will flatten his crop, and also his profits.

And all the time employment falls. Machines do the work for the agri-businessman, and the small farmer cannot tailor his produce to the demands of the supermarket. Land begins to fall idle, and villages and small towns die. Dublin and Belfast already have far too big a proportion of the population of the country, and for those who are not there already, a shoppers' bus will get them there. Soon what is not already engulfed will become in effect giant suburbs, dependent on the cities for all their services. In a scenic area, as the historic villages decay, still more strings of patioed weekend cottages will spring up. The land becomes just so much more scenery, no longer the site of family life and labour, just a Hollywood backdrop.

Most Irish people are unaware of what is happening to their countryside. Litter-louts are promoting that happening. Informed opinion arises from knowledge, and in this book various experts endeavour to show that the tapestry of our countryside, even if tattered and torn in places, still has many areas of interest and beauty. We must all struggle to see that that interest and beauty passes on to our children.

FRANK MITCHELL crowned his academic career when he became Professor of Quaternary Studies at Trinity College Dublin in 1965. The chair was specially created to accommodate his numerous interests. He was President of the Royal Irish Academy from 1976 to 1979, and was elected to the Royal Society in 1973.

All his life Professor Mitchell has been studying – and in the field as much as the laboratory and library – Irish geology, geography, meteorology, botany, zoology, archaeology and human history. It is this impatience with the traditional frontiers between disciplines that makes him a notable teacher.

THE ISLAND OF IRELAND

Frank Mitchell

Earth, sky, water – Ireland has them all in plenty. The quartzite sugarloaves of Wicklow, Connemara and Donegal may be bare of soil and offer exhausting screes to the climber, but on the central lowlands the rock may lie buried by more than one hundred metres of glacial deposit. Rock types change with astonishing rapidity; north of Lisdoonvarna in Clare a few paces will take us from the bare soil-free limestone of the Burren up onto fine-grained impervious shales; the rock pavement decked with flowers gives way to rush-covered sodden slopes. In central Wexford light, well-drained soils produce good malting barley; along its coasts farmers struggle with a wet sticky clayey soil carried in by ice from the floor of the Irish Sea.

We are no longer compelled to look up to the sky, we can look down from it as well. How our weather-forecasters must bless the coming of the satellite. They no longer have to struggle to build up patterns of lows and fronts from data received from various stations; one glance at the satellite image shows it all. How long a given pattern will persist is the problem with Irish forecasting. Will that procession of lows up the east side of the Atlantic continue? Can that anticyclone over Scandinavia build westwards to cover Ireland? The skies not only bring us banks of cloud, they also bring us masses of birds, some to breed, some to enjoy a frost-free winter, some *en route* to distant parts. The Irish sky has always something to show – a cloud, a bird or even a jet trail.

Because of its high rainfall and high humidity, Ireland has water a-plenty. It has the largest lake in the British Isles, Lough Neagh, with a valuable eel fishery, and thousands of small tarns, with small fighting trout. It has rivers, most of them distinguished by tortuous courses to the sea, and important areas of wetlands, many now under threat from drainage. On the whole the Irish countryside is the land of the wellington boot.

The Countryside from Space
The Climate of Ireland
Ireland's Geology
Land of Flying Visits
Island of Birds

Opposite
Satellite image of Ireland.
Grassland is green, arable
land is pale-coloured, bogs
are brown and high
ground is pink.

THE COUNTRYSIDE FROM SPACE

John Feehan

We see the Irish countryside, whose beauty and detail form the subject matter of all the chapters that stretch away into the distance through the pages that lie ahead of us, with the perception of creatures whose eyes and other senses are very close indeed to the earth. We see with eyes that rise no more than two metres above the earth's surface; our horizons are limited by the reach of our eyes, for which the countless other worlds and suns that people our immense universe are mere stabs of light in the forgotten darkness. And yet in the 8000 years that have gone by since the earliest men and women stepped ashore on this island, we have extended our horizons over the reach of the remembered past, to bring the dimmest reaches of lost time into our present. Now we stand on the threshold of looking upon the moment the very universe was sparked into being.

Of course we continue to live and work within our own small time and space. The fabric of our culture, created in its entirety from the materials of the earth beneath our feet, is sewn together and measured on our terms and dimensions. After 8000 years we have covered the entire surface of Ireland with its thin gossamer, the many-patterned hues of which are analysed in such loving detail in this book.

In our lifetime, within the short space of a single generation of human time, we have learned how to stand back from the earth: learned to see it with, quite literally, detached eyes. Of course *remote sensing* is actually much older than this – every time we point a camera we are delegating to eyes other than our own the task of sensing and recording the environment. Colour film has steadily increased its sensitivity and resolution, and ways have been developed to measure the way things reflect bands of the electromagnetic spectrum, such as infra-red, which our eyes are not capable of seeing unaided. However, in the last twenty-five years remote sensing techniques have grown enormously in range and power: we can never see the countryside in quite the same way again, now that we see it from space.

The great remote sensing development of recent years has been the growth of satellite imagery. It is only fifteen years since the first in the Landsat series of earth resource survey satellites was launched by the United States. Two of the Landsat series, Landsat 4 and 5, are currently in orbit, and the first Russian equivalent, Meteor 30, was only launched in 1980. These are what are called *sun-synchronous* satellites: satellites which keep in time with the sun. Their orbit takes them almost over the poles, and is so adjusted that it is passing over any one place on the earth's surface at precisely fixed intervals.

In addition to the *multi-spectral scanner* (MSS) of the earlier Landsats, which recorded data in four wavebands (green, red, near infra-red and infra-red) and had a resolution of 80m – which means that the smallest area of the earth's surface it can distinguish as a separate unit measures 80m square – Landsat 5 has on board the *thematic mapper* (TM) which records data in seven wavebands in the visible, near and middle infra-red spectral bands with a resolution of 30m, and in the thermal infra-red with 120m resolution.

The French SPOT (Système probatoire d'observation de la Terre) satellite was launched on 22 February 1986. It has a different sensor system, the HRV (high-resolution visible) operating in either *panchromatic* (black and white) mode with a resolution of 10m, or *multi-spectral* (three bands) with a resolution of 20m; it also has an important new capability – stereoscopic vision. Like Landsat, it is in a nearly polar, sun-synchronous orbit but at a higher altitude of 832km, and its revisit cycle is slower, at twenty-six days. This is too slow if you are trying to monitor phenomena which develop over a few days or even weeks, but SPOT compensates for this to some extent through its ability to look sideways as well as straight down.

In addition to these countryside-imaging satellites there are many others which specialise in other aspects of the environment. Most familiar of all is Meteosat, whose imaging activities have brought such depressing accuracy, some would say, to our weather forecasts.

As it rotates around the revolving earth, Landsat is constantly *imaging* the surface in never-ending strips of vision 185km wide. But the sensors on board the satellite are not cameras; they are not using film to record the way features at the surface reflect the different wavelengths of visible light. Instead, they measure directly the levels of reflectance in particular parts of the visible and invisible radiation spectrum, and transmit these endless sets of figures directly back to earth. They are stored on tapes, which the highly sophisticated computers we are now learning to live with can read and translate into patterns of colour. These patterns of colour may correspond to the real colours of the earth's surface, but the individual bands can be combined in whatever way we wish, and translated into whatever colours we wish – *false colours* – with results which often show up the structures and relationships at the surface very much more clearly and dramatically.

These patterns of colour, and the reflectance values they represent, are influenced by a whole array of factors – the nature of the vegetation, the soil and its moisture regime, the

Angel's-eye view of Dublin extending out through the Phoenix Park and the surrounding countryside, taken from 832km on 3 March 1986 (SPOT data, © CNES 1986).

underlying geology and so on. In theory, everything at the surface of the earth has its own unique reflectance pattern or *spectral signature*, but in practice we have a long way to go in understanding how the many variables at the surface interact to produce a particular signature. In other words, we have a problem understanding what these colours correspond to in terms of what is actually on the ground. The computer has to be taught the *meaning* of these colour patterns by somebody who knows the ground and its moods in detail – somebody who can point out for instance that the dark brown corresponds to uncut raised bog, the pale brown is bog which has recently been cut, the buff colour is the recolonised bog margin and so on. But once this has been done satisfactorily, the satellite should then be able, with the help of the now tutored computer, to

map the rest of the country's bogs without further human help – and the same applies to all other kinds of land cover.

One of the real advantages of remote sensing is that it provides a tool with the potential to cover the ground quickly and regularly, and to provide accurate, detailed and systematic information on what is there at any given time, so that developments can be monitored and change evaluated without a labour-intensive ground survey that would take many people months or even years to complete, perhaps at great expense. But it does have the disadvantage of not being able to penetrate cloud, and in a country such as Ireland that is a very great drawback, and is one reason why there is great interest in developing satellite-borne *radar*, which is not affected by cloud in this way.

In a sense, the blind sensors of the satellite register more of reality than we do, because even though they are sensitive to only three colours out of the rainbow which washes our senses, they also register colours in the part of the rainbow that is below the horizon of our seeing. Our world is green because our eyes register the green light which vegetation so strongly reflects back into the atmosphere in all its variety of tone and hue, nowhere more vividly than in the Irish countryside. But the stream of infra-red falling upon the earth's surface, which we can't see, is even more strongly reflected by vegetation, and is more affected by changes in the vegetation – as the plants set about implementing their cold season strategies in autumn for instance, or when they are affected by disease or water stress. There are no lyrics about the beauty of

15

Slieve Bloom, 7 February 1983. Upland blanket bog shows up as pink on this false-colour image, dotted by patchy white cloud. Blocks of coniferous woodland are green, built-up areas and areas of bare ground show up pink and the pale green areas are pasture.

the infra-red earth, but if our eyes could see a bit lower in the spectrum there would be. Now with the help of our eyes in space we can 'see' the stream of infra-red radiation, though it has to be translated into visible colour for us to do so. This is why much satellite imagery is reproduced in 'false colour' – in order to allow us to see more clearly than we normally can. In this sense too it is a truer picture of the pattern of radiation at the surface. It also allows us to see the relationships and balances between features in landscape, townscape, seascape, with a clarity that has never been possible before.

One of its most important applications of satellite imagery in Ireland to date has been in the study of fracture patterns in Irish rocks – important since the large base metal deposits at Silvermines, Navan, Tynagh, Gortdrum and many other places are all located along major rock fracture systems, and the new

information from the satellite imagery, used in conjunction with all the available ground information, should prove to be of great value in the selection of new targets for exploration. The last few years have seen a rapid expansion in remote sensing activities in Ireland. Much of this has been in association with the EEC's Joint Research Centre, which has been encouraging member states in the European Community to explore the potential applications of the new generation of satellites in the less favoured areas of the community. There are several important questions which this new research programme will help to answer. Can the new satellites discriminate reflectance patterns with sufficient sensitivity to be able to tell the difference between various types of grassland and other plant communities, and the soil moisture regimes accompanying them, so as to be able to monitor the kind of change that

follows arterial drainage schemes? To what extent can remote sensing replace conventional methods of forest inventory, and be used to monitor the growth and progress of crops? Can it be used to monitor developments in important or sensitive ecosystems, such as uncut bogs?

JOHN FEEHAN was born in Birr in 1946. He read geology and biology at Trinity College Dublin and has worked as a teacher in Ireland, England and central and southern Africa. His research interests include environmental survey methodology and pollination in African mistletoes; he has published books, papers and articles on environmental history, biology, geology and archaeology. He is married with two children and is at present working on a new television series covering various aspects of the Irish landscape.

THE CLIMATE OF IRELAND

Thomas Keane

Ireland lies in middle latitudes. Our climate is largely determined by the prevailing westerly winds and our position on the western seaboard of the European landmass. The main features of the Irish climate are mild winters and cool summers, fairly high precipitation and relatively low sunshine amounts. These characteristics are due to the warm water of the North Atlantic Drift which has a moderating effect on air temperature over the country and which keeps the relative humidity high.

The country lies close to the main track of the North Atlantic depressions which usually pass out of the North Atlantic between Scotland and Iceland. The associated frontal weather systems with active precipitation regularly sweep over the country. Occasionally, and mainly during winter, deep depressions approach the country more directly, producing gales or storms to accompany the rain.

Despite the country's relatively small size, distinct climatic differences are discernible between regions. The climate is slightly continental to the south-east and more maritime to the north-west, so there is increased windiness, greater cloudiness, more precipitation and cooler summers in the north-west compared with the south-east. The most significant characteristic of the Irish weather is variability superimposed on a temperate nature.

Past climates

Climate trends over time are usually small compared with the annual variability of the elements and are therefore difficult to distinguish from annual fluctuations. Temperature is the simplest indicator of climate changes, but our knowledge of past climates comes from clues in the landscape, such as growth of bogs, tree rings and the debris of flora and fauna. Even up to the sixteenth and seventeenth centuries instrumental and regular observations were not yet available.

Cold and warm spells
Viewed over epochs, cool conditions gave way to rising temperatures about 10,000 years ago. Forests covered the country. The climate became drier and a climatic optimum was reached some 2000 years later. This coincided with the first arrival of human beings. A wet but warm period followed, which promoted the growth of marginal fens and marshes, leading eventually to the build-up of raised bogs. The climate reverted to being cold and disturbed with increasing wetness about 2500 years ago. With this deterioration in climate, thick layers of climatic peat were formed in upland areas. The climate again improved during the early Christian era. A secondary optimum occurred in the early Middle Ages between AD 1000 and AD 1400, known as the Medieval Warm Epoch, which reached a climax about AD 1200. Farming was possible in Iceland and Greenland, in areas now frozen. A stormy era occurred during the thirteenth and fourteenth centuries, and the advance of vineyards in these islands ceased abruptly. A general cooling took place which culminated in the Little Ice Age from AD 1430 to AD 1850, during which there were long and severe winters and short summers. There was a decline of agriculture and wheat growing was abandoned in northern Europe, the crop becoming marginal in Ireland.

The potato famine
The spread of potato blight, *Phytophthora infestans,* to Ireland in 1845–6 led to devastating social and economic consequences for the Irish race. In 1845 the potato crop in Europe was attacked for the first time by blight, a disease which had occurred in the United States of America over the previous two years. The source was a new potato variety imported from America and from Fig. 1 you can see how the disease

Oats thrive under cooler and wetter climatic conditions than barley or wheat, so they have always been important in Irish agriculture.

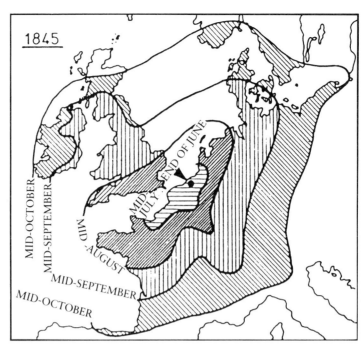

Figure 1

The spread of potato blight in 1845

spread out to vast areas of Europe causing great distress. In one month in 1845 the potato blight rotted the tubers all over Europe. Devastating effects on the population of Belgium and Switzerland were alleviated only by the grain harvest, although yields were low. As the disease was late reaching Ireland in 1845 the crop was dealt only a glancing blow and harvest was only a quarter below normal. However, infection was carried over through a mild winter and poor growth conditions in 1846, especially over Ireland, brought renewed attacks of the fungus which wiped out the crop before development. Widespread starvation and fever, together with massive emigration, led to a sudden decrease in population by about 2 million from the pre-Famine peak of 8 million. We now know that the fungus is carried over from year to year in the potato tubers, and the spread of the disease during the growing season is favoured by prolonged spells of warm and humid weather. Without effective control the potential for an epidemic continues to the present day.

Is the weather getting worse?

During the final decades of the nineteenth century and the early decades of the twentieth, a warm and dry period prevailed which reached a maximum in the 1930s. The agricultural revolution of the last 150 years took place against a background of improving climate. The growing season in the 1930s was about one month longer than in the Little Ice Age, and the frost-free season was also significantly longer. Since the 1950s, however, the climate has tended to become cooler, wetter and duller. In particular there has been a tendency for cooler springs and summers, but little change in autumn and winter.

18

Each season's weather varies from year to year and certain seasons are recalled in conversation long after they occur. The variations in the summer weather over a number of years can be shown by means of a simple index. The Poulter Index applies to the summer months of June, July and August. Based on weighted values of the monthly mean air temperature, total sunshine and rainfall, the resulting index provides a single value to express the quality of each summer season.

The summer index for each year over the period 1880 to 1986 at Phoenix Park, Dublin, shows considerable year-to-year variation, with high values of the index, representing the warmer and drier summers, occurring in 1887, 1933, 1975 and 1976. Low values occur in 1912 (minimum for the period), 1958, 1985 and 1986. Based on mean decadal values of the index, peak values occur in the 1930s and 1940s; the index for the current incomplete decade (seven years) is proving to be exceptionally low.

The climate today

Precipitation

Fig. 2 shows the mean annual rainfall (precipitation) based on data for the period 1951–80. In low-lying areas, the annual amounts vary from about 750mm in the east to over 1300mm in the south-west, west and north-west. These differences represent over 75 per cent more precipitation in western regions than in some eastern coastal areas. Year-to-year variations in annual precipitation are very great and annual totals at Birr ranged from 617mm in 1971 to 1112mm in 1960. While annual precipitation in Ireland is not excessive compared with some tropical regions, the average number of rain-days is high, amounting to 270 days in western areas.

There is enhanced precipitation in upland areas, the increase amounting to roughly 150mm per annum for every 100m rise in altitude. Many of the exposed summits therefore receive over 3000mm annually, but areas to the lee of mountains can be in a more

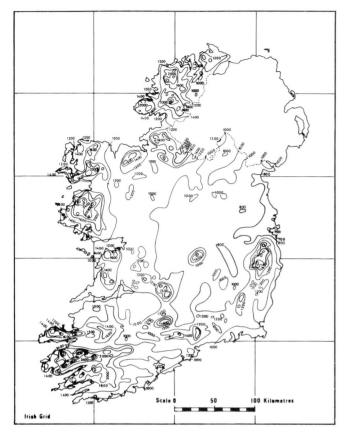

Figure 2

Map of Ireland showing the annual rainfall

favourable position.

Annual water balance

A proper moisture balance is of vital importance to successful farming. Annual precipitation exceeds evaporation by about 150mm in the east and by 800mm in the west. While the average precipitation does not vary from month to month in Ireland as much as in the continent of Europe, nevertheless there is less precipitation in spring and summer months than in autumn and winter. In contrast evaporation is low in winter and reaches a maximum in summer. The moisture balance changes in spring from the winter surplus to a deficit of moisture during the summer. The summer deficit (in the soil) is usually significant for an extended period in the east but rarely sufficient to inhibit growth in western areas. Surplus moisture in the soil can lead to poaching (cutting up) of the grass-covered surface by cattle and to difficulty in travel over fields.

Temperature

Temperature is an important element controlling crop growth. The mean annual temperature over Ireland varies from 9°C in parts of the north-east to 10.5°C in the extreme south-west. There are also strong inland and coastal influences. Coastal areas have considerable advantage if a long, cool growing season with low risk of late spring frosts is needed. For heat-seeking crops such as wheat, the higher temperatures occurring inland in summer are a decided advantage.

The regional differences in the frost-free season can be considerable. The mean date of last air frost in spring can vary from the first week of March in southern coastal areas to the first week of May in the midlands, representing a difference of up to seventy days.

Harsh weather can be severe on wildlife. Ponds and lakes can become frozen, the ice- and snow-covered ground making foraging extremely difficult. While such conditions are not as frequent in this country as in continental Europe, and are usually of short duration, nevertheless, spells of up to ten days occur with reasonable regularity. The longest recorded spell in this country extended from 27 December 1962 to 2 March 1963. There are also many years in which extended periods of harsh weather did not occur, most notably of late in the winter periods of 1969/70 to 1975/6. Because of the lower temperatures prevailing in upland areas, snow is more frequent (an average of fifteen to twenty days annually compared with five to ten days in lowland areas). With stronger winds prevailing at the higher levels, blizzard conditions are also more common.

Sunshine

High sunshine duration is of importance not only because global radiation is the source of energy in the assimilation of organic matter in growing crops but also it is of significance for the health of the human race. Annual hours of bright sunshine vary from less than 1200 hours on the mountains of the south and west of Ireland to over 1600 hours in the south-east. The range in Britain is greater, with values for the south-east of over 1800 hours. Amounts received in nearby continental areas

19

range from 1400 hours in eastern parts of the
Netherlands to 1800 hours in the north of
France and 2000 hours in the mid-western
coastal areas of France. The decrease in
sunshine with altitude is about 5 per cent per
100m. As evaporation is strongly dependent
on sunshine, it is little wonder that farmers in
the west of Ireland experience much more
difficulty in the saving of hay than their
counterparts in France or indeed the south-
east of Ireland.

Wind

Because of our location off the north-west of
Europe and near the tracks of the North
Atlantic depressions, Ireland has a windy
climate. Western and upland areas suffer the
greatest disadvantage from increased
windiness. The mean annual wind speed
along the west and north-west coasts is nearly
twice that of the south midlands.

Persistently strong winds can damage
plants and cause stress to animals. The impact
of the wind on vegetation can be
considerable. While 7 metres per second is
well below the upper threshold for successful
tree growth (which is considered to be an
annual mean of approximately 10 metres per
second) the exposure of the unbroken coasts
such as in north County Clare, 'where no
trees can succeed, particularly in the
windswept Burren', is more inhospitable than
the indented coast of south Kerry which
break the force of the wind.

As wind also increases with altitude,
upland areas (more than 300m) in central
Ireland can experience winds of strength
equal to the exposed coastlines. The wind
pattern is complicated further by wind flow
around mountains or by the funnelling of
wind through gaps in the peaks.

Trees near Roundstone, Co.
Galway, frozen into wind-
blown form by the harsh
westerly winds from the
Atlantic.

Table 1
Percentage frequency of wind directions* in each of the principal compass point sectors

Period	Southerly 140°–220°	Westerly 230°–310°	Northerly 320°–040°	Easterly 050°–130°
	%	%	%	%
April–Sept	32.6	36.4	18.8	12.2
Oct–March	42.9	30.8	12.4	13.8
Annual	37.8	33.6	15.6	13.0
Month with max frequency	Oct	July	Apr	Feb

* Averages based on data (1963–86) at Birr, County Offaly

Birds migrating to or from this country can
be aided or impeded by tailwinds or
headwinds they encounter *en route*. Table 1
shows the frequency of winds blowing from
the principal compass point sectors to
Ireland. There are distinct differences in the
frequencies of southerly and westerly winds.
In the summer half of the year, April to
September, westerly winds are more in
evidence, whereas during the winter half,
October to March, southerly winds have

greater frequency. On an annual basis,
southerly winds are dominant but westerlies
also have a high number of occurrences. The
maximum monthly frequency of westerlies
occurs in July, whereas southerlies peak in
October (but are also common in subsequent
months to January). Northerly and easterly
winds have low frequencies and except for the
northerlies in summer are fairly evenly
distributed. Peak frequencies of the northerly
and easterly winds occur in April and
February respectively.

THOMAS KEANE BSc is the agricultural
meteorologist in the Meteorological Service
in Dublin. He is co-ordinator of AGMET, an
interdisciplinary group of agricultural and
meteorological scientists from An Foras
Talúntais, ACOT, the Meteorological
Service, university departments, agricultural
colleges and the Department of Agriculture.
He is general editor of AGMET's
publication *Climate, Weather and Irish
Agriculture* (AGMET Dublin 1986).

IRELAND'S GEOLOGY

John Feehan

The rocky framework which lies at the heart of every landscape normally only appears at the surface. It is seen on the mountains, in the rivers and along the coasts, where the elements have stripped them bare of their mantle of soil and vegetation, or in quarries where they have been gouged out to provide the raw materials on which our civilisation so depends. For it is rocks which provide us with the stone, metals, oil, gas, coal and chemicals which keep our civilisation afloat.

The rock framework of Ireland is a mosaic of the greatest complexity, whose origins go back to the very beginning of time. Ireland as we see it today only began to take on its modern character some tens of millions of years ago, though weathering has wrought profound changes since Ireland first appeared as a discrete geographical entity on the earth's surface.

The various pieces in the enormously complex rock jigsaw that is Ireland were fitted into place at different times over the long course of the earth's history. The earliest pieces were laid down as long as 2000 million years ago, and the final pieces were slotted in only tens of millions of years ago at most – all a very long time before the first people set foot on our little island. Perhaps the best way to appreciate the overall geological picture is to

Above right
Old red sandstone exposed in the bed of the River Barrow near Clonaslee, Co. Laois

Above left
Satellite image of Co. Donegal showing north-east to south-west trending folds which are the legacy of the great period of mountain building which occurred 400 million years ago.

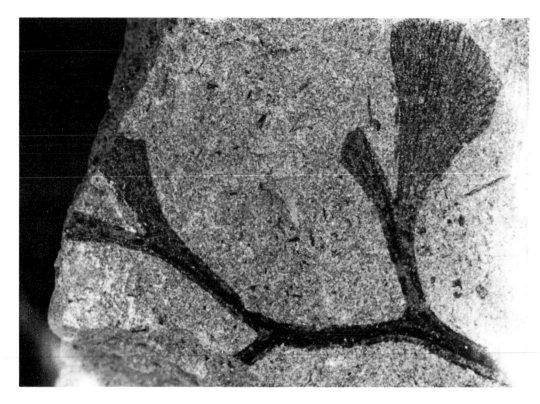

Left
Rocks contain a detailed record
of the evolution of life on earth
in the fossils which are
sometimes found in them.
Here is a fragment of a tree fern
from old red sandstone in Co.
Offaly.

Opposite
The calendar of geological time

look at the largest and most important elements in the jigsaw, while remembering that there is a multiplicity of other smaller pieces which may be extremely important to an understanding of some particular aspect or corner.

We can usefully begin our review of Ireland's geological history by setting ourselves down in the era of earth history called the lower Palaeozoic between 400 and 600 million years ago. For much of lower Palaeozoic time, a great ocean stretched across the part of the earth's surface where Ireland is situated today, and in its waters, sands and muds washed in from the distant land built up over millions of years. The retrospective geologist now gives the name

Iapetus – in Greek mythology Iapetus was the father of Atlas – to this great ocean, and this ancient Palaeozoic ocean was in a sense the forerunner of the Atlantic. This Iapetus Ocean gradually narrowed during the later part of the lower Palaeozoic, as the continental masses which bordered it on the north-west and south-east approached each other and finally collided. The thousands of metres of marine sediments in between were folded and contorted, the pleats of the folds running north-west to south-east, and they were finally thrust upwards as a vast tract of mountainous country, which the forces of weathering and erosion set to work on straight away. These great surface disturbances were accompanied by other

events deeper down, where granite magma was intruded deep in the earth's crust in Galway, east Leinster, Newry, Donegal and around Foxford; these granite intrusions acted as structural pillars which influenced much that happened later.

The sands, gravels and silts produced by this new episode of erosion at the surface were carried by the extensive river network which flowed southwards across the surface of this new continent; they were deposited as sandbanks in rivers and lakes, and on the floodplains when the rivers overflowed their banks. By the end of the Devonian period of earth history, the great mountains which had been there 65 million years earlier had been reduced to sea-level, and a new ocean began

Era	Period	Millions of years before present	Main happenings
CENOZOIC	Quaternary	2	The great Ice Age Evolution of man
CENOZOIC	Tertiary	65	Himalayan orogeny Alpine orogeny
MESOZOIC	Cretaceous	136	Extinction of dinosaurs Flowering plants appear
MESOZOIC	Jurassic	190	Birds and mammals appear
MESOZOIC	Triassic	225	Hercynian orogeny
UPPER PALAEOZOIC	Permian	280	
UPPER PALAEOZOIC	Carboniferous: upper	320	Early reptiles
UPPER PALAEOZOIC	Carboniferous: lower	345	
UPPER PALAEOZOIC	Devonian	395	Caledonian orogeny
LOWER PALAEOZOIC	Silurian	430	First land plants
LOWER PALAEOZOIC	Ordovician	500	Primitive fish appear
LOWER PALAEOZOIC	Cambrian	570	Multicellular life evolves
PRECAMBRIAN	Proterozoic	2300–2800	Earliest bacteria and algae appear about 3200 million years ago
PRECAMBRIAN	Archaean	4600–4700	Oldest rocks about 4000 million years old Crust of the earth solidifies

to creep northwards over the levelled surface. of the continent. The continental sediments buried under its advance hardened in time to become the series of rocks to which we give the name 'old red sandstone'.

For the next 20 million years, lime-rich muds and other sediments accumulated in the warm waters of these shallow lower Carboniferous seas; in time these too hardened to rock, producing the lower Carboniferous limestone which is Ireland's commonest rock. The marine sediments of the lower Carboniferous were succeeded by deltaic sediments in the upper Carboniferous period which followed; forests of tree ferns, horsetails and other strange plants flourished in this new environment and their remains accumulated and were compressed in time to become coal. At the end of the Carboniferous, new continental collisions in southern Europe folded the Carboniferous sediments and the old red sandstone which underlay them, to form new ranges of mountains, this time with east–west fold axes.

Much of Ireland's geological framework had already been blocked out by this time; nearly half of the country is underlain by rocks of Carboniferous age, most importantly the Carboniferous limestone which forms the great expanse of the central plain. The old red sandstone dominates the mountains of Munster, and the lower Palaeozoic foundation upon which it rests makes up much of the triangle of hummocky upland that lies between Longford, Belfast and Dundalk, as well as much of east Leinster around the granites of Dublin, Wicklow and Carlow; lower Palaeozoic rocks also lie at the heart of the old red sandstone inliers in the south midlands.

Although much of Ireland was once covered by sediments of Mesozoic age, these have long since been stripped away to reveal the Carboniferous and older rocks beneath. It is only in the north-east, in the Tertiary basalts and the chalk of Antrim and in the mountains of Mourne, Slieve Gullion and Carlingford, whose granites were intruded at about the time the lavas were being poured over the Antrim chalk, that these are of real importance in landscape terms. These great igneous events were accompaniments to the opening of the North Atlantic ocean, which broadly defined where Ireland's western front would one day lie.

But trying to condense the 2000 million years of Ireland's rock history into these few lines is rather like trying to condense the pain and excitement and drama of our own human history between the covers of a single volume. At most, they may provide a signpost to an aspect of the landscape which opens a window onto a succession of unsuspected ancient worlds for every explorer of the Irish countryside, and sheds an altogether new and richer light on all we see about us.

LAND OF FLYING VISITS
Roger Goodwillie

Ireland's population of birds, fish and insects is never static. There is constant movement of mobile creatures on and off the island, whether they are arriving 'home' from a sojourn abroad, just dropping in on their way to somewhere else, or coming for a bit of a holiday.

Migration

Migration is the regular movement of animals or birds in response to a changing food supply or a breeding cycle. It is thus a seasonal occurrence, usually involving an outward and a return journey in a single year but, in the case of some fish, over several years. One-way movements also occur sometimes in animal populations. These may be invasions or irruptions, where numbers have built up locally to intolerable levels, or hard weather movements where animals desert an area in one movement and gradually trickle back to it as conditions improve.

True migration is a feature of birds, sea fish, some insects and a few bats. But it also occurs on a smaller scale in frogs, which move to a breeding pond, and in many invertebrates. Soil-dwelling animals, for example, frequently move to deeper layers in summer when the soil dries out and come back to the surface for the rest of the year. Earthworms are an example and they even go into a dormant state (aestivation rather than hibernation) when they have reached the subsoil and are unable to feed.

Biological timing

Day-length is usually the signal for bird migration to begin. It produces hormonal changes that allow a build-up of fat for fuel. Many small birds actually double their weight before undertaking their migrations, especially if they have to cross oceans or

deserts where they cannot come down to feed. Flights of 1000 miles (1600km) and more are not unusual for many species. To be able to put on weight like this it is obvious that migration occurs rather earlier than seems necessary. If the birds waited for a decline in the food supply to indicate that they should be moving, there would not be enough extra food left for them. So the times of migration are somewhat skewed with respect to the seasons. In the autumn our summer birds leave rather early, the swift and cuckoo even in July and August. Likewise our wintering birds, the waders and wildfowl, move out in February and March, long before they·

are due to breed.

Birds coming and going

This regularity of migration is one of its interesting features. The order of the birds' arrival is always the same, even if cold weather displaces the sequence by several weeks. Wheatears and Sandwich terns are the first breeding birds to appear in the spring. They are followed by chiffchaffs, sand martins, willow warblers and swallows. The other warblers and terns come with a rush in early May and the rearguard consists of swifts and spotted flycatchers which wait until flying insects have built up good numbers.

Opposite
The life-cycle of the salmon includes one of the most astonishing examples of animal migration. On their voyage from the sea back to the river of their birth, salmon may have to travel thousands of miles, covering up to sixty miles in a day.

Right
At the end of their nesting season in the high Arctic of Canada, brent geese begin the long flight to their Irish winter grounds, crossing over southern Greenland, Iceland and the North Atlantic. The first birds appear at the end of August and numbers reach their peak in late October.

These land birds leave discreetly over the summer and early autumn with occasional stragglers into October. But evidence of migration seldom ceases. Even in July the numbers of waders on our estuaries begin to increase. These are birds which nest in the Arctic and sub-Arctic. Those that fail to breed arrive first and their numbers swell through August and September. Many birds such as redshank and oystercatcher are only passing through Ireland at this time and will winter further south, especially in west Africa. These are passage migrants but for most of the species a segment of the population seems to stay to winter here. The knot and grey plover as well as the more inland golden plover and lapwing come to stay in October along with many of the wildfowl. The movement of redwings and fieldfares is also obvious then, especially by night though they may not be much seen until November. Our wintering blackcaps and black redstarts arrive too from northern and central Europe.

A special type of migration is undertaken by certain wildfowl to moult. The wildfowl lose their flight feathers all together in contrast to other birds which lose them singly in a sequence. The wildfowl therefore cannot fly for a few weeks and they have to seek out specially safe places to moult. Our shelduck, for example, fly either to south-west England or to the Wadden Sea, where they moult along with most of the European population. Mute swans are apt to gather on particular lakes here to undergo moult and then break up into smaller groups thereafter. Mallard and tufted duck move to large reedbeds and lakes and they grow a special 'eclipse' plumage to increase their camouflage.

Fish migration

Migration is a feature of our native fish species both sea and freshwater. Mackerel and herring, for example, come inshore at regular times of the year. Mackerel spawn from April to June, moving into St George's Channel from the Celtic Sea. The shoals disperse along the coast until October, when they disappear to deeper waters. Herring behave similarly though they spawn in winter and early spring. Following such food, the whales also undertake migrations. The fish-eating porpoises and dolphins are with us in summer and autumn while the larger plankton-feeding species pass the west coast in late spring on their way to Arctic waters.

It is the freshwater fish that undertake the most famous migrations, lasting several years. Both salmon and trout were originally sea fish that began to breed in fresh water, perhaps because of the security from other fishy predators that it offered. Salmon that hatch in one of our stony headwater streams go to sea during their first year. They feed on the continental shelf off the Faroe Islands, Iceland and Greenland and return to the river of their birth one to three years later, having remembered in some way the taste of its waters. How they navigate is largely a mystery though they may, like some birds, have an appreciation of the earth's magnetic field. It seems unlikely that they use the stars, which birds also depend on. Sea trout only spend a year or so in offshore waters and there are also pollan and shad in some of our rivers that make a shorter excursion into fresh water to breed. The eel has one of the most curious migrations. When mature it leaves our rivers to swim westwards to the Sargasso Sea, off the West Indies. There it spawns and dies, leaving the young fish to drift back to Europe on ocean currents.

Insects on the wing
The insects that migrate are mainly strong fliers like the butterflies and moths, the dragonflies and the thicker-bodied flies.
26

There are some beetles that fly long distances, however, and in other countries, grasshoppers and locusts. It is often the case with insects, as with the eel, that different generations make the outward and the return journey. How they know where to go is one of the mysteries of inherited knowledge or instinct. But it is similarly the case with some young birds like the cuckoo which move south several weeks after the adults have gone. Two well-known butterfly migrants are the painted lady and red admiral, while moths are represented by the silvery moth and several hawk moths. The painted lady winters in north Africa and its caterpillars feed on the transitory plant life that appears after the winter rains. Hatching into adults they move northwards into France and the Mediterranean. A few reach our shores in the early summer, but they are more frequently seen in autumn when the second generation, bred in Europe, continue their northward migration. The flights may occur at great altitudes (5000m): presumably updrafts carry the insects to where they are beyond the attention of predatory birds. The return journey to north Africa is made by a depleted population, and it may be that the Irish insects never achieve it. Certainly they seem in no hurry to go and, like the humming-bird hawk moth, may be seen on flowers until hibernation seems the only option. This is what tortoise-shell butterflies do, along with a few red admirals and peacocks. The few that survive begin a spring generation of butterflies that is augmented by migrants.

Dragonflies, with their strong flight, are considerable migrants. Large numbers of darter dragonflies have been grounded by storms while the invasion of a Spanish damselfly into Ireland in 1947 represents a flight of more than 800km. This, however, may have been more of a dispersal movement at a time of population pressure. The movements of lemmings and of ladybirds seem rather similar.

ROGER GOODWILLIE is a botanist and birdwatcher who has been interested in rivers since childhood. He took his primary degree in Trinity College Dublin where he developed a keen interest in peatlands. He received his masters degree in the University of Toronto. He has canoed on several rivers in Canada and Ireland and now works as an ecologist with An Foras Forbartha.

ISLAND OF BIRDS

Clive Hutchinson

Black-headed gulls rest on sand and shingle by the sea, but they are also found far inland where they frequently nest in ponds where there is plenty of protection for their nests.

Have you ever wondered why we have the sort of bird community that we have in Ireland and, in particular, why our birdlife in Ireland differs from that in our neighbour island of Great Britain? Why do we have only two-thirds of the species of breeding birds they have across the water? There are several reasons: we are in a different place for a start – further west and the first or the last stopping place (depending on how you look at it) between America and Europe; our habitats are not quite the same; and we are a smaller island.

Is small beautiful?

The area of Ireland is 84,421 square kilometres, and Great Britain is nearly three times as big. But what has size got to do with it? Well, being smaller means that we don't extend as far north or as far south as Great Britain, but it also means that, according to the widely accepted views on island biogeography developed by MacArthur and Wilson, we are bound to have fewer species than Britain, as smaller islands in general have fewer species than larger ones.

There are several reasons for this difference. In the first place, a wandering bird is more likely to find a large island than a small one, because the larger area has a greater chance of being in the bird's flight track. As a result, the number of rare species recorded in Ireland is likely to be less than in Britain.

Fewer habitats

Secondly, smaller islands are likely to have fewer habitats than large ones. For a small island, we have a great diversity of habitat, but even so, we don't have quite the variety that Britain has: we have no equivalent of the lowland heath and chalk downland of southern England or the high mountains and scots pine woodland of Scotland, and this probably explains why we don't have the bird species typical of these places, such as woodlarks, Dartford warblers, stone curlews, dotterels, greenshanks and crested tits.

Patterns of colonisation

The last reason is slightly more complicated. It has to do with patterns of colonisation. According to MacArthur and Wilson's theory, the species that are best at colonisation arrive on an island first, and as more species arrive, the competition increases, so either potential colonists fail to establish themselves or the increased competition puts pressure on species already on the island and those with smaller numbers tend to become extinct. This pattern ensures that the number of species on an island tends to remain fairly stable, with newly arriving species being balanced by extinctions. And so the fairly low number of species in Ireland tends to remain low.

But what of the species we do have? Having smaller numbers of species doesn't mean we necessarily have fewer birds for our size. In fact the few studies that have been done show that we have higher densities of coal tits, blue tits and goldcrests on our farming land and in our woodlands than Britain. Presumably these birds occupy niches that in Britain would be filled by woodpeckers, marsh tits, willow tits and nuthatches, which we don't have at all in this country, or by pied flycatchers, tree pipits, redstarts and wood warblers, which we do have, but only rarely and irregularly.

A sea-swept shore

Whatever about our poverty of species inland, Ireland has an abundance of seabirds, mainly migrating birds. The country projects into the Atlantic and is surrounded by rich and relatively shallow seas, stretching to the edge of the continental shelf. Birdwatchers at Cape Clear in County Cork were amazed in the early 1960s at the vast numbers of shearwaters, petrels and auks that they were seeing, and at the presence among the commoner species of rarer skuas from the north and, from the south, great shearwaters, sooty shearwaters and Cory's shearwaters.

Since those first observations of bird movements at Cape Clear we now have a clearer picture of the passage of seabirds and know in what direction birds are likely to be passing on any coast. The late summer passage of Manx shearwaters at Cape Clear consists mainly of birds from the breeding colonies on the Kerry islands; but the most remarkable passages are those in which southern shearwaters, northern skuas and

rarities such as Sabine's gulls and Leach's petrels are sometimes seen, and seem to happen when the birds are driven inshore by the weather. This suggests that there are large numbers of seabirds feeding well out to sea which cannot be seen from the land except in unusual weather. Birdwatchers have made trips out to sea in small boats, and it appears that we have higher densities of birds off our south-west coast than Britain has.

Different species of seabird feed close to the coast, offshore and over deep waters, but the most important feeding areas seem to be the boundaries where warm and cool water mix and cool upwelling water brings nutrients to the surface. These support plankton, which in turn supports the fish and squid that the birds feed on.

A westerly outpost

Ireland, on the western fringe of Europe, provides winter quarters for birds from as far west as Arctic Canada, for a number of species which breed in Greenland and for birds which breed in northern Europe east to Siberia. Brent geese ringed on Queen Elizabeth Island in northern Canada have been seen in Ireland. The numbers of great northern divers wintering around the coast are far greater than the Icelandic population can account for, and may well include Canadian birds as well as Greenland breeders. Our wintering knot population breeds in Canada and Greenland. From Greenland alone we receive barnacle geese and white-fronted geese and several wader species. Ireland is the principal wintering area for a number of Icelandic species, particularly whooper swans, golden plovers, black-tailed godwits and redshanks. From Scandinavia and the Baltic come many ducks, waders and finches, and from as far east as Siberia come

our wintering Bewick's swans, grey plovers and bar-tailed godwits. Ireland is a long way from Siberia and Canada, but migratory birds stop off *en route* in Scandinavia and the Baltic or in Greenland and Iceland respectively.

Being on the western edge of Europe, Ireland is the first landfall for many vagrants from north America, but birds from as far east as Siberia such as the tiny yellow-browed warblers also occur every autumn. However, Ireland receives far fewer eastern or southern vagrants than does Britain, which of course is not surprising, given the extra distance such birds have to travel.

Wild and wet

Our high rainfall produces winter flooding which provides refuge for wildfowl, and our milder winter temperatures keep the ground soft and the lakes free of ice, leaving them available for feeding birds driven westward over Europe by wintry conditions. When this happens, teal, lapwings, redwings and other species come flooding into Ireland in search of exposed water or soft ground. When the weather is very bad, birds do suffer, but the populations tend to recover very well, and exceptional mortality is probably rarer in Irish winters than in Britain. The Irish kingfisher population, for instance, seems not to have suffered as much as kingfishers in other European countries in the harsh conditions of 1962/3.

So you see, Ireland is a special place for birds. Although it is a small island with relatively few species it is a refuge for large numbers of wintering wildfowl and migrant seabirds, and there are plenty of birds, around our shores, in our woods, on our rivers and wetlands, and even in our towns, all habitats waiting to be explored by the enthusiastic birdwatcher.

CLIVE HUTCHINSON has been interested in birds since childhood, but always remembers the advice of Miss Geraldine Roche, who worked in the Natural History Museum for many years, that an interest in natural history should be kept as a hobby rather than made a profession. He has edited bird reports, written a number of papers on bird distribution, and written three books – *The Birds of Dublin and Wicklow* and *Ireland's Wetlands and their Birds* for the Irish Wildbird Conservancy and *Watching Birds in Ireland* for Country House. He was the founder editor of the journal *Irish Birds*, now in its eleventh year of publication, and is currently working on a new standard book on birds in Ireland due for publication early in 1989. He has been treasurer of the IWC and is chairman of Cape Clear Bird Observatory. When not involved in ornithology he earns his living as an accountant.

SOME IRISH LANDSCAPES

Frank Mitchell

Landscapes

'Before the hills in order stood. . .' When did the Irish hills arise, or more probably when did denudation dissect them out of long-disappeared masses of surrounding rock? We can see at least three great stages of rock disturbance in Irish geological history, and most of our mountains reflect those movements. Four hundred and fifty million years ago great earth pressures created north-east/south-west folds that ran all the way from Newfoundland to Scandinavia; the trend of the ridges and valleys in Donegal and Connemara are witnesses of those pressures. The east/west ridges and valleys of Cork and Kerry indicate other pressures, this time from north and south 300 million years ago. The Mountains of Mourne are mere upstarts. Sixty-five million years ago great masses of molten rock started an upward welling in that area; today those cores of rock are revealed as granite hills. Here we have the great unanswered question about the Irish landscape: when did our hills and valleys take the shapes we know today? My guess would be a long, long time ago.

In limestone areas we have a hidden landscape of caves and sinkholes, much of it probably as old as the visible landscape above. It holds elegant dripstone formations, and also evidence of animals and people. What can be more romantic than to see claw-scratches on a cave wall, made by a bear rousing himself from hibernation and resharpening his claws before emerging?

The undulating Irish landscape means an indented and varied coastline. The basalt cliffs of Antrim lead on to the sand-spits of Lough Foyle; great stretches of sandy beach lie at the north foot of the sandstone mountains of the Dingle peninsula. Great arms of the sea flood the western ends of the valleys of Cork and Kerry. For this to have happened there must have been changes in the relative levels of land and sea. We return to our opening question 'When?'.

The Sperrins
From Wicklow to the Shannon Estuary
The View from Errisbeg
The Glens of Antrim
The Mournes
Hidden Landscapes
The North Coast
The Burren Uplands
Irish Islands and their Monasteries
Variety in Landscape

THE SPERRINS
Gwen Buchanan

Primitive landscape

The Sperrins are a very old and very beautiful curving ridge of mountains separating the basins of Lough Foyle and Lough Neagh in County Londonderry or Derry. Here you will find ancient rocks pushed and folded and squeezed into jostling horizons of hills and valleys, smoothed down to elegant gentle profiles. These folded hills and valleys have held life for thousands of years – first plants and animals and later people, who have left mysterious signs of their presence all around, especially in the higher parts, the great open spaces where the lark sings, the heather is purple and the views are spectacular, mile after mile.

The ancient Sperrin people did not care about details of geology, but they knew that gold is to be found here and that the rocks resemble parts of Scotland. They knew that the sands and gravels left by the ice-sheets made lighter soils for cultivation than the weathered schists and gneisses of the mountain mass. They used giant boulders, broken off and smoothed by ice in its passage, to make noble monuments to their dear departed and mysterious stone circles, whose use is long forgotten.

People now live lower down in the valleys, glens and foothills, and the uplands are abandoned to open moorland and heather. The trees that once grew there are buried in bog and even the tough mountainy sheep find it hard to survive in the winter. For centuries, though, the uplands came alive again in the summer, when spring produced rough grazing and cattle were brought from the wooded valleys to be herded and pastured away from the precious patches of crop located on the glacial sands and gravels along the valley sides. A 'booley' was a summer residence built by the young folk, whose job it was to herd and milk the cows and churn the butter. Echoing this tradition, young people in the Sperrins still build 'Easter houses', though their origin is long forgotten.

This largely pastoral economy supported a sparse population until the seventeenth century when the Londonderry plantation, organised by the London livery companies, brought a new influx of settlers, mainly from Scotland, where they had followed much the same sort of agricultural regime as they found in the Sperrins. They made more clearings in the dense oak woodland in the valleys, but even by the end of the eighteenth century, the Sperrins' glens and valleys were still woody, especially on steeper slopes that are less suitable for agriculture.

Nineteenth-century landscape

By the middle of the nineteenth century the London companies, alarmed at reports of their condition, began to take a direct interest in their estates in County Londonderry. They sent deputations on tours of inspection and their reports give us the first really vivid picture of life and landscape in the Sperrins. It was a remote region where ancient culture and traditions had survived for many centuries in a world that was full of change. What kind of landscape did the deputations find?

The Worshipful Fishmongers are a good example of a London company which had a fair share of the Sperrins in its 'proportion' or estate. When a long lease of the estate

terminated with the death of King George III in 1820, it was decided not to renew the lease but to inspect conditions at first hand with a view to managing the property themselves through a local agent. John Towgood, a freeman of the company, kept a diary of his trip and drafted the official report of the deputation; another member of the deputation was one William Sturch, who later published a treatise on *The grievances of Ireland; their causes and remedies;* and from these sources we have an insight into their impressions.

London comes to Derry

It is interesting to imagine the reaction of this group of Londoners, setting off by coach from London on St Patrick's Day 1820, visiting Shakespeare's birthplace *en route* via north Wales to Holyhead, where they found the newly introduced steam packet about to make its second trip to Kingstown (now Dún Laoghaire). They sailed, however, but later regretted their choice as they took twenty-one hours to cross, whereas the steamer arrived safely in only eight hours.

They approved of Dublin's fine buildings but were struck by the number of wretched beggars swarming the streets. They journeyed on via Dundalk, Armagh, Dungannon and Cookstown to Moneymore on the eastern flanks of the Sperrins where the Drapers' Company of London had already made great improvements, including a very excellent inn, The Draper's Arms, which they highly approved of after some of their earlier experiences. Their destination was Limavady on the western flanks of the mountains, which they traversed by the Glenshane Pass to Dungiven, finding the scenery very dreary. It must have been one of those grey days, or perhaps the city gents were simply not

attuned to the beauties of uninhabited wild landscape – north Wales was also written off as 'dreary'. But at least they were spared the attentions of the highwaymen who were known to frequent the mountain passes.

They spent a night in Dungiven, a small market town situated at the foot of the bold west-facing basalt scarp of Benbradagh at the head of the fertile valley of the River Roe. The village was in the Skinners' proportion or Manor of Pellipar. The village consisted of one long street of single-storey thatched houses stepped down the slope. Its main *raison d'être* was a weekly market, since the bleach greens were no longer in use. A recently built parish church at the top of the street was admired while the medieval ruins of Dungiven Friary with its ornate tomb of Cooey-na-Gall created a favourable impression.

Basing themselves in Limavady (a Skinners' town further down the River Roe) the deputation set about the systematic inspection of their estate. It was a daunting task for the Londoners, in view of the lack of roads in many parts, but they hired horses and set out, accompanied by a local landlord, with guides to take them through the numerous bogs. Despite this precaution, the landlord himself had to be rescued by horse power from being engulfed in some quaggy mire.

In the mountains they found a landscape of extensive bog, scattered with groups of cabins, set in small patches of arable open fields, hand-cultivated in innumerable strips in which were grown potatoes, oats and occasionally flax. There was usually some meadowland nearby from which hay would be saved for winter fodder. They saw cattle being pastured in the open hill grazing and peat (or turf) being cut and harvested on the

33

turf banks in the bogs. One day they saw a sad convoy of people trailing across the 'desolate landscape', pushing their worldly goods on handcarts towards the port of Londonderry and the dreaded emigrant ships whose handbills were pinned to the doors of some of the poorer cabins. The deputation quickly sensed that disaster was looming and they were seized with the need for drastic action.

The dwellings observed by the deputation ranged from one-roomed thatched cabins scattered in the uplands to better single farmsteads in the valleys. There were a few more pretentious farms with good stone-built and slated houses and offices, providing cottages for their craftsmen and labourers; and lastly the 'seats' of the large landlords who had leased estates directly from the London companies. The established church was also a major landowner, and some fine parish churches and rectories were noted; and the grandest house of all, Downhill Palace, built for Frederick Augustus Hervey, could be seen on the rugged and imposing cliffs to the very north of the Sperrins.

Landscape overpopulated

The overall impression borne in upon the London company representatives was that they were looking at an overpopulated landscape. They concluded that farming was inefficient as the holdings were very small and in many cases held in partnership under the traditional rundale system of agriculture – a system which the London companies deplored, but which politically ambitious local landlords had connived at, as it increased the number of property holders whose votes could be commandeered at election time. Under the rundale system a man's share in the communally owned land could be divided equally among his heirs, so

that holdings became progressively smaller. Income had been eked out by cottage industry, but this had largely collapsed on the industrialisation of spinning and weaving. The potato had made it possible to support a family on a very small holding indeed; even half an acre would have been regarded as sufficient to start a family on and a small thatched cabin could be raised in a day with communal labour, so people married very young and fertility was very high.

The stark reality was too many tenants sharing too little land, and paying rents no longer realistic with the failure of cottage industry. In spite of these despairing circumstances it was remarked that the people were civil and well-spoken and the ragged children were well schooled. Other problems were the prevalence of damp-induced diseases, the lack of any kind of welfare and the abysmal housing conditions of most of the tenants.

Landscape improved

By the time the London companies sold out to their tenants under the 1880s Land Acts they had made considerable changes in the Sperrin landscape. By assisting emigration they reduced tenant numbers. They surveyed and reallocated holdings in compact units of 20–30 acres laid out in squared-off fields with neat thorn hedges. Fields were drained and land reclaimed in formerly unprofitable areas; grants were made for improvements to farmsteads. They built schools, dispensaries, churches, roads, bridges and model farms to promote better agricultural methods. Lime-kilns were built to provide lime not only for agricultural use but also for use in the spate of building. In fact much of the structure of the present landscape was laid down at this time; the regular pattern of small hedged fields with sheltering trees, the solid stone-built farmsteads with gardens and orchards, many distinguished public buildings and many of

the roads we still travel on can be attributed to this period of amendment for earlier neglect.

Some of the London companies were more active than others. Some did not regain possession of their lands in time to do very much before government reform of land tenure overtook them. Even with fewer tenants and improved agricultural methods the London companies were finding it difficult to run their estates on an economic basis.

Landscape depopulated

If John Towgood and the other London merchants were to return today, what would they find? They might fly in over the Sperrins and view their former estates from the air. They would see the great rolling arc of heathery mountains, rearing sharply from the sea in the north, topped by the gaping ruins and the long-gone gardens of the great bishop's palace; peak after peak rising gradually southward to the highest summit of Sawel (680m) on the border of County Tyrone, then dying away gradually south-westward towards Omagh and beyond. The high Sperrins are still wild, uncultivated open moorland; but on many higher slopes the Londoners would be able to see the faint marks of spade rigs now reverting to moorland and at a slightly lower level they would be sad to see that many of the small upland farms have been abandoned, the regular squared fields so carefully surveyed and drained now invaded by rushes, the once neat thorn hedges wild and straggly. In the foothills and valleys they might recognise some of the farmsteads they helped to improve, but often the simple and seemly stone-built farmhouses will have been replaced by a modern upstart of alien origins not indigenous to the Sperrins. Some of their fine public buildings remain, for example the classical sandstone church at Banagher near Dungiven; but they would find the Drapers' village at Moneymore which they so admired on their first visit had lost much of its charm. Many of the Drapers' buildings are still there, but most are abused or neglected, though not beyond recall; some have already been thoughtfully restored and the rest are ripe for restoration, in the light of a growing interest in things of the past.

The Fishmongers' general impression would be of vast improvements in some things and doubtful progress in others. They would not recognise the road they had painfully travelled across the Glenshane Pass; its smooth black waterproof curves would amaze them, while the flashing horseless carriages would probably be treated with the same suspicion as the new-fangled steam packet from Holyhead, 160 years before. They would notice, however, that the *clochán* of Carn just above Dungiven has diminished

35

An early-nineteenth-century engraving of Londonderry

from over forty houses to just one or two; while Dungiven itself, though it still has the same main street, has grown out of all recognition. In fact all the towns and villages have grown enormously, but the life has ebbed away from the open Sperrins. The sad procession of emigrants recorded by the Fishmongers in 1820 has never really ceased and the Sperrins could now be seen as a depopulated landscape.

Depopulation can be exemplified by a typical upland parish, which before the Great Famine in 1845–8 had 9200 inhabitants; in ten years it was down to 7800. By 1951 the same parish had only 3000 inhabitants. The census base has changed since then, but figures from the same area show a great loss in the younger age groups. These figures tell the same story as the roofless cabins and neglected farms. It is time for drastic action once again.

A fresh perspective on Sperrin landscape

Now that London and the home counties of England are so overpopulated, our London merchants might be more appreciative of the wild, uninhabited open spaces of the Sperrins. The descendants of the Fishmongers' tenants are still finding agriculture a borderline

economic activity in what has now been officially dubbed a 'less-favoured area', and some of them are trying to capitalise on their wild open spaces and beautiful scenery. This explains some unusual recent landscape developments which are aimed at bringing people back to enjoy the beauty of the Sperrin landscape without actually having to make a living there, thus providing alternative employment for some of the residents, and a new Sperrin way of life.

So our intrepid Londoners could go to the Ulster American Folk Park near Omagh and see a re-enactment of the emigration story. They would find an original farm and replicas of cabins, a meeting house and forge such as they would remember from over a century ago. They could then see what happened to their surplus tenants as they voyaged on the emigrant ship, and their lifestyle on arrival in America. A few miles further on they would find an unprecedented concentration of ancient monuments, telling the story of Sperrin in earlier times at the Gortin History Park. In a deep narrow Sperrin glen beneath the southern slopes of Sawel they would find a heritage centre portraying life in the Sperrins' uplands as they had seen it themselves at first hand.

Sperrin landscape and culture are now being marketed as never before, and anyone curious enough to explore this remote and largely unknown part of Ireland's beautiful landscape will find a ready welcome among these hidden valleys and heather-topped hills.

GWEN BUCHANAN is a graduate of the Department of Geography at Queen's University Belfast, and now works as a landscape architect.

FROM WICKLOW TO THE SHANNON ESTUARY
A Coastal Journey
Frank Mitchell

The Wicklow uplands

The uplands of Wicklow have a core of granite hills, whose rounded outlines dominate the skyline. The upland area runs north-east/south-west, and is about 40km long and 16km wide. Nearly all this area is above the limit of modern agriculture, and we have hill pastures with furze and bracken, which pass up into blanket bog on the still higher tops. Sheep and a few hardy cattle graze these upper slopes.

Geology, of course, deals in immense periods of time, and no less than 400 million years have gone by since the granite welled up in a porridge-like mass into overlying still older rocks, which have since been largely stripped away by erosion.

The heat of the granite altered these rocks, and, where they were sandy in texture, they were welded into quartzite, a virtually indestructible rock. Today these quartzite masses stand up as isolated peaks, of which the Great and Little Sugarloaf are the most striking. The same rock occurs in western Ireland, and there we have Croagh Patrick in Mayo and Errigal in Donegal.

Where the older rocks were clayey, they were less permanently altered, and weathering has cut them down to lower levels around the granite, and has broken them down into soils of clayey texture. Though not inherently fertile, these soils are well drained, and are productive when well managed.

In relatively recent geological time, beginning perhaps 2 million years ago, the climate of north-west Europe became very much colder, and great masses of ice, like those of Greenland today, dominated the Irish scene. Sometimes the Leinster hills had their own cap of ice; at other times ice formed elsewhere pushed into the area. When the ice around the mountains was melting away,

The Glen of the Downs, through which the main Dublin–Wexford road runs, was cut when meltwater separated one lake from another.

great lakes were dammed up between ice and hillside. Where a hill-spur held up the water, overflow might occur, and the escaping water would cut a channel through the spur. Such abandoned channels are very common round the Wicklow hills, and of these the Glen of the Downs is one of the most dramatic examples.

The ice transported quantities of rock debris as it moved along, and when it melted away, the debris was dumped, often as great masses of sand and gravel.

Ireland's first farmers probably crossed by sea from Wales, and the mouths of the Dargle at Bray, the Vartry at Wicklow, and the Avoca at Arklow would have been attractive landing-points. The farmers would have stepped ashore into a land that was covered with trees from end to end, and it must have been hard to decide where to start on the heavy task of making openings in the woodlands for their herds and crops.

Perhaps the trees were thinner and lighter on the uplands. The early people built big tombs on the upper hill-slopes, and their best known settlement is on the top of Baltinglass Hill at a height of 400m.

Excavation here produced charred remains of wheat and barley with an age of 4500 years, so tillage has been going on in Leinster for a long, long time.

Wexford

Tacumshin windmill near Rosslare is one of only two monuments of major industrial archaeological importance in state care, the other being Ballycopeland windmill in Co. Down. Windmills were uncommon in Ireland except in the drumlin country of the north where the topography was particularly well-suited to them.

The granite hills of Wicklow continue their south-westerly course into Wexford, but as they do so they narrow and drop in level so that when we reach New Ross they have disappeared.

Parallel with the hills we have a broad band of older slaty rocks between 70m and 200m; their south-east boundary runs from Gorey to Duncannon. Here glacial deposits are thin, and the soil qualities are the produce of rock decay. This results in well-drained but hungry soils, which respond well to good management, particularly in fertiliser application. Generally the soils are excellent for tillage, and the old-fashioned title of 'model county' largely reflects the high soil quality together with the relatively low rainfall of the area.

But once we get below 70m we have a different story to tell, as the influence of the former ice-sheets makes itself felt. The Irish Sea is older than the Ice Age, and its floor was draped with thick deposits of marine clay. Great sheets of ice flowed down the basin of the Irish Sea from Scotland, engulfing the clay as they moved along. The margin of the ice 'overflowed' up on to coastal Wexford, depositing a mantle of clay on which the modern soils must inevitably be very poorly drained.

In these areas, neglected fields quickly become dominated by a thick sward of rushes. How to manage these soils is a real problem. When Griffith made his valuation of Irish farmlands in the 1850s, these fields were worked with spades, the weak structure of the soil was not a problem, and fine crops of wheat were grown. A high valuation was assigned, and this persists to the present day. But if the fields are grazed, they 'poach' (become cut up and damaged) all too easily. Farm machinery too may get into difficulties, and with mechanical working it is almost impossible to produce a good tilth. Field drains often give a disappointing result, because the soil is so heavy that the water cannot move even to the pipes.

Perhaps because it has been intensively farmed for so long, Wexford is not rich in surviving prehistoric monuments. But it has the distinction of holding the site where the Anglo-Normans first landed in Ireland. The Normans found the soils of Wexford to their taste, and protected their square farmyards by surrounding them with a bank and ditch. Many such square moated sites still survive.

Wexford has more wind than running water, and windmills were very common; one complete example still survives at Tacumshin.

38

East Munster

After the granite of Leinster had been forced upwards, much of Ireland stood above sea-level, and as the mountains wasted away great sheets of desert sands were scattered far and wide over the country. Then, about 350 million years ago, a sea rich in marine shell life invaded Ireland, and thick deposits of limy shell debris were deposited on its floor. Earth pressures from north and south developed, and the sands, now changed into sandstone, and the shelly ooze, now changed into limestone, were forced into tight corrugated folds running east and west. At some unknown – but much later – date these folds were bevelled by a horizontal surface across which parallel bands of alternating limestone and sandstone ran from east to west. We can see this surface very well as we step out of an aeroplane at Cork Airport, where we have a remarkably level skyline at about 200m all around us.

A panorama near Cappoquin, Co. Waterford, looking east-north-east

We can trace the surface north-east till it ends in what seems to be an old cliff, cut in the south face of the Knockmealdown mountains. It is very tempting to think that this surface is a former sea-floor, ending against coastal cliffs, and that we have here evidence of the changes of level of land and sea that have been going on throughout geological time.

When the sea receded, leaving the surface exposed to the erosive powers of rain and river, the bands of limestone were very much weaker than the bands of sandstone. The sandstone bands still have their flat tops at about 200m, but the limestones have dropped in level to form east/west gutters, providing valleys for the Blackwater, the Lee and the Bandon.

The gutter for the Blackwater continues to Dungarvan, but at Cappoquin the river turns abruptly south and cuts through sandstone ridges to reach the sea at Youghal. The Lee does the same; it abandons its east/west gutter at Cork and cuts through sandstone ridges to reach the sea. As yet no satisfactory explanation has been given for these changes in course.

More recently the process has been reversed, and the sea has gained on the land, drowning the lower parts of the valleys and allowing the tide to flow far inland. The drowned mouth of the Lee forms Cork harbour, and the Bandon has a yachters' paradise at Kinsale.

Glacial deposits are not prominent in this area, tending to occur in the valleys but having disappeared from the ridge-tops. The soils are well drained; those derived from limestone are naturally fertile, and with good management the sandstones also yield well.

These soil advantages are capped by the benefits of southern location. A more genial climate than that of the rest of Ireland brings early growth and heavy cropping, and the farmers of east Cork enjoy the most favourable conditions that Ireland can offer.

Archaeological evidence suggests that the area was intensively farmed in early Christian times by people who were in touch with Britain and the continent. Most farms and settlements were surrounded by a circular bank and ditch, and the latter still survive to be the *rath* or *lios* of the modern countryside.

The big rath or fort at Ballycatteen, near Kinsale, had pottery of eastern Mediterranean origin dating to about AD 600, while a smaller rath at Garryduff near Midleton produced pieces of slate on which had been scratched designs similar to those that decorate the Book of Kells, written about AD 800.

The Dingle peninsula

West of Cork the limestone disappears, the east/west folding takes on a stronger pattern, and mountainous ridges of sandstone separated by drowned valleys dominate the landscape.

The Dingle peninsula, with a central ridge of peaks rising to 700m and culminating in Mount Brandon, over 1000m, is the most northern of the ridges. During the Ice Age these hills, like those in Wicklow, were high enough for local masses of ice to accumulate on them, and from these masses valley glaciers flowed downslope to lower levels. The ice rounded and polished the rock it flowed over, and nowhere in western Europe can we see this more clearly than around the Connor Pass, north-east of Dingle.

As an ice mass formed, severe frost action around it shattered the local rock, and as the ice moved forwards and downwards it carried off the rock debris, and thus created a hollow or *coum* as it is called in Kerry, into which the ice mass settled itself more and more firmly. When the ice melted away a small lake occupied the lower part of the hollow, and Brandon mountain is gutted on its east side by such lake-filled coums.

The ice melted away on the lower ground surrounding the hills, and as it did so it deposited the rock debris it had been carrying as a crude unsorted mixture of stones, sand and silt, all derived from the sandstone core of the peninsula. It probably disappeared about 16,000 years ago.

Prehistoric people have not left much legacy here, but the area was densely settled in the early Christian period, and we can still see the pattern of small irregular fields with farming and monastic settlements scattered through them. There was plenty of stone available and round 'bee-hive' huts, 'cashels' surrounded by circular stone walls, and small

Left
Where a glacier formed on a mountain, it gradually gouged out a deep hollow and when it eventually melted away, it left behind an amphitheatre exposed on the mountainside, which is called a *coum* in Ireland, as can be seen here at the Connor Pass, north-east of Dingle.

Opposite
Here the sediments are sandstones and shales and the rock folds of Cork and Kerry have faded away.

rectangular 'oratories' were built everywhere.

But the glacial debris on which the soils developed had very little primary fertility, and what there was was gradually washed down to lower levels by the high rainfall of the region. Thus the soil developed a pale barren horizon with an impervious sheet of iron pan below, the *podsol* of the soil scientist. The result was one of the worst of soils, being both infertile and badly drained.

Rushes and sedges could grow freely on it, and gradually their debris built up a scraw of raw humus. But the local beaches which were rarely far away had sands with calcareous shell debris and also seaweed, and it came to be realised that it was easy, if laborious, to draw cartloads from the shore and spread it on the land, and thus superimpose a new artificial soil, fertile and well-drained, on top of the infertile podsol. Though the practice is now largely abandoned, the 'sanded' land remains fertile.

The Lower Shannon estuary

When we reach the estuary of the Shannon the east/west rock-folds that dominate much of Cork and Kerry have faded away. The fertile limestone that we saw in east Cork reappears west of Limerick city in undisturbed layers or strata, that slope gently westwards. The limestone was originally deposited as a shelly ooze in clear water, but about 300 million years ago rivers began to carry sands and clays into the clear-water sea, which gradually became so choked with sediment that it turned into shallow estuaries with great swamp-forests, whose woody debris later changed into coal.

Today the estuarine sediments are sandstones and shales, sometimes with thin seams of coal. Unfortunately, commercial deposits of coal, such as still exist in Britain, have – if indeed they ever existed – been stripped away by erosion. But west of a line joining Ennis and Newcastle West the sandstones and shales come in on top of the limestone, and as they are more resistant to weathering than the limestone, their eastern limit rises as an escarpment standing above the limestone plain. This is well seen west of Ardagh, where flat hay-fields give way to steep slopes with rushes.

West of the escarpment lies an impoverished plateau, very different from the rich dairy lands of Limerick. The sandstones and shales are low in nutrients, and the shale debris gives a high clay content to the soil, with consequent impeded drainage.

Rushes, sedges and mosses flourished in the combination of poor drainage and moist oceanic air, and as low temperatures allowed plant debris to decay only slowly, a slowly accumulating layer of plant debris gradually buried the whole countryside under a layer of blanket bog.

However, the land could be got at by digging away the peat, which itself could be burned for fuel. Thus in the pre-Famine period of rapidly rising population the area accommodated many new families, who created their land-holding by digging away and burning the peat, and then growing potatoes in the poor quality soil they revealed.

Their tracks and roads ran on top of the bog, and here the peat was not cut away, so that today many of the roads run on top of embankments of surviving peat, several feet above the level of the surrounding fields.

But there was a limited amount of good land on the flanks of the estuary. The last ice from inland Ireland pushed down the estuary to reach its limit just beyond Kilrush.

The ice had picked up much limestone as it moved across Limerick, and as it melted away great masses of fertile, well-drained, limestone-rich sands and gravels were deposited. These cross the estuary in a great arc, from west of Kilrush through Scattery Island to Ballylongford.

The early monastery on Scattery Island with its round tower and its churches was raided many times by the Vikings. In the fifteenth century the creek at Ballylongford held a rich and beautiful Franciscan abbey, while the mouth of the inlet was guarded by Carrigafoyle Castle. The castle was the scene of many bitter fights before it was finally wrecked by Cromwell's armies.

41

THE VIEW FROM ERRISBEG
Connemara and the Aran Islands

Tim Robinson

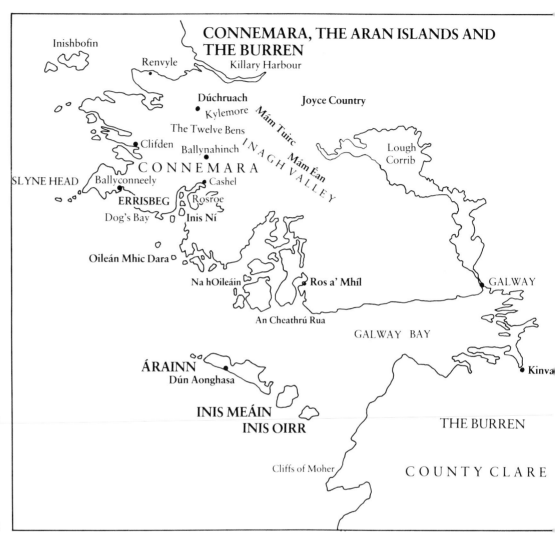

CONNEMARA, THE ARAN ISLANDS AND THE BURREN

In my face, the Atlantic wind, bringing walls of rain, low ceilings of cloud, dazzling windows of sunshine, the endless transformation scenes of the far west. Underfoot, dark crystalline stone, one of the many summits of a dragon-backed hill, the last, beyond which the land tails off into a bleak peninsula, clusters of foaming rocks and a lonely lighthouse. And spread below, to the north, a bewildering topography of lakes lost in bogs, across which scarcely less comprehensible maps of cloud-shadow race inland, towards mountain ranges. Eastwards, a wrinkled golden spread half unravelled by the sea, dotted with the tiny white rectangles of human habitation; off this, to the south, islands, the nearer ones gold too, those on the horizon grey-blue; finally, closing the south-east, another land of grey-blue plateaux.

The hill is Errisbeg, which shelters the little fishing village of Roundstone from the west wind, in Connemara; the portion of the world's surface visible from its summit comprises the suite of landscapes grouped around Galway Bay which it has been my wonderful and wearying privilege to explore in detail over the last fifteen years, the Burren uplands in County Clare, the Aran Islands, and Connemara itself. Most recently I have been enquiring out the names of those lakes that lie on the dark plain below like fragments of a pane of glass flung down and shattered. The elderly men who used to herd sheep, fish for brown trout or shoot the white-fronted Greenland goose out in that labyrinth can recall about two dozen of the names of the larger lakes, and there are a similar number of others, not to mention countless little ones, whose names I am beginning to despair of, all within an area of about thirty square miles. One is called Loch Beithinis, birch-island lake, for while the lakes themselves are often

hard to find among the slight undulations of the bog, the wind-shaped domes of the dense little woods on their islands are visible from greater distances. Crows nest on most of these, and the occasional merlin; some are heronries, and the trees of one have been reduced to skeletons by the droppings of generations of cormorants. The vegetation of these ungrazed islands suggest that but for the omnipresent sheep at least the better-drained parts of such low-lying blanket boglands would be covered with a forest of sessile oak, holly, yew, birch and willow. As elsewhere, it is human activity that determines the texture of what appears at first glance to be untouched wilderness, a fact that complicates the conservationist case somewhat. However, the core of this area, which is becoming known as Roundstone bog, having been spared by forestry and turf-cutting so far, most certainly should be preserved as it is; apart from its ecological uniqueness, it harbours one of the rarest of resources, solitude.

One road winds across this bog, along which the traveller can enjoy a sky undivided

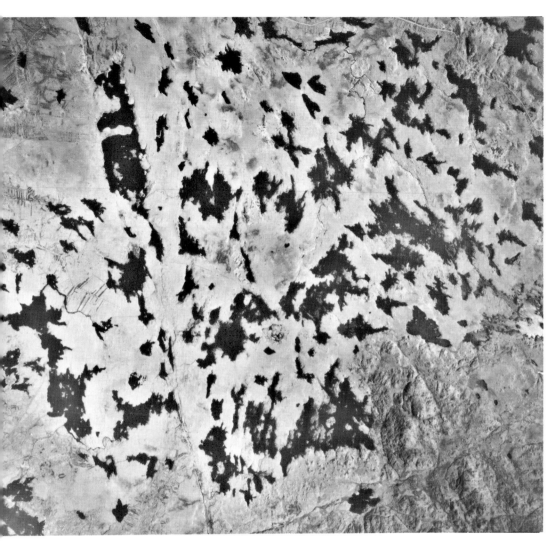

Aerial photograph of Roundstone bog, a unique area of blanket bog with a labyrinthine drainage system of lakes and streams, developed on a low-lying glacially-scoured plain. Errisbeg Hill is at the bottom right. Note the roads fringed with turf-cuttings intruding from the left.

white peak, and one which is not a peak but a massive lump, called Meacanach, probably from an obsolete Irish word meaning a lumpy thing. While the sharper summits are of quartzite, a rock resistant to weathering and inhospitable to vegetation, Meacanach is of kinder stuff, a schist that breaks down into a clayey soil; its southern face is green, and rare alpines lurk on its north-facing precipices. Further east, and separated from the Bens by the majestic Inagh lake-valley, rise the Mám Tuirc mountains, a line of peaks forming a natural boundary between Connemara proper and its eastern province, the Joyce country. Mám Tuirc itself, the pass of the boar, towards the northern end of the range, is hidden from me by the Bens, but I can make out the broad saddle of Mám Éan, the pass of the birds, near the southern end of this range, where the ancient Celts used to celebrate the festival of Lughnasa at the beginning of harvest-time. Later this site was Christianised, and legend brings St Patrick there to bless the lands west of it from that high vantage-point. For the Pattern Day festivities that succeeded to Lughnasa, Connemara and the Joyce country would meet up there, to pray, to drink *poitín*, and to enjoy a blackthorn-stick fight. A few years ago the clergy imposed the alien rite of the Stations of the Cross on Mám Éan, but folk wise to the ancient ways still clamber into a hollow of the steep wall of the pass, known as St Patrick's Bed, and turn

by wires. I can just make it out from Errisbeg, clambering around the knoll called Na Creaga Móra, the big crags, famous in botanic literature as the station of a heather, Mackay's heath, discovered here by the self-taught Roundstone botanist William McCalla in 1835, and otherwise known only from Donegal, and Oviedo in Spain. The other rare heathers of Roundstone bog are the Dorset heath, of which half a dozen tussocks here constitute the entire Irish population, and the mediterranean heath, which grows in the streaming valleys of Errisbeg's north-east

flank, and in Mayo, and is otherwise restricted to Spain and Portugal. It is that mild Atlantic climate that fosters such southern exotics in this almost tundra-like expanse.

Following that road with my eye, I see it disappear north-westwards, where the Protestant spire and the Catholic spire of Clifden show above low hills, the western decrescendo of a symphony of mountains all along the skyline. Due north of me, the Twelve Bens huddle like sheep; there are in fact eleven peaks of between 1700 and 2400 feet in height, with names like Binn Bhán, the

43

round seven times, sunwise.

Although the clustered Bens and the oblique line of the Mám Tuirc peaks look unrelated when one clambers among them, their essential unity is clearer in this view from Errisbeg. They are the remains of one great ridge running from east to west, which dates from the Caledonian period of mountain building some 450 million years ago, when two of the plates that make up the earth's crust were slowly driving against one another, the resultant crumpling being the origin of the mountains of Scandinavia, 'Caledonia, stern and wild' itself, northern Ireland and Newfoundland. A sandstone of even earlier date was pinched in the interior of a giant fold here, and recrystallised under immense pressure to produce the unyielding quartzite of the Connemara peaks. Clay and limestone materials caught up into the outer layers of the fold were metamorphosed into the softer schists and marble that have worn away since then to form the lower land south of the mountains, the corresponding but narrower valleys north of them, and the broad north–south corridor of the Inagh valley.

The blackish crags of Errisbeg itself are of gabbro, a dense basic rock that came up molten from the earth's mantle, probably in the Ordovician period, some tens of millions of years before the Caledonian convulsions. The lovely cone of Cashel hill, rising from the head of the bay east of Roundstone, is of the same rock, and there are a few similar hills north of the Bens, including Dúchruach, the 'black stack', that lowers over the wooded valley and the lake of Kylemore, in perfect sympathy with the nineteenth-century Gothic fantasy of Kylemore Abbey. Thus there are dark hills both north and south of the pale quartzite mountains, preserving the

approximate symmetry of Connemara about its east–west axis.

The ice ages, starting about one and a half million years ago and perhaps not all past yet, have carved up all these variously resistant rocks into the welter of forms that meet the eye today, excavating the valleys between the mountain ranges and the great fjord of Killary Harbour that divides Connemara from the Mayo uplands to the north. Some of the material removed by the glaciers was dumped when they melted back, in the form of the low rounded hills of boulders and clay called drumlins by geologists. These isolated hills, usually of green, arable land, contrast vividly with the dark level bogs on which they are stranded, and they all have individual names. In south-western Connemara such a hill is an *imleach*, perhaps from their rather sharply defined rims (*imeall*, a rim). From Errisbeg I can identify several of them, including

Imleach na Beithe, the drumlin of the birch, and Imleach Caorach, sheep-drumlin, near Ballyconneely to my west.

So, one prehistoric collision of continents, a few hundred million years of erosion, and my almost equally drastic geological oversimplifications, suffice to explain the look of things to the north of Errisbeg. But this tousled fringe of Connemara to the east – can any generalisation hold it together? Immediately below me is Roundstone Bay, most of which is occupied by an island, Inis Ní, which is not quite an island since there is a causeway and a bridge leading into it, and even before that was built people could walk into it over the seaweed-covered rocks when the tide was out – though, on the other hand, very high tides still sometimes make three islands out of Inis Ní. And Roundstone Bay is only a side-issue of Cuan na Beirtrí Buí, the bay of the yellow oyster-bank, which goes on

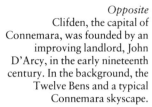

to divide again, facing the incoming salmon with a choice between the outlet of the famous Ballynahinch fishery on the west and Cashel Bay on the east, which delivers them into the hands of the Zetland Hotel's guests. Beyond this dilemma is a broad headland with the ancient name of Iorras Aintheach, the stormy peninsula; it carries the villages of Carna and Cill Chiaráin, and to the south spawns various islands, some isolated and deserted since a generation or two ago, others linked to the mainland by causeways and still populated, others exactly half-way between these two conditions, being accessible at low tide and occasionally reoccupied by the last of their former inhabitants, who gather winkles round their shores or take cattle out to graze there. A little further out is the most precious stone of all this stony littoral, the bare low dome of St MacDara's Island, with its minute oratory dating back almost to the age of the

hermits who sought out such inaccessible retreats all around the coasts of Connemara. Eastwards again, more ramifying bays, with islands strung together by causeways or proliferating out into the spaces of Galway Bay itself, defying and delighting the map-maker.

All this topographical extravaganza has been carved out of granite, which was intruded into the pre-existent rocks a little over 400 million years ago at the end of the Caledonian mountain-building period. It is criss-crossed with joints and faults, which the sea has exploited to bite off archipelagos and prise open the creeks that traverse it in all directions. Without these sea-ways, as I will show, it would be as sparsely inhabited as the boglands and mountains further inland, whereas in fact it is the most densely populated part of Conne-mara. But in spite of the cottages and

bungalows strung out along its web of roads and boreens, this is an intimidating landscape, of glinting pinkish or golden-brown rock-sheets, polished by the ice ages and strewn with glacial boulders, interspersed with tiny cup-shaped tillage plots of black, waterlogged soil, and interrupted everywhere by dark stony or muddy shores upon which high tides heap unbelievable masses of orange seaweed. This growth of knotted wrack or yellow-weed as it is called here, is one of the factors that has made life possible on the acidic granite, for large amounts of it were harvested, both for fertilising the land and for burning to kelp, the main source of industrial alkalis in the eighteenth and of iodine in the nineteenth century; it was the money paid out by the agent of a Scottish kelp-firm resident at Cashel that kept hundreds of families just above starvation level in the 1880s. Even

today one can see rafts of weed being towed into quays all around that intricate coast, for sale to a factory at Cill Chiaráin as a source of the alginates used in thickening agents.

Another resource of this apparently unfavoured coast was its covering of bog, which developed on the impervious granite much as it did on the metamorphic rocks inland. That covering is almost entirely stripped away now, through generations of cutting of the turf that was shipped out of hundreds of little harbours to be burnt in Galway city or on the other side of Galway Bay. But to develop this theme of the strange process by which the bareness of one landscape made another bare, I must now look south, to those islands that lie like clean steel blades along the horizon, so utterly different from the rusty twistings of south Connemara.

Seeing the three Aran Islands from Errisbeg, wrapped in their blue-grey cloaks of monkish remoteness and simplicity, it is hard to credit that a thousand people live out there, manning an up-to-date trawler fleet, profiting from tourism, as well as farming those immemorially stony little fields reclaimed from the bare crags. As I watch, a line of light seeping under them from the bright horizon seems to be easing them free of even that precarious relationship to mainland realities the sea can mediate, and floating them back to the time when *Ára na Naomh*, Aran of the Saints, was a source of inspiration to the monasteries of western Europe. The tall cliffs of Árainn or Inishmore, the largest of the islands, are turned away from me, facing the south-western Atlantic spaces, but I can still feel the thunder of the billows in their recesses, and hear the fierce clamouring of a peregrine falcon swooping along their sheer faces. And beyond the islands, the Burren,

with its flower-strewn hills rising in sweeping terraces to breezy plateaux, cross-hatched by four thousand years of wall-building! Marvels beyond description! I turn again to geology, mother of earth-sciences, for some unifying approach to them.

The essential oneness of the three islands and of the Burren is clearly discernible from Errisbeg; the islands are built of a number of thick, horizontal layers of rock that correspond to those of the Burren, and have evidently been separated from it by long-acting agencies that have not otherwise disrupted their strata. Whereas the visual turmoil of Connemara is a memory-trace of the land's travail, those sober levels to the south are the petrified after-image of a long-departed sea. A hundred million years after the Caledonian events, this area all lay under a subtropical ocean, the waters of

46

Opposite
The terraced terrain of the Aran Islands, rising from a low north-east shoreline to the 300-foot-high cliffs of the south-west coast, facing the Atlantic. The village of Cill Mhuirbhigh nestles in the shelter of a small inland cliff. The general pattern of the stone walls is dictated by the orientation of the principal set of fissures running through the limestone. Dún Aonghasa is on the cliff edge (to the left).

Right
A late Bronze Age stone alignment in Gleninagh near the head of the Inagh valley, discovered by the author in 1985. In the background, bare quartzite peaks of the Twelve Bens.

which pullulated with shelled creatures, from dot-sized Foraminifera to brachiopods as big as saucers. Their remains, piling up together with the corals of the sea-bed for countless generations, compressed into limestone under their own weight, eventually totalled a thickness of over half a mile. Earth movements must have changed the depth of this Carboniferous sea from time to time, as there are thin strata of shale formed from the mud of shallow, coastal waters, between the strata of limestone, and even bands of clay, showing that the surface occasionally rose above the water long enough for a soil to form, only to be submerged again. Eventually, some 270 million years ago, a final upward heave abolished that sea, and since then climates ranging from the tropical to the glacial, and the surges of the modern Atlantic, have been eating away at the limestone, leaving the three islands and the dissected plateau of the Burren, which are even now being reduced in level by a millimetre or so every year through the solvent action of the rain.

Subsequent movements of the earth's crust connected with the opening up of the Atlantic Ocean have exerted lateral tensions on the limestone beds, fracturing them in a system of vertical cracks, of astonishing regularity in places, the major ones running south-south-west, the minor set at right angles to this direction. Flowing rainwater has enlarged these into fissures of all widths up to two feet or so, subdividing the rock outcrops into rectangular slabs, or, where they are very close-set, a rubble of blocks. So the surface, with whatever shallow soil it carries, is extremely efficiently drained. But while the limestone is vulnerable to rain, the shale and clay bands are more resistant. On a hillside it is the limestone exposed between the outcrop of two of these bands that will be removed first, while that overlain by the bands will persist longer, so the hillside is eaten away into great steps; such at least is one scenario that has been proposed to account for the terraced formation of the Aran Islands and the higher regions of the Burren. Therefore the clay and shale is exposed all along the feet of the steep scarps or low cliffs that run across the hillsides, and the rainwater that sinks through the limestone layers and is then conducted horizontally by the impervious shale bubbles out in springs at the foot of these cliffs, washing the shale or clay out with it, to add a soil to the attractions of these particular levels. Even from Errisbeg I can see how the lines of white dots, the cottages and bungalows along Aran's roads, follow the terraces, keeping their heads down below the ridgeline that shields them from the prevailing south-westerlies.

As neighbours, the Aran Islands have come to be closely related in culture to south Connemara; both speak Irish, most importantly, and indeed between them they carry most of the language's hopes for the future. But ecologically and archaeologically they belong to the Burren, limestone being the determining factor. Nearly all the Burren's famous flora is shared with the islands; the

The treeless landscape of the Aran Islands, open to the salt-laden winds of the Atlantic. Gort na gCapall, the field of the horses, is the name of the little village shown here. On the skyline is Dún Aonghasa, a Celtic Iron Age cliff-top fort.

mountain avens is absent but most of its other alpine or northern species such as the spring gentian are present, while the roseroot (in Connemara exceedingly rare and found only on certain cliffs near the mountain-tops) flourishes on some exposed areas of pavement down to sea-level. There are plants peculiar to Aran too. In the wind- and rabbit-mown sward of the highest cliff-tops one can find the purple milk-vetch, recorded nowhere else in Ireland, which is perhaps a relict of the tundra vegetation of immediately postglacial times. And since agriculture is on such a minute scale in Aran's tiny fields, some weeds still occur that have been exterminated almost everywhere else; I have even found the

pennycress, whose transparent disk-shaped capsules used to delight children of previous generations in many rural areas.

Despite such multicoloured mitigations, though, Aran is a desolation of bare stone, like the Burren. But in both places the sheer number of prehistoric monuments shows that this cannot always have been the case. For instance in the Aran Islands there are five megalithic tombs of the type known from their shape as wedge tombs and usually dated to the late neolithic or early Bronze Age (though some archaeologists are now suggesting that they might be earlier). Then there are no less than seven great stone cashels, including the promontory fort of

Dúchathair, and Ireland's most spectacular prehistoric monument, Dún Aonghasa, whose three roughly semicircular ramparts abut onto the edge of a dizzy cliff above the Atlantic and which is visible in silhouette even from Errisbeg; both these forts have arrays of set stones before them, an apparently defensive feature that suggests, by analogy with similar cases in Iberia, an early Iron Age date. The scores of stone huts or *clóchan*s and stony mounds that could well be ruined *clóchan*s, and above all the numerous early ecclesiastical sites, suggest that the early Christian period here was settled and prosperous. In medieval times the O'Briens, the dominant force in Munster, had three

The triple ramparts of Dún Aonghasa. The inner wall is built up of three layers forming terraces on the inner face. Since there is no source of fresh water within this so-called fort, it may be that its main function was ceremonial.

small number of megaliths in the north-west, a spate of recent discoveries has shown that in the neolithic and the Bronze Age a large area around the bays of Streamstown and Ballynakill was almost as rich as the Burren. About twenty-seven court tombs, portal dolmens, wedge tombs and others that do not fit into these perhaps too-neat classifications are now known from the area, while the total of about twenty standing stones and stone alignments makes north-west Connemara show up on a distribution map that was otherwise rather blank between south Munster and central Ulster. This bay area evidently was then, as it still is, the most prosperous part of Connemara, because of its deposits of glacial till and scattered outcrops of metamorphosed limestone.

In central Connemara only a widely spread handful of such megaliths is known (as yet, I should add, for even these discoveries are only of the last two or three years), while in south Connemara there is little or nothing of the sort. Some of these finds have been revealed by turf-cutting, and close to many of them one can make out the walls of fields that predate the growth of the bogs. It was perhaps the arsonist clearance methods of those early farmers, coinciding with a climatic change (from a warmer, drier, postglacial period to the cool, wet times we still enjoy today) that proved too much for the great forests that formerly covered the land and whose roots can be seen in the bottoms of the turfbanks.

The evidence for later settlement is more scattered and ambiguous. There are about a dozen promontory forts, stone cashels and earthen raths, nearly all on or near the western coastline, none of them comparable with the great forts of Aran. More characteristic of the region is the widely

tower houses on the islands (which they lost to the O'Flahertys of Connemara in the 1550s). The O'Briens also added a Franciscan friary to the three already venerable monasteries of Árainn. The record of settlement in the Burren is similarly continuous, and there recent studies in environmental archaeology (such as the analysis of soil from beneath ancient walls and megalithic tombs) is tending to reinforce the impression that the limestone lands remained fertile and productive long after bog had begun to form elsewhere, and that their present stoniness is not of such antiquity as had been thought.

The story in Connemara is intriguingly different. Here, early cultures left abundant traces, but then the trail almost peters out. Middens of seashells, looking much like those in the Dingle peninsula now thought to be of late mesolithic or early neolithic date, occur on several of Connemara's shores. Just below Errisbeg for instance, the sandy spit between the lovely back-to-back beaches of Dog's Bay and Port na Feadóige (the plovers' bay) was evidently a resort of those early food-gatherers, for in the eroded dune-faces one can see blackish layers full of bones, winkle-shells and the heat-shattered stones of their hearths. And whereas only a few years ago the received opinion was that Connemara has little to offer the archaeologist apart from a scattered score or so of crannogs (cashel-like lake-dwellings on wholly or partly artificial islands). Perhaps there were unenclosed forms of settlement too that have left fewer traces, or perhaps the onset of bog development was already concentrating life on the teeming trout lakes south of the Bens. In any case, it is as if Connemara had become a quieter place, when the Burren and Aran were humming with energy. After the Iron Age, settlement seems to confine itself to the coast. The monks of the island hermitages and seashore oratories were notoriously averse to neighbours – tradition repeatedly tells of them departing out of hearing of each other's bells – so the ragged periphery of a deserted Connemara must have suited them well. The seven tower houses (chiefly of the O'Flahertys) were all on the coast, with the exception of one centrally placed, on the lake-island of Ballynahinch, and as far apart as could well be. The bogs, by sealing off the interior, had deprived the coast of its supportive hinterland, and while the wars and resettlements of the Elizabethan and Cromwellian centuries eventually repopulated the coastal fringe with the dispossessed, the centre of Connemara remains virtually desolate to this day. But while Connemara was wrapping itself in bog, the Burren and the Aran Islands remained hospitable throughout, until their continuous millennia of intensive farming reduced them to naked rock, perhaps as recently as the Middle Ages. The difference between limestone on the one hand and metamorphic or igneous rocks on the other has been a dominant element in this divergence of the fate of these lands throughout the rainy centuries of the Atlantic regime: limestone drinks water; granite hoards it.

But then came a strange reversal of fortunes. Since at least the seventeenth century the only source of fuel for the limestone side of Galway Bay has been the peat covering the granite side, and throughout the centuries of Ireland's huge population growth every niche of the south Connemara coastline sheltered a tiny harbour exporting the region's turf to Aran, to Ballyvaughan, to Kinvara, to some little landing-stage corresponding to each village of the islands and the Burren coast. The nineteenth century was the heyday of the Galway hookers, the tar-black wooden workboats with their brown sails, capacious bellies and lines honed by generations of experience of lee Atlantic shores. In 1836 there were just over three hundred sailboats working out of harbours from Roundstone to Ros a' Mhíl, engaged in fishing, general trading and the carriage of turf; the seaways of south Connemara were brimming with life. Even today elderly Araners look back nostalgically to the beautiful sight of the approach of the turfboats bringing their winter warmth. Many other goods crossed the bay with the hookers too: Aran potatoes in payment for turf, *poitín* from Connemara, limestone itself brought back as ballast in empty turfboats and burned in kilns on Connemara shores for lime to whiten the houses and sweeten the land. Connemara cattle used to be taken over to winter on the comparatively dry limestone crags, where they fared much better than in the sodden fields of their home. On the other hand, the Aran farmer used his (Connemara) pony mainly in the winter, for carrying fodder to the cattle out on the crags on 'the back of the island', and for carting seaweed to the fields as fertiliser or to the stacks for kelp-making; in the summer when grass and water were scarce in the islands he could send it back to its native hillsides. Invisible goods were carried in the turfboats too: stories, songs, love even, mixing the folklore and the gene-pools of granite country and limestone land. As two different metals dipped in acid can power a voltaic cell, so all this life-force was generated by the differences between the sterile granite and the fertile limestone, in the common medium of scarcity.

But it was a precarious symbiosis, as the view from Errisbeg reminds me. Just across Roundstone Bay I see a cluster of roofless walls on a desolate promontory, Rosroe, An Ros Rua, the reddish peninsula. 'Rua' is a common place-name element here, and the reddishness is that of poor, brackeny land, of nitrogen-deficient vegetation. Rosroe

Right
Aerial photograph of Cathair an Dúin, Connemara's best-preserved promontory fort, near Renvyle. It is built on a drumlin into which the sea has cut 100-foot cliffs, and its defensive bank is of earth. The building within it was a local defence force lookout post during the second world war. The shadows of old potato ridges demonstrate that much land now disused was intensively cultivated in the last century.

Far right
Loch na Scainimhe near Carna in south Connemara. The round island nearest the bottom left-hand corner of the upper lake on the right is a crannog with a dry-stone wall about 10 feet thick. The larger island to the right of it, close to the shore, is also walled. The seashore is on the left, with its narrow coastal strip of tiny pastures and tillage plots. Bog roads reach out to the turf-cuttings around the lake shore.

depended entirely on its turf trade, and got its potatoes in Aran rather than plant them at home; so, according to local oral history, it 'went down' in the first year of the Great Famine, while other villages survived longer. In those years some Connemara people fled to Aran, lived in little caves of the inland cliffs there and worked for their keep, until the bailiffs drove them out; for Aran, with its better soil, its degree of insulation from potato blight, and its variety of sea and shore food sources, lost nobody through hunger, it is said, whereas in south Connemara in particular the famine grave in the thicket or among the stones of the foreshore is a constant if obscure element of local geography. And throughout these times, as the recurrent famines settled into the chronic misery of the 'Congested Districts' of the turn of the century, the winning of turf proceeded with ever greater desperation; by the late nineteenth century the outer parts of the archipelago known as Na hOileáin, the islands, had not even fuel for themselves, and the stoniness of the limestone lands had been brought back like an infection to An Cheathrú Rua, the 'reddish quarter', and the other peninsulas pointing out to Aran like ever bonier fingers.

It is a dreadful story that is legible in the hard face of south Connemara, but it has a brave little footnote, with which I will end: a brown sail in the bay below brings it to mind. The working life of the hookers dwindled to an end only as recently as the 1960s, though by then most of them were mouldering away in unvisited creeks, irrelevant to the age of lorries, which had rendered the old seaways of Connemara obsolete, and of the various fuels that seemed then to be reducing turf to a historical curiosity. But since then there has been a remarkable revival of interest in these fine boats; several have been prised out of the mud and restored, and a new generation of boat-builders is recalling almost lost traditions of craftsmanship. All summer long the hookers, one or two centenarians among them, sail from regatta to regatta around Connemara, with visits to Cill Rónáin, and, high point of their season, to Kinvara for Cruinniú na mBád, the gathering of the boats.

Galway hookers under sail

This movement, which might seem to be of merely specialist interest, is one of the psychologically most important developments of recent years in these regions, putting the wisdom of the old side by side with the energy of the young, and undoing that dire equation spelled out by Synge between hateful poverty and all the graces of Connemara life.

TIM ROBINSON is a writer and artist who lived in the Aran Islands from 1972 to 1984 and now lives in Roundstone, Connemara. He has published maps of the Aran Islands, the Burren and Connemara, and his book, *Stones of Aran*, received a special award from the committee of the Rooney Prize for Irish Literature in 1987.

THE GLENS OF ANTRIM

Cahal Dallat

The Glens of Antrim cover an area from south of Glenarm to Ballycastle and are nine in number. Starting in the north, Glentaisie and Glenshesk join each other just before they reach the sea at Ballycastle; Glendun meets the sea at the village of Cushendun; Glenaan and Glenballyeamon both meet the sea at Cushendall; Glenariff, the queen of the glens, sweeps majestically down to the sea at the village of Waterfoot; the most southerly of the glens are Glencloy, at whose foot the village of Carnlough nestles, and Glenarm which meets the sea at the village of Glenarm;

all the glens run down to the sea with the exception of Glencorp, which is a traverse glen running in a north/south direction from Glendun to Glenaan.

We can best imagine the glens as being part of a giant hand with ten fingers, and the spaces in between forming a series of short steep valleys running out towards the sea from the eastern edge of the Antrim plateau. These valleys have been gouged out by ancient glaciers after the Ice Age, and as a result drain in a north-easterly direction and look straight across the sea of Moyle to

Glenariff, the 'queen of the glens'. In the 1880s a pathway was made along the water's edge so that visitors could fully appreciate the splendour and beauty of the glen's cascades and waterfalls.

Scotland. They were isolated from the rest of County Antrim by the difficult terrain of the Antrim plateau, with its treacherous flow bog on the west and by a high promontory near Glenarm in the south.

Legends of the glens

The children of Lir who were changed into white swans by their wicked stepmother, Aoife, were sentenced to spend three hundred years swimming on the bleak and stormy sea of Moyle which lies along the north-eastern shores of the glens. Thomas Moore tells their sad story in the 'Song of Fionnuala':

> Silent, oh Moyle, be the roar of thy
>   waters,
> Break not ye breezes your chain of
>   repose,
> While mournfully weeping Lir's lonely
>   daughter
> Tells to the nightstar her sad tale of
>   woes.

The glens are also connected with the story of Deirdre and the sons of Uisneach. King Conor of Emain Macha (Navan Fort) was compelled by his nobles to recall Deirdre and the sons of Uisneach from exile in Scotland, and they are said to have landed at Carraig Uisneach (the rock of Uisneach), near Ballycastle. Deirdre, suspecting treachery, urged the brothers to retreat to Rathlin to await the arrival of their friend and protector, Fergus McRoy, who had been forced under a *geish* (spell or taboo) to attend a banquet at Dunworry, near Torr Head. The brothers refused to wait and hurried on to Emain Macha, near Armagh, expecting King Conor to welcome them with a banquet; but the king had arranged a reception of a different kind and they were all beheaded. Deirdre threw herself on their grave and died of grief and a

54

broken heart.

Finn MacCool mistakenly killed his faithful hound Bran at Doonfin in Glenshesk, and his son Ossian or Oisín is buried in the glens. His grave is marked by a stone circle in the townland of Lubitavish in Glenaan.

But there is nothing legendary about Tievebulliagh and the outcrop of porcellanite from which polished stone axes were made and exported to all parts of Europe in the Stone Age. Other relics of the distant past are the megalithic monuments or dolmens built by agricultural people about 5000 years back and the numerous circular forts or raths which are dotted all over the landscape. These were really solitary farmsteads of 1500 years ago.

The glens in history

The glens have had a turbulent history. Originally in the possession of the Earl of Ulster, they were sold to the Bissetts in the early thirteenth century. In 1242 Patrick, Earl of Atholl, was murdered in his bed in his mansion at Haddington in Scotland. His house was then set on fire to destroy the evidence or to make it look like an accident. The Bissetts were suspected because they had been feuding with the Earls of Atholl for many years, and, although they were able to produce several witnesses who proclaimed their innocence, they were found guilty and condemned to banishment from Scotland. They were lucky to escape with their lives and only succeeded in saving themselves by taking a solemn oath that they would go on a crusade to the Holy Land and remain there for the rest of their lives doing penance and praying for the soul of the murdered earl.

John and Walter Bissett set out from Scotland on their journey of repentance and

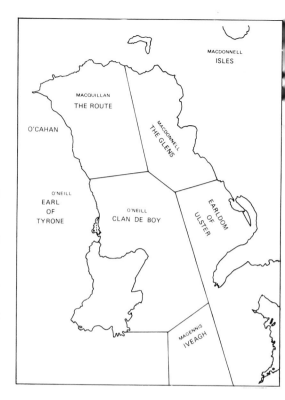

The clans of the glens

whether by accident or design their ship brought them across the 'narrow sea' to Carrickfergus. Here they were met by Richard de Burgo, Earl of Ulster, who made them an offer they found it difficult to refuse. De Burgo was having difficulty in controlling the glens and was very glad to dispose of them to the Bissetts for ready money. Five generations later the last of the Antrim Bissetts, Margery, the daughter of Eoin Bissett and Sabia O'Neill, became the sole heir to the glens.

About this time John More McDonnell of Kintyre, Lord of the Isles, was looking for a wife, and he came to County Antrim to woo the fair Margery who has been described as being very handsome. John and Margery were wed in 1399 and from then on the glens have been in the possession of the McDonnells, who became known as the McDonnells of Antrim. For the next two

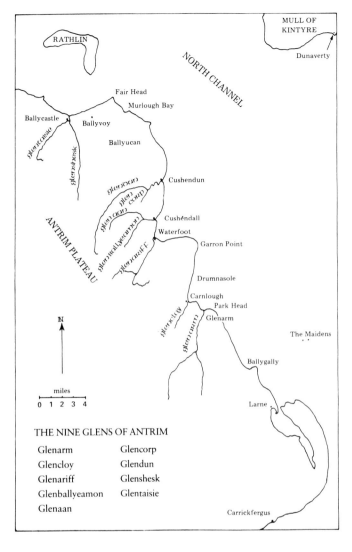

THE NINE GLENS OF ANTRIM

Glenarm	Glencorp
Glencloy	Glendun
Glenariff	Glenshesk
Glenballyeamon	Glentaisie
Glenaan	

for the arrows and Lochaber axes of the McDonnells. Ever after there was a saying in the glens, 'A rush bush never deceived anyone but a McQuillan.'

The McDonnells now added the territory known as the 'route' to the glens, and so controlled the upper half of County Antrim. Shane O'Neill had proclaimed himself Earl of Ulster and, deciding that the McDonnells were becoming much too powerful, determined to banish them to Scotland. In Easter week of 1565 Shane marched northwards from Armagh with two thousand men stopping overnight at various places *en route*, including Dromore, Edenduffcarrick (later known as Shane's Castle) and Clough Castle on the western flank of the glens. He marched down through Glenariff and attacked and burned Red Bay Castle. The McDonnells were only a half-day's march ahead of him and he pursued them to Ballycastle where at the battle of Glentaisie on 2 May 1565 he defeated them and slew seven hundred of their number.

Two years later the same Shane O'Neill was back in the Glens of Antrim to seek help from the McDonnells against the other Ulster clans who had joined forces against him. At first the McDonnells received O'Neill and his thirty or so followers with great hospitality and he was invited to join in the chase of the deer on the high ground above the glen. On the third evening of his visit a banquet was arranged in his honour and there was much feasting and merry-making. The wine flowed freely, perhaps too freely, and a quarrel began between Shane's secretary, Eugene O'Hagan, and a McDonnell over a remark made about James McDonnell's widow. A first-class row developed. Shane foolishly tried to interfere and quick as a flash the McDonnell daggers were out. This was the moment they had been

hundred years the McDonnells spent most of their time and energy in fighting off various claimants to their territory, particularly the McQuillans, the O'Neills and Sir Arthur Chichester.

Slieve an Orra was the site of a decisive battle between the McDonnells and the McQuillans in 1559. The McQuillans, who were assisted by the cavalry from Clandeboy led by Hugh McPhelim O'Neill, made camp on the Orra plateau at the top of Glendun. On the night before the battle, Sorley Boy McDonnell ordered rushes to be spread over

the bog holes which lay between the hostile camps, and over which the McQuillans believed he intended to charge them at early dawn. They were treacherously led to believe that Sorley's road across the swamp had been made sufficiently secure to permit a charge of cavalry, and, resolving to make the first move, persuaded Hugh O'Neill to lead the attack. The O'Neill cavalry rushed out at first light and straight into the swamp where the horses soon sank to their houghs among the thinly strewn rushes and became totally disabled whilst their riders became easy prey

55

waiting for and in a very short time Shane and his followers lay dead. The McDonnell defeat at the battle of Glentaisie had been avenged.

Many other battles and skirmishes took place as well as a couple of massacres on Rathlin Island but eventually the McDonnells became well established as the landlords of the glens. As time went on they began to use their famous Lochaber axes for felling trees and clearing the ground and no doubt their swords were beaten into ploughshares. The inhabitants of the glens are descended from these war-like clans but thankfully attitudes have changed with time and for the past three hundred years the glensfolk have been content to go about their daily occupations of farming and fishing.

The McDonnells of Antrim had castles at Dunluce, Dunaneaney, Ballycastle and Glenarm and it was at Glenarm that they finally settled, where Sir Randal McDonnell, first Earl of Antrim, erected a castle in 1625. Anne Frances Stewart, the Marchioness of Londonderry, whose mother was the Countess of Antrim, would have succeeded to the title of Earl of Antrim if she had been a man. She lived in London where she lavishly entertained England's royalty and nobility,

56

but such was her love of the glens that she was determined to have a castle there which would outshine Glenarm Castle. She erected Garron Tower in 1848 as a summer residence at a cost of several thousand pounds and in order to have somewhere to live while it was being built she had an inn erected in the village of Carnlough. This became the Londonderry Arms and it later came into the possession of her great-grandson, Sir Winston Churchill. He sold it in 1926 when he was Chancellor of the Exchequer. Garron Tower became a hotel in 1898 and in 1951 it opened as a college for boys.

Other historic buildings in the glens include the Franciscan friary of Bunamargie, near Ballycastle, in the vaults of which lie the remains of four Earls of Antrim and two countesses, and where Julia McQuillan, known as the black nun, made a number of prophecies in the sixteenth century which have since come true. There is also Layd church and graveyard near Cushendall, the site of another monastic foundation, and again a burial place for countless McDonnells, including Dr James McDonnell, the founder of the Belfast Medical School, later to become the Queen's University.

Remote and self-contained

The remoteness of the glens and their inaccessibility caused them to have a strong sense of regional unity and a definite affinity with their neighbours on the Scottish coast. There was a ferry running from Cushendun to Dunaverty in Kintyre, Scotland until 1833. In fact it was easier at one time to get to Scotland than to other parts of County Antrim. Richard Dobbs, writing in 1633, and referring to a journey through the glens, says:

There are several high ways but none are good for the lower ways are deep clay and the upper ways are great steep hills. From Glenarm he who would coast it to Coleraine, goes from Glenarm over the mountain to Red Bay and must have a guide, or if he keep the sea near on his right hand. It is very deep in the winter and yet some steep passages ill to ride up and down. Both ways are not to be commended either in summer or in winter. From Red Bay to Cushendun is very good but from thence over Carey Mountain you must have a guide to Ballycastle and you may escape – tho' the mountains seem a continual bog where a man is in danger of sinking with his horse.

Because the area was cut off from the rest of

Red Bay, so called because red sandstone, as opposed to chalk, is plentiful here, with typical glens' ladder-farms on the slopes in the background.

the country, the indigenous population tended to be less affected by outside influences and to retain the old ways of life. This was particularly evident in their customs and their speech. In the Ordnance Survey Memoirs of 1833 we read:

They seem a distinct race from the more southern parishes, both in their features, manners and accent. They are remarkable for their honesty, theft being wholly unknown, although various kinds of property are nightly left exposed and unprotected. They are industrious and very hospitable and obliging in their dispositions, and very peaceable and well-conducted, except that they are fond of whiskey-drinking. Many neither speak nor understand the English language and all speak Irish. Those who do speak English, speak it well and free from any peculiar accent.

Obviously the surveyor who recorded this had noticed that the glens were different. The same surveyor describes the scenery as in the highest degree bold and romantic, consisting of parallel ranges of lofty inaccessible mountains, which form the beautiful glens in between. He goes on to point out that

notwithstanding these formidable barriers, the inhabitants of the glens have sought out several passes whereby they can have access to the mountains' tops from which they procure their fuel; not one of these paths or tracks is in a direct course but on the contrary go zig-zag, taking advantage of the terrain by seizing on such little cross inclined plains as they find best suited to their purpose; some of them are most dangerous. It is by means of ponies and slide cars that they carry the turf from the mountains down these circuitous and dangerous paths, a task which the stranger would deem most impracticable, though the peasantry from habit look upon it with a degree of indifference.

Inroads

The geographical isolation of the glens came to an end in the 1830s when the present coast road was built. Hitherto the old road along the coast from Larne to Cushendall had to climb up and over each successive headland making the journey very hazardous for the traveller. True, Francis Turnley had improved communication by cutting the Red Arch and making a road near the sea between Waterfoot and Cushendall and had blasted a way later known as Turnley's Cut through a protruding crag at Garron Point. But it was a Scottish engineer, William Bald, who suggested that the cliffs should be blasted away down to sea-level and that he could use the blasted rock to make and surface a road and the debris to form a protective battery to resist the onslaught of the sea. This was a military road designed to open up the glens, which were seen by some as being a subversive area. It has since become one of the finest scenic roads in Europe and the famous travel writer, H.V. Morton, could describe it a hundred years later as being 'finer, to my mind, than the Grand Corniche Road in the south of France'.

Although the new road provided access to the glens, it was some time before tourists began to use it. The gentry had time and money to visit and appreciate the beauty spots of County Antrim, but the other classes were too busy trying to eke out an existence to have any time for scenery. Thackeray, in *The Irish Sketch Book*, published in 1843, claims that to describe Glenariff as 'Switzerland in miniature' is totally inadequate for 'in joining together cataracts, valleys, rushing streams and blue mountains, with all the emphasis and picturesqueness of which type is capable, we cannot get near to a copy of Nature's sublime countenance'.

By the 1880s times were changing and a suggestion was made to the railway company that the Glenravel mineral line from Ballymena to Parkmore could be used to provide a passenger service to Glenariff glen and its fantastic waterfalls. The Belfast and Northern Counties Railway Company got parliamentary permission to carry passengers in 1888 and in the following year the company purchased that part of the glen in which the falls lie. They constructed a pathway along the water's edge, crossing and recrossing the river, to give advantageous views of the cascades. At the lower end of the pathway a wooden, chalet-like tea-house was erected and here tourists could recover after their walk down the glen. Day trippers from Belfast could make the journey by train to Ballymena and then by narrow-gauge train to Parkmore. Wagonettes or long-cars conveyed them to the head of the glen at Glenariff post office, where in true tourist fashion they could send postcards saying 'Wish you were here!' A walk of a mile or so of exciting

58

pathways brought them down to the tea-house below. Having partaken of tea they could return by wagonette to Larne and train to Belfast or back by the way they had come.

Gaelic revival

Irish was still spoken in the glens until the last quarter of the nineteenth century, although the use of it had declined in most other parts of the country. To combat this decline, the Gaelic League was set up in Dublin in 1893. As might be expected, the glens were seen as an area where this Gaelic revival would flourish, and a number of influential people in the glens soon became involved. It was decided to hold a great *feis* (festival) where people could compete in Irish dancing, traditional singing and instrumental music, story-telling and history, arts and crafts and hurling. The *feis* held in Glenariff on 30 June 1904 was very successful and there was a great hosting of Gaels in the glen that day. Prominent among the organisers were Francis Joseph Biggar, Roger Casement, Barbara McDonnell, Margaret Dobbs, Ada McNeill

and John Clarke. The *feis* was officially opened by Sir Horace Plunkett, who appealed for a greater interest in Irish industries and among the other speakers was Eoin MacNeill, later to become Minister of Education in Dáil Éireann. The glens *feis* has been held every year since in one of the nine glens, and there is no doubt that it has played some part in preserving the distinctive culture and traditions of the glens.

Eking out a living

Because it was a place apart, old farming methods continued to be used in the glens long after things had changed in other places. The spade and flaghter were superseded by the plough; the sickle and scythe by the two-horse reaper; and the flail and the winnowing sheet by the one-horse threshing machine. Eventually the tractor took over from the horse, but it is interesting to notice how much land previously cultivated by the spade is too steep to be ploughed by the tractor. Remains of cultivation ridges or 'lazy beds' can still be seen on high ground throughout the glens.

Looking down through Glenariff and across the North Channel to the Mull of Kintyre in Scotland.

Maud Cottages, Cushendun: built in 1912 and named after Lord Cushendun's wife

Many people were engaged in fishing and nearly every family was involved in turf-cutting to ensure supplies of fuel for the winter. Although there had been coal-mining at Ballycastle and iron-ore mining at Parkmore and Glenravel, the glens could never be considered as an industrial area. One of the few industries still remaining is the quarrying and burning of limestone at Glenarm for use in local agriculture and for export. There is some boat-building using fibre-glass and other modern materials at Cushendall, and perhaps the fiddle-making at Carnlough is a relic of the toy-making and wood-carving industries which existed at the turn of the century in both Ballycastle and Cushendall.

Conservation villages

The Glens of Antrim have been classified as an 'area of outstanding natural beauty' by the Department of the Environment for Northern Ireland, and Cushendun, Cushendall and Carnlough have been designated 'conservation villages'.

Some of the charm of Cushendun lies in the group of houses built in the style of a Cornish village by the celebrated Welsh architect Clough Williams Ellis in 1912 and named Maud Cottages after the wife of Lord Cushendun. Rockport Lodge at the east end of the village was once the home of the poet Moira O'Neill, whose *Songs of the Glens of Antrim* encapsulate the simple lifestyles and pleasures of glensfolk.

Cushendall's focal point is its Curfew Tower erected by Francis Turnley in 1820, while the picturesque stone bridge over the River Dall has been the meeting place for the villagers for well over a hundred years.

Carnlough has its Londonderry Arms Hotel, to which reference has already been made, and the attractive white limestone bridge built in 1854 to carry the mineral railway over the road to the sheltered harbour which dates from the same time.

CAHAL DALLAT BA MPHIL DIP ED ADMIN is a justice of the peace and was formerly headmaster of Star of the Sea secondary school in Ballycastle, County Antrim. He serves and has served on committees or councils of several organisations to do with health services, the countryside and local studies. He is joint editor of the *Journal of Ulster Local Studies*, author of *Caring by Design* (Department of Health and Social Services NI) and co-author of *Oh Maybe it was Yesterday* (Glens of Antrim Historical Society). He lectures and broadcasts on Ulster place-names and folklore.

THE MOURNES

James Busby

Is there an Irish person anywhere who, on hearing the phrase 'the Mountains of Mourne' does not finish it 'sweep down to the sea'? Was Percy French referring to the mass of Slieve Donard towering above Newcastle and sweeping abruptly to the sea? Or was he referring to Slieve Martin above Portaferry, Knockshee above Killowen, or the way the peaks of Slieve Binian and Rocky mountain sweep to the coastal plain above Kilkeel and Annalong?

A beautiful landscape

Whatever mountain French was referring to, the evocative phrase 'the Mountains of Mourne' conjures up an image of romantic beauty. And it is that beauty that we are concerned with here: and not only the beauty of the mountains themselves, but the whole Mourne countryside, together with the outlying Slieve Croob to the north, the high ground around and the hills and valleys of Castlewellan lying between. This is designated an area of outstanding natural beauty (AONB), and the purpose of this designation is to achieve conservation of the scenic landscape of the area. But what has been happening to the Mourne countryside? And what can be done to preserve and improve it?

Opposite
Riverine scrub woodland in the Mournes.

Below left
'The Mountains of Mourne sweep down to the sea'

Farming

How the land is used is what, more than any other activity, gives the countryside its character. Farming peoples have been modifying the landscape since the dawn of agriculture, and as agriculture intensified in the face of population growth in the nineteenth century, enclosures or fields were extended onto the flanks of the higher ground. The remains of lazy beds high on the foothills of the Mournes bear testimony to the spadework of earlier generations and their struggle to grow sufficient potatoes to feed the family and have some left for sale.

The modern equivalent can be seen on the heather hillsides above Carrick Little and Carrick Big on the south-east side of Slieve Binian. There are artificial green fields, where tracked diggers have gathered and buried surface stones in trenches, which act as drainage ditches, and the ground is levelled and re-seeded with grass mixtures, encouraged with heavy doses of chemical fertiliser. Regrettably, the native heath sward has been reduced for what is a questionable

short-term advantage: in a high rainfall area like this, where nutrients are not available from the granite-derived substratum it is not economic to go on fertilising the land artificially, and in any case the increased productivity is unwanted in these times of surplus.

The heather vegetation is also being damaged by overgrazing or overgrazing combined with heather burning to such an extent that coarse grasses take over and erosion sets in on the steep slopes.

One of the great attractions of enclosed land is the way the field patterns contrast with the high ground in valleys and on the edge of the mountains. Unfortunately open stone walls have degenerated into mere mounds in some parts of the Mourne countryside, but it is the hedges that are in the poorest condition. Few are well maintained and most are gappy, over-mature, and ineffective as stock-proof boundaries or for shelter.

Agricultural grants for drainage and scrub clearance have in the past encouraged the removal of much of the variety and diversity of the farmed landscape. A tree survey completed in 1986 shows that of the remaining trees most are over-mature and among younger trees ash and sycamore are the only species to be represented. Native oak is especially rare in hedgerows or in scrub areas. The most important scrub areas are on steep slopes and associated with the river valleys flowing off the mountains. This scrub can be of hazel, birch, holly or thorn.

The recent declaration of the Mourne AONB as Northern Ireland's first environmentally sensitive area (ESA) includes a positive inducement to farmers to maintain the scenic and conservation value of their farmland. To avail of the ESA grant a farmer will agree a course of action with an advisory officer on conservation work. It may be nothing more than good 'housekeeping' – keeping hedges, stone walls, trees, gates and gateposts in good repair. It is hoped that scrub and woodland planting and wetland management will also be encouraged.

Over the last twenty years the appearance of the farmhouses and farm buildings in the Mournes has changed gradually. More and more urban forms of dwelling have been altering the rural scene. A rich heritage of traditional buildings still remains, but it is increasingly threatened.

The planting of trees around the old farms had the functional advantage of shelter, but also, more than anything else, integrated the buildings into the landscape. The species, apart from scots pine, were usually beech or sycamore. The cypress trees currently fashionable around our country houses do not integrate into the landscape, are frequently of species that do not thrive in our climate, and more often than not simply exaggerate the inappropriateness of the development.

The economic forces which have encouraged intensification and reclamation in the past are also forcing some farms out of business or into part-time farming. Side by side with enlarged fields and intensive silage production we have dereliction of land and farm buildings: bracken-dominated hillsides, rush-covered meadows, abandoned farmsteads. Examples of old *clochán*s like Hanna's Close near Kilkeel or an unchanged nineteenth-century pattern of rural farming, as in the Ardglass valley in the Slieve Croob area, stand as monuments marking the end of a farming era. Variety and interest in the countryside would be immeasurably served if these elements of rural heritage could be safeguarded.

Forestry

Large areas of state conifer plantation have made a significant contribution to the Mourne countryside. Tollymore, the first forest park in the United Kingdom, was opened in 1955. At this time other state forestry areas had 'trespassers prosecuted' signs at their entrances. Upon the framework of the old Annesley estate with its fine deciduous trees and parkland, the foresters of the 1930s created plantations of conifers – larch, pine, spruce and Douglas fir.

The practice of planting different species in appropriate different locations gave Tollymore and other forests of the time a most attractive appearance, reflecting the landscape upon which they were planted. This practice was also followed at Castlewellan and Rostrevor forests, which are now important forest park and recreation areas. However, after 1950 this practice fell from favour to be replaced by a monocultural approach to coniferous plantations, with straight lines of sitka spruce. It is only relatively recently that planting plans have a landscape design element built in from their inception. Similarly, fellings of the pre-war forests, which are now ready for harvesting and regeneration, are being planned with the maintenance of an attractive landscape as a controlling restraint. Regrettably, there have been most unfortunate examples of clear-felling in some very sensitive areas at Castlewellan and Rostrevor. The appearance of the countryside is a resource that should not be compromised for short-term expediency.

Mill Bay

Mill Bay in Carlingford Lough at the outflow of the White Water river is a large unspoiled salt-marsh and mudflat, one of the finest salt-marshes in Northern Ireland. The area displays good transitions from lower eroding faces, through pools, to mature salt-marsh close to the old raised beach. The mudflats are valuable feeding areas for large numbers of wintering wildfowl and waders. These can be seen from Greencastle Point. They include redshank, bar-tailed godwits and golden plovers as well as curlew and oystercatchers. Numbers of wigeon and migrating brent geese feed on eel grass which grows on part of the mudflat. Winter brings mallard, teal, and shelduck to the intertidal area with merganser, grebe and other divers offshore.

An invasive threat exists to this thriving community of plants and animals – *Spartina* or cord grass, a fertile hybrid between a native and a North American species. By means of its extensive system of roots and rhizomes, it stabilises the soft mud of the estuary, while its surface parts collect the debris and silt and raise the level of the mudflats, causing them eventually to become dry. This plant was first noticed in Southampton waterway in 1870, but since then it has covered many tens of thousands of hectares of mudflats from the south coast of England to France and by way of Wales to Lough Foyle. An effort to control its spread is being made by spraying and digging out.

Murlough Bay

Murlough Bay is a mature and stable large dune area over shingle, lying between the beach at Newcastle and Dundrum Bay. Part of the system forms an internationally famous golf course and the remainder is managed as a nature reserve by the National Trust. It has a number of well-developed habitats. Some of the stable dunes have a heath and lichen community. Together with sea buckthorn scrub, this is an important breeding site for

Looking towards the Mournes from Dundrum Bay

birds and butterflies which include respectively grayling and dark green fritillary. On partially stable dunes can be found shepherd's cross, the only place in Northern Ireland, and a unique small dung beetle found nowhere else in Ireland. The marine and intertidal waters, especially in the bay at Dundrum which is sheltered by the dunes, are important wintering grounds for many species, especially large numbers of common scoter. The small visitor centre is most successful and a model for other sites.

Other landscapes

The northern Mournes area is granite and provides extensive areas of upland heath and poor grassland on a granite-derived substratum. Above 300m summit heath contains dwarf willow, crowberry, sheep's fescue and woolly fringe moss, and the rare stiff sedge along with the more widespread ling and bell heather.

In the southern Mournes on Knockshee and Slievefadda are a variety of grasslands on a Silurian-derived substratum, less acid and containing a much wider range of flowering plants. Communities vary from those dominated by gorse and western gorse to large areas where heather alternates with grassland.

Mountain cliffs and crags provide important nesting sites for birds of prey, especially peregrine falcons which have been gradually increasing in number since the 1960s. Kestrels tend to be more common in the foothills and valleys and buzzards can occasionally be sighted.

In a number of places along the coastline from Newcastle to Ballykeel, sea erosion has exposed the history of glacial deposits and also the effects of change in sea-level during the glacial period and since. Between Kilkeel and Cranfield Point, coastal erosion allows us to see a unique series of muds, sands and gravels which are thought to have originated during the retreat of the ice-sheet 17,000 years ago. The sequence is cut by the raised beach at Cranfield Point.

Immediately offshore from Greencastle Pier are Green and Blockhouse Islands – islands of Carboniferous limestone rich in

fossil remains. However, the prime interest here is the breeding colony of terns. The four species – common, arctic, Sandwich and roseate – are represented, the latter in sufficient numbers to be of international importance. However, the islands are rapidly eroding away.

But not only areas of outstanding beauty or with bumper lists of unusual species are worthy of conservation. Every meadow, fen, wood or heath has something to offer, and examples of these must be preserved too. The Mournes area includes a variety of landscapes: hazel and birch scrub woodland with holly on steep slopes of small upland valleys and along stream sides; incised coastal stream valleys, sometimes with old hazel scrub, oak and species-rich swards below cliff-line streams; traditionally managed permanent grassland, nutrient-poor with

The aptly named Silent Valley reservoir in the heart of the Mournes

64

The Mourne Wall is 35.2km long and goes over all the highest peaks in the mountain range.

relatively rich herb associations; lowland heath communities where low grazing pressures have enabled most unusual plant associations to develop and be maintained. All these are environments of natural interest worth keeping as they are.

Mourne heritage

Indivisible from the landscape in which they stand are the special sites which represent the heritage of human activity: the prehistoric dolmens, court tombs and standing stones; the cashels, raths, crosses and church sites of the early Christian period; and the castles, mottes and churches of medieval times. With the help of the agricultural community a good system exists for identifying new archaeological sites as they come to light. The farmed landscape itself is a museum of its use over the centuries, and increasing awareness of this heritage is emerging.

But what of the traditions of the recent past that are in danger of dying out before their value is recognised? What about the nickies and nobbies – the sailing fishing boats and the fishing traditions that went with them from the Mournes coast, the dipping luggers and the herring-men? And then there are the granite quarries and the men whose work paved and kerbed our towns and cities, but whose story is silent in their place of origin.

One positive development in heritage preservation is that Newry and Mourne District Council have kept a water-driven grain mill at Annalong as a working demonstration of this aspect of rural life. The picturesque harbour adjacent would be an ideal location for a fishery museum. The town is one of the places where the granite-working tradition is alive and well. Paper-making was another important industry in the area. All the elements are here for a series of locally based heritage features which are unique to this area.

An outstanding area – but for how long?

Even though the Mournes landscape is recognised as something special and worth preserving, there are problems of management and conservation. The popularity of mountain walks has caused erosion along some routes, and in spite of efforts at repair by voluntary groups, this remains a problem. There are conflicts too between farmers and hill-walkers, and resentment grows in the absence of mechanisms to resolve disputes.

But hill-walkers are not the only source of potential damage to the landscape, though judging by the litter that is taken off the High Mournes in the annual clean-up, some of them might need to revise their attitude to the mountains. Other and more permanent disfigurements to the countryside include inappropriate building, overhead lines and road improvements. Every new house built increases the problem, and the encroachment of the ugly cannot be halted, in spite of the reclamation for agricultural use of many of the worked out gravel- and sand-pits which disfigured the landscape of the coastal plain.

Problems like these can only be solved by concerted and co-ordinated action by the statutory bodies with responsibility for the area. A good sign is the proposal to improve planning regulations to impose tighter control on siting and design in specially scenic and sensitive areas. Let us hope these pious hopes are fulfilled. It would be a sorry loss if responsibility for preservation of the Mourne countryside were to be passed around from one public body or council to the next, with the final result that nobody took the responsibility and the area was allowed to deteriorate.

But behind the statutory bodies must be a concerned, informed and aware public, who will not accept anything less than wise use of this beautiful part of Ireland. Only a committed body of opinion can guarantee the emergence of desirable structures, policies and actions.

JAMES BUSBY is a Principal Scientific Officer with the Countryside and Wildlife Branch of the Department of the Environment for Northern Ireland.

HIDDEN LANDSCAPES
Gareth Jones

Hidden away under the ground, around the coasts and under the sea, is a whole mysterious and often beautiful landscape, accessible at some points to the general public, but normally only explored by cavers and potholers: the limestone caves of Ireland.

Cracks and seepages: how caves are gouged out

Limestone is soluble in rainwater. This doesn't mean that you could dissolve a lump of limestone in a glass of rainwater the way you put sugar in your tea, but over very long stretches of time, limestone can be nibbled away by the chemical action of rainwater. This is because rainwater is a very weak or dilute form of carbonic acid. Rainwater takes up carbon dioxide from the atmosphere and humic acid from organic soils, and so gentle drops of rain become aggressive water which percolates through the vertical joints and horizontal bedding cracks in limestone and attacks and dissolves it. Out of all these numerous seepages the flow gradually concentrates on one pathway, which becomes enlarged to form a cave.

The geological map of Ireland shows large exposures of Carboniferous limestone (330 million years old), but you will only find areas with accessible caves around the edges. That is where the mountains are producing more rainfall and, more importantly, steeper hydrological gradients. Regions where solution of limestone occur are called *karstic* areas, after the famous Karst region in the north of Yugoslavia.

The Irish lowlands were extensively karstified during the Tertiary geological era and earlier tropical times, and they have since been polished by glaciation and buried by the resulting waste material. Before the Ice Age, when Ireland was much closer to the equator,

humid tropical conditions would have produced landscapes similar to those seen in Jamaica, New Guinea or even China. Beneath the glacial deposits we have evidence showing buried poljes (very large enclosed depressions), cliff-sided channels and old sinkholes, and exploration boreholes frequently intercept fossil cave passages up to 10m deep.

Show caves

There are four caves in Ireland that are open to the general public: Marble Arch cave in County Fermanagh, Aillwee cave in County Clare, Dunmore cave in County Kilkenny and Mitchelstown cave in County Tipperary. Each displays a different aspect of cave landscape and we are very fortunate in having so much variety.

Marble Arch cave near Enniskillen is a living river cave, with a dramatic descent from the surface to the Claddagh river, an enchanting boat ride up dark waters and a stroll up a passage 'decorated' with stalactites and stalagmites. The rock architecture is particularly fine, with leaves and pinnacles of rock decorated with scallops. It was visited in 1895 by Edouard Martel of Paris, the father of spelaeology (the study of caves) together with Lyster Jamieson from Dublin. They boated up the river in a collapsible canvas boat. With fine rock structure, sparkling waters and exquisite stalactite formations this must be the most beautiful cave for the casual visitor to admire.

In the Aillwee cave south of Ballyvaughan can be seen a fine example of a half-tube in the roof, testimony to the earliest stages of formation of the cave passage. The little stream that now runs along the inner parts of the cave is a tiny misfit taking the place of the river that once flowed through it. Even some

thousands of years ago, the cave bears who made their pits close to the entrance found it a dry safe home in which to hibernate. The final section of large open cave passage can give the amateur a real feeling of exploring a wild cave.

The Office of Public Works runs the Dunmore cave which is notable for its huge chambers and magnificent 'market cross' stalagmite column. It was mentioned as Derc Ferna (the cave of the alders) in the Annals of the Four Masters. This early book details the slaughter of about a thousand local people in and around the cave by the Vikings from Dublin in AD 928. This was confirmed during the development of the show cave by the discovery of a hoard of coins, all of which had been minted in the forty years before.

Mitchelstown cave near Ballyporeen must be the best decorated of all the show caves, testimony to its great age. The waters that formed these chambers have long departed, to take other routes through the rocks. The great chambers have roofs tilted at an angle of about 30°, which follows the dip of the beds of limestone. In plan the cave has a maze of passages typical of a cave formed principally below the water table. The guides through this complex cave point out a wealth of stalactites, stalagmites and columns, but the flashing crystal beauty of the 'heap of diamonds' is one of the favourite displays. Martel also visited this cave which was discovered during quarrying operations in 1833.

Fermanagh/Cavan

Around the edges of Cuilcagh mountain and Tullybrack mountain, Irish cavers have the most exciting and variable of underground environments. The caves are generally much older than those found in Clare, and since

Cave exploration

It is common these days to wear a wetsuit for cave exploration, since it keeps the caver warm, and lets you slide easily through small gaps. On your feet you wear strong soled boots or caving wellies, and on your helmet you may use either an electric lamp or a carbide light. It is important to learn to cave with experienced friends and always to cave in small groups. You should be able to borrow the equipment if you want to try out the sport.

There are many small caving clubs scattered through the country, and if you want to go caving seek advice from a member of one of these. You can also contact the Spelaeological Union of Ireland through Steven Dowds, 8 Cremore Crescent, Glasnevin, Dublin 9, or attend one of the caving courses run by Gortatole Outdoor Pursuits Centre, Enniskillen, County Fermanagh, or Kilshanny Outdoor Centre, Lisdoonvarna, County Clare.

The Irish Cave Rescue Organisation can be reached through the 999 emergency telephone line.

Top
Gareth Jones wades upstream through the waist-deep Lake 1 in the Skreen Hill passage of Marble Arch cave, Co. Fermanagh.
Since the show cave opened you can now walk 'through' the lake with dry feet.

Bottom
Magnificent rock architecture of the Grand Gallery of Marble Arch cave, Co. Fermanagh. The river flows between sandbanks of reworked glacial deposits.

MINERAL DEPOSITS OF IRELAND

Mineral deposits of Ireland

they have been formed in clean massive limestones, they have developed magnificent large chambers and deep plunging shafts or potholes.

On Tullybrack mountain south-west of the villages of Derrygonnelly and Boho, the mountain streams run off the shale and sandstone top onto the underlying limestone and immediately plunge into a number of magnificent potholes. These shafts have developed along faults and joints, lines of weakness in the rock, and have produced the classic potholing region of Ireland. Chief amongst these potholes is Noon's Hole, named after a Ribbonman who made an involuntary descent in 1826. The 80m drop is broken by a series of ledges, but as the potholer slides down the high-tech rope, he or she is captivated by the daylight from the narrow entrance, slanting down to illuminate the grooved and dripping walls of the shaft, as they belly out to become a 10m × 5m ellipse. There are two parallel shafts at the bottom: one ends in a sump pool, and the other is dry; only the slim can squeeze through the narrow passage that runs off. For a number of years, cave divers were the only people who could get through from these narrow rat-holes, via a 36m dive, into the fine stream passages of the downstream Arch cave, but recent explorations have yielded a bypass for the dry-cavers. The inaccessible passages of Arch cave were always described by the divers as being the most magnificent, with the best formations, and now the dry-cavers can see for themselves. The downstream end is blocked by an even more formidable series of floodable canals and 150m or more of complex sump, before the dark peaty waters finally emerge at the impressive entrance to Arch cave, known locally as Ooghboraghan.

The other major pothole on the mountain is Reyfad Pot, which has been connected to the adjacent caves of Pollnacrom and Polltullybrack to form the deepest (179m+) and third longest (7km) system on the island. The entrance shaft is a more sombre place than Noon's Hole, but the final 24m pitch breaks into the roof of a 15m high and wide passage almost giving the explorer that most unexpected feeling in a cave – agoraphobia! Most of the cave consists of passages of the same dimensions, more or less filled with extensive deposits of sand and boulders. This is a very old system, whose history may extend back for millions of years. As cavers climb up and down the 10m high sand-dunes, their feeble lights attempt to penetrate the distant darkness. These huge passages must have been practically filled with sediments during the glacial periods, but the little streams now occupying them are slowly carving out their courses and removing the fill

to reveal the original dimensions. In places where the streams do not run, it is often just possible to make some progress in the very roof of the passage, because of compaction of the sediment as the water is drained away. In these areas a small gardening trowel can achieve miracles in excavating a body-sized channel. Hidden in remote areas of this vast system, there are small grottoes whose brilliantly coloured formations shine all the more brightly in contrast with the general sand and mud colours seen everywhere else. In the small amount of this cave so far explored, there are at least three young streams which pursue totally independent courses. You enter through Polltullybrack, which is a very young postglacial cave, requiring the caver to crawl, usually on his belly, for about 150m. This journey may take

an hour or more, usually lying in freezing water, until the cave breaks into the roof of an underground shaft. An exhilarating 54m abseil (sliding down a rope with metal clamps) drops you into the main Reyfad system. Another stream sinks in the Pollnacrom complex, which is currently inaccessible, while the New River, the third and largest, arrives from the surface in the Shower Room, runs for about 10m and disappears into a boulder choke, an impenetrable pile of boulders. In 1978, a breakthrough was made into a large downstream extension, which ran for nearly a kilometre into the heart of the mountain. Two sumps have been dived and a remote 12m pitch descended before exploration ground to a halt in a gloomy flood-prone region kilometres away from the nearest cave.

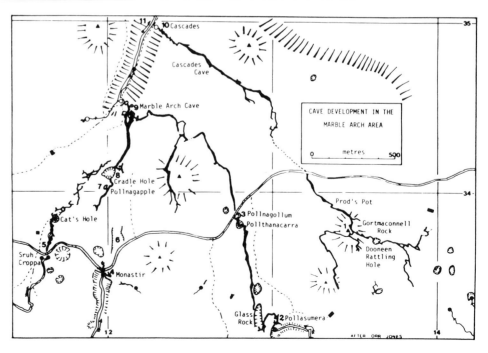

70

Other caves on this mountain include the linear system of Pollaraftara which is notable for the inclination of the passageway caused by its development along a geological fault, and for the long series of canals which must either be boated in a rubber dinghy or swum by those wearing wetsuits. Next to the village of Boho are the Boho caves, which are a highly flood-prone maze of passages, where it is very easy to get lost in the jagged walled passages.

The Marble Arch cave on Cuilcagh mountain has associated with it a wealth of smaller caves, which are ideal for the developing caver to explore. Since these are also very old caves, many of the passages cross over each other as in Upper Cradle Hole. Ancient rock collapses, such as those in Pollnagollum of the Boats, provide endless hours of amusement in a three-dimensional puzzle that requires amazing powers of contortion and controlled emaciation. Close by is the long system of Prod's Pot, whose 66m-deep entrance pitches are so narrow that they can nearly all be climbed, by the expert, without ladders. The long twisting stream passage below is reminiscent of a Clare cave, until a complicated series of six sumps bars the way to the downstream extension connecting to the Cascades Rising cave. The water from this is captured by the local council for a water supply. Further east again the small cave of Tullyhona is noted not only for its formations but also for the tightness of its entrance squeezes, which have denied access to many an outsize suitor.

At the west end of Cuilcagh mountain, the source of the Shannon river has been traced to the Pollahuna or 'Shannon cave'. The entrance to this cave features a permanently unstable series of boulder chokes. These periodically close the cave until a new way through is engineered. Similarly, within the cave there are a number of loose boulder piles which have led to one major cave rescue so far. Interestingly, much of the water is derived from streams in County Fermanagh. The water rising in the Shannon Pot has been found to issue from narrow impenetrable slots at a depth of −8m (8m below the surface of the water), below a tangle of submerged trees.

Clare

The Burren is a classic area of cave development set in the finest karstic landscape in Ireland. Streams run off the shale caps of the low hills of Slieve Elva, the Cullauns and Knockaun mountain of the west Burren. They disappear as soon as they reach the limestone, to enter long twisting canyon passageways. In big caves like Poulnagollum–Poulelva or Doolin–St Catherine's these may be up to 8m high and 3m wide. Frequently they are so narrow that the caver must brush against the sides while wading in the shallow streams. Occasionally, as in Poulnagollum–Ballyshanny, although the passage is still 3m wide, progress is only possible by crawling on your side in the very bottom of the passage, where it is marginally wider.

It is considered that most of these west Burren caves are very young (post- or late-glacial in age) since their entrances relate directly to the shale caps. Poulnagollum–Poulelva is the largest cave in Ireland – presently over 13km long, with a typical dendritic (branching) plan. It has a longer history than some of the other caves and because of erosion a number of its entrances are now situated well away from the shale boundary. Although the younger, upper entrances are close to the shale/limestone boundary, the main one is Poulnagollum Pot, where a steep scramble down and a crawl through boulders shortly brings the explorer to the main stream passage some 30m below the ground. The magnificent passageway meanders downstream for nearly 3km, passing waterfalls, deep pools and stalactites. Eventually the water seeps off to the side, the passage diminishes into a hands-and-knees crawl, and route-finding past the edge of the Maze becomes a problem. Then a crawl through an artificially enlarged section connects Poulnagollum to Poulelva, and the cave emerges at the bottom of the 30m pothole entrance of Poulelva. A waterfall cascades out of a passage half-way up the shaft and if a ladder or rope has been placed here beforehand, the explorer can climb or prusik (climbing ropes assisted by metal clamps) up to the surface.

This is the pattern repeated all over the west Burren, of long narrow twisting streamways. In some of them water is a stronger feature such as in the Coolagh river cave with its short sections of swimming or deep wading. This is also the case in the Doolin–St Catherine's system. But this older system has many interesting features, not least the fact that it is one of the few examples in this part of Europe where a major cave passes underneath a river – the Aille river. You can go right through the cave and out at the other end. You start in a small crawling swallow cave, which gradually gets bigger as it accepts more and more tributaries. It is notable too for its dry high-level passages, its well-decorated grottoes, and for the place where water leaks through from the Aille river as the Aille Cascade which, being warmer than the main cave water and atmosphere, often steams like a shower bath. After a hands-and-knees crawl for a hundred

metres or so the caver again returns to
daylight up the 12m ladder climb of
Fisherstreet Pot – conveniently close to
Gussy's pub on the other side of what is, in
normal water conditions, now the dry bed of
the Aille river.

But in the west Burren can also be found
one of Ireland's jewels in the cave of
Pol-an-Ionian. At the end of a painful hands-
and-knees crawl of 450m, a large chamber is
reached in which hangs the longest free-
hanging stalactite so far discovered in the
world. At 7m it is a dramatic sight.

Also around the coast of the Burren there
are numerous sites for those most specialist of
extreme sportspeople, the cave divers. During
the last few years they have been exploring
submerged caves off the coast and have so far
linked two sets of passages together.
Although water has much better visibility
than in inland caves, there are occasional
problems with the halocline. This is the
boundary layer where fresh water from the
land mixes with salt water from the sea,
causing a haziness and change in refractive
properties. A highly significant breakthrough
is the discovery of passages which are leading
inland towards the main cave systems.

Another recent development by local
cavers has been the discovery on Knockaun
mountain, of a pothole – Poll na gCéim – in
this area of mostly horizontal cave
development. This plummets 75m in four
pitches until it levels off and passes through
four sumps (completely flooded sections of
passage). Two further small pitches follow
and the entry of a decent sized waterfall
suggests that they have joined the major
stream from the nearby Poll Balliny. With a
depth of 120m already and further potential
of 120m, this might one day be the deepest
cave in the country.

In the east or 'high' Burren, cave development is much older and relates to a period before the removal of the shale caps in the area. At Kilcorney, the Cave of the Wild Horses is famous not only for its mud, but also because, although it is normally a sink, during heavy rainfall it acts as a spring and water rushes out of the cave to form a small lake.

Other cave regions

Caves can be found all over Ireland: limestone caves in at least ten of the thirty-two counties and sea caves in at least four more. Major areas are located in Sligo/Leitrim, Monaghan, Galway, Tipperary, Cork, Waterford and Kerry. Major isolated caves are worth visiting in Antrim, Donegal and Roscommon.

The Sligo/Leitrim area is renowned for its potholes which descend up to 84m (Pollnaleprachauns, north-west of Manorhamilton), but mostly through fairly grotty cherty limestone, where the walls of the potholes are festooned with brittle ledges which break away as soon as you put any weight on them. The debris also accumulates at the bottom and chokes the continuing passages, so that very few of them have much lateral extent. Other major sites at Ramson's Pot (70m deep north of Manorhamilton), Polticoghlan or Pulthy (also 70m deep east of Drumshanbo) fit the same picture.

However, at Geevah, north-west of Ballyfarnan, there is a small karstic area which contains a wealth of deep holes and promising sites. Here the Carrowmore system with its entrances of Seighmairbaun and Pollnagollum descends to 142m by a series of messy crawls over wet pebbles and boulders, and a handline descent to a final passage to a sump. This dead, undecorated cave is one of the most challenging and fulfilling. Only a few metres away the 133.5m deep Polliska Pot drops in a series of pitches to the same base level, a total contrast in spelaeological style.

Finally, one must mention the Truskmore massif, where the summit potholes close to the transmitter are Ireland's highest cave entrances. But the yawning maw of Dermot and Grania's cave perched high above the isolated valley of Gleniff is part of an ancient cave system totally truncated by the glacier that formed the valley.

Near Ballintra there is a charming little system where the Blackwater river flows through what used to be a continuous cave. However, most of the roof has gone and it is now possible to indulge in the most contradictory sport – open-air caving.

In Mayo, another Aille river can be found flowing off the Partry mountains to sink into a cave noted for its long canals and recently for its deep and intimidating dives. The connection with the spring 3km away at Bellaburke seems to lie at a constant depth of −30m. This will have to wait for technology to overcome the problems of decompression involved in such an extremely long and deep dive before it can be explored.

At Cong, the waters of Lough Mask flow entirely underground to Lough Corrib. They can be seen in some of the small caves scattered around the isthmus. The springs at Cong are amongst the most powerful in the world, producing several times the normal flow of the River Liffey. Again, this is an area set aside for the cave diver, though it may be years before they are able to cope with conditions underground and underwater.

Near Carrickmacross in County Monaghan is a small series of fairly grotty holes which do not draw an overwhelming rush of caving visitors. Nevertheless, the Aphuca cave, with the waist-deep wade half in mud and half in water for over 400m, is still yielding its secrets both to the caver and the cave diver. Nearby Poll'D draws those who can bear the smell to explore a small cave noted for its brittle rock, its tight squeezes and its occasionally flooded 12m pitch to the far reaches.

At the other end of the country, Cork has a number of small caves, many of the maze variety, reaching their acme in the caves of

Cloyne, where so far over 2.4km of passages have been surveyed in an area as small as 4 acres (less than 2 hectares). These are generally crouching sized, interconnecting on a bewildering scale, and can only be fully explored during the summer, since the winter water table floods most of the routes. This is a phreatic system, meaning that it is still evolving whenever it is flooded.

Crag cave at Castleisland in County Kerry has recently been extended to give a total of nearly 4km of passages. This is an old cave with the river flowing at a lower level and abandoned crawl-ways and chambers criss-crossing above it. The Tralee–Castleisland valley has numerous caves and is fast becoming one of the main caving regions in the country.

One of the most unusual cave sites is at Kingscourt, where the gypsum mines occasionally break into cavities in the rock, which behave entirely like limestone caves. The mines used to have a problem with water flooding them until one day they broke into a cave, which drained the whole excavation.

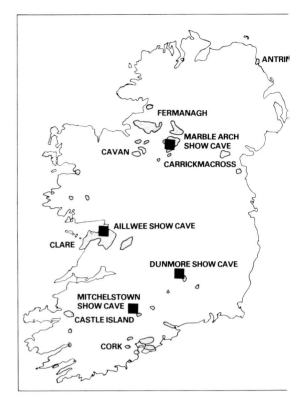

The caving areas of Ireland

GARETH LLWYD JONES MSc is a Welshman living and working in Dublin. He studied at both Queen's University Belfast and Trinity College Dublin, and he is a micro-palae-ontologist, which means he studies micro-scopic fossils. He manages Conodate, a biostratigraphic service for the mineral and oil exploration industries, advising them how old their rocks are.

MR JONES has been caving and climbing for twenty-five years, most of it in Ireland. He is author of the guide to *The Caves of Fermanagh and Cavan* (Watergate Press 1975), and took part in a television documentary on the Marble Arch caves in Fermanagh. He instigated a dig by the Ulster Museum in Pollnagollum–Pollthanacarra, which uncovered human skulls and other remains 4500 years old. In 1975 he took part in an Irish expedition to the Gouffre Berger near Grenoble in France, then the second deepest cave in the world. He has been chairman of the Irish Cave Rescue Organisation and Irish correspondent for *Descent* for many years. He has published articles on both spelaeological and geological topics in a wide range of journals.

THE NORTH COAST
Bill Carter

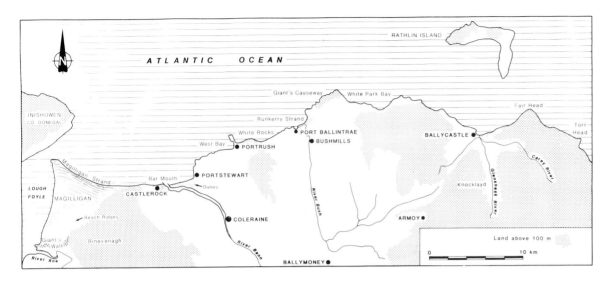

The 'north coast', running from the mouth of the Foyle to Torr Head

The recent designation of the Giant's Causeway on the north coast of County Antrim as a UNESCO world heritage site (the only one in Ireland) confirms what many Irish people already know: that the north coast is one of the most spectacularly beautiful shorelines in the world. The mix of black basalt, white chalk, green grass, blue sea and yellow sand is almost unique. Were the air and sea temperatures a little warmer and the cultural ones a little cooler, the north coast would certainly rival the Algarve or Dalmatia as a holiday centre. But then perhaps some of the character and beauty would be lost. . .

The 'north coast' of Ireland is a colloquial term referring to the area between the mouth of the Foyle and Torr Head, all of which, with the exception of the extreme western part, lies within County Antrim. The coast is rugged – steep cliffs interposed by sandy beaches and dunes, and crossed by the rivers and estuaries of the Foyle, the Bann, the Bush and the Shesk. Offshore, Northern Ireland's only inhabited island, Rathlin, lies 7km across a treacherous strait, where waves and currents meet and many lives have been lost.

The distinctiveness of the north coast derives from its natural resources. Over the years these have been tamed and modified by people, yet the character still shows through.

The volcanic inheritance

The north coast is cut into volcanic rocks of Tertiary age. Around 60 million years ago, north-east Ireland was the scene of extensive volcanic activity, and basalt lavas poured out from vents to cover the area between Ireland and Scotland with an igneous rock plain. These lavas infilled the pre-existing chalk (karst) landforms, pouring into solution holes, through caves and baking the chalk limestone into a hard rock, completely unlike the soft chalks of southern England. The lava flows were intermittent, with often several million years between eruptions, allowing tropical vegetation and soils to form. Today these soils are preserved as red, weathered horizons (laterites) often including plant remains. The cooling of the basalts was highly variable. Those lava surfaces that were exposed to air or water cooled rapidly, often forming contorted skins, not unlike those that form on custard. However, at depth the lava cooled more slowly, often trapping gas and liquids in bubbles (vesicles) or contracting to form the columnar structures now best seen at the Giant's Causeway.

Much of the Tertiary landscape is still with us. If you travel east from Castlerock towards Coleraine on the Crannagh road you ascend a long hill in a series of steps. The treads of these steps are the flow tops, and the risings are where lava flows came to a halt 50 to 60 million years ago. Erosion and weathering since Tertiary times have exposed many of the features of volcanic Ulster in the cliffs of the north coast. Volcanic vents push through the chalk near Ballycastle and west of Port-ballintrae, dykes and sills criss-cross the landscape, often forming prominent bluffs in the cliffs or across the shore. At the White Rocks near Portrush, volcanic bombs of basalt are embedded within chalk; at first this appears anomalous, until you realise that the chalk was completely disintegrated by a volcanic eruption and was redeposited, together with the bombs. Such rock faces bear witness to the explosive events of the Tertiary era in north-east Ireland.

The coastal landforms

It was towards the end of the last glacial period 15,000 years ago that the modern coast began to take shape. Of great importance in coastal evolution is the rise and fall of sea-level. The relative positions of the sea and land change in concert with variations in climate and the 'weight' carried by the land. Thus when the climate becomes colder the sea-level falls – as more of the world's water is locked up in ice – and when the climate warms – and the ice melts – so the sea rises. In this manner the sea-level fluctuated about 130m during the glacial periods. However, a complicating mechanism is that if ice covers the land, the land is depressed; and when the ice is removed, the land rises, albeit very slowly. Together these factors mean that the course of sea-level on the north coast is complex: 16,000 years ago the sea was probably several metres higher than today, by 10,000 years ago it was at least 30m lower, thereafter rising rapidly to about + 4m at 6500 years ago, and subsequently falling and perhaps rising again.

We can deduce these changes in sea-level by 'interpreting' the expression of the coast. The early, high sea-levels are marked by raised beaches, especially further west in County Donegal around Malin Head. The low sea-levels of 10,000 years ago are preserved in buried land sediments, that have been found in boreholes near Magilligan Point and dredged from the mouth of the River Bann. The rise of 6500 years ago is well preserved as

Left
The Causeway cliffs consist of basalt flows, later eroded by ice and water.

Opposite
The mouth of the Bann at Portstewart is marked by sand-dunes and shoals.

a raised cliff inside Lough Foyle. At this time the lough was open to the Atlantic, and the glacial clay cliffs were severely eroded by waves. The coarser boulder material from these cliffs was transported south, collecting in a series of gravel ridges near Bellarena called the Giant's Walk and at Culmore, near Derry. As the sea fell away again, great quantities of offshore sediment were brought ashore. First came the gravels, forming ridges, and then quantities of sand, blown up into dunes and covering the ridges. This is well seen at Castlerock, Portstewart, Portrush,

Runkerry and White Park Bay. The sand-dunes are little more than 5000 years old. We have a radiocarbon date from Articlave, near Castlerock, from oak leaves trapped between two dunes, of 5300 years ago, making this the oldest Irish dune so far discovered.

The beaches and dunes of the north coast were formed largely between 2000 and 5000 years ago. Sediment accumulated in numerous embayments, but the most impressive deposit is the great triangular mass of Magilligan, sitting at the mouth of Lough Foyle. This feature, one of only two

have confidently proclaimed that the river mouth is being deflected west, indicating a strong longshore current running from Portstewart to Castlerock. Many times I have been told this tale; sadly it is not true. A more plausible explanation is that the river mouth became fixed about 5000 years ago at a point on the coast where the river current coincided with a strong coastal current, generated by waves, called a rip. Once these two currents had joined, they swept the local sediment into stable patterns of bars and channels, and remained there until 1884. In this year, work was finally started on 'improving' the navigation of the river mouth, to allow ships a safe passage to Coleraine. The game of improving the Bar Mouth has continued ever since; some of Britain and Ireland's best engineers have played with the problem, suggesting moles, breakwaters and dredges. Today a dredger, the *Bar Maid*, regularly digs out the sand and takes it out to sea, from where it cannot return to fill in the river mouth. The port of Coleraine is thriving, but the river mouth is becoming dangerously unprotected, and big waves are moving into the sheltered estuary behind.

Portstewart Strand is a superb beach, 3km long, hard and flat, and backed by some of the most spectacular sand-dunes in Ireland; little wonder it is exceedingly popular with visitors, especially as they can park their cars on the sand. The beach and dunes are now owned by the National Trust, but the previous management of the site has left a sad legacy. The sand-hills are falling apart, the fragile dune grasses have succumbed to thousands of trampling feet, and the loosened soil has blown away. Huge hollows now mark the locations of old paths and the wind funnels and accelerates through and over the dunes, taking more sand as it goes.

(Dungeness is the other) coastal depositional forms to appear on the TV weather map, consists of hundreds of parallel sand ridges, which grew seaward as the sea-level fell. Originally the ridges were separated by low, waterlogged troughs, often filled with alder, willow and reeds. Magilligan has now been drained and farmed, but remains of the old vegetation are still to be seen in the low cliffs along the Foyle. These cliffs bear witness to another event, a great sandstorm that engulfed Magilligan about 1000 years ago. We do not know if this was a natural event or whether it was triggered by human activity, but a wind-blown sand sheet smoothed the old ridges making many hard to pick out, except in dry weather from an aeroplane or perhaps from the viewpoint at Gortmore.

The human influence

Man's love affair with Magilligan has been tempestuous; in the pre-Famine days of the late eighteenth century, the population of the area rose dramatically. The sand-dunes were dug up for potatoes, and used for rabbit warrens. There was a bustling fur and meat market each Friday at Benone, the rabbits going to Belfast. So popular was rabbit farming that contemporary accounts claim the animals were 'planted' by digging a hole in the sand hills and popping in a rabbit. However, these activities took their toll, and by the time of the Famine the sand was blowing again and the land was abandoned.

To the east, Magilligan passes, almost without interruption, past Downhill and the now-ruined Bishop of Derry's summer residence (or palace) to Castlerock and Portstewart. Between these two seaside resorts is the mouth of the River Bann, locally called the Bar Mouth. Generations of geography students have studied the map and

As the molten lava cooled, so shrinkage caused the formation of the columnar structures now best seen at the Giant's Causeway.

(cusps) often seen on the north coast beaches.

The mark of recreation is indelible all along the north coast. While visitors sustain the local economy, it is sad to see the unattractive trappings that accompany them: the mile after mile of caravans around Portrush, with not a tree or bush to screen them; the picturesque harbour at Portrush overshadowed by a giant, screaming funfair; the damage and vandalism to the dunes and the lack of consideration of many in littering the streets and beaches.

Portrush is the centre of these neo-tourist activities. Thirty years ago, 70 per cent of the resort's visitors stayed in hotels and guesthouses, now only 10 per cent do: the rest have gone to caravans and self-catering flats. The main street – locally called the 'Trench' – is full of gaudy amusement arcades and the Victorian railway station is another funfair. People have indelibly altered the natural coast at Portrush, through ignorance and greed. On the West Strand, a sea wall was built between 1947 and 1963, to solve an erosion problem that never existed, as well as to provide a promenade for visitors. Unhappily the sea wall cut off the beach from the dunes; this action is tantamount to taking the wheels off a car and wondering why it won't move. The beach and dunes have a relationship rather like the one a client has with his or her bank. The client (the beach) saves a little money (sand) each month in the bank (the dune). These savings are against a rainy day: the client may need them in a hurry, and the bank will oblige by repaying. During a storm the beach needs its sand back, so it takes it from the dune. This sand is spread out over the beach, forcing the storm waves to break further offshore and so lessen the risk of damage. In the absence of its dune, the West Strand at Portrush has been unable to cope

Restoration of the dunes will be a long and arduous job, one not appreciated by the summer tourists, who cannot perceive the damage they are causing.

At first sight the wide sandy beaches of the north coast seem to be a bathers' paradise, but the water is cold, and the rip currents can be treacherous. Many swimmers – and floaters – get dragged seaward every year, trapped in the strong currents. If caught, don't swim against the current, but swim sideways or even seawards and you will soon enter calmer water. Better still, take precautions before entering the water – don't

swim where the breakers seem to be lower and don't swim near rocks or near stream outlets. If you climb up to a vantage point it is easy to spot rip currents as streaks of foam and water crossing the breakers. Often rips are remarkably regularly spaced: at Portstewart and Castlerock they are almost always 400m apart, at Runkerry 100m and in White Park Bay 300m. This rhythmic pattern is due to a conjunction between the incoming waves and secondary waves trapped at the shoreline, imperceptible to the casual observer. Similar but much smaller trapped waves cause the regular ups and downs with storms, and the sea has stripped its sand away. In 1968 it was possible to jump off the promenade onto the beach, in 1987 you would risk a broken leg, as the drop is nearly three metres. This trend will probably continue until all the sand has gone.

Another disappearing beach is at Portballintrae. This is a sad story that has gone unexplained by the many engineers who have tried to solve the mystery. Until the 1930s, Portballintrae had a fine beach, wide, flat and sandy. Today there is no sand, only a rocky strip between the slumping cliffs and the sea. Why should a beach, almost 5000 years old, suddenly disappear? The answer lies in a single untoward act, in 1895, when the fishing pier at the north-west side of the bay was extended and rebuilt in stone, replacing an old open wooden pier. This pier altered the wave pattern inside the bay, causing a strong current to develop which has flushed the bay of sand. The consequences of the 1895 project took nearly eighty years to fulfil, a delay which makes it hard to apportion blame. The engineers have tried groynes, sea walls, cliff reshaping and other tactics, but all to no avail. The horse has bolted. The only solution would be to remove the pier and bring back the sand by lorry.

Lorries, in fact, figure in the greed that has blighted many of the north coast's finest beaches. Many local landowners have an ancient right to 'take sand', similar to rights to cut turf or graze common land. Unfortunately this right has become abused by people with lorries and tractors with trailers taking vast amounts of sand from the beaches at Castlerock, White Park Bay, Runkerry and Portrush. There is no more fresh sand, once removed it will not come back naturally (at least not until the next ice age!), so every lorryload means that much

White Rocks beach, a popular rocky shoreline on the north coast

less. On those beaches with relatively little sand, uncontrolled removal can lead to erosion; the pervasive erosion that has threatened the famous fifth hole on Royal Portrush Golf Club, was triggered by unchecked removal of sand from the adjacent beach in the 1950s. Attempts to curb this problem have led to many angry confrontations.

The Giant's Causeway

The Giant's Causeway is the 'jewel in the crown' of the north coast. We have already noted how the basalt columns formed, but in the Causeway they reach their most glorious expression. While the Causeway itself is spectacular, so too is its setting, in the amphitheatre of the glacial and marine hewn cliffs. The National Trust, which owns and manages the Causeway, has made great efforts both to make the site accessible to the many thousands who come each year, and to retain its awesome beauty. No tourist impediments now spoil the view, souvenir shops and ice-cream parlours are hidden over the cliff top.

To many the Causeway is a timeless scene, yet since it was first brought to the attention of the scientific world in the late seventeenth century, the rocks have suffered from erosion. From the masses of drawings and photographs we can trace the disappearance

of individual columns, the collapse of arches and rock falls on the cliffs. More subtle changes have also occurred; visitors, however careful, have disturbed the birds, which no longer nest here in great numbers, and the vegetation has suffered from generations of flower pickers.

A word of warning

The north coast owes its living to its natural resources, especially its magnificent scenery. Yet the landscape is changing, often slowly and without warning. We should make greater efforts to understand these changes if our valuable heritage is not to be lost to future generations.

DR BILL CARTER is senior lecturer in Environmental Science at the University of Ulster. His academic interest is in coastal studies (geology, ecology and management) and his other interests include cooking, jogging, gardening and bringing up two very lively children. He has published over fifty papers on the coast of Ireland and three books, including a forthcoming volume, co-edited with Tony Parker of University College Dublin.

THE BURREN UPLANDS
Crossing the Pass

Tim Robinson

Seen from the Aran Islands, from Galway city or from Kinvara, the Burren imposes itself as an entity; its battered walls, rising steeply from the waters of the Atlantic or Galway Bay, or from the stony plain of Gort, which is almost as low and level as the sea itself, admit no doubts as to where it begins. Ambiguity creeps in only from the south, with the gentle rise of the shale-and-bog country and its irregular cessation, revealing the limestone strata underlying it; hence towns like Lisdoonvarna and even Lahinch can quibble their way into the region. But the word *boireann* means a rock, or a place composed of rocks, and to be true to ancient intention one should confine the name to the limestone region, with the reluctant inclusion of the shale-capped hill of Slieve Elva which runs into it from the south and rises just a little higher than the rest of its hills.

However, once one is within the Burren, this geological prescription is not enough to guarantee a sense of its unity. The place is a plateau sundered by valleys, some of which open onto the sea and others close in on themselves, and its heights are all so close to the 1000-foot mark that none offers a panorama of the whole. In my initial explorations I felt that the place was outmanoeuvring me, that wherever I penetrated, it withdrew and lurked elsewhere. But then, one autumn day (a day, it turned out, that had come down through hundreds, perhaps thousands, of years) I was privileged to hear the vast, slow heartbeat of this place of rock. I had been visiting the ruins of Corcomroe Abbey, where in the early thirteenth century the Cistercians had coaxed the stones of the Burren into conformity with the spirit of Gothic Europe, and I was walking back to the farmhouse I was staying in at Lough Rask near Ballyvaughan. The still and

sunlit afternoon achieved perfection as I climbed the pass from Turlough, and I paused, feeling the wholeness of the Burren like a fruit mellowing on the branch. A herd of cattle was being urged up the rugged track; the cries of men and barks of dogs rang to and fro between the bare hillsides. At the saddlepoint their way diverged from mine and wound on up into the heights.

I learned later that this was one of the two periods upon which the Burren year hinges, for it is the uplands that provide 'winterage' to graze the cattle on, while in summer they are kept near the houses in the lowlands, where they are more easily watered and their calves tended. It was a pattern I was familiar with in the Aran Islands, though there the seasonal movement between the little patches of improved land around the houses and the crags is of smaller compass. Perhaps it was the Celts, whose unit of wealth was the heifer and whose stonework is everywhere in the

Burren, who initiated this alternation between upland and lowland pastures, or rather the particular form of the custom that marks this region. For what I saw that day was the exact opposite of the ancient practice once general in western Ireland.

The two seasons of the Celtic year were articulated by the movement of cattle and their attendants between winter quarters in permanent lowland settlements and the mountain pastures only habitable in summer. In Connemara, for example, the O'Flaherty chieftains and their retinue took up residence in temporary dwellings every summer, and this custom of 'booleying' (from *buaile*, a milking pasture) persisted among the peasantry until late in the last century, it being the womenfolk who spent the milking and buttermaking season in little huts of stones and sods on the hillsides while the men attended to the tillage, fishing and kelp-burning below. But the Burren is different. A

spell of hot weather that would make the Connemara hills delightful will reduce the Burren's uplands of thirsty limestone to waterless deserts; conversely in winter when Connemara's hillsides are streaming quagmires, the Burren's are relatively dry underfoot, and the Burren farmer can take advantage of the residual Gulf Stream mildness that plays around his land, and leave his cattle outdoors.

Of course the visitor who drives into the Burren past those northern hillsides that from a distance look like the flanks of huge salmon closely armoured with silvery-grey scales, or from the south along roads that cross square miles of the bare rock-sheets so aptly called 'pavement', must wonder how anything could survive on what such a terrain has to offer, winter or summer. But as it happens the harder, purer limestones that take on such a hostile polish occur mainly on the lower and intermediate levels and so make a disproportionate contribution to one's first impressions, while the upper strata are of a dolomitic limestone, richer in magnesia, and break down into a light soil supporting a nutritious vegetation. Also, even the barest-looking areas have little pockets of lush grazing here and there around the springs and the seepages at the foot of the scarps that run across the hillsides.

This pass that, crossed with a time-hallowed day, gave me a hint of the specificity of the Burren, is called Mám Chatha, the pass of battle, for history has penetrated it, as I shall tell. A walk that winds through it will supply themes enough for this brief evocation of a region that exceeds it in all dimensions. I begin at Turlough, the village south-east of it, and end at Lough Rask, to the north-west.

A *turlach* is a hollow in which a lake comes and goes, not fed by streams or springs but filling and emptying from below through openings in its bed, as the general level of groundwater held in the fissured rock fluctuates in sympathy with rainfall. Since the phenomenon is almost unknown outside the limestone regions of Ireland, the Irish term for it has been adopted generally (anglicised as 'turlough' on the natural but mistaken assumption that the second syllable has something to do with *loch*, a lake). The village is named from a fine example of this unusual landform, and there is another just north-west of it; between the two, most of the strange features of a turlough can be examined here when the water is low or absent.

Since different plants can tolerate different degrees and probabilities of immersion, the flora of a turlough is arranged in zones that follow the contours of the hollow. Where a turlough is surrounded by hazel scrub, this diminutive forest will stop short around its rim as neatly as if trimmed by a landscape gardener, and its inner face will be

81

embellished with flowers of hawthorn, rowan and guelder rose. Slightly lower comes a contour line of a blackish moss with the lovely name of *Cinclidotus fontinaloides*, which is almost diagnostic of periodic flooding. The grassy bowl within is usually well grazed and rich in flowering herbs; the common sorts of violet are replaced at the lower levels by the pallid *Viola persicifolia*, a rarity in Ireland, where it is almost restricted to this specialised station in life. In the centre, pondweeds root in muddy dregs around the natural drainholes.

Sometimes in summer one finds that the empty bowl of a turlough is sheeted in what looks like rough whitish paper, laid over the vegetation; I remember being baffled by this phenomenon on first coming upon it in the Aran Islands. It is made up of the matted and bleached remains of microscopic algae, which have multiplied countlessly in the sun-warmed waters and then been left high and dry when the turlough emptied. Algal paper, as it is called, can appear with mysterious suddenness overnight; in Germany, where it has only been recorded about a dozen times, it is called meteor paper, as people imagined it had fallen from the sky.

A bare, limestone landscape without surface streams, in which the drainage is subterranean, is termed a *karst*, from the name of such a region in Yugoslavia. The Burren is a karst that has been worked over by glaciation; the bowls of the turloughs are depressions that have been gouged out by the glaciers, or are formed in deposits of glacial drift. Other karstic and glacio-karstic features of the Burren can be seen on the hillsides around Mám Chatha, such as, to the east of the pass, a row of steep conical pits which were once swallow-holes of some long-vanished stream, and a ravine formed by the

collapse of the roof of a cavern excavated by water flowing underground. These impressive works of water date from a time when the shale strata that still overlie the limestone to the south were much more extensive than they are today, for erosion is slowly stripping them away. A stream running off the impervious shale will be acid with bog-water, and on reaching the limestone will soon dissolve itself out a swallow-hole by eating away at the fissures and enlarging them; the rest of its course to the sea will be underground, with perhaps some reappearances in turloughs and springs. As the area covered by shale contracts, the stream will abandon its first swallow-hole and punch through another one closer to the retreating boundary of the shale; one can see the process at work around the margins of Slieve Elva today (and it is because of this creative implication with the limestone topography that one must include such shale areas in the area to be thought of as the Burren). This is the location of the famous potholes and caves of the Burren, which the wetsuited experts can follow for, in one case, over eight miles. Their latest discovery has

been of a section of dry cave near Doolin, which can only be entered through an opening on the seabed and a quarter of a mile of submarine passage; the river that formed this system must have been flowing when sea-level was much lower than it now is, perhaps at the end of the last Ice Age. For the family party on a Sunday outing there is the Aillwee cave south of Ballyvaughan, further west along the ridge from Mám Chatha; here one can stroll through over quarter of a mile of tortuous caverns, sprigged with tastefully illuminated stalactites.

Just east of the summit of the pass are the scars of old open-cast mining of fluorspar, the glossy purple crystals of which can still be turned up in the spoil. Fluorspar is formed out of calcite (the pure white and crystalline version of calcium carbonate) by the action of hot fluorine gas, and the fact that at one time there were such fumes rising through the fissures here is part of the evidence for the existence of granite deep down under the limestone. In fact it seems that the Burren is underlain by an extension of the Galway granite that is exposed on the north side of Galway Bay. Perhaps it was because of this

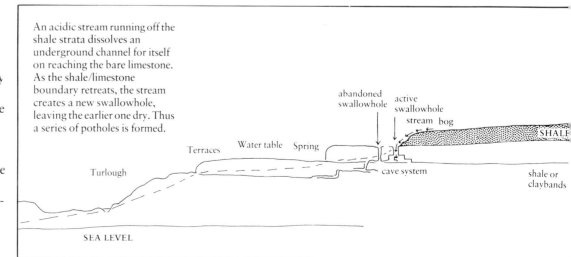

An acidic stream running off the shale strata dissolves an underground channel for itself on reaching the bare limestone. As the shale/limestone boundary retreats, the stream creates a new swallowhole, leaving the earlier one dry. Thus a series of potholes is formed.

solid basement that the limestone strata were so little disrupted by the Caledonian uplift, some 270 million years ago, that left them as a plateau with only a slight southwards inclination. Only at the two ends of the upland area is there substantial folding or faulting: the giant steps with which the furthest hillside of Árainn (Inishmore) descends north-westwards into the sea are slightly warped and cleft by faults, while the terraced sides of Mullach Mór, a hill in the south-east of the Burren, are so curved as to make it look like a layer-cake that has sunk in the cooking.

But it is on the nature of what is immediately underfoot, the broken stone of such hillsides as those around Mám Chatha, that the Burren's paradoxical fame for barrenness and floral luxuriance is grounded. The limestone offers plants some very specialised habitats, of which two form a strikingly complementary pair. Down in the grykes, as the enlarged fissures are called, all is shadowy, still and dank; ferns such as the hart's-tongue and maidenhair thrive in this atmosphere from a Victorian bottle-garden. But the horizontal surfaces (the clints) between the grykes are dry, exposed to strong winds, and searchingly grazed by cattle, goats and rabbits. Wherever a thimbleful of humus has accumulated some plant will root, of a sort adapted to these spartan conditions rather than to, say, the hurly-burly of a luxuriant buttercup-meadow.

So, close to the maidenhair fern, which is a plant of the mild, Atlantic side of southern Europe, one finds here species associated with severe Arctic or northern European climates, such as the vivid blue spring gentian and the delicate, ivory-silk-petalled mountain avens, the two stars of the late May Burren show. A profusion of the usual lime-loving plants,

notably thyme, various saxifrages, eyebrights and orchids, occur on all but the barest surfaces; even the most uncomfortable-looking rubble puts forth woodsage and the lovely burnet rose. Right next to these one will find lime-haters like the heathers colonising some deeper, well-drained pocket of soil from which the high rainfall has leached out the lime. Sheltered slopes of neglected land carry dense hazel scrub, and it is worth fighting one's way through its outworks of bramble to see the miniature forest glades, dim, green, humid, bewitched by moss and lichen, where the wood sorrel and wood anemones flower virginally in the spring, and the rarer broad-leaved helleborines more sophisticatedly in high summer.

All this is uniquely interesting and beautiful, but not very profitable for the landowner, who naturally is tempted by the availability of EEC grants to have his hillside sprayed with fertiliser by helicopter, the result being a more mundane but productive pastureland, at least in the short run. The financial, legal and moral persuasions necessary to preserve the Burren from such 'improvement' have not yet been discovered. But at present the northern and southern graces of mountain avens and maidenhair fern still evoke each other out of the rock, year after year, by sharing out its wetness and dryness, its windiness and its shelter.

Once, when groping my way down in torrential rain to the summit of Mám Chatha from the hills south of it, I came across an ancient stone-walled enclosure about a hundred yards across, which was not marked on the Ordnance Survey maps nor had been included in the otherwise almost exhaustive one-man survey of the Burren 'forts' conducted by T.J. Westropp in the 1900s. It

consisted of a very dilapidated and irregular semicircular arc of wall springing from the face of a steep scarp crossing the slope just above the saddlepoint; whether its purpose had been military, watching over the pass, or peaceable, for the corralling of cattle at a half-way stage of their seasonal migrations, I could not tell. It is only one (but a very large and unusual one) among hundreds of walled enclosures, some of them magnificently situated and visible from afar, others so much degraded and enmeshed with more recent fences that they can hardly be distinguished from the fields around them.

The majority of the three or four hundred ringforts in the Burren are roughly circular and often about twenty yards across, with simply built dry-stone walls a few feet thick, and they served as cattleyards around small huts, the individual farms of Iron Age and early Christian times. But a large number are more imposing, even in ruin; they have walls up to five or six yards thick, rising in two or three terrace-like steps inside; a few of them still retain their lintelled doorways; some are surrounded by one or two outer walls, while Baile Cinn Mhargaidh, near Kilfenora, has an *abattis* of set, slanting stones around it like the two cliff-forts of Árainn. Despite such forbidding externals these great cashels may not have been built with sieges in mind; their outworks may have reflected communal prestige; their interior terraces, it has been suggested, are better adapted to viewing ceremonials within than repelling the foe without. Perhaps such monuments served various purposes, sacred and profane – but since the Celts who built them could not confide their intentions to writing, less is known about the cashels of the Burren than about the Egyptian pyramids.

Cathair Mhaol, the low-topped

(dilapidated) fort, at the foot of the slope just west of Mám Chatha, is typical of these almost anonymous ruins. Like so many others it is deeply obscured by thickets; to fight one's way through them, groping to and fro until one can stretch out a hand to the mighty masonry, is to experience the past in all its difficulty of access and its indubitable reality: here was the pride of some long-settled and prosperous community, and it lies overthrown among brambles. But it is not just the individual monuments, the scores of cashels and hundreds of lesser ringforts that lie awaiting attention in the Burren; there are webs of ancient field-walls, large tracts of the agrarian landscape from which such monuments drew their sustenance, a stone document of the life of that late Iron Age and early Christian period, scarcely smudged by more recent use.

And interwoven with that landscape there are earlier ones, fainter but still legible, of the Bronze Age and the neolithic period. Not one of the Burren's sixty or so wedge tombs has been investigated; their dating to 'the end of the neolithic and the beginning of the Bronze Age' has become a received idea which many archaeologists suspect is outworn. The famous dolmen at Poulnabrone, a portal tomb with a huge and rakishly poised capstone, which has had the misfortune to be adopted as a touristic mascot of the region and featured in countless vapid come-ons, has now been excavated; it turns out to date from the middle rather than the late neolithic: it is 500 or 1000 years older than had been thought. Modern archaeological techniques could well overturn all current assumptions about the course of settlement in the Burren, but even the prospects of a cursory listing of the monuments of this, one of the world's richest and most complex prehistoric landscapes, are fading for lack of funds.

84

Meanwhile the land-clearing bulldozer is busy everywhere, steered by ignorance and fuelled by greed.

However, since the Burren has scarcely been picked over by the professionals, the amateur has every chance of making worthwhile discoveries – or at least of bringing to the notice of academia what has long been known to the locals. Coming down northwards from Mám Chatha once, I stopped to investigate two grassy mounds, each by a spring. Unable to make anything of their outward appearance I kicked a bit of turf off one and pulled out a small stone from its interior; it crumbled in my hand, and appeared to have been in a fire. A farmer I met further down the slope told me that these mounds were *fulachta fiadh*, the cooking-places of ancient huntsmen. On looking up the subject later on, I learned that such mounds of burnt stone are common field-monuments in many parts of Ireland, that they are usually horseshoe- or kidney-shaped (as these are) with traces of a wooden trough in the indentation of their perimeter; the water in the trough was brought to the boil for the cooking of meat by dropping heated stones into it, and periodically the debris of shattered stone would have to be dredged out and flung aside, so building up the characteristically shaped mound around the site. When I mentioned these particular cooking-sites to an archaeologist, I was told that, no, the Burren was not *fulachta* country; although a few had recently been discovered near Kilnaboy, where the Burren merges into the lakelands south-east of it, in general they were features of wet lowlands east of the Shannon, and not to be expected on limestone hills. However, having learned to recognise them, I noticed several more in the north of the Burren, and a geologist who was following out the spring-lines for his own purposes began to record them almost throughout the area, wherever water appeared on the surface. The only example of

Opposite
Thrift growing in a crack in the limestone pavement of the Burren.

Right
The glaciers that ground across the Burren in the ice ages tore chunks off the rocky hillsides, which were dumped when the ice melted back. Since then these glacial boulders have been sheltering the ground immediately underneath them from the erosive effect of rainfall, and now stand on little pedestals, showing that the general level of the rock surface has been reduced by several inches since the end of the last Ice Age.

the Burren *fulachta* to have been studied properly as yet is close to a turlough south of Carran; it was found to date from the Later Bronze Age, about 3000 years ago.

Finally I come down to Lough Rask itself, a lake that is responsive to the tides although it is a quarter of a mile inland, and which occasionally reveals itself to be a turlough by disappearing into its own muds. Herons nest in the tall trees around it, and bee orchids flower on its banks; it is a beautiful place, but its legend is horrific. In 1317 when two chieftains of the O'Briens were vying for supremacy in what is now County Clare, one of them, Donough, passed the lake with his army on their way to the fateful battle at Corcomroe. They saw a loathsome hag washing a heap of severed limbs and heads in the lake (the long description of her in the account of this campaign must be one of the foulest passages in medieval literature); she told Donough that her name was Brónach Boirne, the sorrowful one of Burren, that

these limbs were those of his army if he pressed on to this battle, and that his own head was in the middle of the heap. They tried to seize her but she flew up and hovered above, spewing curses on them. But Donough told his men that she was the demon-lover of his enemy Dermot and was seeking to discourage them; so they marched on (through Mám Chatha, the place-name suggests), accompanied by crows, ravens and wolves, and by nightfall most of them were dead and laid out within the abbey of Corcomroe. The battle was not without consequence, for, having consolidated his power, Dermot went on to defeat de Clare, the Norman lord of Bunratty Castle, in the following year, and it was another two hundred years or more before the region ceased to be under Gaelic rule.

Passes are impressed upon the physical landscape by great forces of nature – in this instance the glaciers of the ice ages. Subsequently history follows these ways of

least resistance and scores them into the cultural landscape of lore and place-name. In one's own mental map of a region it is the weight of significance they are made to bear that incises the passes so deeply. Mám Chatha stands here for two complementary rites of passage: the indefinitely repeated seasonal migration of cattle between upland and lowland, and the crossing of a threshold between prophecy and the reality of death in battle upon a particular day in history. Tracking the past and present of this landscape through Mám Chatha, I meet 'the sorrowful one of Burren'; and it is under her shadow that I think of its future. For Brónach Boirne is not just a banshee, the other-worldly but time-serving retainer of some local dynasty. She is the reapparition of the ancient Celtic divinity of the territory, a nightmare to the usurper, a vision of beauty and fruitfulness to the one who cherishes it. Should she make herself visible to our exploitative generation, it might well be as the vile prophetess of doom. Indeed our heads could be in the middle of the heap – for if we cannot save such a place as the Burren from spoliation, there is nowhere safe on the surface of the earth.

IRISH ISLANDS AND THEIR MONASTERIES

Michael Herity

Of the many islands off the Atlantic coast of Ireland over thirty, between Malin Head in Donegal and Mizen Head in Cork, have early monastic remains. Many of these are well-known, like Inismurray, the Aran Islands and Sceilg Mhichíl. The names of the founders of some are known to us, Molaise of Inismurray, Fechín of Ardoileán (High Island), Brendan of Inis Gluaire (Inishglora), men who in the sixth or early seventh century chose to live in pious seclusion on these lonely islands.

Today the sea journey to Sceilg Mhichíl, 13km off the Kerry coast, takes about an hour and a half in good weather by modern fishing boat. By currach (or *naomhóg* as it is called in Kerry), even with a sail up, it would have taken at least twice as long in early Christian times. The landing at several of these islands is difficult and can be made only in calm conditions with just the gentlest swell on the sea; this is particularly so at Ardoileán. The currach, drawing only a few inches of water and so manoeuvrable as to be almost a live thing on the waves, is perfectly adapted to landing on these rocky or sandy shores.

In summer the islands are places of great natural beauty where fishermen and naturalists live for short periods in tiny huts or restored dwelling-houses. Cormorants perch on rocky promontories fringing the islands, kittiwakes, seagulls and puffins build their nests in security on the now deserted fields and outcrops, many choosing nesting-places among the ruined monastic buildings which are frequently situated in the most sheltered places on the islands. In June, islands like Ardoileán are carpeted with sea-pink, and later with masses of daisies. Inishkea North is like a tropical paradise in summer, with wide white sandy beaches and aquamarine inshore waters. Other islands like Caher, Duvillaun More and Ardoileán

present less hospitable, rocky shorelines. Some trail fringes of dark slippery seaweed over the rocks at high tide.

The opening lines of the twelfth-century poem 'St Columba's Island Hermitage' as translated by Kenneth Jackson recall the sea in summer mood: 'Delightful I think it is to be in the bosom of an isle, on the peak of a rock, that I might often see there the calm of the sea.' Whereas in summer the sea, in benign mood, only laps the rocks, in winter, in savage mood, it beats and sounds on the cliffs and inlets, driven by gales from the west or north. In these conditions, which only the lighthousemen can describe for us, it must have been dangerous to venture outside the oratory compound.

It is appropriate that at a number of the islands with monastic remains one of the first sights to greet a visitor is a cross-slab close to the landing-place, where hermit or pilgrim could kneel to give thanks for a safe journey. The monastic remains themselves follow a pattern which varies only in its detail: a small church or oratory, often dry-built with patient craftsmanship, is the focal point; some as at Ardoileán and Caher Island are enclosed within a tiny stone compound. Close to the church, often at its east end, is the *leaba*, the tomb or reliquary of the founder saint, marked by slabs, some cross-inscribed, or a shrine built of carved slabs as originally existed at Ardoileán. The shrine of the saint is often a focus of pilgrimage. So too are *leachta*, small stone-built rectangular 'altars', often crowned by cross-slabs; on Inismurray one has the so-called 'cursing stones' turned prayer-stones and only exceptionally used to call down a curse. Usually placed close to the oratory, at Caher and Inismurray the numerous *leachta* extend out beyond the central focus of buildings to make the stations

of a *turas* or pilgrimage round.

Close to the oratories on these sites are the living-quarters of the monks, stone-built *clocháns* or beehive huts. These and the oratory form the nucleus of the foundation, usually encompassed by an outer enclosing wall which also includes within its bounds a small monks' graveyard. The outer wall at Ardoileán has wall-chambers, tunnel-like spaces built into its thickness; similar wall-chambers are built into the massive cashel wall at Inismurray and into the enclosure around the church at Caher Island. Wells, marked by cross-inscribed slabs at Rathlin O'Birne and Ardoileán, are a further recurring feature, as are small lakes close to the monastic settlement. That at Ardoileán feeds a mill-stream on which a horizontal mill was turned, overlooking the sheer cliffs of Cuan a' Mhuilinn (the mill cove) below.

MICHAEL HERITY is Professor of Archaeology at University College Dublin and Dean of Celtic Studies. He has published numerous academic papers and textbooks and has a special interest in early Christian monuments.

Dalkey Island

View from the south-east of St Begnet's Church on Dalkey Island, less than 400m off the coast of Dublin. The church, which has *antae*, projections of the side walls beyond the line of the gable, a typical feature of Irish early Christian church construction, stands within a small enclosure. The bell-cote at the west end is a later medieval addition to the building. A cross-in-circle incised on a rock outcrop, which can be seen in the photograph opposite the west doorway of the church, suggests a foundation close to the introduction of Christianity. The modern buildings in the background lie between the two small harbours of Coliemore and Bulloch on the mainland. Boat trips to the island can be arranged from Coliemore harbour in the summer.

Rathlin O'Birne

Evening light on the monastic remains on Rathlin O'Birne Island (Rochuil), about 1.5km off Malin Beg in south-west Donegal. A hermitage was founded here about AD 500 by Assicus (Tassach) of Elphin, St Patrick's metalworker. The nucleus consists of an oratory, hermit's cell and well-house, built of the pinkish felstone of the island and enclosed within two adjoining rectilinear enclosures. There are simple cross-decorated slabs on the roof of the well-house and on two *leachta* within the outer enclosure. Beside the well-house, above the landing-place, stands a schist slab with a wreathed Chi-rho (symbol formed of the first two letters of 'Christ' in Greek) on its east face and a cross-in-circle on its west. This nucleus is linked by an outer roughly semicircular enclosure, resembling that of Colmcille's monastery on Iona, the ends of which are anchored to the natural boundary provided by the shoreline. In the background of the picture, in cloud, is Slieve League. On the left is the village of Malin Beg.

88

Inishkea North

The Bailey Mór on the island of Inishkea (Inis Cé) North, a granite-based sandy spit over 1.5km long, lying about 4km west of the Mullet peninsula, County Mayo. This and the neighbouring island, Inishkea South, were inhabited until the 1930s. The houses of the islanders now stand derelict along deserted streets. Towards the south-east tip of the island are three sand-hills called baileys by the locals. The Bailey Mór, the largest of these, is over 150m in diameter and 18m high.

Cross-slabs and remains of buildings on the summit of the Bailey Mór on Inishkea North. Parts of this small foundation were excavated by Dr Françoise Henry in 1938. The excavations uncovered three dry-stone buildings of the early Christian period on the north-east slope of the bailey. A hut site excavated by her in 1950 produced large quantities of broken shells of *Purpura lapillus*, a shell from which purple dye can be extracted. A number of early Christian carved cross-slabs were found on the island. Some are now in the National Museum, Dublin.

Clare Island

Opposite

Clare Island (Oileán Cliara), County Mayo, is the only inhabited island of this series, with a population of over two hundred. There is a regular ferry service to the mainland at Roonagh Quay. Legend connects Gráinne Ní Mháille or Grace O'Malley (*c.* 1530–1603), with the island and with the fifteenth- or sixteenth-century tower house which overlooks the harbour.

Above right

Clare 'Abbey' is a small late-fifteenth-century nave and chancel church. The church also has remains of fifteenth- and seventeenth-century paintings on the founder's tomb, east wall and chancel vault. At the east end of the churchyard is a tall pillar with a cross inscribed on its east face, probably the only Christian foundation.

Below right

The crest of the Ó Máille family with the legend *Terra marique potens* (powerful on land and sea) is in the ruins of the 'Abbey'.

Duvillaun More

Cross-inscribed slab on the tiny island of Duvillaun More (Dubhoileán Mór), County Mayo. Some 5km off the southern tip of the Mullet peninsula, the island has been abandoned since the early years of this century. The photograph shows the east face, with compass-drawn Maltese cross-in-circle, of a large plank-like early Christian slab. On the west face of the slab is a depiction of the crucifixion. It stands at the west end of a grave known traditionally as the Tomb of the Saint, apparently the reliquary of the saint who founded the hermitage here, whose name is now lost. Immediately north of the slab are the dry-built remains of a tiny church. Both stand at the east end of an oval enclosure measuring 30m by 20m.

Inis Gluaire

Fishermen's marks towards the west end of the island of Inis Gluaire (Inishglora). The stone-built cones appear to be built on the *leachta* of a pilgrimage round. Inis Gluaire (island of purity), 2km off the coast of the Mullet, County Mayo, is the site of a foundation of St Brendan the Navigator in the sixth century. The remains of an early monastery at the east end of this now uninhabited island consist of three churches, three *clochán*s, part of the monastic enclosure and further stations. The photograph shows part of the Mullet peninsula, near Cross Point, on the horizon.

Mason Island

Mason Island, south of Carna, Connemara, County Galway; remains of a hermitage and of dwelling-houses abandoned about 1952. The enclosure of the hermitage is rectilinear, at the south side is a church, north of this is the burial area, a prominent feature of which is a *leacht* with a limestone cross-ornamented slab facing west. In the north-west corner of the enclosure is a second *leacht* with standing slab. In the background are Mweenish Island and the hinterland of Kilkieran.

Caher Island

View from the south-east of the hermitage on Caher Island (Cathair Phádraig or Cathair na Naomh), with dried-up pond now filled with irises in the foreground and Croagh Patrick to the right in the background. Cathair Phádraig is a small island off Killadoon in south Mayo and 6.5km from Inishturk. The foundation is attributed to Patrick. A tomb at the east end of the church marked by a flat decorated grave-slab and a headstone with a Greek cross-in-circle is traditionally known as Leaba Phádraig. The present church is a building of the fourteenth or fifteenth century, erected on the site of the original church. Within the rectangular enclosure are cross-slabs, facing west, in the north-east, south-east and south-west corners, and a *leacht* east of the church with cross-slabs and Leac na Naomh, a rounded stone of conglomerate about 60cm in diameter which may have been a 'cursing stone' of the type known at Inismurray. In the east wall of the enclosure there is a wall-chamber, 5m long, roughly 1m wide and 50cm high, entered from the enclosure. To the east of the enclosure extend two arrays of four *leachta* with decorated cross-slabs, the stations of a *turas*. Although the island has not had permanent inhabitants in modern times its surface is extensively ridged; compare Clare Island.

Inismurray

Cross-inscribed slab on the *leacht* known as Altóir Beag within the cashel or monastic enclosure at Inismurray. The cashel is in the style of prehistoric stone forts like Staigue and Grianán Ailigh and the great forts of the Aran Islands. The extant buildings are entirely monastic: Teampall na bhFear (the church of the men), Teampall na Teine (the church of the perpetual fire), Teach Molaise (Molaise's house), which houses the tomb of the saint, Leaba Molaise, and a *clochán*. Besides Altóir Beag there are two further *leachta* within the enclosure, one of which has, as well as two cross-slabs, about fifty rounded stones, some cross-inscribed, the Clocha Breaca or cursing stones. There are also a number of wall-chambers built into the walls of the cashel and a wealth of cross-inscribed slabs. The *turas* or pilgrimage round takes pilgrims to sixteen stations, many with decorated cross-slabs, around the perimeter of the island and within the cashel.

Left
Clasaidh Mór, the principal landing-place at Inismurray (Inis Muireadaigh) Island, looking towards the mountains in the vicinity of Lough Melvin. The island, named after Molaise, also known as Muiredach, who established a foundation here about AD 525 is 7km off the Sligo coast and can be reached by boat from Mullaghmore. Another landing-place is called Port a Churaidh (landing-place of the currach) as at Iona. Inismurray was inhabited until 1948. It is now a bird sanctuary and the eider and shelduck have established themselves since 1948.

Sceilg Mhichíl (Skellig Michael)

The monastic remains on this needle of rock, 13km west of Bolus Head in Kerry, are on a series of adjacent terraces sloping to the south 190m above the Atlantic. The northern terrace contains the focal remains, a dry-stone oratory and burial ground with cross-slabs at the east end and six *clochán*s fronting an open space running in a rough arc from north to west. In the open area are two wells. North of this group is a second tiny boat-shaped oratory, sited at the top of the cliff. The Monks' Garden occupied a lower terrace overlooked from the north by the main enclosure.

The monastery is reached by three flights of stone stairs climbing steeply from the sea. On narrow shelves around the South Peak, at 230m, are the remains of a hermitage. The foundation is traditionally attributed to St Finán.

Ardoileán (High Island)

View from the east of St Fechín's hermitage on Ardoileán (High Island) off the coast of Galway, north-west of Clifden, founded about AD 635. The photograph shows the remains of the dry-built church with its west doorway and *clochán*s to the east and south of it. The enclosure is open at the south side with an enclosing wall at the west containing a large wall-chamber. George Petrie described a decorated stone reliquary, the Tomb of the Founder, which stood at the east end of the church, in 1820. The lake visible on the left of the picture feeds a mill-race with the remains of a horizontal mill.

Miners, settled on the island in 1828 by the Martin family of Ballinahinch, sank a deep shaft close to the south-east landing to exploit copper. Near here they built two huts, robbing building stone from the monastery. Above the landing place is a decorated cross-slab. The island is a mass of sea-pink in early June and puffins nest in and around the monastery. The island was owned by the poet Richard Murphy, who has written a cycle of High Island poems. In 1985 he offered the island to the people of Ireland and it is now in state ownership.

St MacDara's Island

East face of a granite cross-slab above the landing-place on St MacDara's Island (Oileán Mhic Dara) off the coast of Connemara, near Carna. The Latin cross with expanded terminals is created by a single ribbon-like strand left in relief; raised bosses are placed in the quadrants between arms and stem. In the background is the stone-roofed church of St Sionnach MacDara, restored in recent years. Its features imitate cruck construction, a building tradition in timber, here translated into stone; a reproduction of a carved finial found on the site has been placed on the gable at the west end in the recent reconstruction. Immediately east of the church stood the tomb of MacDara. To the north and west of the church there is a monastic enclosure. The church of MacDara is featured on the 28p postage stamp.

VARIETY IN LANDSCAPE

Frank Mitchell

North-west Mayo

The Nephin Beg hills are the highest part of a great arc of high ground that runs from Bengorm on Clew Bay to Maumakeogh on Sligo Bay. In the Nephin Beg range we can see a series of ice-cut coums just as dramatic as any Kerry has to offer.

West of the arc of hills we find what is today the most desolate landscape in Ireland, a great sheet of blanket bog, with a very small population concentrated on the coastal strip.

But it was not always so. Before humans came this area was forested, just like the rest of Ireland, though here the pine was dominant. We can still see the pine-stumps everywhere at the base of the peat, and even see them disappearing below tide-level in shallow bays, for sea-level was then lower than it is today.

This part of Ireland was just as attractive as the rest of the country when the first farmers came here about 4500 years ago. They laid out fields of about 10 acres (4ha) surrounded by stone walls: they lived in large rectangular wooden houses, and they buried their dead in elaborate tombs built of large stones in the megalithic manner.

Then something happened, perhaps the climate became cooler and moister, and plant remains began to accumulate where the ground was badly drained, and the formation of blanket peat began.

There is much evidence for another phase of farming activity about 3000 years ago. The areas that had not yet been invaded by bog were cultivated in ridges and furrows, essentially similar to the *iomaire* (so-called lazy beds) of today's farmers, presumably also worked by spades.

Dr Séamus Caulfield has shown that these ridges are common below the peat around Belderg, and Professor Michael Herity has also found them much farther to the east around Bunnyconnellan, where the road from Ballina to Tubbercurry is climbing up the slopes of the Ox mountains.

Thus, 1000 years before the birth of Christ, the north Mayo landscape was fantastically different to what it is today. Instead of an abandoned wasteland of bog, we would have seen great expanses of farmland being cultivated with spades, just as Clare Island was cultivated in pre-Famine days.

On Clare Island we can still see the ghost lazy beds of 150 years ago. Strip away the peat of Erris and we will see the *iomaire* of 3000 years ago.

Before the Famine, Clare Island was very densely populated. The lazy beds that were worked with spades 150 years ago can still be clearly seen.

The sheepwalks of the west

Throughout the agricultural history of Ireland cattle have been of the greatest importance. But there are areas particularly favourable to sheep. They can do well in the uplands, as we have seen in Wicklow, but they thrive especially on dry limestone soils such as we have in east Galway, south-east Mayo, and south Roscommon. Here we find the large heavy sheep of the Galway breed. Wet soils must be avoided, as these bring heavy fluke infestation.

It was the Cistercian order, which reached Ireland in the twelfth century, that introduced the commercial rearing of sheep for wool, as well as many other advanced agricultural practices. There were many important abbeys in these parts, for example, the Cistercians were at Boyle and the Franciscans at Claregalway.

Before sheep became popular, cattle probably outnumbered them by ten to one, and it was cattle-ranching that made this area the preserve of the kings of Connacht in early historic times around AD 500. Queen Maeve herself is supposed to have had her palace at Rathcroghan, and the royal initiation ceremonies took place at Carnfree.

Because grazing, and not tillage, is dominant here, the ground has been less disturbed than in many parts of Ireland, and circular stone cashels and old field boundaries have survived in large numbers.

Sheep are very active animals, and must be very carefully enclosed if they are not to stray across the countryside. Stone is plentiful on the thin soils where they thrive, and so there is no scarcity of material for walls. Wall-building was a traditional art, and there are local variations in the pattern and sequence in which the stones were laid.

Before the coming of cotton in the nineteenth century, and synthetic fibres in the twentieth, wool was the staple fibre for cloth, though smaller quantities of flax and hemp were also produced. Europe had an insatiable appetite for wool and woollen cloth, and control of the wool trade was a powerful economic weapon.

England was constantly trying to impede the export of wool and woollen cloth from Ireland in order to maintain its own monopolistic position. Before the Industrial Revolution all spinning and weaving was carried out by hand, and cottage industries based on these crafts provided an important supplementary source of cash for rural families.

Left
This striking pattern of field walls of various ages superimposed on one another lies 7km south-east of Tuam. The oldest features are the two circular cashels (one cut across by a recent wall); they date to about AD 1000.

Opposite
Between Athy and Carlow the modern river cuts across a great area of well-drained sands and gravels washed out of former ice. The area has rich soils and large prosperous farms.

The Barrow valley

The Slieve Bloom mountains are a ridge of harder older rocks which now stand up above less resistant younger limestones, which still surround them – and doubtless once covered them also, just as limestone once covered the older sandstone ridges of east Cork.

The River Barrow starts its zig-zag course on the north slope of the hills, dropping down to the midland plain. Here at about 100m it turns north-east until it meets a surviving higher ridge of limestone south of Killeigh.

Then, making a right-angled bend, it flows south-east to Mountmellick, where it turns to the east and flows between huge areas of raised bog to the north and higher limestone to the south. At Monasterevan it turns sharply south-south-east and enters an area of very badly drained alluvium, which marks the floor of a large lake which existed here at

the end of the Ice Age and for some time thereafter.

The middle reach of the Barrow (continuing in the same direction) leaves the former lake-basin in a narrow channel near Kilberry. Ireland's early hunter-fishermen came here for fish and wildfowl, and it was also an important crossing-point in later prehistoric time. When the exit channel was drained by the Office of Public Works to reduce flooding, numerous bronze weapons and other articles were found.

The river then gradually turns to the south and continues through Athy and Carlow as far as Goresbridge. When the Ice Age was ending, the ice shrank slowly backwards up this part of the valley, washing out of itself as it detached great masses of limestone gravel and sand.

Thus, for a distance of about 40km, we have a broad ribbon of some of the best land in Ireland, only limited by a tendency in the more sandy areas to lose too much water in prolonged dry periods. Farmyard manure is much in demand here. Open texture means easy tillage, and great crops of barley and sugar-beet are raised. Permanent pasture is out, but short-term leys give good silage and hay for bullocks.

South-west of Goresbridge, low open country leads on to Thomastown, but the Barrow, already less than 30m above sea-level, continues directly south through Graiguenamanagh where it enters a gorge whose walls rise to over 70m, cut through the granite ridge that links Brandon hill to Blackstairs.

Only some complicated, but as yet unravelled, geological story can explain why the river pursues such an enigmatic course. Still in its granite gorge at St Mullin's it begins to feel the effects of the tide; it emerges from its gorge above New Ross, and flows on through open country to Waterford harbour and the sea.

Strongbow followed the Barrow valley in his northward march from Waterford to Dublin in 1170, and the Normans were quick to recognise the agricultural potential of the middle reaches, good land to grow their wheat, and a good river to turn their mills. They set up numerous earthen forts and farmsteads along its course, with a central stronghold in the great stone castle at Carlow, built about 1205.

Drumlin country

When an ice-sheet can no longer advance, but is melting away, the water in its upper layers drains away through the rock debris the ice was carrying, and the debris is deposited on the surface that had been below the ice without being sorted in any way, so that large boulders and the finest of sand are mixed up together. There has been no pressure on the debris, and the deposit can be quite loose in texture, as are the hummocky deposits at Screen in Wexford. Sometimes, the base of still advancing ice has picked up so much debris that it can no longer transport it all, and it sheds some of its load by extruding it onto the ground below, much as toothpaste is extruded from a tube. This extrusion takes place under the pressure of the weight of the overlying ice, and emerges as a hard and tough deposit known to the geologist as *till*.

Normally the till is extruded as a relatively flat sheet, like rolled-out pastry, but sometimes it has a rucked surface, and small closely packed oval hills, separated by intervening depressions, are created. Such small hills of till are extremely common in parts of Ireland and were indeed first scientifically described here, and so their international name, *drumlin*, is founded on the Irish word for diminutive hill, *droimín*.

Drumlins are at their most dramatic when their bases are surrounded by water, either by the sea, as in Clew Bay and Strangford Lough, or by a lake, as in Upper Lough Erne. They extend in a broad belt from Donegal Bay through Sligo, Leitrim, Fermanagh, Monaghan, Armagh and Down till they reach the Irish Sea.

Due to compaction, the till is dense in texture, with the result that water finds it difficult to soak away, and on the whole drumlin regions have poor soils. Leitrim is the worst off of the counties. Only one-tenth of

Left
It is almost impossible for farming to hold its own in drumlin country, but the soils and climate seem to be suited to forestry.

Opposite
Trim Castle was one of the strongest castles ever built in Ireland. It was surrounded by a great wall with towers, some of which served as gates, and an inner castle, or *keep*, was erected in the space within the wall.

the soil there is well-drained; sixth-tenths are poorly drained, and much of this lies on steeply sloping drumlin sides. The remainder is bog, lake or river, much of it occupying the low ground between the drumlins.

The vast majority of drumlin farms cannot produce a family income comparable to that of a family of industrial workers. It seems almost impossible for farming to hold its own here, but on the other hand the soils and the climate appear to be most suitable for forestry. There is no good growing timber, however, unless it can be sold profitably. Here one immediately thinks of pulpwood processing, but this industry is in serious difficulties in Ireland. The whole economics of extensive afforestation will have to be very seriously studied.

A countryside studded with wooded drumlins and lakes is difficult to traverse, and such a drumlin belt forms a natural barrier. Where people had stripped the trees off the drumlins, however, they could not present much difficulty to an invader. But difficulty could be re-created by cutting a ditch and bank across the cleared drumlin, and so filling the gap in the defensive line. Such ditches were dug in the centuries before the birth of Christ; when they were abandoned they came to be regarded as a furrow thrown up by the snout of a supernatural pig, and the Black Pig's Dyke threads its discontinuous way across the country from the vicinity of Dundalk to the Atlantic coast.

The plains of Meath

In prehistoric times the plains of Meath centred on the Hill of Tara, in early Christian times Kells was important, in the medieval period Trim was the focal point, and today Navan is dominant.

Most of the area is floored by limestone, with a few higher areas of shale above the limestone. The country undulates between 70m and 130m above sea-level, and the Boyne and its tributaries wind slowly through it. The glacial deposits are rich in limestone debris, but the local shales add a quota of clay to the soil, which tends to have a heavy texture. Such soils are more suited to grass than tillage, and throughout Ireland's recorded history these have been proverbial lands for fattening cattle.

Though the Hill of Tara is only 170m high, it commands a remarkable view of the surrounding countryside, and equally can itself be seen from considerable distances.

It was first occupied about 4500 years ago, when neolithic farmers erected a megalithic tomb to receive the cremated remains of their community. About 3750 years ago Bronze Age people, attracted by the already existing mound, added a thick skin of earth to it, and in this they buried their dead. One youth had been entombed still wearing a valuable necklace, which contained among others beads of amber from Scandinavia and of a glassy compound from Egypt. Thus those who buried him were traders with far-reaching connections in Europe.

Most of the earthworks we see on the hill today probably stem from the Iron Age, the centuries immediately preceding and succeeding the birth of Christ, when iron was displacing bronze as the metal for everyday use. Another mound, the so-called 'Rath of the Synods' has also been excavated, and it again revealed trading connections, this time with the Roman Empire.

When Christianity became established in Ireland about AD 500, the Hill of Tara lapsed into obscurity, and was perhaps even avoided because of its long-standing pagan traditions. By AD 800 Christian Kells had risen to importance, and even today a stone-roofed church, a round tower and four carved high crosses – to say nothing of the Book of Kells – still remind us of that importance.

From their first appearance greedy Norman eyes were attracted by the rich lands of Meath, and by 1200 the great castle at Trim had been erected. A walled town grew up around it, and abbeys and castles sprang up in the vicinity, and indeed Trim, and not Dublin, might well have been the capital of Norman Ireland. Its importance continued into the seventeenth century, but after that it subsided into the market town that we see today.

Navan lacks important early remains, but it lies at the junction of the Boyne and the Blackwater, and when power-driven factories began to displace cottage handcrafts, the town had plenty of water power. Though the factories have changed to other sources of power, Navan remains an industrial town. It is now known to be sitting on vast deposits of lead and zinc, and a new element is entering the Meath landscape with the large-scale extraction of ore.

The Bann valley

In prehistoric times early fishermen were catching eels and salmon, which they first split and then smoked to build up a good reserve. Today, the eel fisheries of the River Bann are still important.

Sixty million years ago there was tremendous volcanic activity in north-east Ireland. Volcanoes spouted ash and molten lava, and at intervals long cracks opened in the ground, pouring out vast quantities of molten rock which spread out and cooled to form successive layers of a dark, fine-grained rock, basalt.

The volcanoes have since weathered away to stumps, but a great saucer-shaped area of basalt still covers much of Antrim and Derry. The modern Lough Neagh, Ireland's largest lake, lies on the floor of the saucer, whose rim forms the black cliffs that we see on the Antrim coast road, at the Giant's Causeway, and east of Dungiven.

Sometimes, the intervals between lava flows lasted long enough for soils to form and plants to grow before the next flow arrived. The soils and plant debris were sometimes preserved between the layers of basalt, and their study tells us that at that time Ireland had a warm, tropical climate, utterly unlike that of today.

The Lower Bann is the only river that escapes out of the saucer, and it carries the overflow from Lough Neagh northwards from Toomebridge to the sea at Coleraine.

Water that drains from limestone is rich in calcium, and many water animals and plants use the calcium to build up protective or supporting skeletons. The water from the basalt is rich in silicon and in Lough Neagh millions of microscopic free-floating plants known as diatoms protect themselves inside tiny boxes, largely made of the oxide of silicon, a substance very resistant both to heat and to chemical change.

When the plants die, the boxes float away into the Bann, where they are trapped by the stems of the grasses in the water-meadows. This process has been going on for thousands of years, and gradually a thick, white cheesy layer of diatomite (which can be cut into blocks like sods of turf) has accumulated.

When dried, diatomite is commercially very valuable, because the little boxes make it full of airspaces and porous. It is used in insulation, in filtration, and to absorb liquids.

Today, the eel fisheries of the Bann are very valuable, and they were also important in prehistoric times. Seven thousand years ago early fishermen were catching eels and salmon, which they first split and then smoked to build up a food reserve. Archaeologists digging near the base of the diatomite can still find the ashes of their fires and the broken flint implements they threw away.

The Slieve League peninsula

Slieve League (601m), on the south-west of the peninsula, offers some of the most spectacular cliff-scenery in Ireland.

Farming in Ireland has changed almost out of all recognition in recent years, but it is still possible to find some old-time landscapes, where little has changed in the last hundred years, except that the population has fallen and fallen. To find such traces of the past, it is necessary to go where access is difficult, the terrain is broken, and the soils are poor. The Slieve League peninsula in south-west Donegal is such a place.

The peninsula is bounded by four high rock ridges, arranged like the edges of the diamond on a playing-card. The ridge from Ardara to Kilcar cuts it off from the rest of Donegal. The glaciated valley of Glengesh – very similar in form to Glenmalure in Wicklow – which leads back from Ardara, fails to cut through the ridge, and the road has to climb up the valley head with many hairpin bends, still a severe test for motor-rally drivers. The road from Killybegs has to climb to 200m to cross the ridge into Glencar.

The other three ridges face the sea, and at

Slieve League in the south-west, and Slieve Tooey on the north, the quartzites of the ridges drop into the sea in some of the highest cliffs in Ireland. The north-west-facing ridge, from Malin More to Slieve Tooey, is not so high, and is breached by two valleys running west into the sea, the larger at Glencolumb-kille and the smaller at Port. St Colmcille and his followers were not the first to reach this relatively sheltered 'desert', as such lonely places were called in early Christian Ireland, though isolation was the only feature such 'deserts' shared with the barren sands of Egypt to which early hermits withdrew.

St Colmcille's day is still marked by a circuit of stations, and the first station visited is the ruin of a megalithic tomb. There is quite a cluster of such tombs in the vicinity and the peninsula must have been settled as early as 3000 BC. The Columban settlement must also have been relatively dense as there are many slabs and pillars with decorated crosses in the valley.

But it is at Lougheraherk, at the head of the Port valley, that we get our glimpse of the past. The surrounding rocks have been greatly changed by earth pressures and movements, but they did contain some beds of limestone. Much of the limestone has been removed by erosion, with consequent creation of small basins, but enough has been left to give some fertility in an area of otherwise barren soils. Surrounded by an area deeply covered with bog, one small fertile basin is still farmed; a mosaic of small fields is cultivated without machinery, with small meadows, with potatoes in lazy beds, and with oats in broader rows, but grown on the ridge-and-furrow principle.

In many parts of Ireland we can see such broad ridges lying fallow, and in Wexford we can see the still broader ridges in which wheat was formerly grown, but Lougheraherk is the only place in Ireland in which I have seen oats growing in small ridged patches.

THE NATURAL HABITATS
Frank Mitchell

Because of its relatively restricted size, both latitudinally and longitudinally, we cannot expect to find the range of habitats in Ireland that we would expect in other larger areas. Also the generally low altitude, nowhere rising above 1050m, means that northern plants and animals, such as the capercaillie, which still survive in the Scottish highlands, can find no refuge here. Similarly the high humidity prevents the development in sandy areas of dry heathland, such as we find in southern England. But despite these restrictions, there is a wide and important range of habitat in Ireland.

Woodland habitats are hard to assess because they are limited in area, and what there are have been affected by human activity through the millennia. I doubt if there are any truly 'native' woodlands in Ireland, in the sense that there are no trees that have continued in apostolic succession since their ancestors entered Ireland early in the postglacial period. For the coniferous trees only the juniper and yew are native – that is if we accept that the pine died out in medieval times and was subsequently re-introduced. The American conifers, only planted on a large scale since the beginning of this century, have yet to establish distinctive habitats.

It is ironic that two of our habitats, the bogs and the wetlands, which previous generations of naturalists tended to ignore as 'dull', have suddenly leapt into importance, not because they have become intrinsically more exciting, but because in neighbouring countries they have been largely destroyed by drainage, and we are now following in the same regrettable direction. Closer examination shows that both raised bogs and blanket bogs are far from dull, but are closed ecosystems of very considerable complexity. Wetlands, studied in detail, also yield a great deal of ecological information, and by their very existence provide important refuges for birds, both resident and migrant. How splendid it would be to hear the call of the bittern again in Ireland! Our still surviving bogs and wetlands must be preserved.

PEATLANDS OF IRELAND

Margaret Cruickshank

Left
Pine stumps lie unearthed in the boggy landscape following the cutting of bog for turf.

Opposite
Drainage channels cut through the peat

Peat or turf is undecomposed plant material and a peatland is anywhere that peat accumulates to more than 30cm depth. Fungi and bacteria normally cause the decay of dead plants, but in a peatland their growth is inhibited either by low temperatures or by wetness, which deprives them of oxygen.

Peat formation in a wet climate

In our climate wetness is the important factor, so peat growth begins in lakes and ponds, on the higher mountains and on the wetter parts of the west coast. For peat to form in a lake the water must be invaded by plants. Reeds and sedges are important colonisers and they grow first as a floating mat or scraw, rooted in semi-fluid mud. In shallower water the bogbean and marsh potentilla may also contribute to such a raft, and willows may become established in it. There are other sites less frequently flooded where sedges and

groundwater and the bog becomes rain-fed or ombrotrophic.

Raised bogs

There are two main types of peatland in Ireland: raised and blanket bogs. Raised bogs are typified by the red bogs of the midlands, raised above the level of their surroundings by the growth of peat for perhaps 5000 years. A raised bog is generally based on a shallow lake and the old shell mud or marl is often visible when drains are later cut through the peatland. But the bog acts as both a sponge and a dam, supplying water to its margins and preventing surrounding waters from draining away. The soil becomes waterlogged and peat forms directly on it, spreading the bog ever outwards till it reaches an esker or other high ground. In this way, a raised bog can grow out of its initial basin coalescing with its neighbours and giving rise to great tracts of bogland.

In preglacial times the central lowlands probably had well-organised, if sluggish, rivers making steadily for the sea. But during the Ice Age there was much ice here, and when it melted away the debris it was carrying was dumped down irregularly, often blocking former valleys and diverting rivers they had held. Great volumes of water accumulated as the ice was melting, and these were carried away from beneath the ice in sub-ice tunnels. If the meltwaters changed their courses, a tunnel might be abandoned, and this gradually silted up with sand and gravel.

The irregular surface of the glacial deposits trapped much water in shallow lakes in which muds accumulated, while the dry ground became covered with forest; the lakes will have teemed with fish and wildfowl. Gradually, sedges and reeds invaded the lake margins, and obliterated the open water,

grasses (moor grass) are predominant.

A peatland at this stage is called a fen, and for it to become a bog *Sphagnum* moss must invade. *Sphagnum* is a key element because, alive or dead, it holds water like a sponge: a handful may contain 98 per cent water. It also has a great capacity for trapping nutrients from water either from groundwater or from rain. For every nutrient it scavenges, it releases an equal part of acid and so its surroundings become acidic. Along with the waterlogging, this also inhibits the breakdown of dead plants so that peat builds up. Eventually it rises above the reach of

107

The bog purple with heather

depositing a layer of sedge peat on top of the earlier lake-muds. As the years went by, hummock of *Sphagnum* was built upon hummock, and gradually a dome of peat rose above the level of the former lake. Once initiated the process went on and on, and the peat spread sideways as well as upwards, until wide areas of the midlands had disappeared beneath great domes of raised bog. The great Bog of Allen in the central plain is the classic raised bog. At one time it was 100,000 hectares in extent.

By the standards of the midlands, northern raised bogs are small and none have survived disturbance by human agency intact. Field surveys have already earmarked the best remaining raised bogs in Northern Ireland for

conservation – large bogs, which have extensive domes with pool–hummock complexes. There are classic individual bogs, but some of the best occur in clusters. These are truly bog wilderness places, with several domes, each up to half a mile across. Seen from the air, they look like a batch of extra large, but not-too-well-risen brown loaves, often nibbled round the edges by peat-cutting, and sharply separated from the green fields around them.

Blanket bogs

Blanket bog is the type of peatland that develops directly on a mineral soil if it is subjected to enough wetness. The total amount of rain is obviously important, but it

is its distribution throughout the year that is critical. Blanket peat only forms beside oceans where onshore winds bring frequent light rain. In Ireland 250 days a year with rain seem necessary for it to happen.

Similar peatlands are found in Scotland and Norway and in New Zealand and Argentina. On the lowlands close to our west coast extensive areas of Mayo and Galway are covered, whereas to the east such rainfall is only experienced by the higher mountains. Good areas of blanket bog remain, for example in the Slieve Bloom mountains, in Sligo and Cavan and in Wicklow, though here peat-cutting has reduced the area.

Despite their easterly (and therefore drier) location, the high basalt plateaux of County

Peat-cutting by spade has been going on since prehistoric times. As there are virtually no coalfields in Ireland, bogs have acted as the main source of fuel for 1000 years or more.

Antrim have some of the most extensive blanket bog in Northern Ireland – over 30,000 hectares of it, and that doesn't include several large forests planted on bog. Around their edges blanket bogs originally thinned away rather unevenly towards their lower limits, but the margins now have diverse vegetation from centuries of human interference, the exact nature of which is rarely obvious or simple. Cutting, burning to 'improve' the sward and grazing by sheep are all involved. As a result, the edge may be quite difficult to recognise, and it can be rather irregular and complicated. At higher levels, because rainfall is greater, and the ground more waterlogged as a result, the blanket of peat is thicker. Gully erosion has attacked it

over large areas. This is characteristic of bogs in all the high mountains and can be quite spectacular, as for example on Trostan (551m).

Blanket peat is extensive in the western uplands of Northern Ireland. In the Sperrins it caps the high ridges, but cutting and erosion have left little of it undisturbed and some has disappeared into the forests of Glenshane and Loughermore. What remains, especially near roads, is attractive to the new cutting machines, and parts of the Sperrins are now covered with the creeping black scars which these leave behind. Further south, vast peatlands, with many individually named bogs, extend southwards across west Tyrone and into Fermanagh.

How the peat starts to form on soil is an interesting question, for it appears that it has covered ancient farmland and forests. For instance, tree trunks and branches are often seen where blanket peat is eroding, and these are the relics of pine forests that flourished on the hills about 4000 years ago. As well as this evidence, peat is now being cut off a former landscape in Mayo, revealing field boundaries and cultivation ridges of long ago. In both cases, severe leaching of nutrients must have occurred, the rain washing them deeper and deeper into the soil out of the range of plant roots. A poor vegetation of moor grass and mosses must have colonised, producing acids which added to the leaching effect. This chain of events culminated in a cover of bog cotton, heather and cross-leaved heath, with some *Sphagnum* which gradually swamped the pine trees and preserved their roots. The thickness of the peat is generally 1–2m, much less than the 4–7m of a raised bog, but there are places in the mountains on cols or other flat areas where 4m of peat is found. Here *Sphagnum* is much commoner than elsewhere and even pools and hummocks can develop.

Turf-cutting

Just as humans may have caused some of our peatlands to form, we are also responsible for their destruction. Turf-cutting is an obvious pressure on the bogs, and it has been carried out since prehistoric times. For a settled population it is a much easier fuel to use than wood. It requires only a spade instead of an axe, a saw and a wedge. There are virtually no coalfields in Ireland, north or south. So it was that peat-cutting by spade became ubiquitous as the only source of domestic fuel. Culturally, therefore, bogs have been central to Irish life and have supplied the main fuel for 1000 years or more. It was a fuel of rich and poor alike, used in the monasteries of Holycross, Fore and Castledermot as well as in the smallest thatched cabin. It was imported into the towns and every load was the source of some early taxes to the city of Kilkenny, for example.

Cutting affected small units of peatland until this century when machinery became available for the drainage of whole bogs at a time. Bord na Móna was set up in 1946 and it has gone from strength to strength, helped by the various oil crises. Ireland now gets more of its fuel from turf than any other country in the world except Finland, and this has meant the drainage, cutting or other modification of 90 per cent of our raised bogs.

110

Left
Like snow in May, bog cotton covers an area of recently burnt blanket bog.

Opposite
The Pilgrim's Way esker running alongside the uncut Mongan Bog in the Irish midlands.

Hand-winning of peat for fuel extends far back into human history, but has been most important since the seventeenth century. By that time, as the careful research of Eileen McCracken has shown, wholesale clearance of forests had removed one indigenous source of fuel.

A whole folklore grew up about turf, as shown to us eloquently in the writing of Estyn Evans, particularly in his *Irish Folk Ways*. The scenes have been captured and perhaps idealised on canvas by well-known artists and in poem, story and song by writers and musicians. But what would they and what should we ourselves make of the new machines?

Cutting by spades, designed for the task, carefully extracts blocks of peat from a vertical wall in the bog. It is done in early summer so that the peat can be left to dry in time for next winter's fires. Meanwhile, the newly cut wall dries ahead of the next cutting. Over time, as the wall retreats, cut-over bog grows, and as we have seen, it can be reclaimed for agriculture or abandoned to wildlife. Left this way for centuries, bog plants would accumulate sufficiently to create a second generation of peat. Such bogs are broken ground and wet, not very attractive to agriculture, but diverse habitats for all manner of wildlife. They can be seen as one way of re-creating the fens and bogs that we have so much diminished.

Such cut-over bogs may be brought back into productive use by the new machines, though they are not the only places where machines are used. Cutting by machine is quicker and so eats up the bog faster. In the

though it is run over by the machines and during the summer growing season it is starved of light as long as the sausages lie on top of it to dry. It seems also that machines cause some damage to the vegetation and pack down the surface; unsightly black patches have been left behind.

Such cutting in already cut bogs appears to be less problematical than cutting the remaining intact bog by machine, especially the blanket bogs which, it will be recalled, form in areas of high rainfall – one cannot 'turn off' rainfall. Problems in the endless rain of wet summers in 1985 and 1986 require little imagination to visualise. Many who bought their machines in the two much drier preceding summers (1983–4) were bitterly disappointed. Sometimes it was found that the bog was too wet and soft, and the machine drowned in the bog – an expensive error! Less seriously, on some bogs cutting had to stop, and on others peat that was cut could not be adequately dried.

Less costly in money, but very costly ecologically, are the areas of bare peat. On some, cutting will continue, providing that drainage can be maintained – and that is easiest on lowland raised bogs because of lower rainfall, but blanket bogs may be attacked by gully erosion. Some bogs show signs of being colonised and healed by the peat-forming bog plants themselves, so that peat may regenerate in the same way as in the hand-cut bogs.

Bogs act like huge natural sponges to soak up rainfall and release it slowly to nearby rivers. If the regulating sponge of blanket peat on the hills is damaged or removed extensively, there may be consequences for rivers, and those living near them in the valleys below – as well as leaving an unsightly mess on the hills themselves. Cutting bogs

early 1980s machines were welcomed both by peat-cutters and by government agencies charged with encouraging rural enterprise. One approach is to remove the bog surface, layer by layer. This is commonly done on lowland raised bogs, where the upper *Sphagnum* peat is harrowed to loosen it, so that it dries quickly (if it does not rain). It is lifted by a large 'vacuum cleaner' to be taken away and baled as horticultural peat, for which there is now a good demand in Ireland, and more especially in England. A spectacular example, using very large machines, can be seen on the huge raised bog at Ballymacombs More, near Bellaghy on the north side of Lough Neagh, where an already hand-cut bog is being stripped by the Bulrush Peat Company. The surface *Sphagnum* peat of the old dome is highly prized by gardeners to add

texture to their soil. In the early 1980s parallel drains were cut across nearby Sluggan Bog, until then one of the best remaining raised bogs, to strip it in a similar way.

The lower layers of raised bogs are formed by fibrous sedge peat and require a different approach. They can be removed by tractor-drawn sod-cutting machines which are also widely used on blanket bogs. Most of the machines are small, but they make up for that by their large number. They cut and extrude long peat 'sausages' from well beneath the living vegetation (up to a metre or more), to lie on the surface to dry; in doing so, the sausages shrink, crack and this helps them to break up into convenient pieces for burning. It is claimed that cutting below the surface will allow the vegetation to survive, even

Left
High-tech peat extraction at
Bellaghy, Co. Londonderry

balanced community needs for survival, and encouraging people to burn the hills for a new flush of growth for grazing.

We have to balance the economic needs of rural people with conservation needs and duties. The best remaining bogs are in urgent need of protection in order to survive. Better knowledge from surveys, backed by necessary finance and legislation from government, could lead to better use of our peatland. Such efforts will only succeed if we can raise the consciousness of the wider public about the countryside: some live and earn a livelihood in it, and others visit it to enjoy a break from town living. Only with dialogue between all concerned can rational, balanced decisions be taken and implemented to save and develop this most characteristic part of our countryside – its peatland.

extensively by machine to provide rural employment and incomes may create high costs within the same rural economy. Benefits and costs must be balanced, but with high unemployment the pressures to exploit peatland by machine-cutting in order to sell fuel or horticultural peat are strong.

The distinctive countryside of cut peatland has been conserved in Brackagh Bog beside the Upper Bann, near Portadown and in the larger Peatlands Park further west at the Birches. Brackagh shows how peat-cutting can actually create fens. Most of the upper acid peat layer has been cut away, leaving pools in the underlying base-rich fen peat, which become rich habitats for both plants and wetland animals. So peat-cutting is not always totally destructive to conservation

interests. In a complementary way, the Peatlands Park is developing conservation, educational and recreation roles. By careful management of different types of peatland, it will show how it formed, and how it has been and is currently being used. Outside conserved areas some of the remaining peatland is being revitalised by the introduction of new machines, which have helped to make production economically viable again, to provide much-needed local employment.

A more insidious pressure is from peat erosion which is obvious on the higher hills and almost impossible to stop. Its cause is not well understood, and probably complex, but sheep must contribute by removing into their bodies the nutrients that such a critically

MARGARET CRUICKSHANK MSc is a graduate of London University and now teaches part-time in the Department of Geography, Queen's University Belfast. She has been interested in peatlands for over two decades, starting with a research degree on the Pennines in England and more recently has been involved in research in Northern Ireland, the results of which have been published in academic journals. She is presently supervising a survey of peatland in Northern Ireland for the Department of the Environment (NI).

OAKWOODS

Roger Goodwillie

Oakwood is the natural forest cover for most of Ireland and at one time it must have covered everything except the lakes, raised bogs and higher mountains. It was not, of course, made of oaks and nothing else. In the rich soils of the midlands, elm and alder were mixed into it; and in the poor soils of the mountains, pine and birch. The first forest clearance took place just over 5000 years ago as the neolithic (late Stone Age) farmers arrived from Britain, but substantial amounts of oakwood remained till AD 1550. Then the industrial demand for oak took hold and large amounts were required for buildings, for ships and for barrels. In addition, the wood was used to make charcoal for iron-smelting, and the bark was stripped for tanning leather. These pressures led quickly to the downfall of the last oakwoods, and were gone to all intents and purposes two hundred years later. Even the small timbers for barrel staves had to be imported after 1770.

Surviving oakwoods

The few remnants of oakwood that have survived grow on rocky shallow soils in Munster, Donegal and Wicklow. The soil is acidic, derived from sandstone or granite, and its nutrient content is relatively low. These woods can only give a poor impression of the oakwood of old, though in a handful of places – for example Abbeyleix, Tullamore and Portlaw – something better does survive.

Layers in the woods

The appearance of a typical oakwood is of oak above and holly below, but several other trees and shrubs occur at a low frequency. Birch and willow spring up in any clearing or in the brighter conditions on the outskirts of the wood and they will persist then for sixty years or so, despite encroachment by the shade-bearing oaks. Ash is often present around streams, and rowans find a perch on

A rich bryophyte ground flora is a feature of old oak woodlands such as this one in Killarney.

113

rocky outcrops at the higher levels. In the understorey or shrub layer hazel is widespread and hawthorn may occur sporadically. Where they have been introduced by humans, the rhododendron and laurel may flourish, benefiting, like the holly and yew, from their evergreen habit during the winter half of the year. Oak itself is a light demander, so seedlings do not generally survive beneath a continuous canopy; they require breaks caused by the death or windthrow of individual trees. Then there may be a surge of new regeneration as seedlings strive to fill the gap.

The ground layer of an oakwood on an acid soil will usually have extensive patches of woodrush and fraughan with hair grass in the brighter places, wood sorrel in the darker. A deeper and richer soil will bring in brambles, celandine, herb robert and wood sanicle with bluebells in abundance. Ivy may form large patches on the ground as well as on trees, provided grazing is not too intense. Honeysuckle is more scattered but equally characteristic as is that retiring plant tutsan which grows singly, never in company.

Ferns and mosses are always conspicuous in Irish woods; the hard fern, the male fern and the lady fern being frequent in the mountain oakwoods, and shield fern on the better soils. In the west the mosses add a new dimension to the trees, responding to greater humidity and covering the trunk and lower boughs. They allow other plants to get a hold too like the polypody or the delicate filmy ferns. Some of the mosses extend up into the tree canopy growing anywhere that water tends to lodge. They co-exist with a wide variety of green and grey-green lichens some of them up to 10cm long or more. The lungwort is the largest. Flattened and pitted like some sort of tree seaweed, it is often taken

114

Left
A small tortoiseshell feeding in the outer margins of an oakwood

Opposite
A curious fox cub peers from the oakwood undergrowth

to indicate very long established woodland, perhaps continuous in history with the ancient oakwood.

Insects and invertebrates

The oak itself plays host to many more insects and invertebrates than any other tree species in this country, so the animal community of an oakwood is rich. Much of the activity takes place in the canopy. Caterpillars, aphids and beetles feed on the new leaves in spring and summer and only come to ground to overwinter or pupate. The purple hairstreak is the butterfly of the oakwoods and the adults may sometimes be seen (with binoculars) flitting about the leaves in July. Down below in the glades there may well be speckled wood butterflies and the fast-flying fritillaries, which as caterpillars feed on violets. Shake out a piece of lichen and the chances are you will get several bark lice, small speckled insects with short bodies.

You may never see gall wasps, but many sorts are active in oakwoods and you will find their products: the spangle galls on the back of oak leaves or the marble galls (oak apples) on the stem shoots of older trees. Galls are the plant's response to chemicals that the young wasp produces and they serve neatly as protective houses for the larvae. When fully grown the wasp tunnels its way out leaving an obvious hole. Oakwoods are also the place for beetles and up to 40 per cent of the Irish beetles may be found there. There are beetles

not be forgotten.

Jays have a function in seed dispersal for the oak, for they bury larders of acorns for later use. In this they resemble the red squirrel. It is only by such means that the oak may spread and colonise new ground, because its seed otherwise will stay very close to the parent tree. Wood mice also feed on acorns when they are available, as well as holly and rowan berries. The oak has a peculiar fruiting pattern, like a number of other trees. Some years there are no acorns at all, whereas in others (mast years) they are everywhere – so abundant in fact that the animals that feed on them could not possibly find them all. In this way some seedlings become established and perpetuate the wood.

The other mammals of the oakwood are hedgehogs and shrews on the ground and bats, notably long-eared, in the air. Stoats and foxes will visit, particularly if there are rabbits available, and badgers will make a sett where there is a good depth of soil. Depending on the richness of the site they will feed on the bluebells, bulbs and other roots and invertebrates within the wood or travel outside to nearby farmland.

in the leaves and flowers, beetles in the bark and wood and beetles in the ground. The specialists in old rotting timber are the longhorn beetles with their curving antennae.

Birds and beasts

Feeding on these vegetarians are a host of predators, most noticeably the birds. The goldcrest, blue tit and coal tit are constant members of the fauna, feeding largely in the tree tops and on ivy. They are joined in summer by the chiffchaff, willow warbler and spotted flycatcher and occasionally the redstart or wood warbler. These all depend on the abundance of insect life brought out by the tree leaves. The treecreeper, catching insects on the bark of the trees, is also characteristic but difficult to see while the blackbird and robin as ground feeders would be hard to miss. One of the less obvious birds of lowland oakwoods is the woodcock since it is active only at night. Occasionally by day you may flush it from a clump of brambles or bracken but you may more often see evidence of it having probed for worms in muddy places. The largest birds to be found consistently in the wood are hooded crows and woodpigeons but there will usually be sparrowhawks and jays at low density. Both species are noisy at certain times of the year. The insistent screaming of young sparrowhawks to be fed often penetrates through the leaves in summer while the alarm screech of the jay, once heard, will

MOUNTAINS
Seán Ryan

Structure of the Irish mountains

Ireland is often described as a saucer shape of flat level midlands, surrounded by mountains on the edge, and almost all our mountains are located in a broken rim around the island. The basic rock structures are very old, mostly pre-Carboniferous and Tertiary. What we see today are these basic structures, much altered by glaciation. The glacial period had a profound effect on our country and especially on our mountain landscape.

Where a glacier formed on a mountain, it gradually gouged out a deep hollow and when it eventually melted away, it left behind an amphitheatre exposed on the mountainside, which is called a *coum* in Ireland, a word that is very common in our mountain place-names, for example Coumeendubh, Coumasaharn and Coumcallee in Kerry. As the ice gradually retreated the process of weathering and erosion continued to work into the cliff face, eating back further and further towards the mountain summit. A coum usually has a steep cliff with a slope of boulder scree at its foot and a flat stony bottom occupied by a mountain lake. When strung out in succession along a valley floor leading off a coum, these are called pater noster lakes because they are strung out like rosary beads. In a severe winter, these high lakes will be completely frozen over. Many of them have descriptive names, like Loughnabpreachaun (lake of the crows); or Loughnambreacdearg (lake of the red trout) which may refer to the char, a species of fish which still survives as an arctic relict, though now recorded in lower and larger lakes. Some mountain lakes have quite beautiful names like Loughna-huisceguirme (lake of blue water) situated at approximately 600m on Mangerton in Kerry.

Where two coums have been formed back to back, and have cut into the mountain from opposite sides, a high wall of rock may be left in between, culminating in a thin airy ridge, called an *arete*, its crest shattered and splintered by frost action. An example is the connecting ridge between Beenkeragh and Carrauntuohill in the Macgillycuddy's Reeks, County Kerry, between Coumeenuachterach and Coumloughra.

The glaciers carried along boulders and rock-dust on their surfaces, just as we can observe today in the Alps and the Arctic. An accumulation of this debris was left dumped by the retreating glacier at its head, or snout, as a large amount of loose rock, boulders and gravel, as can be seen at the outlet of many mountain coums, now largely overgrown with vegetation, and usually forming a dam containing a lake on the coum floor. Debris was sometimes also pushed out to the side and frequently forms the side ridges of a coum, often traversed by hill walkers making for the heights. These heaps or ridges of debris are known as *moraines*.

The signs of the passage of the ice can be read everywhere; for it is the severity of the glaciations that has determined the

116

Opposite
Aerial view of the mountains of the Dingle peninsula.

Right
The signs of the passage of ice can be read here in this panoramic picture of the Wicklow mountains.

topography of the mountains we see today rather than the parent rock itself, though it can generally be said that harder rocks have persisted and softer rocks have eroded more quickly. Some mountains were only partly ice-covered, their summits standing free as a *nunatak*. It is generally thought that some Irish mountain tops, for instance the Galtees in County Tipperary, probably escaped the last two cold stages.

These ice-sheets and local mountain glaciers did not suddenly vanish. Small local glaciers must have lingered on for very long in the high mountain coums, until gradually they too disappeared in a warming climate which began about 10,000 years ago. The process of soil formation through erosion and weathering had begun.

Human influence

The influence of the Irish people on the mountain habitat has been mostly concentrated on the submontane zones, those roughly between 300m and 600m. Not all changes were brought about by human activity, however, and we must consider our influence against the background of the consequences of climatic change.

Above 600m it is not really known to what extent we have influenced the mountain environment. We did use higher pastures in Ireland, especially in the peak populations of pre-Famine times. The remnants of old potato ridges (lazy beds) and dry-stone fences can still be found above 300m, but rarely if ever above 600m. These stone fences must date back to well over two hundred years ago because they were to keep out wolves from cattle, which presumably had been brought up high for summer pasturing. Sheep grazing and burning are possibly the extent of human influence above 600m, and over-stocking may be one reason for summit erosion on plateau bogs.

Today the mountains contain some of the last living links with the retreat of the last glaciation. The relict populations of arctic type insects found on the summits remind us of their long history, and it is no haphazard coincidence that our two truly montane animals, the grouse and the mountain hare, are endemic subspecies.

Over 750m, a distinctive upland bog type is found on certain summit plateaux, containing a moss and lichen vegetation with particularly northern characteristics. A good case could probably be made for considering all ground over 600m (about 0.3 per cent of the country) as areas of scientific interest.

The question of conservation is complex. Nature is not static, and the dynamic interacting of biological forces which we can now witness in the mountains will mean that the areas to be conserved will in the future be unlike what they are today. The future is as important as the past, however, and we can do a lot to safeguard it. Environmental pollution on these great open slopes could have consequences far beyond what their limited physical size might indicate. It is easily forgotten that the mountains are vast catchment areas of rainwater, where many rivers have their head waters, and any pollution up here could affect all life downstream.

It is perhaps the sense of wildness and freedom which is the single most important aspect of our mountains. They are rugged and still remote, places where one has to rely on one's own judgements and abilities, and where the noises, smells and wastes of industrial society have not yet penetrated. There one can feel the rush of cold air, taste pure clear water, smell the aromas of bog and heather, hear waterfalls in the valley far below, see the swift movement of incomparable cloudscapes and walk for a whole day without meeting one other person. In many, many ways they are our last and only wilderness.

Extracts from *Wild Ireland*, Country House, 1984

SEÁN RYAN lives in Cork and is interested in mountain ecology and especially in the red deer herd in Killarney National Park.

THE FLOW OF THE RIVER

Roger Goodwillie

Water flows downhill, so naturally rivers run from the mountains to the sea. Since the hills in Ireland lie mostly near the coast there are two main types of river. Those that rise in the seaward side of the hills run quickly to the coast and they are often acidic and rocky. The others, which rise on the landward side, make their way slowly and at times rather aimlessly towards the sea, their richer water flowing past banks of silt and mud. Where there is a depression in the landscape their waters tend to accumulate as a pond or lake until they can overflow to continue their journey. The Shannon lakes lie in such depressions, perhaps scoured out by ice in the Ice Age, but Lough Neagh is an even clearer case. The rivers flow into this basin from all sides and their converging pattern is only broken in the south-east corner where the Lagan flows towards Belfast.

The headwaters – that is the waters near the source – of any river are forever eating back into the hillside enlarging their sphere of influence. Their narrow valleys become broader and they come to take drainage water from a larger and larger area. This process is easy to see on eroding blanket bog or on the seashore where a spring flows out on a sandy beach. By this erosion the stream can capture water that formerly went in different directions. This is what the Lagan seems to have done. Its course lies on soft sandstones and it has worked back to the south-west to divert the flow of the river from Dromara which used to reach Lough Neagh. River capture is quite common: it may be noticed too on a map of the southern part of the Wicklow mountains with the Derreen river.

The course of the river

In their path to the sea, rivers choose the lowest land even before they start to erode it.

It is therefore a bit disconcerting to find that many of our main southerly-flowing rivers have dug through sizeable hills rather than following a seemingly easier route around these obstacles. The Slaney, for example, having risen on the west side of Lugnaquilla, should tend to flow into the Barrow, but instead it turns south-east and ploughs across the mountains in the gap of Bunclody. The Barrow itself has cut a gorge below Graiguenamanagh and the Nore a similar one at Inistiogue. They isolate Brandon Hill in between with its curiously named settlement, the Rower. The Shannon strikes southwards through the Slieve Bernagh hills at Killaloe rather than flowing out onto the Clare lowlands at Scarriff. The Cork rivers are famous for their idiosyncratic behaviour. Both the Lee and the Blackwater run nice gentle courses eastward from the mountains until they are almost within sight of the sea. Then they turn abruptly south at Cork and Cappoquin and dig their way through three or four separate ridges of rock before releasing their water into the sea.

To find answers to these paradoxes we must go back to the glacial period and beyond. Where the course of a river now cuts through a hill there may have been a time when it flowed at a higher level on a surface now totally vanished. Flowing on this surface it cut its valley into the new rock below, working deeper and deeper while the former supporting rock was weathered away. Alternatively the hills may have risen so slowly that the river has been able to keep pace, cutting its valley through the rising ground. There is nothing strange about land rising in this way: geologically speaking it happens all the time. The raised beach around most of our northern coast and in places elsewhere shows that the land has risen out of

the sea by up to 8m in the relatively recent past. Old sea caves occur quite regularly on the landward side of the coast road.

There is also the complicating factor of ice to remember. Before the coming of the glaciations the central plain may have been a karstic limestone landscape as the Burren is today. There were hills about but the rock was full of holes and passageways. The Dunmore and Mitchelstown caves are probably relics of this time and there have been many other vertical pipes found that once took surface water down to nether regions. Before glaciation, therefore, our midland river systems may have been very different to what they are today.

The legacy of the two ice advances that took place is seen in physical changes to the hills. There may be similar changes on the lowlands also, but they lie concealed beneath a sheet of rock waste or glacial drift. This drift has an equally great or even greater effect on the rivers. For one thing it allows them to flow on the surface again. In a limestone region such as the Burren, where drift is almost absent, rivers flow largely underground, though they sometimes briefly visit the surface. The Fergus, for example, disappears eight or nine times on its journey to Ennis, and its tributaries spend practically all their time hidden from view. Glacial drift is also piled into moraines, drumlins and eskers. In a flat lowland these deposits may control the course of the river. The Shannon in fact has eroded no valley in the middle part of its course. Its gradient (slope) is too flat and its flow too slow to mould the landscape. It contrives to flow south as a sort of moving lake, hemmed in by nothing but soft glacial deposits and bog. The absence of meanders (bends) suggests that it is no normal river.

Drift can have more dramatic effects: it

may block a former valley and force a river to change its course. The Liffey in Kildare offers an example, for it used to flow westward from the Wicklow mountains to the Barrow. After the retreat of the ice it found the Curragh deposit of sand and gravel directly in its way and had to cut a new course through Kilcullen and then on to Leixlip. The Vartry river in Wicklow was blocked at Roundwood and was diverted south-east, where it is still cutting a fine valley, the Devil's Glen. Similarly the Bush river in Antrim had to abandon its former course down to Ballycastle in favour of a longer and less visually attractive route to Bushmills. Glacial excavation is common where the ice was confined by hills, and several modern rivers follow the path of the glaciers. The Newry river flows down an ice-cut channel into an ice-cut fjord in the shape of Carlingford Lough. The Slaney follows such a route at Ferrycarrig near Wexford while the Erriff's course in Mayo has been so modified by ice erosion that its flow may actually have been reversed. The Shannon at Killaloe is subject to two glacial modifications. Here the ice seems to have branched the Slieve Bernagh ridge in the same way as it took the bite out of the Devilsbit mountain nearby. It also left enough debris at Scarriff, including drumlins, to block the former outlet of the river. Behind this block the water now flows back to Lough Derg in the Scarriff river. The main Shannon has to head southward through its new gap and it plunges – or plunged before the power station was built – over the falls at Ardnacrusha as if in relief. The presence of a waterfall such as this is a clue to a fairly recent change in the river's behaviour, as on a longer timescale it disappears into rapids or riffles.

When the ice melted it released a great quantity of meltwater capable of cutting sizeable gorges. The Glen of the Downs in Wicklow illustrates its potential for erosion. All of our southern rivers and later many of the others must have taken unimaginable volumes of water to sea at this time, for the ice had been up to 1000m thick. It seems likely that it caused one other peculiarity of these rivers, the fact that the sea comes a long way inland up their valleys. Sea-level was lowered during the Ice Age when so much water was frozen into the ice-mass. It did not quickly return to normal and the rivers cut deep trenches down to it, burgeoning with their debris-filled flood waters. The rise of the sea eventually drowned the lower parts of the valleys, partially filling them with sediment, but allowing the navigation by ships that today is such a feature. Elsewhere too melt-waters were important, and it is thought that the Owenmore finds a glacial spillway through the arch of the Mayo hills at Bangor.

Rivers and us – then and now

In almost every part of Ireland there are stretches of river which seem unspoilt and apparently quite free from the influence of human beings. You have probably walked along a river bank which is slightly elevated so that the view is alternately the wide stretch of callow land away from the river and the long reach of the river itself, possibly punctuated by a weir or other feature. The masonry bridge in the distance is so hallowed by time that it seems to have been there for ever. But as they travel down from the mountains to the inhabited lowlands, rivers come more and more under the influence of human activity, and have done for centuries.

The elevated bank which makes walking so easy may well be the spoil heap thrown up during one of the many drainage schemes hand-excavated by starving labourers in the famine years. The weir, whose sole function now appears to be to improve the landscape, may be all that remains of a long-forgotten attempt to capture fish or to provide power for a local mill. The bridge, known for centuries past as the old bridge, was once the brash new bridge that replaced a succession of wooden bridges, which had in turn replaced a ford or a ferry. Ditches, banks, side branches, weirs and bridges, the presence of stands of butterbur, *Petasites hybridus*, or balsam, *Impatiens*, the absence of trees or the occurrence of planted poplars and willows all tell of the ceaseless interaction of people and rivers over the centuries.

Human activities generally have an enriching or *eutrophying* effect on rivers and few waters have retained the nutritional level they had when people first reached our shores. First of all, people cleared the forest; this gradually changed flow conditions in the river. Trees intercept a good proportion of the rain that falls on them, they catch it on their leaves and it evaporates back into the air without ever reaching the ground. They also build up a thick layer of dead leaves and branches on the soil and a good layer of roots below. Both of these absorb rainfall, which is used by the trees themselves and also by soil life. A beech forest evaporates 60 per cent of the year's rainfall through its leaves alone, certainly in a continental climate.

So what form did our rivers take in post-glacial times? Flows must have been much lower through most of the year and run-off after rain much slower than today. Is river flooding quite a modern phenomenon brought about by forest clearance? This is definitely so in many parts of the world today, but in Ireland it is more likely that winter rains falling on a saturated forest floor have always run off quite rapidly into rivers,

119

The River Erriff near Leenane in Connemara

causing discharges, erosion and flooding. But the frequency of flooding must have been increased by human activities, and spates in the April–October period must now be an occasional factor in river life that was not there before.

We cannot know for sure how human activity so long ago has affected our rivers, but we know something about the relationship between people and rivers in more recent times.

Draining the land

Most of the rivers of Ireland have been affected, at least over part of their length, by works of arterial drainage undertaken to provide adequate outfalls for land drainage or the development of bogs.

Arterial drainage is the most severe form of management for the river. It is carried out to speed the flow of water to the sea, preventing floods and lowering the water level in the channel so that field drains can empty into it. The means to achieve these ends are to widen or deepen the channel and to eliminate obstructions to water flow. Speeding up the river flow is liable to increase erosion on bends, and therefore the channel may be straightened or canalised and the banks protected with stonework or concrete. Bringing machinery in to do this work and to dispose of the soil necessitates the removal of trees, so the appearance of the river as well as its habitats for river life are drastically altered.

Once drained, flow in the river changes in character. The extremes of high and low flows are often intensified. There is less storage capacity in the catchment, so run-off is more rapid and the river reaches its peak discharge more rapidly after a rainstorm. Likewise low flows become lower as drained

120

agricultural land cannot supply a steady flow. In an extreme summer a drained river may not even be able to water cattle. Most aquatic organisms are adapted to quite a narrow range of flow conditions and if these are exceeded one way or the other in a drained river they cannot survive. Also water depth is normally reduced by drainage and there is less physical space available to water plants and animals.

Every river channel is subject to periodic scouring by floodwaters and to the gradual transport of rock and soil from the mountains to the sea. Thus they may recover from this most drastic form of scouring. Where the draglines have not gone below the gravel layers in the channel, recovery seems to be very rapid. Beds of water crowfoot again expand and larger numbers of invertebrates occur. Exceptional numbers of trout may also be found but when examined it turns out that they are all young fish of one to three years.

There are probably more fish present than before drainage and over a thousand may inhabit a kilometre stretch. But the fish are slow-growing and in poor condition because the dredging has done away with the deeper pools in which larger fish used to find shelter. Abundant food is available for the younger trout in the form of mayfly nymphs and fly larvae and a population explosion takes place in the fish. However, few survive long after their first spawning, and the large trout that made the Maigue or the Robe great trout rivers for the angler have vanished for ever.

Extracts from *Irish Rivers*, Country House, 1985

CONIFEROUS WOODS

Roger Goodwillie

The occurrence of coniferous woods is quite a modern phenomenon in Ireland which began falteringly in 1750 but only took off properly about 1900. Though the scots pine occurred widely in the past, as shown by the abundance of its roots under peat, it is thought to have died out some 1500 years ago. Conifers were first introduced to gardens and parks, and afforestation, if it occurred at all, involved oak, beech and sycamore. At first the conifers came from Europe, including scots pine, larch, Norway spruce and silver fir. It was not until the early part of this century that it was realised that conifers from the west coast of North America grew superbly in our climate also. They dominate the plantings of today: 45 per cent of planted trees are sitka spruce and 40 per cent are contorta or lodgepole pine. The balance is made up of larch, Norway spruce, Douglas fir and noble fir (for Christmas trees).

The land that is usually available for afforestation is peaty or otherwise poorly drained. It is common therefore to turn it over with a plough, creating ribbons of peat in which trees are planted. This is useful for weed control, because by the time the heather and other plants have regrown, the trees have got away to a good start. The clearance also does away with any shelter the existing vegetation could offer, so you may sometimes see damage on a new plantation after late spring frosts.

Good habitats in the early stages

For the first ten years after planting, the trees and other plants produce a cover of low scrub which is most attractive to other wildlife. The site is fenced so that domestic animals do not graze it. There is abundant cover for small mammals like mice, shrews and the bank vole as well as for foxes, stoats and many birds.

The red squirrel is typical of coniferous and mixed woodland, and although widely distributed it is a shy creature and therefore rarely seen.

Stonechats quickly move into a plantation from the stands of gorse where they usually live and the willow warbler and reed bunting are not far behind. Hen harriers may come to nest in hilly areas and may sometimes be seen in their display flights over the forest. Grasshopper and sedge warblers enliven such places in the summer with their songs while redpolls and linnets may pop up anywhere on a nearby tree. All in all it is a rich bird community that replaces the moorland one of meadow pipit, skylark, red grouse and merlin.

Birdlife in later stages

It is transitory, however. As adjacent trees meet, the ground beneath becomes shaded and the plants that grow there die out. Life becomes concentrated in the tree canopy and the bird community changes to a more limited one. The chaffinch, goldcrest, robin and wren become the most frequent species, though blackbirds and thrushes may feed along rides or paths, nesting nearby. The smaller birds may reach spectacular numbers: 591 pairs of goldcrests per square kilometre have been counted in Norway spruce woods, with 273 pairs both of robins and chaffinches. Larger birds include the woodpigeon, which finds a secure roost and nesting site in plantations, though it feeds on farmland outside. Hooded crows and long-eared owls also move into a forest as the trees become larger, while in winter hordes of roosting starlings may pile into a forest, sometimes killing the trees with their abundant droppings.

Pests

The goldcrests and coal tits feed largely on aphids in the tree tops. Conifers have been introduced without a good many of the pests that prey on them in their native haunts. But

A fine display of sitka spruce numbered for felling

this means also that there may be no natural controls on a pest that does arrive. The green spruce aphid is one such animal. Its natural host is the Norway spruce, but it has spread its attentions now to the sitka, where it can reach plague proportions. Like all aphids it sucks the sugary juice of the plant and the needles turn yellow and fall off when sufficiently pierced and sucked. In extreme years a tree may become practically leafless. There are also a number of woolly aphids, the type that burrows into the bark of a tree. It then produces a fuzz of white threads to keep itself dry and also discourage predators looking for it. One of these does so much damage to silver firs that the species cannot be used as a forestry tree. Such pest problems are a consequence both of using introduced species and growing them in monoculture – single species stands of uniform age. A diversity of species and of tree ages would limit the severity of any particular pest attack. At the same time it would make present forestry practice, which depends on clear-felling and replanting, impossible.

Life on the forest floor

The darkness of the forest floor inhibits the growth of most woodland plants as also does the litter fall of dead leaves and twigs. Forests

This female sparrowhawk is a woodland bird of prey and will follow its quarry even when it seeks the shelter of the trees.

may also be 'brashed' when the lower dead branches are broken off to reduce the size of knots in the timber. They are then left on the ground. Close to clearings or paths, however, there are always a few species of plant and under more mature trees the range may be wider. Wood sorrel is often frequent, sometimes with tormentil, foxgloves or wavy hair grass. Ferns and mosses require the least light of any plants to survive so a limited range will usually be present. It is a good place to begin a study of either group because of this fact.

The floor of a coniferous wood is also a good place to find fungi. These plants grow on dead organic matter in the soil and produce fruiting bodies above ground every so often, usually in autumn. There are such toadstools of every hue: many are yellowish or brownish and relatively inconspicuous until you have seen one. Then there are pinks and greens, purples and oranges. The orange peel fungus (*Peziza*) is one of the brightest, often growing on a path. In a good fungus year there may be twenty different varieties in a small woodland plot from the tiny bootlace fungi on individual twigs to the corky flanges of *Fomes* on the conifer stumps. Many of them are edible to slugs and squirrels and many are soon colonised by the grubs of fungus gnats which must grow from egg to pupa in a very few days, before the fungus withers and decays.

Trees are felled in blocks in a working forest and the flood of light that then reaches the ground creates an immediate response in the vegetation. Small-seeded plants like willows, willowherbs and ragwort may colonise the first year, followed by grasses, brambles and elder. If there is rhododendron in the area, its seedlings may soon appear and the Himalayan honeysuckle may also invade. Together these plants form a tangle of growth in a few years which favours foxes and wintering woodcock but makes replanting trees very difficult. Surprisingly few conifer seedlings grow of their own accord around a forest because their seeds need a longer cold period than our winters provide before they will germinate.

HEDGEROWS
Declan Doogue

Left
Various forms of fuchsia grow well in gardens but one, *F. magellanica* now thrives in exposed western districts where it is often the only hedge-forming species to be seen.

Right
The white umbrella heads of cow parsley festoon the roadsides of lowland Ireland in April and May. Uncut verges such as this provide an increasingly valuable alternative habitat for displaced wildlife.

The Irish woodland flora is sadly impoverished, but luckily this is partly offset by an extensive network of hedgerows, covering most of the agricultural lowlands which constitutes a habitat whose richness is totally out of proportion to its area. Where woodland has been cleared, certain species, in particular those of the margins and clearings, manage to maintain a hold in the hedgerows. The hedge is never merely a line of thorny bushes: trees, shrubs, woody climbers and a large number of flowering plants, ferns, mosses, liverworts and lichens find a place to live in the hedgerow. Many of these in turn support a surprising diversity of insects and other invertebrates and provide shelter and food for various small animals and birds.

Hedges are in general either planted structures or they have been modified by humans in some way, in order to enclose and delimit landholdings and restrict or prevent the movement of farm animals. When properly tended they become a kind of living fence, which even in the present day can still prove an effective barrier to cross-country passage. When their upkeep is neglected, gaps appear, as individual bushes or trees die. When this happens, they cease to be useful as barriers, and so the hedges can become redundant. In tillage areas they may be simply scraped out, as the level of mechanisation of planting and harvesting increases.

Hedgerow species

Hawthorn is the usual hedging shrub in Ireland, as it is able to thrive on a variety of soil types. Other thorn-bearing species are occasionally planted, notably gorse and blackthorn. In the course of time, through

wind and bird-assisted dispersal, the seeds of other shrubby species make their way into hedgerows. Brambles (blackberry bushes), dog roses and woody climbers like ivy and woodbine become established, protected in their earlier stages by the planted species in the hedge from browsing. Once the bridgehead is established, many other species of animal and plant can become part of the community.

There is a shortcut in the lengthy business of establishing a hedgerow: the landholder can leave existing lines of trees and shrubs when clearing scrub and woodland. In this way certain hedges are given a head start in the process of species accumulation.

The relationship between the age of a hedge and the number of species of woody shrub it contains has intrigued botanists, geographers and local historians, and in recent years various attempts have been made to 'date' hedgerows by reference to their species numbers. In Ireland, attempts to apply the 'one species per century' rule are complicated, because, with our reduced flora, the pool of potential hedge-forming species is fewer. In addition, the background flora from which any hedge may derive its members varies so much from place to place that a 'poor' hedge in one area may have more species than a relatively rich one elsewhere. It has also been pointed out that as certain hedges become older, tall trees may form dense canopies, shading out more light-demanding species.

For anyone contemplating local hedgerow studies the ideal would be to find a selection of detailed estate maps dating back several hundred years before the advent of the Ordnance Survey six-inch survey. Sadly this is seldom possible. Some idea of the differences between old and new hedges may, however, be gained by comparing the shrub flora of roadside hedges with those of adjoining field hedges. Depending on locality, certain species like hazel, holly, spindle and even ash may appear commoner in the roadside – and generally older – hedges. Age is not of course the only reason for this greater richness. Many roadside hedges have a stream or drain running alongside, thus providing sufficiently moist conditions for willows and alder to survive, even on occasions long after the water has been piped. Townland and parish boundaries, because of their greater antiquity, may also possess richer hedgerows, but again these boundaries may be related to some ancient watercourse or other topographical feature.

In some parts of Ireland, the ramparts of the larger hill-forts have been incorporated into the present-day field system, and are now overgrown with scrub. They may prove to have a significantly different flora. (Recent work in the Isle of Man has shown that the ancient trackways converging on the Tynwald – the historic parliament – have certain bramble species not found elsewhere on the island.)

As one moves around the country, it becomes very obvious that the shrub flora varies from place to place as well as from habitat to habitat. While certain species such as hawthorn are almost ubiquitous, other species display an ecological and superimposed geographical distribution. The field rose, so common in south-east Ireland on various soils, thins out dramatically as one moves north and west. Spindle, common on the lime-rich ground of the central plain is much rarer to the north and south. Higher ground (and all that that entails by way of lower temperatures, greater exposure, higher rainfall and subsequent leaching of the soil), has acid-ground species like mountain ash, spring and autumn gorse, broom, birch and holly. In the lowlands ash, privet, hazel and spindle are the characteristic species, and where these lowland hedges adjoin bog margins they are enriched by a bewildering array of acid-ground willows, guelder rose and alder, producing a shrub or small tree flora with, on occasions, more than twenty species in ten 30-metre sample lengths.

At least sixty Irish trees, shrubs and woody climbers have now been found in Irish hedgerows. Several are of interest as species of considerable rarity in these islands. *Sorbus hibernica*, the Irish whitebeam, is widespread in the midlands as a small tree. Though closely related to other whitebeams it is apparently an Irish endemic, and has been featured on Irish postage stamps. Another, very different whitebeam, *Sorbus devoniensis*, which has brown fruits, turns up occasionally in hedges in south-east Ireland. Otherwise, it is known only from Devon and Cornwall. Many of the central plain hedges, especially those associated with the esker landscape, contain the rose *Rosa agrestis*, one of the sweet-briars, but with a very distinctive leaf. This species has become quite rare in Great Britain as a result of hedgerow removal and scrub clearance. As well as these species, the frequency of shrubs like guelder rose, purging buckthorn and spindle give our hedges a distinctly Irish aspect. We lack (at least as definite natives) species like field maple and wayfaring tree, both widespread in the south of England.

Herbs

A large number of herbaceous plants now find their main refuge in hedgerows, not because they need the hedgerow habitat, but because they are suppressed by grazing and ploughing in nearby fields. Other shade-tolerant species like lesser celandine, wild arum and wood anemone, would not normally thrive in the open anyway, and find the hedgerow habitat quite to their liking, provided the shrub cover is not cut back too severely. The sheltered and undisturbed conditions provide over most of Ireland suitable ground for species like robin-run-the-hedge, primroses, violets and ground ivy, while on the outer fringe tall species such as cow parsley, hogweed and hedge woundwort thrive. On more acid soils wood sorrel and foxglove are commoner and, where drains

adjoin the lowland hedges, they are often choked with wetland species like meadowsweet and great hairy willowherb.

Insects

Most flowering plants have a selection of insects and other small creatures that feed upon their various parts. Nettles and thistles have large numbers of weevils and plant bugs that eat their leaves and suck their juices. Many are covered by huge numbers of aphids that are in turn eaten by various ladybirds. The flowers of cow parsley and hogweed bear flowers that attract large numbers of flies and small beetles. Butterflies like the silver-washed fritillary (whose larvae, incidentally,

feed on the leaves of violets) may be seen on the flowers of brambles in late summer, along with the much commoner speckled wood butterfly. Earlier in the year, wood white butterflies lay their eggs on the abundant bush vetch. Crab spiders lurk in the flowers of various plants, waiting to pounce on small nectar- and pollen-seeking insects. The variety is endless and may best be appreciated on sunny mornings in July and August, but is of interest at any time of the year. Were it not for the scarcity of oak (which has many hundreds of associated insect species) in the modern Irish countryside, many of our hedges would be even more valuable.

Hedgerows threatened

Hedgerow management in Ireland has been described as a sustained exercise in self-control, but the restraint exercised by landowners until recently is lessening. Many hedges are now pared down to the point where they can no longer flower or set seed. For some reason, stud farms throughout the country seem to have espoused the new order of neatness, and many of the hedges in the generally better-tended landscape of north-east Ireland are equally disappointing. County councils quite reasonably demand that when hedges become a public nuisance they must be cut back. The landowners, often through a contractor, then decide to do a 'good' job, which means one that will last a few years. A variety of tractor-based saws and flails are now used, often in an indiscriminate manner, cutting back both trees and shrubs to the same level. While the shrubs may recover from this treatment, tree saplings are another matter. What the long-term impact of such practices will be remains to be seen, but as the extensive beech plantings of earlier times go into decline and elms continue to suffer from the Dutch elm disease outbreak, the immediate prospects are less than good.

The rate at which the hedges themselves have been removed has become a matter of concern in recent years. For non-naturalists their removal is a blunt confirmation that a somewhat idealised way of life has ended, surrendered to the prairie landscape and electric fence. For naturalists, the hedge is often the only zone of diversity on the monocultural landscape. Rates of removal are related to many factors – the relative profit margins of arable versus pastoral agriculture, the pattern of land-ownership and succession, the cost of maintenance, the topography of the terrain itself. The removal of a single field hedge here and there makes little difference. The dismantling of an entire landscape is an entirely different matter. Despite their man-assisted origins, the prospect exists that in the twenty-first century hedgerows may be one of the few pieces of wilderness to survive. Whether they will be allowed to do so remains to be seen.

Left
Honeysuckle or woodbine *Lonicera periclymenum* has found hedges an ideal support for its twining stems and conspicuous flowers which produce tight clusters of red berries in autumn.

Right
The large (10cm) flower heads of guelder rose, *Viburnum opulus*, appear in May and June in hedges in lowland Ireland.

DECLAN DOOGUE is a primary school teacher with a particular interest in wildlife, especially in land and freshwater molluscs, canal wildlife, millipedes and woodlice, plant geography, the flora of Dublin and Kildare and conservation. He was formerly chairman of the Irish Biogeographical Society and president of the Dublin Naturalists Field Club. At the moment he is engaged in research on the botanical composition of hedgerows with special emphasis on the taxonomy of roses. He is co-author of the *Atlas of Distribution of Irish Woodlice* (An Foras Forbartha 1982), author of various articles and papers on the same topic and on the subject of natural history.

WETLANDS

Roger Goodwillie

A constellation of water crowfoot blossoms in a shallow lake. Although wetlands are noted chiefly for their spectacular birdlife, they also have a rich and distinctive flora.

Watery habitats are particularly well developed in Ireland because of the low-lying nature of the land and the abundant rainfall. In addition glaciation and the dumping of ice-borne material has so complicated the natural drainage that water takes a long time to reach the sea. This is especially true in the drumlin areas and throughout the midlands. Human beings have been trying to speed the flow of arterial drainage over many years and we have been successful in certain places.

However, there remain a few of our river catchments where drainage has not been carried out, most notably the main channel of the Shannon, and which consequently are unique in Europe.

A wetland develops where drainage is impeded for some reason, perhaps because of the shape of the land, where a basin is surrounded by higher ground from which water flows at certain times of the year, or because the soil may not be free-draining enough to carry away surplus water because of its peat or clay content. Rainfall or flood water is held long enough to inhibit the growth of terrestrial plants and favour those of marshes. A marsh is usually thought of as a wet community on a soil containing some mineral matter. Given time, sufficient dead plant matter may accumulate to produce an organic soil and a fen, which, as it continues to build up, may become a bog as it loses contact with the groundwater.

128

Sunset on the callows. The flooded grasslands or callows along the Shannon have densities of nesting waders as high as any part of Britain or northern Europe, as well as an enormous number of winter visitors.

Callows and turloughs

Two Irish specialities along this graduation are callows and turloughs. Callows are the flat fields and marshland in the floodplains of the larger rivers. They are flooded when the rivers burst their banks and slowly dry out as the floods subside. Tributary streams and ditches run through the callows and there is often a channel at the landward edge of the floodplain against the valley side. Because callows receive one or several silt-carrying floods in the year, they have rich soils and are seldom fertilised. Their grasses grow rank and tall and are mixed in with many herbs such as meadowsweet, the yellow and purple loosestrifes, and sometimes the marsh pea and water parsnips. Moor grass invades sites that are less frequently flooded and it promotes the development of peat and perhaps, in the end, of raised bogs. The Suir valley is full of such bogs, as is the Shannon around Lanesborough and south of Athlone.

Turloughs resemble callows to some extent. They are hollows in limestone country that flood when the water table in the ground is high. When the water table goes down they dry out and, since they receive no surface drainage, they become grasslands rather than marshes. The flooding can occur at any time of the year and in a very few days. This inhibits the growth of bushes and trees so the turlough may appear in summer as an ordinary field crossed by walls or telegraph poles. A blackish moss is distinctive on such structures. The water enters and leaves a turlough through cracks in the rock and these can usually be found in some corner. One of the largest remaining turloughs is Rahasane in Galway and this has a river flowing through it. It is a largely independent feature, insulated from the porous rock beneath by its clayey bed. However, at times of flood, the river adds its surplus load to the turlough creating a hybrid turlough-callow.

The plants of turloughs grow in a firm muddy soil and are often so closely grazed and trampled that they are hard to identify. Grasses predominate like creeping, bent and marsh foxtail but you may also pick out the leaves of silverweed and cinquefoil as well as the creeping buttercup and water pepper. Around the edge the creeping willow, stone bramble or dewberry will take advantage of any irregularity, while, with luck, two or three sedges can be found. The fen violet is the doyen of the flora with water germander in the Shannon basin.

Marshes and fens

There are many variations in the theme of marsh and fen. Whether the feed water is acid or alkaline has a great bearing on the flora, but the length of time of flooding and the depth of water are also important. The classic riverside or lakeside fen is a reedbed consisting of reeds with clubrushes in the deeper water and bulrushes in the shallower. The reedbed is a mysterious place of swishing stems constantly in movement. Old stalks crackle underfoot and the new ones shoot upwards to flower at 2–3m. It is a world strangely empty of animals and birds unless there are sedge or reed warblers or, in the autumn, roosting swallows. Only the water

rail is at home at ground level, the other warblers, the several herons and harriers of Europe never having reached our island outpost or having been driven from it by people.

Alkaline fens are often based on the black bog rush or saw sedge and may be quite floriferous away from the taller vegetation. There will be several different sedges present, with orchids such as the marsh helleborine and the marsh orchid, willowherbs and St John's wort. Big mossy patches may have the white grass-of-Parnassus on them, as well as the bog pimpernel and marsh pennywort. Where mineral soil is not far away the marsh marigold, flag iris and spearworts will also be found. An absence of lime in the water may be shown by certain species, for example the bog violet, the marsh St John's wort and the larger birdsfoot trefoil.

Wetland birds

Fens and marshes have tall vegetation exploited by large birds for nesting or small birds for food. The snipe is a year-round specialist, the mallard and teal more fleeting. Callows and turloughs have short grass vegetation much more suitable for grazing by geese and wigeon. By their openness they offer security to birds that spend their time in flocks, so they are intensively used for wintering. The Shannon callows are famous for their flocks of wildfowl and waders, particularly plover. Whooper and Bewick's swans swim around on the floodwaters, grazing on plants beneath the surface.

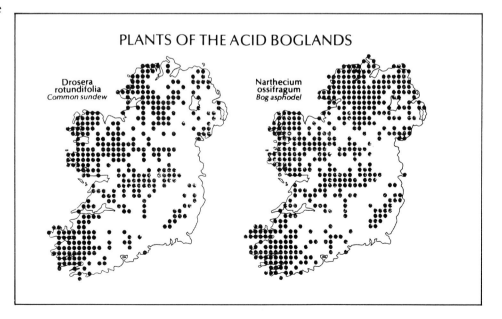

PLANTS OF THE ACID BOGLANDS

Drosera rotundifolia
Common sundew

Narthecium ossifragum
Bog asphodel

Wigeon and white-fronted geese feed in the fields adjacent to the floods and roost on the water or on nearby bogs. Pintail, teal, mallard and shoveler feed at the water's edge while lapwing, golden plover and curlew probe or pick invertebrates from the soil. In spring they are joined by black-tailed godwits getting ready for migration to their breeding haunts in Iceland.

Invertebrates and insects

Turloughs generally have smaller numbers of birds because they themselves are smaller and susceptible to disturbance. They also have a limited range of animal food since the fluctuating conditions are difficult for many organisms. Any successful invertebrates will have to withstand sudden drying out and rewetting. A few snails can do this, some by shutting themselves tightly into their shells during drought. Otherwise, the commonest creatures are crustaceans, which can survive dry periods as eggs or can creep away into the rocks beneath. The prime example of an animal adapted for turlough life must be the fairy shrimp whose eggs can survive many years of drying and which can multiply in a few weeks when its habitat is flooded.

By comparison fens and marshes seethe with insect and invertebrate life. The numbers of swifts, swallows and martins that feed there is an indication of the richness, but the flies, beetles, bugs and moths are themselves quite obvious. A lighted open window brings in a multitude of midges, crane flies and moths in a very short time.

This alert otter will find plenty to feed on amongst this classic riverside vegetation.

SEASCAPE AS HABITAT
Strangford Lough
R.A. Brown

Sheltered bays and inlets on the western shore of Strangford Lough

Strangford Lough, the largest inlet on the County Down coast, reaches northwards for some 33km from the rugged channel that links it with the Irish Sea. Although virtually enclosed by the Ards peninsula, it is almost entirely marine in character. Its waters, its contorted 150km shoreline, and its scatter of small islands combine to create a gentle scenery that holds some of the richest maritime wildlife in Ireland. The importance of this wildlife has been recognised by the creation of the Strangford Lough wildlife scheme, run by the National Trust, and now in its twenty-first year of looking after the

interests of the wildlife. The story of the lough, however, reaches back to much earlier times.

Rocky origins

The lough's origins, some 400 million years ago, lie in the creation of a shallow depression or basin in the ancient Silurian slates and shales that underlie much of County Down. This basin, formed from the same pressures that thrust up mountains in England and Scotland, was later obscured by the deposition of a number of sedimentary rocks, but there is relatively little evidence of these

today, with the notable exception of the precipitous Scrabo Hill at the north end of the lough. Here soft sandstones have been protected from erosion by a thick layer of hard igneous rock. The result is an impressive outcrop that contrasts sharply with the low-lying farmland and mudflats below its slopes.

Drumlin territory

Today the most widespread features of Strangford Lough's scenery are the much more recent beds of boulder clays deposited by melting glaciers at the end of the last Ice Age – about 12,000 years ago. Over much of

The lichen *Xanthoria parietina* flourishing on folded sedimentary rocks just outside the mouth of Strangford Lough. The presence and condition of this lichen are indicators of the purity of the surrounding air, for it cannot tolerate sulphur dioxide pollution of more than around 200 parts per million.

have become truncated during some 10,000 years of wave action.

The Narrows

In the south of the lough the blanket of glacial deposits is much thinner, and here we see the ancient Silurian slates and shales poking through to the surface. As a result, the scenery takes on a more rugged appearance, dry-stone walls are the most frequent field boundary, and everywhere, betraying the shallow nature of the soil, gorse (or whin) bushes grow, bursting into brilliant gold flowers in springtime. It is in the south of the lough, probably because of faulting in the underlying rocks, that Strangford's connection with the Irish Sea is found. The Narrows, as this channel is called locally, runs for about 9km and is only half a kilometre wide in some places. It is here, in these turbulent waters, fringed by rocky shores and guarded by the Angus Rock lighthouse at their entrance, that the secret of Strangford Lough's wildlife lies.

It has been calculated that about 350 million cubic metres of water must flow in and out of the lough with every ebb and flood of the tide, and, of course, this must pass through the Narrows. As a result this small channel carries some of the fastest sea currents in north-west Europe, with the water flowing at about 16km an hour on a good spring tide. Depths exceed 30m in many places, but where the water is shallower, the uneven nature of the bottom is betrayed by a series of whirlpools and upwellings, as the water surges through. Anyone standing on the shore at Portaferry or Strangford can watch these currents take effect as the ferry struggles across, forced sideways by the rush of water.

This extraordinary topography exerts a

the lough these can be seen as rounded, and rather fertile little hills or drumlins, forming the typical 'basket of eggs' scenery. There are few places in Ireland, except perhaps Clew Bay in County Mayo, which show this very distinctive type of scenery so well. Where the drumlins lie in the lower parts of the Strangford Lough basin, they are partially submerged, creating small islands and tortuous water channels. Many have a wave-cut notch, or raised beach, about 4m above the shore, which shows that sea-levels must have been higher in prehistoric times. Nearby the islands merge almost imperceptibly with

the contorted bays and headlands of the mainland, nowhere more so than on the western shore of the lough, which is sheltered from the strongest prevailing westerly winds. Here a patchwork of small, and often incredibly green fields, bounded by hawthorn hedges and dotted with small farm cottages, reaches down to sheltered bays that are almost lake-like in their tranquillity. The eastern shore, by marked contrast, receives the full force of the weather. As a result, the drumlin islands have generally been eroded to low shingle banks and reefs, while the shoreside drumlins of the Ards peninsula profound influence on the lough's waters and their underlying sediments. In the Narrows itself, virtually all materials are swept away leaving a bottom of bedrock and massive boulders. Further in, as the currents gradually slacken, an intricate succession of cobbles, gravels, sands and muds are deposited, with the finest silt only settling in the areas of very least water movement. Added to this are different degrees of exposure to the prevailing winds and different shoreline types. So there is an almost infinite combination of different habitats for marine life in the lough.

Other aspects of the water are important too. The mixing of waters in the Narrows results in an even distribution of nutrients, small food particles and microscopic plants and animals (plankton), all of which get swept into the lough. Equally, the mixing ensures that generally most of the lough is about the same temperature, and the extremes of summer heat and winter cold are avoided. Not only is this immensely important to the wildlife, but it allows lough-side farmers a longer growing season than is normal for this part of Ireland.

A rich marine environment

Because of this unique combination of effects, the lough's marine life is exceptionally rich. Over 2000 species of marine animal have already been identified, and it is likely that the list is far from complete. This marine life is of international importance, and because about 70 per cent of all the marine animal species found on the Ulster coast occur in Strangford Lough, it is irreplaceable in a local context. As well as being of importance in its own right, the marine life is essential to the populations of seals and nesting and overwintering birds. Conservation of all of Strangford Lough's wildlife is dependent to a very large extent on the success of the lough as a marine environment.

A great many of the lough's marine animals are 'filterers', trapping their food as it is swept past them by a range of specially adapted tentacles, gills, and siphons. They eventually fall prey to other animals in the lough and so constitute one of the principal means by which energy from all the drifting food can be transferred to the other animal populations. Nowhere are these filtering animals more in evidence than in the Narrows with its powerful currents. Large plumose anemones, coloured in a range of brilliant oranges, yellows and white, grow on the rocks like large flowers. Soft corals, relatives of their robust tropical counterparts, encrust

A common seal pup basking on the rocks: the number of common seals reaches its peak in June when many give birth to pups.

boulders and stones. These and massive sponges literally carpet large areas of the bottom swept by the powerful currents.

Further into the lough, dense populations of brittle stars, up to five hundred in a square metre, trap food particles by extending their arms into the current. In muddy areas, horse mussels not only assume the role of major filtering animals, but by growing in extensive, densely packed beds, these long-lived animals provide hard shell surfaces for other animals like barnacles and sponges to fasten onto, where otherwise there would only be soft mud. In other areas, the bottom is covered in a silt so fine that the slightest movement creates a cloud that may take an hour to settle. Here lifestyles are very different. Gone are the encrusting organisms, for there is nowhere for them to attach themselves. Instead, living in a maze of burrows and tubes

are shellfish, Dublin Bay prawns, burrowing worms, and even burrowing species of anemone.

Meandering over these communities, and indeed very much part of them, are the predators. Starfish like the bright red sunstar, crabs, and octopus live on the vast populations of bottom dwellers. Shoals of fish move throughout the lough. Sand eels and other small fish feed on the plankton. Mackerel, coalfish, cod, along with ballan wrasse and the brilliant blue-striped cuckoo wrasse, prey on the more mobile animals living on the bed of the lough. Probably because of the rich fish stocks, the lough holds the largest accumulation of common seals in Ireland, with as many as seven hundred present in late June when the pups are born. There are also a small number of grey seals, which usually pup in the autumn.

Throughout the lough, both species may be seen basking on rocks, but particularly in the Narrows, where large numbers can often be spotted from the shore roads. Their curiosity is considerable; visitors pausing to view seals may well find themselves a subject for interested inspection.

Occasionally other sea mammals and large fish are seen. Porpoises, one of the commonest small whales in the waters around these islands, regularly occur, while pilot whales (known locally as herring-hogs) can be seen at the entrance of the lough, probably attracted by rich stocks of fish. Also at the entrance of the lough, basking sharks can occur. These impressive but harmless plankton feeders have declined somewhat in recent years, because they are fished for their livers. Finally, the most infrequent visitors, but probably the most spectacular, are killer

A small flock of brent geese. In late October the lough holds two-thirds of the west European population of this arctic breeding species.

whales. Their last appearance was in 1982 when seven entered the lough. On this occasion little was found out about their activities, but it is likely they took large fish and possibly young seals.

Although much of this submarine life remains somewhat inaccessible, human activities have exerted their effect. Excessive levels of trawling and dredging have not only severely curtailed the small locally based fisheries, but they have damaged many areas of the lough's bottom, hindering the chances of recovery. Proposals to construct a tidal barrage for electricity generation would have the greatest effect on all the marine life, however, by its potential effect on the tidal currents and nutrient balance of the lough. Without a wider appreciation of the lough's importance for marine life, and effective control and planning to protect it, the lough's marine animal communities will remain at risk, to the detriment of wildlife and human interests alike.

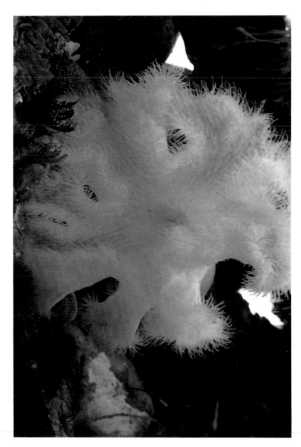

Left
A rich community of soft corals in the Strangford Lough Narrows – an area with some of the fastest sea currents in north-west Europe

Opposite
A roseate tern landing by its nest. This is now one of the rarest breeding sea birds in Europe and the subject of deep international concern.

Life on the shore

If the waters and the bed of Strangford Lough are spectacular for their wildlife, the shores are scarcely less so. Varying from wave-battered outcrops of bedrock in the Narrows, to the glacial gravels, boulders and mudflats within, the lough exhibits a remarkable range of shore types. In sheltered localities dense growth of brown seaweeds provides shelter for large numbers of animals less able to cope with exposure to air. Rock pools provide an equally important habitat.

One of the most extensive intertidal habitats in the lough are the mudflats. Dismissed by some as boring and unattractive, these do in fact have their own beauty, changing from hour to hour as the tides move over the stretches of shining mud.

136

Apparently devoid of life on the surface, these muds and fine sands are host to millions of burrowing worms, small shrimps and shellfish, and each particle of mud or sand has its own community of microscopic organisms. Some animals occur in vast numbers, the small snail *Hydrobia* may occur in densities of over a thousand in a square metre. Growing on the muds are extensive swards of eel grass, their root systems binding the substratum together. In late summer the whole of the north end of Strangford Lough assumes a greenish hue as these plants reach their peak of growth. These mudflats play a fundamental role in maintaining the balance of water quality in the lough. Waste products are filtered, consumed and broken down by the myriads of microscopic bacteria and larger burrowing organisms.

Overwintering birds

Perhaps the most readily visible evidence for the importance of the lough's shores, particularly its mudflats, comes from the populations of overwintering birds. Numbers of these often exceed the criteria conventionally applied for both national and international importance. In this respect Strangford Lough plays a fundamental role in providing a major link in a chain of estuaries and inlets along the Irish Sea coast. All of these areas provide an essential series of feeding and shelter stations for wildfowl and waders migrating from the more rigorous winters of their northern breeding areas, to exploit the relatively mild conditions of the Atlantic climate.

The most notable example of these birds

tufted duck, and occasionally scaup occur. The lough is noted for its swan populations – mute swans occur in the lough the year round, while populations of Icelandic whooper swans are present in November and December, though recently they have tended to spend more time on nearby farmland.

The populations of overwintering waders are no less impressive. Massive flocks of golden plover, knot, bar-tailed godwit, oystercatcher and dunlin may be seen circling over the northern mudflats – a startling sight as their wings reflect the low winter sun. As the tide ebbs, they can be seen out on the mud, probing and pecking for the millions of small worms, shrimps and snails. While many of these species are widespread about the lough, others specialise in particular localities. Black-tailed godwit, for example, occur only in the very sheltered bays of extremely soft mud on the western shore of the lough. Turnstones tend to specialise in areas of weed and shingle, which they can flick over to feed on small shrimps, while purple sandpipers are usually confined to the rocky shores at the entrance of the lough. Virtually all the overwintering waders are seen in their densest numbers at high water when they roost on saltmarsh fringes, rocks and sand spits. Even at small sites, numbers may reach several thousand birds as flocks driven off their feeding grounds by the rising tide arrive to rest, digest their food and preen.

For both wildfowl and waders, Strangford Lough in winter means one thing: an extremely rich and sheltered area for winter feeding. However, the food stocks are depleted as the winter progresses, and many species employ complex foraging strategies to maximise their food intake. By careful selection of food type, location and numbers feeding in any area, the birds are able to

comes in the form of the pale-bellied brent goose. These small but rather attractive geese, which nest in the high Arctic of Canada, are one of the world's most northerly nesting birds. At the end of each nesting season, whose success depends upon the dubious chances of the very brief Arctic summer, the brent, with their newly fledged young, begin the long flight towards their Irish winter grounds. Crossing southern Greenland, Iceland, and the North Atlantic, the first birds usually make their appearance on Strangford Lough at the end of August. From their first arrival, the numbers of brent rapidly increase as more flocks arrive, descending from high over the lough. By the time numbers reach their peak in late October, the population may exceed 15,000 birds, or about two-thirds of the whole west European population.

At their peak numbers, the flocks are an impressive sight, with as many as 4000 birds moving as a single flock in response to tidal movements. As the tide ebbs, the brent can be seen following the retreating water's edge grazing on the swards of eel grass, which are their preferred food. Occasionally there are brief low-level flights as nearby areas become exposed. Then, with the turn of the tide, the process is reversed, finally resulting in the accumulation of very large flocks once more, floating a few yards offshore waiting for the tide to drop again. With this type of grazing pressure on the eel grass stocks, the food is rapidly depleted. Gradually the flocks disperse to other parts of the lough, or elsewhere in Ireland in their hunt for food.

Brent are not the only wildfowl to come to the lough in large numbers. Wigeon, though much reduced in numbers may still exceed 2000 birds, while mallard, teal, pintail and shoveler are all very regular winter residents. In the open waters of the lough, goldeneye,

A female merganser on Strangford Lough. The merganser's beak is specially adapted for feeding on fish.

survive the worst January and February weather when food stocks could be much reduced. In this respect the lough's westerly position may be something of a bonus, since winter conditions are much less extreme than in Great Britain and Europe. It does mean, however, that the success of the lough as a habitat for overwintering birds is dependent upon their access to food stocks. To this end, much of the work of the Strangford Lough wildlife scheme has been directed towards management of the foreshores by control of shooting, designation of disturbance-free refuge areas and general shoreline conservation.

Spring nesting

With the gradual arrival of spring, the whole emphasis of birdlife shifts. The shores and mudflats take on a slightly deserted appearance as the flocks of overwintering birds pass through and away to their northern breeding areas. Instead, the 120 or so islands scattered about the lough take on the role of supporting a new wave of arrivals. Many of these islands are quite large, with areas of woodland, herb-rich meadows and small farms. Others are tiny, little more than spits of sand and shingle capped by a few maritime weeds, and often it is these that attract the nesting birds, probably because of their isolation. These birds are no less dependent on the marine life of the lough than the overwintering birds were, and at this time many are dependent on the fish populations of the lough as the shoals move in with the warmer waters.

The first half-hearted attempts at nesting can be as early as January, when mild spells may induce herring gulls to scrape a few twigs and grasses together. However, it is usually the lough's resident mallard that are actually the first to lay eggs. The first clutches generally appear in late March, and like the eggs of the other wildfowl nesting on the lough, are laid in carefully prepared, well hidden nests of down, dry grass and twigs. Shortly after, greylag, Canada and barnacle geese start laying, again in nests well concealed by vegetation. Later, merganser and shelduck nest, the latter often selecting rabbit holes on the larger islands, while a recent development has been the appearance of gadwall and eider duck to the list of nesting wildfowl.

By the end of April the two colonies of cormorants have become well established. Easily spotted on their high turret-shaped nests of dead seaweed, the cormorants are attracted to these islands by the rich boulder shores festooned with weeds, an ideal habitat for the eels and small fish that they live on. By contrast, the oystercatchers and ringed plovers nest on sand and shingle beaches with virtually no nest preparation. This, together with the irregular speckles and dashes on their eggs provides a very effective camouflage, and often it is only the presence of the bird feigning injury a few yards away (as a distraction tactic) that reveals the presence of a nest to the observer.

Summer visitors

Of all the species nesting on the lough's islands, it is the terns that usually attract the greatest interest and attention. These graceful, white fish-eating birds, often called sea-swallows, spend their winters on the African coast – even as far away as South Africa. Their summers on Strangford Lough commence with the April arrival of the first of the four species – the Sandwich tern. These are the most numerous, recently exceeding 1500 nests spread through about four or five islands. They are easily detected: high-pitched raucous calls, reckless dives for food and constant disputes over nesting sites are the hallmarks of a vigorous Sandwich tern colony. Later, common and arctic terns arrive. Both of these are notoriously fickle in their choice of nesting sites, and at least twenty-six islands are known to have been used. Roseate terns, so named because of a very faint pink flush on their breast feathers, are the rarest species on the lough. They are now the subject of deep international concern

because of their declining numbers throughout Europe and elsewhere. Usually the latest to arrive, they generally nest amongst common and arctic tern colonies, probably because they are incapable of mustering enough pairs to create secure colonies on their own.

All the species of tern prefer to nest in densely packed colonies, where their combined aggressive behaviour generally keeps predators at bay. Usually the nesting is on open ground of short maritime weeds and grasses, or actually on the shore of the island. Common terns often lay on the fringes of dead weed at the top of the shore, and this makes them particularly vulnerable to spring tides, which can result in the whole nest being washed away.

As with cormorants, the attraction of the lough for terns lies as much in the availability of food as in the range of safe island nesting sites. The rich plankton in the lough during the warmer months ensures a ready food supply for enormous shoals of sand eels. Thus where areas of turbulence cause accumulations of plankton and fish, the terns will often be present, plummeting into the restless water from heights of over 15m. Often the water seems to boil as thousands of these tiny fish rise to the surface and dive again. In late summer, when mackerel are present, they too will pursue the sand eels, and in turn provide an attraction for hungry porpoises and seals.

Conservation of the nesting birds, particularly sensitive species like the terns, involves a careful balancing of interests. The lough is immensely popular with yachting people, and part of its charms are the pleasures of island visiting. Where sensitive species are nesting, the National Trust erects signs asking people not to land and

co-operation is excellent. There are, however, many other islands where visitors do no harm at all; and the Trust owns several of these and actively encourages people to come ashore. In this way it is hoped that people are encouraged to enjoy the lough while at the same time the nesting of many important species is protected.

Autumnal journeys

Finally, the lough's waters gradually lose their summer warmth. The terns accumulate on sand bars and spits in preparation for their long journey down the European coast to Africa. At the same time, the first of the autumn's brent geese are arriving; bar-tailed godwit, still bearing the remnants of their summer plumage pass through or stay to overwinter on the lough. After a summer of growth and development, the eel grasses, weeds and millions of small mudflat animals have regenerated and will support the thousands of birds through the winter. And so the cycle begins again.

R.A. BROWN PHD has been Head Warden of the Strangford Lough Wildlife Scheme since 1982. His doctorate, awarded by Queen's University Belfast, was on the subject of the ecology of bivalves in Strangford Lough. He has spent two years in Sweden researching the breeding cycles of deep-water mussels and three years in Jamaica developing an oysterculture industry; he has also been involved in the conservation of hawksbill turtles. He has published many scientific papers and articles on wildlife for newspapers and magazines.

WILDLIFE IN THE COUNTRYSIDE

Frank Mitchell

The range of wildlife to be found on an island will depend firstly on the nature of its climate and the range of habitats it can offer. It will further depend on the length of time that has been available for immigration. Life on an island can be wiped out by a volcanic explosion, as was the case with Krakatoa in the nineteenth century. Life can also be wiped out by cold, and it seems likely that only a very small number of specially adapted plants and animals survived the short period of extremely harsh climate that Ireland suffered about 11,000 years ago.

Balanced immigration into an island can only take place if land-bridges are available. Crossing a stretch of water is only possible for a very limited number of organisms, and opportunities for crossing must always be chancy. We know that sea-level was low and Ireland was joined to Britain when the climate was cold, and that it subsequently rose as the world's ice-masses melted away. At what rate did it rise? For how long did an adequate land-bridge – adequate in the sense that the bridge itself must have had some range of habitats that made it possible for a wide variety of plants and animals to use it – last? These are topics of acute controversy among naturalists; geologists say the cut-off came early; some botanists and zoologists say the bridge lasted for thousands of years; I ally myself with the latter group.

But all the factors mentioned above do have effect, and Ireland has fewer types of animals and plants than Great Britain, which in turn, being itself an island, has fewer than the continent of Europe.

Humans too made additions to – and also subtractions from – the wildlife of the country. Some, like the domestic animals, were beneficial, some like the rabbit were dubious, some like the grey squirrel were disastrous. The native wolf was wiped out, but the introduced mink may yet turn out to be more dangerous. It is already disturbing riverine habitats, and may yet spread into other ecological niches.

Introduced Plants and Animals
Birds
Owls
Flora
Bird Song
Snails and Slugs
Fish
Mammals
Insects

INTRODUCED PLANTS AND ANIMALS

Roger Goodwillie

Humans have affected the countryside in obvious ways, by clearing woodland, growing crops and keeping livestock, by draining rivers and wetlands and by building houses and roads. In doing so we have altered the natural fauna and flora. Woodland animals like deer and woodpeckers have been reduced or exterminated, while grassland species like the rook and starling have multiplied beyond all previous levels. But there is another more subtle way that we have affected our wildlife; by bringing in plants or animals that did not reach the country by themselves. These introductions may today be inseparable from the native stock, having settled into natural communities as if they were always here.

The frog, for example, may have been an early introduction, as many ancient writings note its absence. Lizards are mentioned in twelfth-century manuscripts but not frogs, and there are no frog bones found in archaeological sites. It is unlikely that the St Patrick legend, which says that the saint banished all snakes, toads and frogs, would have arisen if there had been frogs in Ireland.

In other cases, introductions may remain distinct, either by their aggressive ability to colonise or through holding onto an association with humans. *Spartina* grass on mudflats looks like an introduction: it grows in pure stands and is obviously still spreading in many places. But if we did not know its history (it was imported earlier this century) we might think it had experienced a natural genetic change similar to the one that allowed the collared dove to spread across Europe from the Balkans in a mere fifty years. Poppies and garden speedwells also follow humans wherever they cultivate, but what about the mallow or the wild lettuce? Both grow close to habitation but also in wild

142

places, the former in sandy ground, the latter on the Burren rocks.

Accident or design?

Introductions take place intentionally or by accident. The grey squirrel, for example, was brought to Castleforbes in Longford in 1911 and released on an estate. From there it has spread to cover fifteen counties and shows no sign of stopping. The fallow deer and the rabbit were introduced for food by the Normans. It was the practice to establish rabbit warrens in coastal areas where the animals could be cropped at intervals. But the rabbits soon left the confines of the warren and, until myxomatosis, they populated the country so densely as to have a considerable economic effect. The house mouse and brown rat, by contrast, are most likely to have arrived by accident, as stowaways in a cargo of grain or fodder. In former times the black rat was called the Irish rat: it was mentioned as being here before 1200. The brown rat is a comparative newcomer, arriving in 1720. It

was so successful, however, that it has all but eliminated the black rat.

The Irish mammal fauna has probably been more influenced by introductions than any other group. It contains an assortment of species that suggests a series of chance introductions rather than an orderly sequence of colonisation in postglacial times. Field voles, for example, occur naturally north to the Arctic tundra and they should have got here long before wood mice. And if the field vole 'should' be in Ireland, the hedgehog should not, as it is a slow mover dependent on woodland cover.

In fact out of the twenty-nine mammals in Ireland there is reason to believe that thirteen (or 45 per cent) have been brought in by humans. In the plant kingdom the figure is nearer 20 per cent. For insects and other invertebrates we cannot say for certain, as the distribution of the fauna is not well enough known for us to pick out species with implausible natural ranges.

It is certain, however, that a number of

Opposite
Rabbits were introduced by the Normans for food. They populated the countryside densely until the onset of myxomatosis.

Right
One drawback with introductions is that if they survive they are likely to spread and possibly become a nuisance. Such is the case with rhododendron, the 'beautiful' pest, which is affecting areas all over the west of Ireland and threatening the native woodland.

'garden' insects have been introduced with ornamental plants and the fauna of arboreta and other gardens frequently contains a few surprises. Out of thirty-seven bark lice, for instance, a significant number are most common in parks and gardens and often feed on non-native trees. Before the disinfection of aeroplanes was common, many foreign insects arrived at Shannon, especially mosquitoes. Nowadays the car ferries must be responsible for assisted passages from Europe, while cargoes of wood and fruit may conceal small tropical animals. In this way spiders, grasshoppers, crickets, moths and many beetles have arrived in several ports. If the cargo includes the Colorado beetle it generally makes the news, but there are many other insects with the potential to become established here, and some that already have done so. An acorn barnacle arrived in some way in England from Australia forty years ago. From there it has spread naturally and has now become one of our commonest species.

Problems with introductions

The trouble with introductions is two-fold. On the one hand they obscure the natural development of flora and fauna in Ireland, the legacy of historical and climatic factors. With the introduction of *Spartina* to estuarine muds for example, the unique Irish tendency of tasselweed to grow in full salt water rather than in brackish water may be destroyed for ever. The very existence of the moneywort, one of our southern plant species, may be threatened by an aggressive trailing willowherb brought in from New Zealand.

The other drawback with introductions is that if they survive they are quite likely to spread to the extent of becoming a nuisance. The reason for this is that they arrive without their natural controls, whether these are their own pests or special climatic factors to which they have become adapted. Rhododendron for example is not eaten by any Irish animal, either mammal or insect. It has evolved a tiny wind-dispersed seed to allow it to colonise scattered clearings in woodland. In Ireland it found woodlands so closely grazed that they resembled a continuous clearing. Having been introduced into gardens near oakwoods, it had ideal conditions for spread, and from about 1900 it has gone from strength to strength. It is in every sense a pest, though some would say a beautiful one. Not only does it infiltrate itself into any available woodland, spreading to produce an impenetrable tangle of stems, but it then shades out seedling oaks and all other plants, so that in the long term the wood cannot survive. Rhododendron is affecting areas all over the west of Ireland from Cork to

Spurge laurel belongs to a group of plants introduced in the eighteenth and nineteenth centuries in estate parks and woodlands. Several of these plants secured such a foothold that they can now be considered as established members of the Irish flora. A few, such as rhododendron and day laurel, are proving to be very undesirable aliens.

Donegal and is proving a costly problem to those who would retain our native woodland.

Some other introductions may not be pests. It is thought that all 'coarse' fish like perch, roach, bream and pike were brought in by humans, some of them introduced by the monasteries to the large rivers they are situated beside. They fill an empty niche in our rivers, especially now that pollution makes some of the lowland stretches unattractive to trout. They feed the otter and the heron and satisfy a large number of anglers.

Are the sycamore, beech, horse chestnut, the wall valerian and the fuchsia also collectively a bad thing? The purists think so at any rate.

144

Importing disease

Introduced species may carry disease. The Dutch elm disease was brought here by beetles imported in elm bark. A similarly harmful disease has appeared in our native oyster which can be carried by the foreign oysters sometimes grown. And there is a potentially lethal crayfish disease introduced into Britain and the rest of Europe by an American species of crayfish. But it is a fact of life that introductions will continue to happen as travel and transport become a human preoccupation. We must prevent as many misguided importations as possible and contain the accidental introductions as best we can. Ireland still has a unique flora and

fauna and also a disease-free status that we have yet to fully appreciate.

BIRDS

Clive Hutchinson

Let's visit a variety of Irish habitats and see what we find there.

Coast

Seabirds and waterfowl are the most studied groups of birds in Ireland. This is partly because their habitat is threatened by reclamation, pollution and disturbance, and partly because these birds are rather easier to count than passerines skulking in woodland.

Rocky shores

More than 85 per cent of the coast consists of rocky shores, but much of it is low-lying. There are about nine seabird colonies with more than 10,000 breeding pairs. Of these only Lambay Island off the Dublin coast, Great Saltee off the south Wexford coast and Rathlin Island, Antrim, are away from the west coast. The largest colonies are in Kerry, where some tens of thousands of Manx shearwaters, storm petrels, gannets and puffins breed on the Blaskets, the Skelligs and the appropriately named Puffin Island. These are the largest storm petrel colonies in the world. The colonies close to the Irish Sea have large numbers of razorbills, guillemots and gulls.

The rocky shores support wintering populations of turnstones and a few purple sandpipers. Oystercatchers, curlews, redshanks and greenshanks also winter on the rocks or in small inlets on the rocky shores. The outer Ards peninsula, in County Down, has up to 1900 wintering turnstones, a surprisingly high number.

Soft shores

Less than 15 per cent of the Irish coastline is sandy beach, mudflat or salt-marsh. These shores, however, incorporate a large inter-tidal zone and are important for wintering

The largest colonies of puffins in Ireland lie off the coast of Co. Kerry – on the Blaskets, the Skelligs and the appropriately named Puffin Island.

waders and wildfowl. It is now widely accepted that a wetland holding more than 10,000 ducks, geese or swans, more than 20,000 waders or in excess of 1 per cent of the flyway population of a waterfowl species is of international importance, and on these criteria eighteen Irish estuaries qualify.

The sandy shores on the west coast support quite large winter populations of ringed plovers and sanderlings. As well as winter waders, sandy shores also support some breeding terns, though the colonies tend to be small and widely dispersed.

Above the high tide line

The cliff-tops provide feeding habitat for

choughs from Wexford west to Kerry and north to Donegal. Recent studies have shown that regular grazing of pasture on cliff-tops and the absence of fertilisers provide an abundance of invertebrates accessible to a long-billed bird. Choughs have not declined in numbers over the past ninety years except in Northern Ireland, where fencing of the coastal strip has led to a reduction in the number of pairs from twenty-one or twenty-two to nine or ten over the twenty years from 1963 to 1982.

On the west coast, grassy islands are the main wintering ground for barnacle geese, which breed in west Greenland. The Inishkea Islands in Mayo hold nearly half the Irish winter population and these birds have been studied since 1961. Many of these islands also provide secure nesting sites for arctic, common and Sandwich terns.

There is a small amount of sand-dune machair in the west, stable dune grassland with sands enriched by calcareous shell fragments. It is heavily grazed and frequently includes wet pools and marshes. A survey of fifty-one machair sites in the summer of 1985 found 604 breeding pairs of waders.

Wetlands

In winter the open waters of the inland wetlands provide feeding and relative security from predators for ducks and geese, mainly from breeding areas to the north-west and north-east. The damp edges provide grazing for the wildfowl and also attract lapwings, golden plovers and curlews, which can locate food more easily on soft than on hard ground. In summer, ducks and grebes nest on the larger waters, little grebes, moorhens and grey wagtails on the rivers and ducks and snipe on the marshes.

Lakes

Lough Neagh has a surface area of 383 square kilometres and in summer it holds well over five hundred great crested grebes, much the largest breeding concentration in the country. In winter it is of European importance for the huge numbers of wintering waterfowl it holds. The flocks of up to 1700 scaup are much the largest inland concentration in Europe; the numbers of goldeneye (5000–9000) are among the largest in Europe and the flocks of pochard (up to 17,000) and tufted ducks (up to 6200) are much lower in recent years than the gatherings of 30,000 each which were recorded in the mid-1960s, but they are still by far the largest in Ireland or Britain.

Lough Corrib in Galway, with an area of some 170 square kilometres, is the second largest lake and it too is a shallow lake with a large diving duck population in winter. In the 1970s it was known to have a large flock of pochard in late autumn, presumably completing their moult, and in winter there were about 10,000 coots at peak. Numbers appear to have declined somewhat in recent years.

These two lakes are much the most important for birds, principally because they are so shallow. The other large lakes – Lough Derg (116 sq km), Lower Lough Erne (110 sq km) and Lough Conn (50 sq km) – are deeper and of less importance in winter. However, a number of the midland lakes, especially Loughs Iron, Owel and Derravaragh, have sizeable winter duck populations.

In summer great crested grebes, mallard and tufted ducks nest on most lakes. Common scoters nest on the Lough Erne system, on Lough Conn and increasingly in small numbers on other lakes. There are large colonies of black-headed gulls, common gulls and lesser black-backed gulls on the western lakes and smaller numbers of great black-backed and herring gulls. Common terns are the most widespread terns breeding on lake islands but arctic and Sandwich terns also nest on islands away from the sea, though in small numbers.

Flooded meadows and marshes

The water table in the west of Ireland rises with winter rain, the slower-flowing rivers flood and the few remaining turloughs ('disappearing' or 'dry' lakes) fill with water. This flooding produces large areas of water where ducks, geese and swans can graze, relatively safe from predators; it drives invertebrates up to the surface where lapwings, golden plovers and curlews search in the soft ground for prey; and it covers such large tracts of country that startled birds can find feeding again after a short flight when they are disturbed.

The callows or flood meadows on both sides of the River Shannon between Athlone and Portumna, on either side of the River Suck in Roscommon and on either side of the Little Brosna in Offaly and Tipperary are the finest examples, though the Blackwater callows in Waterford are also superb. Here wigeon graze on the edge of the water in great flocks of several thousand birds, whooper swans graze out in the middle of the flood and large flocks of golden plovers wheel about. Black-tailed godwits probe in the soft alluvium, and the more common curlews and lapwings can be seen in most fields. At some of these sites white-fronted geese winter in small numbers, feeding on the callows and usually roosting on the surrounding bogs. The feeding appears to be very rich in spring for numbers of wigeon and black-tailed godwits normally reach a peak in March on the Little Brosna, apparently because many birds of Icelandic origin assemble here before departing to their breeding grounds.

Much of the west of Ireland is termed 'unimproved agricultural land' and this is typical snipe country. Snipe breed in quite

147

small numbers, though widely, but in winter
the damp pastures, flooded water meadows,
marshes and bogs are filled with immigrants
from Britain, Iceland and the Baltic states.

Rivers

Because the central plain is so flat, most Irish
rivers are sluggish in their upper courses, but
they tend to run much more rapidly as they
come close to the sea. Moorhens are common
on almost all rivers and kingfishers, dippers,
grey wagtails and reed buntings breed on
most. In recent years the spread of mink on
rivers has been seen as the cause of some
reduction in bird numbers.

148

Mountain

Golden plovers once nested on high ground in
the south, east and midlands, but now only
remain as breeding birds in the north and
west. Ring ouzels almost certainly continue to
nest in small numbers in most of the
mountain ranges in the country, though they
are difficult to track down. Ravens were once
true montane birds but have increased and
spread into the lowlands. The principal birds
of high ground are meadow pipits. At
Glenveagh, County Donegal, the birds of
upland heath and bog were censused in 1980
and a very limited range of breeding species
was found. Meadow pipits, skylarks, wrens
and wheatears were found up to the summits.

A few golden plovers and red grouse also
nested and there was a scattering of kestrels,
merlins, peregrines, ravens and ring ouzels.

In winter most birds leave the mountains,
though snow buntings are known to occur at
this season in the Donegal mountains.

Bogland

Raised bogs are of considerable importance
in winter as snipe habitat and, in certain
areas, they support roosts of white-fronted
geese. Unfortunately, they are declining
rapidly in extent as Bord na Móna crops the
turf. Conservation of a representative sample
of bogs has been widely sought because of the

scarcity of the habitat. The results of only one study of birds on Irish bogland have been published. As part of a study aimed at improving habitat for red grouse, P.J. O'Hare and Dr A. Watson sampled Mayo blanket bog in 1968–71 by using dogs to flush birds. They found that meadow pipits were the most abundant birds, dominating in heathery areas. Skylarks were numerous on flat bog and snipe on well grazed wet areas with rushes and bog myrtle. Species diversity was low and densities of bird appeared to be much lower than on a similar area in Britain.

The same authors recorded passing birds in spring and August. They found white-fronted geese in spring each year on bogland lakes or flying towards them. Golden plovers were seen on one occasion and a few birds of prey were seen. Overall numbers of birds were clearly very low, though it was clear that the availability of dead sheep in spring supported a high population of scavengers.

Farmland

Just under 70 per cent of the land area of the Republic and more than 80 per cent of the area of Northern Ireland is 'improved land' under crops and pasture. The current agricultural regime, with its emphasis on grassland, was not always in place and the effect of change can be measured broadly by looking at the changes in numbers of quail and partridges.

Quail are believed to have been common in Ireland in the eighteenth century and certainly increased in the first half of the nineteenth century. By the Famine they were common breeding birds in most parts of the country. At Easky, County Sligo, the normal bag for a day's shooting would be five to ten brace. After the Famine, numbers declined and by 1880 none were believed to nest in Ireland. There were occasional revivals and quail have bred in small numbers in parts of Ireland, particularly in Louth and Kildare, at intervals this century, but they have never returned in numbers.

The reason for the decline was attributed at the end of the nineteenth century to the structural change in agriculture after the Famine as the amount of land under tillage collapsed. Quail nested in the cultivated small-holdings which covered the country before the Famine and, it was argued, the change in habitat was so marked after the Famine that quail disappeared.

Partridges are now rare breeding birds, nesting sparsely in the south-east, midlands, east and north. In 1900 they were reported as having been long in decline as a result of the decline in wheat-growing and an increase in shooting pressure. In the early 1960s they were considered to be holding their own, but there has been a recent, marked decline and in the early 1980s partridges could only be found in the midlands and at a scattering of locations in the north and east.

The decline of cereal-growing after the Famine appears to be the principal cause of decline. More recently, changes in farming methods since the early 1960s have probably caused it. Partridges need good nesting cover, low predation levels and an abundance of

149

insects. In Great Britain modern farming methods have been shown to have reduced the numbers of these insects, thus reducing chick survival rates.

Stock doves feed largely on weed seeds and newly sown grain on ploughed land. They are recent colonists, having first bred in Ireland in 1877, and increased steadily until the 1960s. The breeding distribution is centred on the tillage counties but is not restricted to them, and the arrival of the species post-dated the decline in tillage after the Famine. However, survey work for *The Atlas of Wintering Birds in Britain and Ireland* in 1981/2 to 1983/4 shows a more restricted distribution than in the early 1970s, with the largest numbers not unexpectedly concentrated in the cereal-growing areas. This contrasts with the British position where stock doves are less dependent on the cereal-growing areas, apparently because the intensified use of weed-killers has reduced the availability of weed seeds and stock doves now favour areas of mixed pasture and tillage.

Rooks occur at higher densities in most parts of Ireland than in Britain. This reflects their requirement for mixed farming with a preponderance of pasture. Good grassland is required to provide food for the young in the summer and grain is required in autumn when the number of insects declines in grassland. Cowpats are an important food source because of the number of insects they attract.

Woodland

About 5 per cent of the land surface of Ireland consists of forest, most of which is planted coniferous woodland.

Deciduous woodland

Census work has been carried out on the birds
150

of sessile oak, yew and planted broadleaf woodland, mostly in Killarney. This has shown that the most numerous species in oak woods are chaffinch, robin, goldcrest, blue tit, coal tit and wren, these six comprising 75–85 per cent of the breeding bird communities. In two yew woods visited in Kerry, the six most abundant species were the same as in the oakwoods. However, coal tits were less common and blackbirds more common in the yew. In planted broadleaf woods the four most numerous species were robins, goldcrests, chaffinches and wrens, but species diversity was higher in this habitat than in oak or yew wood.

Coniferous plantations

The annual planting of state forests in both the Republic of Ireland and Northern Ireland has had a noticeable effect on hen harrier numbers, which increased from the early 1950s to a peak in the mid-1970s, the spread corresponding with the development of plantations on hillsides throughout much of the country. Hen harriers nest in young plantations and the maturing of many forests and the clearance of marginal land following Ireland's admittance to the European Economic Community appear to have been responsible for some decline in the late 1970s.

Norway spruce and sitka spruce woods in Kerry were surveyed in 1973, and the highest density of birds on any survey plot was found in the Norway spruce wood with 180 pairs per 10 hectares, of which forty-nine were goldcrests. The number of species, at fourteen, was very low. Goldcrest densities were much the highest recorded in any habitat in Britain or Ireland. The sitka spruce wood had fewer birds and only eight species were found. Again, goldcrests were the most numerous species with chaffinch and robin in

second and third place as in Norway spruce.

Conservation

The various bird habitats which have evolved or been modified by humans in Ireland have provided the conditions within which those bird communities which occupy the country must survive. Modification of these habitats can have a marked effect on their bird populations and people's activities are the principal cause of changes to the landscape or its vegetation. Conservation is mainly about the careful planning of the landscape and the future of the Irish avifauna depends on the influence of conservationists in the future.

OWLS
James Fairley

Barn owl

Apart from some rare visitors, Ireland has only three owl species: the barn and long-eared owls, both widespread and resident breeders, and the short-eared owl, essentially a winter migrant. All three hunt over open country rather than woodland.

The barn owl, sometimes called 'white owl', is indeed largely white, though the back and top of the head are finely speckled with yellowish buff. The face is heart shaped. This bird is usually seen at dusk as an almost luminous form, or at night in car headlights but it is sometimes abroad in daylight in winter or when feeding chicks. It roosts in hollow trees, rock crevices, occasionally old jackdaw nests and in isolated lime trees with the dense mesh of twigs called 'witch's broom'. However, roosts are commonest in buildings, particularly ruins, and this, along with the noises emitted by the owl, gives rise to stories of ghosts. For besides screeching, a snoring sound is made. Breeding is from late April.

The long-eared owl is barred and mottled brown and grey and has two tufts of feathers on the head which give it its name. Roosts are nearly always in evergreens, especially conifers, where, during the day, the owl perches on a branch close to the tree trunk. Eggs are laid from about late March, mainly in disused birds' nests. The young betray their presence by their calls, which are rather like the noise of a rusty gate. The adult song is a triple hoot.

The short-eared owl has bred only a few times in Ireland and is rarely seen in summer. It is similar in colour to the long-eared but the 'ear' tufts are shorter and virtually invisible at a distance. These owls, often seen in groups, are abroad mainly in daylight and are typical of really open country such as bogs, marshes, newly forested hillsides, sand-dunes and coastal areas generally. The flight is slow, with regular turns and glides, and often low. They will settle on any convenient perch and frequently on the ground. They tend to be silent.

Owls, along with many other birds, regurgitate indigestible parts of their food in the form of pellets. So an owl pellet is a neat parcel of fur, feathers and bones. The bones may be identified and give a good idea of the diet. Irish owl pellets are sausage shaped and 20–80mm long. Those of the two eared owls are grey, while the barn owl produces fat black ones.

Food varies with local conditions: for instance, barn owls roosting near a dump will catch many rats. By weight the average diet of this owl is usually 50–75 per cent wood mouse and up to 30 per cent rat. Around 75 per cent of the long-eared owl's food is wood mouse but only about 15 per cent rat. Birds and house mice are also taken by both owls, and the barn owl, though not the long-eared, eats a lot of pygmy shrews. Being so tiny, though, these are much less important than the two major preys. Bats are, rather rarely, caught by both species. The short-eared owl feeds on much the same prey, but rats form the majority of its food in Ireland, for wood mice are nocturnal. In the south-west, where bank voles occur, they figure substantially on the menu of barn and short-eared owls. Unfortunately nothing is known of the diet of the long-eared there.

FLORA
Roger Goodwillie

A field in north Tipperary ablaze with dandelions in May. Rare plants occupy a special place in the Irish flora, but the beauty and interest of common plants are often overlooked.

The origins of the Irish flora must be looked for overseas because practically all our vegetation was destroyed by the several ice advances of the glacial period. As the ice melted the flora reinvaded the country, spreading across lands that were then dry because of lower sea-levels but have now been flooded. These land bridges lay between Wales and Wexford and between Scotland and Antrim. Plants and animals spread across these as their populations rose rather than by a concerted migration. The spread was slow, often to be measured in metres per year. One can imagine the wind-dispersed seeds of willow or dandelion travelling several kilometres with a following wind, but what about the oak, the hazel or the gorse? A maximum spread of a hundred metres or so is just about possible given an exploratory squirrel or jay for dispersal. It has been calculated that for the oak to have reached our shores before the country lost its connection with the rest of Europe, it must have travelled at 100m a year.

Distinctive distributions of plants

On a human time-scale the distribution of plants in Ireland appears to be stable. Plants seem to be largely controlled by habitat, but there are also some distinctive distributions

The strawberry tree (*Arbutus unedo*) is the most impressive of all the rare plants of Mediterranean origin found in Ireland, where it can grow to a height of as much as 12m.

that probably result from historical factors. The arctic-alpine plants form one such group. These are species that were widespread soon after the Ice Age but have retreated northwards or to the higher mountains in Europe in the face of new immigrants, better suited to the present climate. They grow on our higher mountains and are at their most numerous in the north and west: the mountains of Munster have rather few of them.

There is also a group of 'Scottish' species common in northern Britain and Europe which have remained in north and north-west Ireland, having entered presumably by the northern route. The wild lovage on coastal cliffs from Donegal to Down is one such plant; the meadow horsetail and the narrow-leaved pondweed are others. Some of the northern plants have such a restricted range that they may be on the point of becoming extinct. Alternatively they may be relatively recent arrivals, perhaps having got here even after the intervening land had become covered by sea. We can think in terms of bird transport for the cloudberry, which grows on one mountainside in Tyrone and perhaps early human introduction for the two large cranesbills that occur 'wild' in Antrim.

The southern element in the flora consists

153

of species that occur in Spain and Portugal and sometimes in the Mediterranean. Their occurrence here so far north has aroused widespread interest. Chief among the plants are the Kerry butterwort and Kerry lily, the moneywort and a group of three or four heathers including St Dabeoc's heath. The arbutus, cottonweed and mediterranean orchid are three which extend eastwards to Turkey. Immigration into Ireland by this group must have been by the coastal fringes of France and Britain since the plants do not survive severe frost. Evidence of such a route is shown by the arbutus which still occurs in Brittany.

Another fascinating part of the flora are those American or amphi-Atlantic plants which grow in that continent and also on the western edge of Europe. Some of these are probably modern introductions but a number are under no shadow of suspicion. The pipewort, American lady's tresses and the waterweed *Naias* are examples. The distribution of *Naias* gives a clue to what may have happened to these plants, for fossil remains show that it was widely found soon after the Ice Age. It has gradually become restricted to western Ireland since then. This still does not answer the question how these plants crossed the ocean. Probably this occurred much longer ago when the Atlantic was a narrower sea and Greenland was ice-free. It may not be a coincidence that the 'American' plants are all lake or marshland species and are thus available to migrating waterbirds – the major travellers of the natural world.

A wet and windy island

Looked at in a European perspective, Ireland is rich in evergreen woody plants like holly, ivy, gorse and yew. Similar species which

154

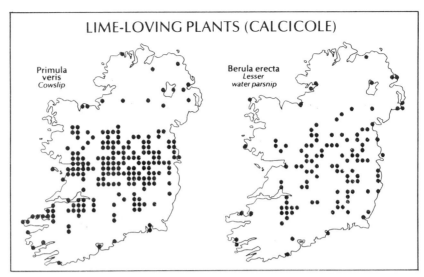

LIME-LOVING PLANTS (CALCICOLE)

Primula veris
Cowslip

Berula erecta
Lesser water parsnip

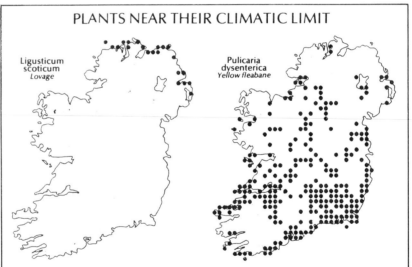

PLANTS NEAR THEIR CLIMATIC LIMIT

Ligusticum scoticum
Lovage

Pulicaria dysenterica
Yellow fleabane

flourish once they have been introduced are the laurel and rhododendron. Such woody plants can only retain their leaves in a mild winter climate and it is noticeable that gorse suffers often in frosty winters. The summer greenness of the vegetation is also remarked on by visitors, the absence of a summer drought being the reason here. The frequent wetting also suits many epiphytes – small plants, especially mosses and lichens, that grow on trees but without drawing nutrients or water from them.

The effects of exposure are obvious over much of the country, as we live in a particularly windy region of the world. Not only do gales dwarf the vegetation in coastal areas but they mean that trees lean eastwards anywhere that they are not sheltered. Gales play havoc with newly expanded leaves in the spring and a gale in April or May may kill the

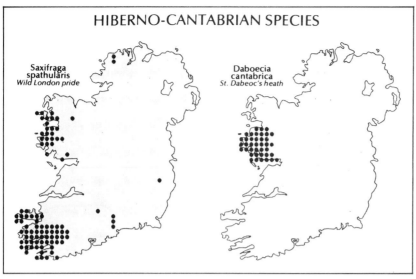

HIBERNO-CANTABRIAN SPECIES

Saxifraga spathularis
Wild London pride

Daboecia cantabrica
St. Dabeoc's heath

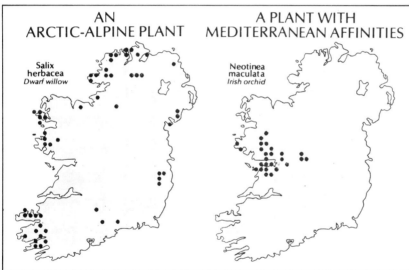

AN ARCTIC-ALPINE PLANT

Salix herbacea
Dwarf willow

A PLANT WITH MEDITERRANEAN AFFINITIES

Neotinea maculata
Irish orchid

midlands, including cowslip, carline thistle, marjoram and biting stonecrop. This is best developed in the Burren where it has the added distinction of including an arctic-alpine species, the mountain avens, and also some of the southern ones like the maidenhair fern and madder.

Certain plants seem to require free drainage rather than an acid or alkaline soil and they may be most frequent on the eskers and other glacial deposits around the country or on sand by the sea. Indeed some species which have a general distribution in Britain are restricted to coastal sands in the wetter climate of Ireland. Many of the annual clovers fill this role as does the hairy birdsfoot.

The human factor

Human influence on the flora is to be seen everywhere, not only in the gross changes of replacing woodland with pasture or tillage and replacing these in turn by concrete. The introduction of grazing animals like the sheep and the rabbit also has had a major effect on many vegetation types. The use of lime mortar in stone walls has allowed plants that formerly grew only on exposed limestone to spread throughout the country. In the same way the railways and canals have offered lines of migration for particular plants; the aquatic flora of the Shannon has spread across the midlands to Dublin. Plants of disturbed soils (generally weeds) have been transported as impurities in crop seeds or stuck onto straw or implements. Some are new species from outside the country, but others are natives, restricted at one time to riverbanks or shingle and sand on the coasts. Plants such as the creeping thistle, curled dock and sow thistle have spread to the limits of cultivation from very small beginnings.

majority of leaves on beech or hazel for many miles inland. The ones that survive will lie on the eastern side of the tree and this causes branches to grow in this direction. Wind keeps the treeline low throughout the country, from about 150m in the west to 350m in the east.

Plants are largely controlled by habitat: thus wetland species are at their most numerous in the Shannon basin, bog plants in the mountains or on the central plain. The richest woodland would lie on the deep lowland soils if it was let, but humans have banished it to the rockiest mountain soils where nothing agricultural will grow. Here the woods shelter a distinctive group of plants that require acid soils. Foxglove and broom, fraughan and heath bedstraw are some of these that are allergic to lime. By contrast, there is a characteristic flora of the limestone

155

Furze in bloom

The bee orchid: found mainly
on limestone areas of the
countryside

156

BIRD SONG
Roger Goodwillie

Not all species use their voice for song: the mute swan produces a singing sound with its wing tips.

North-western Europe is one of the world's best places for bird song. Male birds here rather than developing colour have specialised in song as a way of attracting mates. Once evolution is set on such a track only the best songsters manage to breed and the process of improvement is reinforced.

Sabre-rattling
Song is a form of display, an action that communicates information. As well as using it to attract mates the male bird advertises its presence with song. It confronts rivals and maintains a territory suitable for nesting. Often it has a number of song posts around the edges of this patch of land which help to define it. Song is an exercise in sabre-rattling: usually a vehement song is enough to keep males apart and they seldom resort to fighting. Often a song in one territory is answered by a song next door and you may notice wrens and chaffinches competing like this.

Song time
At certain times of the year singing takes a lot of the time of a male bird: a chaffinch has been counted singing 3300 times in twelve hours. Usually there is a peak of song activity early in the morning and late in the evening —

157

the dawn and dusk choruses. Before there is light enough to feed, practically every bird seems to be singing, forming a jumble of song which is beautiful to listen to but deadly to disentangle. Rooks and jackdaws wake up first and though the 'caw' of a rook is not generally considered a song, it serves the same purpose in a treetop rookery. Robins and blackbirds also sing early and a pheasant may crow. Then in rapid succession come the mistle thrush, song thrush, wren and dunnock. The tits and goldcrest, the chiffchaff and willow warbler are next and last come the finches, the chaffinch being particularly late. Thus waves of different species' songs occur which help them hear one another. It means also that the blackbirds are generally feeding when, a half-hour later, the chaffinch sings.

The sequence of species changes little and occurs roughly in opposite order in the evening. Pheasants are usually more vocal at night and their loudest crowing occurs as they fly up into a tree to roost. This must tend to draw attention to them, but ground predators are their main danger so it cannot matter. Once in the trees they may respond to loud noises, especially sonic booms, as they and their relations are sensitive to low notes such as wing flapping. Some birds sing at night when in the stillness their voices carry well. Both the sedge and grasshopper warbler do it as do the corncrake and nightjar, two species now very rare.

As with other parts of breeding behaviour, song is initiated by day-length. Once the days start to lengthen in January, several species are inclined to sing, though they may be depressed temporarily by cold weather. Robins have been singing most of the winter, since they hold territory then, and they will be joined occasionally by a wren. Mistle

158

thrushes sing from their high perches in February, regardless of wind, while the song thrush and the dunnock may be heard too. The great tit waits for a bright sunny day before it sends its loud 'see-saw' echoing through the trees, while blackbirds soon start up also, generally in March. At the peak of song, many birds sing in strange places: they may release a snatch of song on the ground or in flight. Other species like the skylarks, meadow pipit and whitethroat habitually sing from the air.

In good voice

Most birds produce sounds with their syrinx, a voice organ just above the lungs rather different to our larynx. Various membranes and air chambers play a part, as the bird has no lips or mouth cavity to modify the sound. Their complex system of air sacs allows some birds to sing continuously even while breathing: the grasshopper warbler is the

prime example, singing for minutes at a time without apparently drawing breath. The control of the voice is complex and many songs are made up of notes much too rapid for us to hear. Slowing the song of a wren down on a tape, for example, shows that it sings fifty-six notes in five seconds, while the slowed willow warbler song resembles a mynah bird.

Not all species use their voice: the mute swan produces a singing sound with its wing tips that is just as effective, as does the male goldeneye. The snipe also uses a mechanical method to mark its territory. This is 'drumming' in which the outer tail feathers vibrate with a bleating sound as the bird swoops downwards.

Individual styles

As well as identifying the species, a bird's song also may identify the individual or the population to which it belongs. Starlings

often develop a personal style, the bird mimicking sounds it has heard in its youth. Many starlings use the curlew's call, and you may hear sparrowhawks, hens and even a ringing telephone coming from a single bird. More generally, birds have dialects, and for this reason some of the recordings made in other countries do not sound quite like Irish birds. The chaffinch is a good example. Not only does each male have the ability to sing several songs, but chaffinches in Bandon sound different to those in Belfast or Belmullet. Chaffinches introduced into New Zealand have developed a song so different that it puzzles many people.

Alarms and signals

It is sometimes difficult to draw the line between a bird's song and its calls. Does a jackdaw or a magpie sing, or a woodpigeon call? Calls can communicate more things than songs. Practically every species has an alarm call, a short incisive call that may mean the difference between life and death. Even the woodpigeon may use its wing claps as an alarm call as well as in display. Different species may respond to others' alarm calls in a way that they never do to songs. Thus a blackbird 'chinking' after a cat will bring robins and dunnocks out to join in. The thrushes also have a specific call, a high uniform squealing note which they use when they see an aerial predator. This can be given by blackbird or song thrush and because of its simplicity is very difficult to locate.

Calls used as threats, in distress and in contact complete the repertoire of most species. The contact call of long-tailed tits moving as a flock through bushes is the best way of finding this bird and treecreepers are also more often heard than seen. The brood of pheasants keeps together with piping calls as do birds migrating at night like curlews, whimbrels and redwings. Every young bird has a food call also, often completely different from the adult calls. It usually has an insistent quality even to our ears, urging the parent to hurry up. Town pigeons are a good example, as are starlings, blue tits and even young hawks and long-eared owls.

SNAILS AND SLUGS

Declan Doogue

Anyone who has witnessed the spectacular emergence of large numbers of snails following a heavy shower in summer will be left in no doubt as to their fondness for moist conditions. They will also recognise the importance of the shell as a water-retaining device, conserving the vital body fluids during prolonged dry spells. When drought threatens, certain species can seal themselves up in their shells, constructing a temporary seal called an *epiphragm*, across the mouth of the shell.

Snail habitats

Smaller species can dig down into the soil where a cooler microclimate prevails: larger species, especially those of sandhills and other very dry habitats, climb up on vegetation where cooler breezes provide a much more tolerable environment than that of the often scorching sands below. Although a short walk across most Irish sand-dunes will reveal the presence of thousands of shells, the reality is that very few species have managed to become established in such a severe habitat.

In order to grow their shells, snails need plenty of lime, which they get from their environment. Although a small number of species can get by in lime-deficient areas, the number of species encountered in calcium-rich localities is usually much higher. Lime is usually abundant in sand-dunes (and on sandy ground inland) but conditions are often too arid for snails. In wetlands nearby – dune slacks near the coast and fenny ground inland – a number of quite rare species may still be found. If there is a little deciduous woodland, so much the better, as several species are to be found in quantity in decaying leaf litter and seldom elsewhere.

Sheltered spots for slugs

In upland areas – especially on moorland – very few snails can live. There is simply not enough lime available. Various species of slug (which do not have a rigid external shell) can survive, however, provided there are sufficient shelter sites. The lack of an encumbering shell helps them to move up and down within the soil. Many can move about quite rapidly in the open when weather conditions are suitable (warm moist nights are best) to feed on a variety of foods. Because most of their body weight is taken up with water (which they can shed whenever necessary) they can squeeze into surprisingly small spaces such as the underside of stones and logs. By jamming themselves between the soil and the underside of a rock they can reduce the amount of body surface exposed to the air and so retain moisture.

Garden pests

The preference of certain snails and slugs for rubbish has enabled them to invade and become pests in gardens and agricultural land. Root crops can suffer badly and flower seedlings are often devastated by the attacks of two or three notorious slug species. In the

past century a number of slugs have invaded Ireland. How these species managed to get into the country is not clear – perhaps as eggs on imported flowers and vegetables. Even the garden snail (or pooka) which has so many traditional folk-rhymes associated with it, is not above suspicion of introduction. These nuisance species are the ones with which most people are familiar.'

The biogeographical questions

It is the less obvious species, however, that are often of the greatest biogeographical interest. There are two species, the Kerry spotted slug (*Geomalacus maculosus*) and the Pyrenean glass snail (*Semilimax pyrenaicus*) that exist in substantial numbers in parts of Ireland but are unknown in Britain. The question arises as to how they came to be here but not across the water. The Kerry spotted slug is known from the Iberian peninsula (Spain and Portugal) and one or two spots on the west coast of France. The glass snail is known from various parts of the mountains in the south of France. Is it a case of 'survivals and new arrivals'? Are we looking at species that have died out in Great Britain but continue to live in Ireland (perhaps for climatic reasons) or

might these and other species be examples of introductions by humans at some time in the past? The Kerry slug seems to occupy habitats that have not been interfered with by people in south-west Ireland – woodland and lichen-covered rocks are its usual habitats. The *Semilimax*, for many years known only from estate woodland in the Mellifont, Collon and Monasterboice areas of County Louth, has been found recently in a number of wooded sites in other parts of the country. Is it spreading – native species do not usually do this without good cause once they have settled into a particular habitat – or are we

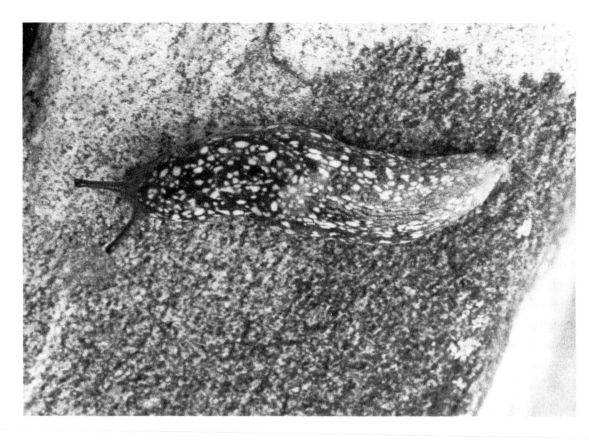

The spotted slug, *Geomalacus maculosus*, sometimes called the Kerry slug (although it can survive in west Cork), is known elsewhere in north-west Europe only from Brittany, but also lives in north-west Spain and Portugal. Its mottled coloration (dark greenish grey with white or yellow spots) provides an excellent camouflage on lichen-covered rocks on 'soft days' in Glengarriff, Kenmare and Waterville.

looking at an example of increased observer activity turning up other natural populations?

The fens and other wetlands of the midlands have a number of small snail species, including *Vertigo angustior*, unlikely to be seen by even quite diligent naturalists. For many years this species was thought to be extinct in Britain (dead shells had been found in various parts of the country) but has been discovered recently in a new site. It is, however, much commoner in Ireland – as are several other closely related species.

Sand-dunes from north County Dublin and up as far as Termonfeckin in County Louth contain numbers of the large and conspicuous *Theba pisana*. Thought by some to be an ancient introduction into this country, this edible snail is often seen where the ground has been cultivated in the past.

Many households are pestered by a large slimy-green slug that comes out at night, often making its appearance in kitchens. On certain nights they may be found crawling over old walls where they appear to be feeding on the green algae that grow in such places. In some instances they even climb into milk bottles left at the doorstep. These are almost certainly the slug now called *Limax maculatus*, which is well known throughout Ireland. It is much rarer in Britain, where it is replaced by the equally slimy but yellow *Limax flavus*. Its full biogeographical tale remains to be told.

The snail and slug fauna of most of the Irish woodlands is very poor. Coniferous forests do as little for molluscs as they do for most other groups. Even our broad-leaved woodlands are often deficient in species for a variety of reasons. The remnants of lowland deciduous woodland that have survived prove that at least some woodland species arrived and dispersed themselves on the island. One of the best examples of this is the long, pointed snail *Cochlodina lamellata*, almost an inch long, still found in a few woods around the country. It should not be confused with the much commoner *Clausilia bidentata* found on walls, in moss and under logs almost everywhere. Another example is the largest Irish slug *Limax cinereoniger* (which is reputed to be up to 9 inches (22cm) long when extended), another species widely recorded in the past which appears to be getting much rarer as a result of woodland clearance.

We can gain some idea of the snail fauna of the past by examining the preserved remains of their shells in buried soils. Snail shells decompose only slowly in suitable ground. Many of the smaller species may be recovered from the samples in an almost undamaged state (although they have usually lost their colour). It then becomes possible to gain an impression of the way the environment of a particular area has altered with the passing of time. Patterns of climatic change, woodland removal, agricultural spread and human habitation can be detected thousands of years after their occurrence. Future researches may be able to clarify which species are truly native to Ireland and which are not.

FISH
Robert O'Kelly

Ireland is a land of waters, surrounded by sea and covered in lakes and rivers. We have 144,585 hectares (357,000 acres) of lakes, which is roughly one-fiftieth of the total area of the country; there are also some 13,800km of main rivers and at least another 12,800km of tributary streams and 3220km of coastline.

Fish in fresh water

The Irish freshwater fauna is poor compared with that of Great Britain, which in turn is poor compared with that of continental Europe, where some 130 different fish species exist. A total of thirty-four species of fish have been recorded from fresh water in Ireland. Of these eight species are predominantly marine and are only occasional visitors to fresh water. A further fourteen species are thought to have been introduced. This leaves a possible total of twelve indigenous fish species.

The salmonids

Even when Ireland was in the grip of the Ice Age at its fiercest, an area of the country, roughly south of a line from Dingle to Carnsore Point, remained relatively free of ice, and rivers in this area were colonised by migratory salmonids (salmon-like fish): it is thought that populations of salmon, trout, char and pollan were present.

As the Ice Age ended, about 10,000 years ago, releasing its icy grip on the countryside, rivers and streams began once again to flow freely. Glacial lakes formed in the mountain valleys and in the lowland depressions. Underneath the ice-sheet, Ireland and Great Britain had been joined by a land-bridge lying across what is now the north Irish Sea, but before the ice finally disappeared this land-bridge had subsided, Ireland was cut off from Britain, and the newly formed rivers could

now only be colonised from the sea.

As the great ice-sheets melted and the land-bridge between Ireland and Scotland was flooded, the newly formed rivers were slowly colonised by anadromous salmonids (fish that swim upriver to spawn) such as the char, trout and salmon. The barren, gravel-laden rivers probably attracted the salmonids as ideal spawning areas which also provided a safe haven for their young.

As conditions stabilised in the newly formed freshwater catchments and stable food chains were formed, sub-groups of these early salmonids lost their migratory instinct and established resident populations. Irish trout and char now largely consist of resident stocks, although sea trout or sea run brown trout do occur in most small coastal streams and in maritime lake systems about the coast. The Killarney lakes also hold stocks of a non-migratory species of thwaite shad which is unique to Ireland, and resident populations of pollan have been recorded from Lough Neagh, Lough Erne and the Shannon lakes.

Until quite recently it was assumed that all races or strains of particular salmonids were genetically similar and that differences in shape, coloration and preferred habitat, noted by earlier taxonomists, were in fact due to their geographical location. However, work carried out by scientists on Lough Melvin has shown that there are three genetically distinct races of brown trout. Because of subtle differences in behavioural characteristics, these races have maintained their genetic integrity over time.

Geneticists have found also that there are two major strains of salmon in Ireland, the ancient celtic strain, and the more recent boreal strain. The celtic salmon inhabit the southernmost rivers such as the Lee and the Cork Blackwater, and must be the

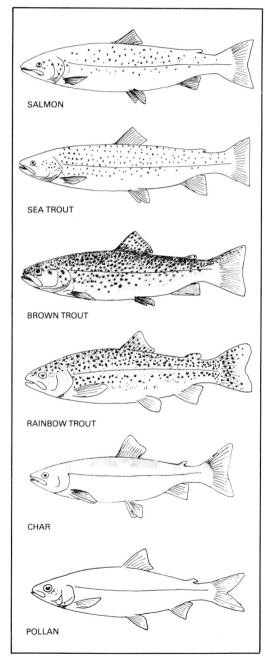

SALMON

SEA TROUT

BROWN TROUT

RAINBOW TROUT

CHAR

POLLAN

descendants of the original native salmon that lived in southern rivers through the Ice Age. The boreal salmon colonised the remaining Irish rivers after the Ice Age. There is a theory that there may also be two equivalent strains of sea trout in Ireland. Within both the celtic and boreal strains it is now known that genetically distinct riverine stocks exist, and each major tributary may even have its own genetically distinct strain.

Given the genetic evidence now available, great care must be taken when stocking rivers or streams with salmonids to ensure that the strain being stocked is of wild origin and as far as possible is genetically compatible with the resident population. We do not fully understand the significance of these subtle genetic differences which the scientists have identified, but they may well have a survival value for the fish concerned.

Coarse fish

Since many of the non-salmonid species of freshwater fish, the cyprinids (carp-like fish), pike, perch and so forth, have a low tolerance for salt water, they cannot have got here by sea, but they must have colonised our rivers through inland river systems, before the land-bridges linking Ireland and Britain to mainland Europe had disappeared. The Thames was once a tributary of the Rhine and it flowed across 'Doggerland' (where the sea area of Dogger now is) to the North Sea. Many coarse fish species invaded Britain through this route before the land-bridge disappeared about 9000 years ago.

The term 'coarse fish' is normally reserved for the cyprinids, pike and perch. However, it does include such species as the eel, minnow, stone loach and gudgeon. Documentary evidence exists to show that at least seven species were introduced into Ireland within the last four hundred years or so. Indeed, the Irish name for the most ubiquitous of these exotic species, the pike, is *gaill-iasc*, which literally means foreign fish or the foreigner's fish. Nor is there any name for pike in the old Irish language.

The first documented evidence for the importation of tench and carp was in 1634. However, monastic settlements probably imported the latter species from Britain and Europe long before that date. Both species require high summer temperatures to spawn and self-sustaining populations were only established in isolated areas. However, both

As the Ice Age ended, about 10,000 years ago, sub-groups of the early salmonids lost their migratory instinct and established resident populations in Ireland. Irish trout now largely consists of resident stocks, although sea trout or sea run brown trout do occur in most small coastal streams and in maritime lake systems about the coast.

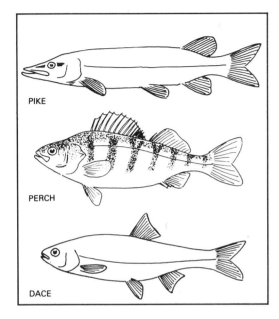

PIKE

PERCH

DACE

species are highly prized by anglers, and throughout the 1950s and the 1960s the Inland Fisheries Trust carried out successful stocking of both carp and tench on carefully selected waters. The programme was highly successful and stocks of large tench in particular are now a feature of many inland and east coast coarse fisheries.

Roach and dace were unknown in Ireland before 1889 when they were accidentally introduced into the Cork Blackwater by a British pike angler. Both this occurrence and a further introduction into the Fairywater in County Tyrone are well authenticated. However, since 1968, populations of roach have established themselves in many large catchments throughout the country. They are now firmly established in the Erne, Shannon, Corrib, Boyne and Liffey catchments and

pose perhaps the greatest single threat to our native trout fisheries in the midlands and west.

The rapid spread of roach may be attributed to sport anglers using the fish as live bait for pike and frequently discarding their surplus bait, and to the intentional stocking of roach into various waters by well-meaning groups of coarse anglers. These practices still continue today despite legislation banning the unauthorised movement of live fish.

Their ability to dominate a catchment in such a short period of time is based on an exceptionally high fecundity rate and maturation at a young age. Research on roach from the River Annalee in County Cavan has shown that both the males and females mature at three years of age. The minimum

Angling for wild game fish is fast becoming a very lucrative sector in the Irish tourist industry, one reason being the scarcity of supply in Europe.

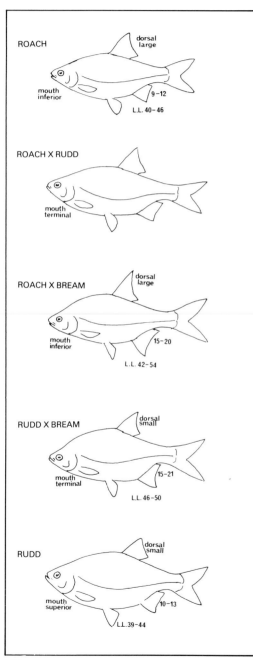

ROACH
dorsal large
mouth inferior
9-12
L.L. 40-46

ROACH X RUDD
mouth terminal

ROACH X BREAM
dorsal large
mouth inferior
15-20
L.L. 42-54

RUDD X BREAM
dorsal small
mouth terminal
15-21
L.L. 46-50

RUDD
dorsal small
mouth superior
10-13
L.L. 39-44

size of maturity for males can be as low as 8cm, while females can mature at 10cm. However, if growth is faster and these critical lengths are attained earlier, maturity may be reached at two years of age, at least in the males. The fecundity or egg-laying capacity of roach is truly exceptional. For instance, one 400g fish was found to contain 136,000 eggs. At one spawning site on the River Annalee it is estimated that over 270 million eggs were laid in an area of 80 to 90 square metres.

On the positive side, roach provide excellent sport for the coarse angler and many match-angling venues benefit greatly from the presence of roach. However, unauthorised introductions into new waters and the subsequent fisheries management problems which this has caused should serve as a salutary lesson to those considering such introductions.

Cyprinid species also hybridise readily and the presence in a fishery of good stocks of rudd/bream or roach/bream hybrids in an area may act as a key attraction to visiting coarse anglers. In contrast to most hybrid animals, cyprinid hybrids are fertile. They may average 2kg or more at spawning time, when they are most accessible to the lake shore angler.

Our freshwater fisheries have developed a real economic value in recent years. Freshwater angling has now grown into a valuable component of the tourist industry, contributing £28 million annually to the economy. This represents only a fraction of the full earning potential of the sector, since there are over 4 million anglers in Britain, 30 million registered anglers in the USA and equivalent numbers of anglers in Germany, France and the Benelux countries.

Visitors from the sea

Freshwater estuaries also hold a variety of species which are principally sea dwellers, but which visit estuaries and bays either to feed or to spawn. Chief amongst these are the lampreys, shad, mullet, flounder and bass. The lamprey and the shad spawn in these areas while the other three species follow the ebb and flow of the tide searching for food. In the past number of years shad and mullet fishing has become very popular, particularly in the estuaries of the large southern rivers.

Sea fish

The glacial history of marine fish species is far more difficult to trace than that of the freshwater species. However, we do know that some inhabitants of our seas have been present for some considerable time. Sharks, for example, first appeared during the Devonian period, more than 300 million years ago, and by the close of the Cretaceous period, some 63 million years ago, their evolution was essentially complete. They have remained more or less unchanged since that time.

Ireland is fortunate in the diversity and abundance of fish species which are present around our coast. Because of the influence of the Gulf Stream, or the North Atlantic Drift, as it is also called, our shores are occasionally visited by species such as the trigger-fish and the flying-fish which are normally confined to the Mediterranean and the tropical Atlantic. We also have resident populations of warm water species such as the bass, which are at the northern limits of their distribution.

To exert such an influence on the distribution and abundance of marine fauna around our southern and western coasts, the North Atlantic Drift must contain enormous quantities of warm water. It has been calculated that near the American coast the current transports 50 million tonnes of water per second. As it crosses the Atlantic, side currents move southwards and by the time it reaches the south-west of Ireland it is only carrying 10 million tonnes per second. Here the current divides and sends out branches northwards which eventually reach south-west Iceland, west Norway and the southern Barents Sea. The mild winters which we normally experience here in Ireland are largely due to the solar energy trapped in the ocean some two to three years previously, in the area of the Caribbean and Sargasso Seas.

Ireland also marks the southernmost limits for the distribution of species of cold deep waters, such as the torsk, which is frequently recorded off our coast but is normally associated with the far North Atlantic. Because of this convergence of cold and warm water species, well over two hundred species of marine fish have been recorded from Irish waters and many more remain to be discovered.

Sea fish populations are composed of both migratory and sedentary or localised species. The migratory fish may make annual north/south journeys of several thousand kilometres while the sedentary species are unlikely to be encountered outside of an area several kilometres square.

Fisheries scientists have for many years used fish tags to trace the movements of individual fish. Subsequent recaptures of fish over several seasons provide valuable clues to their migrations and movements. Work on fish movements carried out by Irish scientists during the 1960s and 1970s has certainly resulted in some unexpected surprises. Tope tagged off the Irish coast have been recaptured as far afield as the Porcupine bank, the Azores, Gran Canaria, the Algerian

and Spanish coasts of the Mediterranean, the north Spanish coast in the Bay of Biscay, off the north-west French coast and off the Isle of Wight. The greatest distance travelled by a tope tagged in Irish waters was over 3520km. In contrast, populations of the mighty skate, which grows to over 100kg (220lb), are exceptionally localised in Irish waters and few have been found to travel more than a couple of miles from the tagging site. For this reason skate populations are susceptible to over-fishing and strict conservation measures must be observed to maintain the stocks. Monkfish and ray are also very localised in their distribution.

The diversity of species encountered by fishermen along the coastline is very much dependent on the bottom type being fished. A sandy bed normally means catches of ray, flat fish and pelagic or mid-water species such as mackerel and tope. Rough, rocky areas strewn with kelp, particularly in deep water, are populated by conger eel, ling, pollock and coalfish. Old wrecks are particularly good locations for encouraging species diversity and up until recently they provided a relatively safe haven against intensive commercial fishing. However, with the advent of mid-water gill netting, even these areas are under severe pressure.

Even more surprising than the diversity of marine species is the actual densities of fish present. During 1986 it was calculated that the western European stock of mackerel, which includes our Irish stock, consisted of 4500 million fish, weighing 1.5 million tonnes. This stock is currently appreciably lower than it was before the intensive high technology fishing which has taken place in recent years.

The number of eggs laid by some common sea species is also quite startling. A single

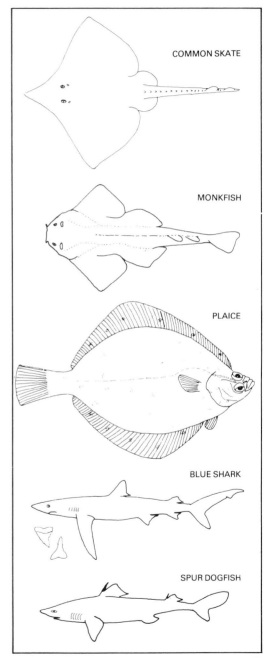

COMMON SKATE

MONKFISH

PLAICE

BLUE SHARK

SPUR DOGFISH

plaice may lay between 50,000 and 500,000 eggs, depending on her size. Most of the larvae of sea fish are free-floating, although some, such as those of the herring, are sticky and adhere to rocks and seaweed on the sea-floor.

The males of the shark family are equipped with claspers which hold onto the female during copulation and facilitate internal fertilisation of the ova. These animals are viviparous, that is to say the young are born alive, rather than hatched from eggs. The number of offspring varies depending on the species and the length of the female. Spurdog fish normally produce three to four young but may produce up to twelve. Blue shark can produce twenty-five to fifty young and these may vary in length from 40cm to 45cm.

Sea fishing

Although Ireland is surrounded by water, we have, for historical reasons, no great tradition of seafaring. We are not a martime nation in the way the Faroese or Icelanders are, who for centuries have travelled great distances over hundreds of miles of ocean in search of migrating stocks of fish. However, our sea-fishing industry is steadily growing and during the twenty-year period from 1963 to 1983 the total fish landings increased seven fold, from 27,000 tonnes to 206,000 tonnes. Salmon landings averaged 1100 tonnes during the same period. During 1986 the ten most important commercial species were as follows:

Species	Total catch ('000kg)
Mackerel	70,011
Herring	34,614
Horse mackerel	23,275
Whiting	6,983
Cod	4,362
Plaice	2,075
Haddock	1,992
Saithe (coalfish)	1,661
Megrim	1,359
Monkfish	1,266

So it is manifestly clear that our ability to harvest fish has improved

Left
Each year Ireland's clear waters produce many specimen fish such as this fine 9kg+ pike. Although highly regarded as a sport- and table-fish in France and the Benelux countries, pike were formerly considered freshwater vermin by Irish anglers. There has been a complete reversal of attitudes in recent years and by-laws have now been introduced imposing a bag limit of three pike per day and a possession limit of ten pike. The fine sporting qualities of this most voracious of predators have at last been recognised.

Opposite
Killary Harbour
Many of our estuaries and bays are now being used for the rearing of shellfish and fin-fish. It is now confidently predicted that by 1990 Ireland will be producing some 10,000 tonnes of farmed salmon each year.

immeasurably since the days of the currach and the half-decker. The largest boat in the Irish fleet is now a 213ft supertrawler capable of taking up to 2000 tonnes of fish. To put this in perspective, one three-day trip could provide a meal for 2 million people with a value of over £100,000.

With this improving technology, a great deal more research into the biology of the commercially important stocks is required if they are not to be irreparably damaged by over-fishing. More emphasis must go on scientific management and less on blind exploitation.

Sea angling is also a very important commercial sector. It is estimated that it generates in the region of £12 million annually in tourist revenue. The fishing is often done for the less important commercial species and is normally carried out close to the shore. In recent years conflict has arisen between commercial and angling interests regarding the sharing of commercial stocks. The time would now seem opportune to introduce a system of inshore zoning to protect recruitment areas and to enhance sport-fishing.

The fishing industry, both marine and freshwater, is valued at £100 million and it gives employment to 13,000 people. It is based on a naturally self-renewing resource and it has the potential to increase greatly in value, but it will only attain this potential if it is managed in a rational and scientific manner.

WHEN TO FISH

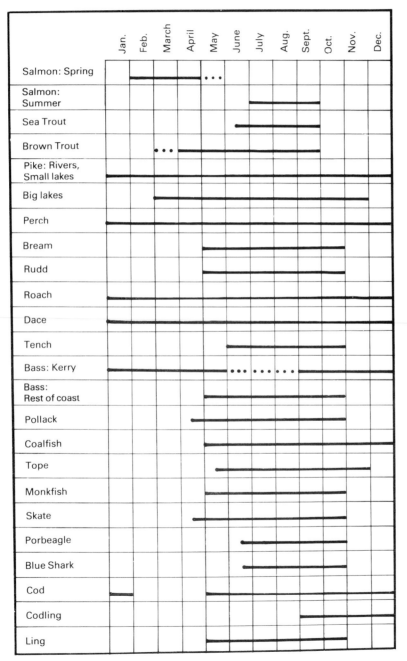

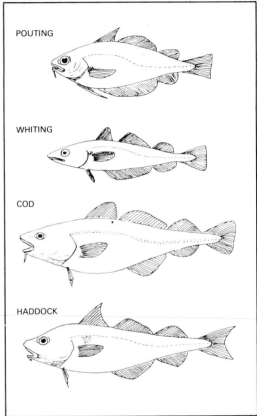

POUTING

WHITING

COD

HADDOCK

MAMMALS

James Fairley

Ireland has decidedly fewer mammals than Great Britain and a number of familiar species are missing, such as dormice, harvest mice, moles, wild cats, roe deer and weasels, though the Irish stoat is habitually referred to as 'the weasel'.

Ireland's only shrew, the pygmy shrew – both the smallest and possibly the most numerous of all Irish mammals – is present almost everywhere that there is some ground cover. Superficially resembling a tiny mouse with a long, mobile snout, it is a ferocious predator of insects, woodlice, spiders and suchlike creatures. It hunts in leaf-litter, in the mat of vegetation below herbage and in crevices. Because it is so inconspicuous, it is perhaps most often seen when brought in by cats.

Hedgehogs are common in cultivated ground, scrub, woodland, parks and city suburbs, but for the best chance of spying them one must go out at night armed with a torch. Compared to other mammals they are then simple to find, for they are noisy feeders (mainly on insects, snails and earthworms) and, when disturbed, roll into a ball. Unfortunately this means that they are most frequently seen squashed, as road casualties. Hedgehogs hibernate: generally from about October to February.

Ireland has a mere seven species of bat, less than half the number in Great Britain. All prey exclusively on insects and are quite harmless to people: they neither spread disease nor 'get in your hair'. The improbability of the latter is obvious when one considers that their echolocation system enables them to catch tiny insects in pitch darkness. Bats are often seen on the wing in the country at dusk in the warmer part of the year. All seven species hibernate but individuals may still be abroad on mild winter nights or, quite exceptionally, during the day. The best place to see them is by a slow-flowing river or lake, fringed with hardwood trees, on a clear summer evening after sunset.

Bats roost in secluded places such as caves and hollows in trees, and in roof-spaces, and often have separate summer and winter quarters. Indeed some move regularly round a series of roosts each year. A colony which takes up residence in a roof-space – most likely in early summer – will usually have moved on by autumn. *Then* is the time to block entrances if the guests are unwelcome.

The most abundant species of bat is the pipistrelle, which may form colonies of hundreds and can pack itself into

A young otter comes ashore to feed on an eel

171

Wood mouse

extraordinarily confined spaces. The long-eared bat, readily identified as its ears are about as long as its head and body, often hangs freely from the horizontal. The only other species to do this is the lesser horseshoe – found only in the south-west from Mayo to Cork – which characteristically cloaks itself entirely in its wings while roosting. Other species comprise the Leisler's, Natterer's, Daubenton's and whiskered bats.

The fox – though killed in winter in large numbers for its skin – remains common nearly everywhere and its range extends well inside city boundaries. It is most easy to see in the first hours of daylight in early summer, when the adults are still busy hunting to feed cubs. Local enquiries and careful observation downwind may be rewarded with a view of the cubs at play. The most apparent evidence of foxes is their droppings: similar to those of dogs but composed mostly of hair, feathers and bone fragments.

Badgers are also widespread and numerous particularly in agricultural land, scrub and woodland. Their burrows, or setts, are often enormous affairs. Discarded bedding – hay and other dried vegetation – is sometimes visible outside, and badger paths, though narrow, are particularly well defined. Although these mammals are omnivorous, earthworms are the most important food and shallow scrapes on the ground bear witness to foraging for them.

The stoat may be seen nearly anywhere in the countryside, throughout Ireland, but most likely by hedgerows, or dry-stone walls, or at the roadside. This animal frequently shows little fear of man and, if it should take cover at first, will return if the observer will simply stand still. Its distinctly bounding gait as it crosses a road is characteristic and readily distinguishes it from a rat, which

172

scuttles. The Irish stoat is a separate subspecies although, surprisingly, it is also found in the Isle of Man. Unlike the British form, the line between the brown upper parts and the white beneath is not straight, but irregular; moreover the border of its ear and, almost always, its upper lip are not edged with white. Most illustrators seem to be unaware of this! In the north, Irish specimens are also smaller than in Great Britain, although in the extreme south the differences are scarcely noticeable. The food seems to be mainly rodents, rabbits and birds, and it is interesting that after the rabbit population was drastically reduced by myxomatosis in the 1950s stoats were said to have become scarcer.

Unlike most other countries in western Europe, Ireland still has plenty of otters. They even frequent the rivers in some of the larger towns. On nearly every river and lake, wherever there are sufficient fish, there are otters; and on the coast they are probably even more plentiful. For those who neither fish nor live in remote districts, glimpses of

otters are rare. On the other hand, a search for their signs is usually rapidly rewarded. Footprints and paths are easily spotted once one can recognise the droppings or 'spraints'; these vary in size and shape but are usually blackish when fresh and crammed with fish bones, giving them a spiky appearance. They also have a sweet, musky, fishy odour. They are deposited on prominent minor topographical features by the water: on large flat stones, on ledges round bridges, on either side of a drain entering a river, or on grassy mounds, where the conscientious manuring can result in the grass becoming a particularly virulent green. Analysis of spraints yields useful information on the diet: mainly fish, frogs (especially when these are breeding in early spring), crayfish and the occasional water bird.

Another member of the weasel family found in and around water is the American mink. However the otter is ten times the heavier and most wild mink appear almost jet black, so the two animals are not to be confused. Introduced for fur farming in the

1950s, the mink settled in the wild through escapes and deliberate releases in the 1960s. It is now established and breeding nearly everywhere, except for most of counties Clare, Galway and Mayo. It is more often seen than the otter and has a more varied menu, including large proportions of birds and mammals. Despite much public alarm, it is unlikely to do significant damage to our native fauna.

The pine marten, Ireland's rarest mammal, is cat-sized and weasel-shaped, with a bushy tail. The fur is chocolate brown with a creamy orange patch at the throat. The marten bounds rather than runs, and from a distance this, and the tail, are distinctive; close up, the creamy insides of the ears are absolutely diagnostic. This animal is an agile climber, at home in the tree-tops, though moving about and foraging on the ground. It prefers fairly open forest with an understorey but it also occurs in the hazel scrub of the Burren, County Clare. It eats a variety of food including significant quantities of fruit.

Above
Pine marten
Below
Pygmy shrew

Today this species is essentially limited to the west, from Sligo to Clare, and to the area of the Slieve Bloom mountains, with a few other isolated pockets, such as Portlaw, County Waterford. In Northern Ireland the distribution is not so well documented but there is a fair scattering of recent sightings.

Both the common seal and grey seal (which is the commoner!) occur around the Irish coast, though only an expert will be able to distinguish them in the water. Seals are rather less likely to be seen near eastern shores south of Dundalk Bay.

173

Of Ireland's three deer species, the fallow is the most widespread. Brought in by the Normans, it is still kept in parks, but most of the population is wild and descended from escapees. Fallow are particularly associated with forest and tend to be localised, but are absent only from the extreme north-west, south-east and south-west.

Sika deer, introduced in the nineteenth century, are found over much of County Wicklow, around Killarney and the Iveragh and Beara peninsulas in the south-west, and in counties Tyrone and Fermanagh.

There are red deer in County Donegal – especially around Glenveagh – extending into County Fermanagh; in the mountains around Killarney, which hold the only native red deer; and in County Wicklow, though these animals have largely hybridised with the sika there.

Rabbits are present throughout the country and are a common sight, as is largely the case with the Irish hare. The latter, like the mountain hare in Great Britain, is a subspecies of the arctic hare, characterised by a completely white tail and shortish ears which scarcely reach the tip of the nose when pulled forward. The Irish hare had a red-brown coat which may whiten partially in winter. Complete whitening is rare. The brown hare, the common hare of England and southern Europe, has been introduced into Ireland from time to time for coursing. It has survived, at least in parts of the north-west, where it is sometimes referred to as the 'thrush hare' because the dark underfur showing between the long outer hairs can give it a speckled appearance. The black upper surface of the tail and its longer ears, which can be stretched forward to beyond the nose tip, are enough to tell it apart from the Irish hare.

The red squirrel is typical of coniferous woodland but may extend into mixed or hardwoods. It is widely distributed and locally common. Nevertheless, it is a retiring rodent and therefore infrequently encountered. To see one, set out shortly after dawn in summer; move quietly and halt often. The best clue to the presence of squirrels is stripped conifer cones, with only the central core and its ragged scale bases remaining. Grey squirrels are, in fact, more typical of hard or mixed woods and may even move into parks, gardens and hedgerows. If the audacious grey is about, it will almost certainly be seen. Grey squirrels were introduced into Ireland in 1911, to County Longford, but are now found over a wide area, mostly east of the River Shannon, though not in the extreme north and south.

The wood mouse, or long-tailed field mouse, competes with the pygmy shrew for the title of the commonest Irish mammal. It occurs almost everywhere there is some cover, though not necessarily ground cover (even the open floor of a beech wood will do, for there is canopy above), but it is absent from bogs and built-up areas. It is wood-brown above and white beneath and the eyes and ears are bigger than those of the house mouse. Incidentally, the latter, mostly a nondescript grey, hardly qualifies as a mammal of the countryside, because, except on islands, it is almost entirely restricted to buildings or their immediate vicinity. Wood mice are strictly nocturnal: the alert observer may sometimes glimpse them crossing the road in the headlights of a car. At such times, when they wish to move fast, they leap.

A further rodent, the bank vole, is about the size of a mouse, but more rounded and generally dumpier, and it has rich chestnut fur. It was first discovered in Ireland in 1964 and was probably introduced within the previous twenty years. It is gradually spreading and colonisation can proceed as fast as 4.5km annually. At present it is established over most of counties Cork, Limerick and Kerry, in substantial parts of Clare and Tipperary, and it has also reached south Galway. It is usually commonest in dense ground cover.

The brown rat is unfortunately still a familiar mammal of the countryside, but mainly in agricultural land. The black rat is almost certainly confined to dock areas of ports.

DR JAMES STEWART FAIRLEY is a Statutory Lecturer in Zoology at University College Galway. Born in Belfast in 1940, he graduated from Queen's University in 1962 and obtained his doctorate there in 1965. His extensive studies of Ireland's wild mammals have lead to the publication of more than a hundred scientific papers or notes, and four books: *Irish Wild Mammals: A Guide to the Literature*, privately published, 1972; *The Experienced Huntsman* by Arthur Stringer (editor), Blackstaff Press, 1977; *Irish Whales and Whaling*, Blackstaff Press, 1981; and *The Irish Beast Book*, Blackstaff Press, 1975, 1984.

INSECTS

Declan Doogue

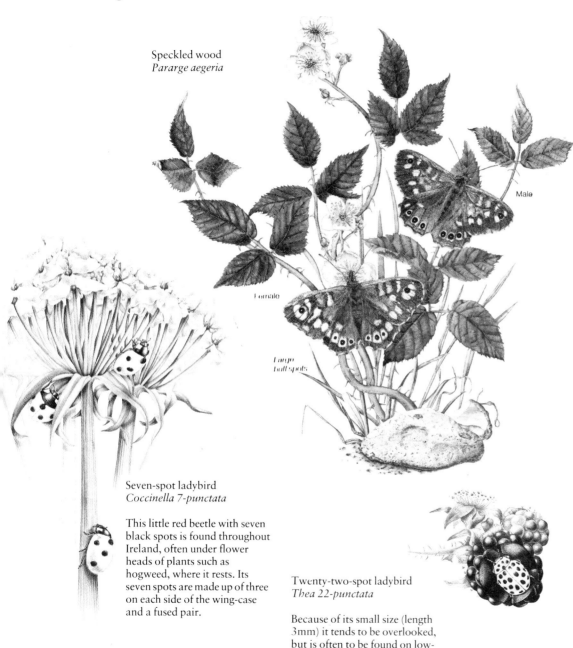

Speckled wood
Pararge aegeria

Male

Female

Large
buff spots

Seven-spot ladybird
Coccinella 7-punctata

This little red beetle with seven
black spots is found throughout
Ireland, often under flower
heads of plants such as
hogweed, where it rests. Its
seven spots are made up of three
on each side of the wing-case
and a fused pair.

Twenty-two-spot ladybird
Thea 22-punctata

Because of its small size (length
3mm) it tends to be overlooked,
but is often to be found on low-
growing vegetation, such as
creeping buttercup.

Hedgerows

Hedgerows and their associated herbaceous
vegetation provide both food and shelter for
many different kinds of insect. On windy days
highly mobile species can move to the lee side
of the hedge where they can continue to fly
and feed on the nectar provided by various
flowers. Butterflies such as the wood white
and speckled wood are characteristic of
roadside hedges and are joined by meadow
browns and ringlets all of which find suitable
food plants for their larvae. In late summer
'nests' of black caterpillars may be seen on
webs on nettle-heads. These mature usually
to become small tortoiseshells and peacock.
When the verges remain uncut the umbrella-
shaped heads of cow parsley and hogweed are
visited by large numbers of flies and beetles of
various kinds. The saucer-shaped flowers of
certain plants like buttercups and roses act as
sun traps and provide a suitable warm microclimate for the more heat-demanding species.
As well as the web-spinning spiders, others,
the crab spiders, live underneath flowers and
wait to pounce out on unsuspecting visitors.
The tiny aphids ('greenfly' and others) that
feed on the plant are themselves eaten by the
larvae and adults of various species of ladybird. The seven-spot, twenty-two-spot,
fourteen-spot (brown with cream spots) are
all commonly encountered, and the easily
recognised two-spot may be an increasing
species. In areas of intensive agriculture,
hedgerows are one of the few places where
wildlife can survive. The structural diversity
and range of food plant enables a great
variety of insects to thrive. When the hedges
are excessively trimmed and the verges mown
back almost to ground level, that variety is, at
best, severely curtailed.

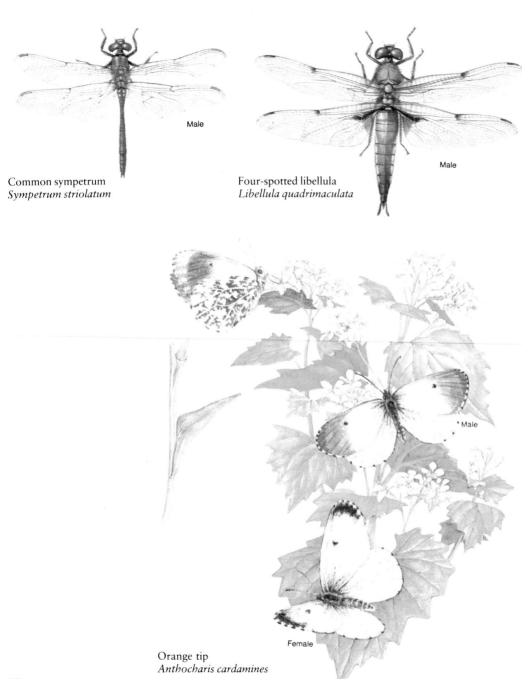

Common sympetrum
Sympetrum striolatum

Male

Four-spotted libellula
Libellula quadrimaculata

Male

Male

Female

Orange tip
Anthocharis cardamines

Wetlands

The fauna of Irish wetlands is in many ways richer than that of most of our other habitats. Our Atlantic position ensures a rain supply throughout the year so that there is usually no acute dry season. The wetlands themselves, of many different types (base-rich fens, base-poor peat bogs, lake shores, callows, canals, dune slacks and marshes), support their own distinctive animal (and plant) communities. Where wetlands have patches of open water the fauna becomes even richer. A cocktail of new microhabitats is provided in such pools where a number of creatures have adapted to life both on and beneath the surface. Pond skaters and predatory spiders work across the water-top feeding on creatures that have become trapped in the surface film. Underwater, the larvae of dragonflies and water beetles feed on creatures almost as large as themselves. In clean waters with a high lime content many different kinds of water snails and large freshwater mussels may be found. Where the aquatic emergent vegetation is varied the fauna tends to be correspondingly enriched and even on nearby ground where one can walk dryshod, butterflies such as the orange tip and marsh fritillary lay their eggs on plants of the moist grasslands – lady's smock and devil's bit, respectively. All our wetland habitats are threatened, often from quite remote sources – illegally dumped toxic substances can find their way into river systems and cause immense damage to fish life. Deepening, straightening or widening a river in one place may cause a lake level to drop many miles upstream. Excessive nutrients from slurry and fertilisers can grossly modify and degrade the local aquatic flora and fauna. Although there have been some successful local efforts to protect some of our endangered wetlands, community vigilance is still necessary.

Woodlands

Broad-leaved deciduous woodland supports many times more insects than do the coniferous forests that have been planted over much of the Irish uplands. Long-established native species, such as oak, have many hundreds of species feeding on their leaves, twigs, roots, decaying trunks and leaf litter. Unfortunately, by now most of the Irish lowland oakwood has been removed. In contrast, very few Irish creatures are the unpalatable new arrivals like spruces and firs. The difference is apparent not only in terms of the creatures that eat the leaves of the living trees, but also in the flora of the ground layer and the insects that it supports. The broad-leaved forest, especially in early spring, has a number of herbs that flower before the leaf canopy which develops in the late spring reduces the amount of light reaching the ground. The evergreen coniferous forests have a permanently reduced light level which partly explains their desolate appearance when viewed from within. Most of the creatures that live in coniferous woods are also very resilient species and can do quite well in other habitats as well. Certain ground beetles, woodlice and centipedes that can also live on building sites and rubbish heaps occur in large numbers under logs and stones. A small number of beetles, however, including the eyed ladybird *Anatis ocellata* and the rare *Neomysia oblongoguttata* (pale brown with cream streaks), may be found occasionally.

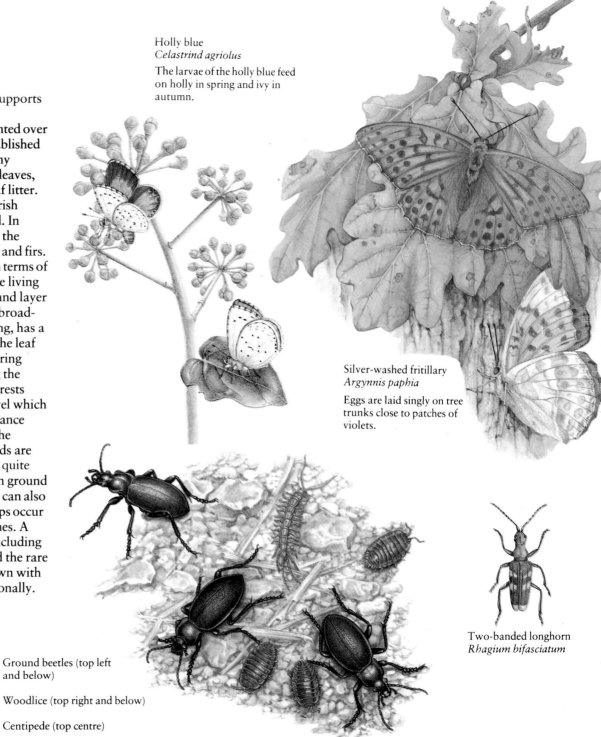

Holly blue
Celastrind agriolus
The larvae of the holly blue feed on holly in spring and ivy in autumn.

Silver-washed fritillary
Argynnis paphia
Eggs are laid singly on tree trunks close to patches of violets.

Ground beetles (top left and below)

Woodlice (top right and below)

Centipede (top centre)

Two-banded longhorn
Rhagium bifasciatum

THE TAMING OF THE COUNTRYSIDE

Frank Mitchell

Ever since farming began in Ireland some 5000 years ago, man has been disturbing the countryside in various ways and to various extents. His influence was at its greatest at two periods, the first 150 years ago, and the second the last forty years.

When Queen Victoria came to the throne Ireland's population was growing rapidly and at a still increasing rate, and there was little concern about the perilous dependence of 7 million people on a single source of food, the potato. More and more land was needed, and potato-patches replaced the natural vegetation farther and farther up the hill slopes. And with the need for food went the need for fuel. Except for the demesne trees within walled estates, no wood was safe from the fires of the cabins. Trees were cut down, hedges were uprooted, the countryside became a monotonous sheet of potatoes. For the first time substantial quantities of peat were dug, but the cuttings merely nibbled at the edges of the bogs, and there were few serious attempts at major drainage schemes. If sand and seaweed were thrown on the bog surface, potatoes could be grown there as well. When the population was drastically reduced by famine and emigration the countryside made some recovery.

In the 1950s the Marshall Plan injected new life into agriculture, in the 1960s industry boomed, in the 1970s the Common Agricultural Policy of the EEC brought an enormous increase in farming profitability. Again the countryside suffered. Great areas of upland were seeded with grass, in cereal country hedges were swept away, coniferous plantations increased indiscriminately, great machines were set to drain the wetlands and to strip away the bogs. The concentrated potato production of the nineteenth century did not bring any pollution in its wake, but pollution is Ireland's new bogey. Both industry and agriculture now produce toxic wastes, and the problems of their disposal have not yet been tackled effectively. Drastic measures are necessary if further damage to the countryside is to be minimised.

THE CHANGING FLORA

Declan Doogue

Left
Traditional low stocking levels allow herb-rich grassland to maintain itself. Extra fertiliser, improved grass growth and high levels of grazing seriously reduce the floral diversity.

Opposite
The cowslip, *Primula veris* (foreground), a plant of lime-rich grasslands, has become much rarer in certain areas, because of the ploughing-up and reseeding of its traditional habitat.

If a naturalist from the turn of the last century were to fly over present-day Ireland, he or she would notice a number of startling changes in the landscape. Towns have increased in size, the number of tilled fields has decreased, grassland is lusher and more extensive, great bare brown expanses mark the worked-out sites of many of the huge bogs of the central plain, medium-sized lakes have shrunk and some of the smallest have disappeared entirely (although they are still marked on the OS maps). An increase in agricultural productivity, expressed as beasts per acre or tonnes per hectare, has resulted in the incorporation of much marginal land into an intensive agricultural system, reducing the structural diversity of the countryside, picking off the fragments of remaining wilderness, bringing a sameness to the land and its wildlife.

Gross destruction – the clear-felling of a primeval wood the size of an average town, or the complete removal of a peat bog larger than the Phoenix Park – attracts public attention through sheer visual impact, but such disappearances are often only the final step in a sequence of related events. The giant cutting and flailing machines that scarify the surfaces of the midland bogs kill very few rare plants. Those were well dead already, killed off by the drainage operations that were needed to let such huge machines operate. What survives bears little relation to what went before. Infilling of quarry pools, insensitive urban planning, extensive conifer plantations, are all one-way processes that

leave little scope for rehabilitation

In practice many species of flowering plants (and their associated fauna) have become threatened, not only by the direct destruction of their habitat but by less obvious modifications of their living places. Rare plants are rare because they require combinations of living conditions that are themselves exceptional. As pressures like drainage or grazing increase, certain stress-sensitive species are edged out by other more resilient species that thrive under the new

conditions. Until quite recently, cowslips were considered a fairly routine component of the flora of well-drained lime-rich soils in central Ireland. They have become much rarer nowadays, persisting on roadside banks that adjoin the fields in which they were once abundant. Silage production and efficient pastoral farming demand a dense grassy sward, and nothing else. Rosette-forming species such as plantains, daisies and dandelions reduce the amount of space available for grass production. Herbicide

sprays see off most of the competition. Ploughing and reseeding finish the job. To the farmer, cowslips are just another weed. By the time their absence has been noticed, the chances are that other less conspicuous but more sensitive species have already been lost.

The performance and success of the more vulnerable species is watched by conservationists in much the same way as voting patterns in marginal constituencies are scrutinised by political commentators. They give advance indications of the changes that are taking place in the environment. Carline thistle, salad burnet, marjoram and kidney vetch have all suffered severe reductions of their inland ranges, although some continue to do well in the less heavily managed sand-dunes of our coast. Green-winged orchid, once a widespread species in midland Ireland is now a candidate for official protection under the Wildlife Act in the Republic. (It is already protected in Northern Ireland, as is the cowslip.) The spectacular yellow mountain pansy, always a rarity in Ireland, has now become almost impossible to locate in many of its former sites.

These are the casualties of a system where high land prices, interest rates and labour costs exact the maximum returns from the land. Similar economic pressures apply to arable farming. Although the decline of certain cereal-crop weeds such as corn-cockle (through improved seed-screening techniques) is not necessarily a matter of great concern, a number of annual species of acid arable land have all but disappeared in certain parts of the country. The combination of herbicides and applications of lime to the soil may have accounted for the decline of species like corn marigold, field woundwort and the weed form of wild pansy. Each was once common and can now be found with

181

regularity only on the acid soils of south-east Ireland, often on the edges of sugar-beet fields.

Many of the weeds of light sandy soils have also suffered. Some, however, produce seeds that lie dormant in the soil for long periods. Several species not seen for years suddenly spring up when their seeds are brought to the surface. Provided that good seed is then set, their extinction is at least postponed. In places on the east coast, parts of the sand-dunes are occasionally cultivated and then let lie fallow for some years. Between the abandonment of tillage and final grassing-over an interesting crop of weeds appears. A poppy with spiny fruits, *Papaver argemone*, is characteristic of such conditions, and the tall spikes of white mignonette have been appearing, albeit sporadically, in the same patch for more than a century, only to disappear again without notice.

Our aquatic flora has also experienced considerable modification at the hands of people. Deepening and straightening of rivers and the infilling or drainage of ponds and even small lakes have changed or destroyed habitats. The waters of many of our lowland rivers have become artificially enriched with nutrients from fertiliser run-off, domestic sewage and agricultural slurry. This enrichment does nothing to help clean-water species such as the water crowfoot, *Ranunculus penicillatus*, which was once common even in the Liffey just outside Dublin city. (It may still be found abundantly in many swift-flowing streams where the scale of human activity is less.) Interestingly, these same nutrients seem to promote the growth of species such as the fennel-leaved pondweed, a plant whose leafy parts bear a close superficial similarity to the crowfoot. This pondweed now grows in great quantity

182

This fly orchid is threatened because of drainage schemes throughout the countryside.

in some lowland rivers, often in the exact sites where the crowfoot once flowered. It would be unwise to suggest that a direct ousting has taken place. Rather a combination of oxygen depletion and excessive enrichment has enabled one species to prosper while disadvantaging the other.

Other aquatic species of stagnant pools and slow-moving drains seem little perturbed by this enrichment. Provided that their habitat is not actually filled in or drained, species such as *Zanichellia palustris* and *Ranunculus tricophyllus*, another pondweed and crowfoot respectively, seem, if anything, to be getting commoner in some circumstances.

A dramatic example of the manner in

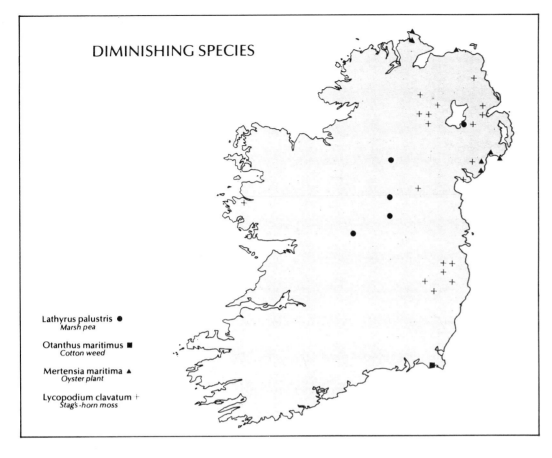

DIMINISHING SPECIES

Lathyrus palustris ●
Marsh pea

Otanthus maritimus ■
Cotton weed

Mertensia maritima ▲
Oyster plant

Lycopodium clavatum +
Stag's-horn moss

which a native species can colonise disturbed land habitats is provided by rosebay willowherb. Once known mainly from upland situations – cliffs and scree slopes – it may now be found in quantity in lowland Ireland on bog margins, railway sidings and urban wasteland. (In Britain, it spread dramatically on bomb sites after the second world war.) Whether the plants that colonised lowland Ireland originated from wild stock or came in from some other source has not been established with certainty. The plants, when mature, produce thousands of tiny seeds with parachute attachments which undoubtedly aid dispersal – but then many other species possess similar mechanisms, and have not as yet become invaders.

Such opportunism has, however, been displayed by many species now widespread in Ireland. Pineapple weed, so called because of its fruity-smelling flower heads, was first noted in Ireland in 1894, and has now spread throughout the country, growing on a variety of wasteland and pathways. Canadian pondweed, first noted almost sixty years earlier, flourished in the waters of the main canals to such an extent that navigation was actually threatened. Its colonising zeal abated substantially in later years. No such abatement is discernible in the case of the tiny creeping speedwell, *Veronica filiformis*, whose bright blue flowers cover many suburban lawns in late spring, delighting some people, infuriating others. Introduced as a garden plant, it has found lawns a most acceptable habitat, and thrives there, apparently unhindered by the fact that it seldom sets seed in our climate.

Many other introduced species have become pests outside gardens. The giant hogweed, *Heracleum mantegazzianum*, brought in originally as a quick-growing and spectacular-looking cover plant, has escaped with ease from the estates and gardens where it was first planted, and now forms stands three to four metres high on the banks of rivers. Its stems produce a juice, which, in the presence of sunshine, causes severe discomfort and blistering of the skin. Many children have suffered badly as a result of using its large hollow stems as jousting poles or blow-pipes.

The spread of species such as giant hogweed, rhododendron (which severely disrupts the ecology of many of our native oakwoods) and cord grass (now covering many important salt-marshes, which are feeding grounds for vast numbers of birds, especially in winter), was originally a matter of morbid curiosity to certain naturalists. Their increase has now become a matter of concern to all, as they become allied with the many other forces that combine to threaten the remains of our indigenous flora.

THEN AND NOW
Farming in the Republic

Paddy Smith

In no other EEC country do the cattle outnumber the people. There are nearly two of them to every one of us in the Republic of Ireland – proof that our countryside is still devoted predominantly to the practice of farming.

And what else would you do with the countryside, for goodness' sake, except farm it? I hear you exclaim. Well, early in March 1987 the British Minister of Agriculture, Michael Jopling, felt it necessary to give his farmers what we in Ireland would regard as a rather astonishing reassurance: 'Farming will remain a major activity in our countryside.' A major activity, mind you – not the only activity, or even the predominant one.

This declaration came as a direct result of EEC-inspired proposals to 'protect' the countryside by preserving it roughly as it is now. In certain specified areas, land improvements such as drainage and reclamation would be actively discouraged and farmers would be paid not to grow crops where they had not grown them previously. This reflects the growth of the conservation movement as much as the existence of the immovable mountains of surplus food.

But Britain is totally different from Ireland, because farmers are in such a small minority there (240,000 farmers in a total population of 56 million). Isn't that right?

Not if you face up to the facts. In 1901, only 28.3 per cent of the population of the Republic of Ireland was in urban areas. It was to be sixty years before there was any significant change in this proportion, but from 1961 change was so rapid that by 1971 Ireland was no longer a rural society – 52.2 per cent of our people were urbanised. Moreover, at that rate, over two-thirds of the population (68 per cent) will be classified as urban dwellers by the year 2000, with the

figure standing at a massive 82 per cent in Leinster. Farmers have not woken up to this trend yet, and unless they do they will be faced with the same controls as their colleagues in Britain.

It is the actual appearance of the countryside that is at stake here. This matters to hundreds of thousands who travel through it and, indeed, to the many who only read about it. If it changes too fundamentally, it will matter even more.

But has it changed all that much? Lean across the average farm gate with me and, if you have eyes in your head at all, you will see that it has, enormously.

Mechanisation

That gate we're leaning on, for instance. You must have noticed by now that it is made of tubular steel and not the half-rotting two-by-four timber so common as recently as fifteen years ago. It may still be tied in place by a length of baler twine, but that is purely a reminder of the strange mixture of the modern and the primitive that is Irish farming. It is a physical statement that some of the most advanced farming in Europe can co-exist alongside some of the most backward.

The gate is wider than you remember, isn't it? That is easily explained: it has to be in order to make way for the bigger farm machines in use nowadays. However, even though farm mechanisation has increased enormously, there are still only just over 145,000 tractors on Irish farms – a startling figure when you consider that there are upwards of 190,000 farmers. Furthermore, as recently as 1970 there were only 84,000 tractors – at a time when there were even more farmers than at present.

Question: How do the others get along

without this most basic of farm tools? Answer: Some of them do have tractors but these vehicles do not show up in the official figures because they are never registered for road tax purposes; the rest simply do without.

The single biggest reason for widening a farm gate, in many cases, is the increase in size of the combine harvester. Some of these can cost as much as £100,000 and it is no surprise, therefore, to learn that there are now a thousand fewer combines than the 6300 there were in 1970. A significant number of them are in the hands of farm contractors, who hire out their services and equipment to farmers, since few farmers want to make a very large investment in a machine that works only a few weeks of the year.

On the other hand, it is surprising that a mere one-third of dairy farms have what most people would have thought was an essential requirement – a milking parlour. Granted, the number has doubled since 1976, but it confirms that a large number of dairy farmers – who are generally accepted as being in the vanguard of intensification and efficiency – have to put up with daily hardship, mainly out of economic necessity.

Fertilisers

Still leaning over the gate with me? We can learn a lot more about the countryside simply by allowing our gaze to wander a bit further away. For starters, we can add another colour to the forty shades of green we are credited with having, by noting the blueness in the tinge of the grass in the field in front of us. That forty-first shade has been induced in the sward by the liberal use of fertiliser, notably nitrogen, on the grassland that goes to make up 90 per cent of the agricultural land of Ireland.

Fertiliser is a major expense to the serious farmer and, on a well-stocked dairy farm, nitrogen accounts for nearly one-fifth of the total farm costs. An annual bill of £200 million is collectively paid by Irish farmers, with £120 million of this being spent on nitrogen alone. The community at large accepts that the grass needs to be 'pushed' that little bit hard to get the vital extra grass, but the liberal use of nitrogen is one of the issues that is almost bound to cause friction between town and country in the future. This is because it was discovered very recently that some of the nitrogen not being taken up by the farm plants and grass is finding its way into the public's drinking water, with possible detrimental implications for health. The main concern is that nitrate concentrates in fresh water may be one of the causes of 'blue baby' syndrome. Traces of nitrogen have been found in groundwater as well as in rivers, and it is feared that a cumulative build-up has now gone too far to be reversed. The 'migration time' of nitrates can be up to several decades, so the present nitrate concentrations only reflect the fertilising rates of many years ago, when they were substantially lower. In Ireland, the measured rates in water at present are well below the World Health Organisation danger levels, but the rate of nitrogen use before the mid-1970s was also low. The reason for concern is that the means of filtering nitrates out of water is a hugely expensive process and is, effectively, impracticable.

In the Middle Ages, Ireland's farmlands were governed from strongholds such as this tower house, but from the mid-seventeenth century onwards the focus of the farmed landscape began to shift elsewhere.

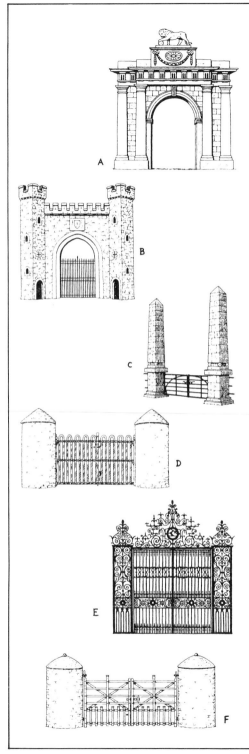

GATEWAYS define the place of entrance to the enclosed spaces of field, homestead and demesne. Field and farm gates were generally the product of local craftsmanship; with the increase in the size of farm machinery many have been removed and, together with their stone pillars, replaced by modern gates and concrete or metal posts which are usually devoid of local character. More elaborate gateways are found in many nineteenth-century demesnes, but in all there is the same statement of pride and care.

A Mote Park, Co. Longford: a grand and elegant arch forms the entrance to the demesne.
B Slane, Co. Meath: one of the battlemented Gothick-revival gates servicing Slane Castle.
C Russborough, Co. Wicklow: a perfectly ordinary farm gate flanked by a pair of ostentatious obelisks.
D Near Fethard, Co. Wexford: a locally made iron gate supported by home-made pillars with conical caps.
E Castlemartin, Co. Kildare: extremely elaborate wrought-iron gates protecting the estate of Dr A.J. O'Reilly.
F Mourne district, Co. Down: traditional design of locally made gates and pillars.

Part of the problem is the spectacular results that fertiliser use produces and the consequent very human response that if some nitrogen is good, then more must be better. You need to be a bit of a prophet to get the best out of the fertiliser you spread: if it rains too soon after spreading, the nitrogen is simply washed – or 'leached' – into the nearest drain, and if it does not rain soon enough after spreading, the fertiliser is ineffective. So fertiliser tends to be spread more often, because it sometimes goes to waste.

Pollution

Over-use of nitrogen is one of the more subtle forms of pollution. Another is as plain as the nose on your face, with which you can smell it – slurry. The spreading of animal manures on land has long been recognised as a supplementary means of fertilising it. But slurry, by definition tending to be a liquid, has a habit of running downhill into water-courses and thence into rivers, and has become as much of a nuisance as a benefit, now that the community objects to having its fish killed and its drinking water contaminated. In the Netherlands, where they have more than 12 million pigs (as against one million in Ireland), the problem of slurry disposal has got so big that it has arrested the expansion of the pig herd.

Another source of farm pollution in Ireland is the run-off of effluent from silage pits. This can be serious, because of the runaway increase in the amount of silage made in this country, entailing the addition of millions of gallons of acid to the ensiled grass. The wetter the grass when stored in the pit, the more acid is needed, thus creating a vicious circle of liquid, because few farmers are equipped to handle the large amounts of noxious liquids that need to be disposed of safely. No planning controls are applied to silage pits, and this means that they have been laid down in all sorts of compromising positions, which aggravates the problem of run-off.

Farm building

Farming is singularly free of planning restrictions. To a very large extent, the authorities depend on the common sense of farmers, but this attitude allows them to build anything under a certain height anywhere they want to on their land, as long as it doesn't interfere with a stream or river, or isn't constructed right up against a public road. This liberal attitude was adopted to encourage farmers to develop their farms, without feeling that there were planning obstacles in their way. In a country where, up to a few years ago, most farm animals were wintered outdoors, it was important that housing should be provided so that cattle and sheep would thrive in the average five-month winter. Ninety-one per cent of farms with cows (either beef or dairy) now have housing for them, although only 40 per cent of farms with cattle have housing. The corresponding figure for sheep is only 5.2 per cent, but the housing of sheep in winter is still a relatively new idea, although it should catch on fast here with the renewed interest in sheep as a lucrative farm enterprise. (There were 8000 new entrants to sheep farming between 1983 and 1987.)

Soils

But, stop! We are wandering away from our main activity, which is enjoying the view across our imaginary average farm gate. What we cannot see from here is what is beneath the surface of the field in front of us. The landowner does not know either, unless

he or she is progressive enough to want to find out. You can do this by having soil tests carried out on the farm, tests that will tell what type of soils you have (and there are dozens of different ones, with all sorts of exotic names – rendzina, grey brown podsolic, regosol) as well as what elements the soil needs to make it fully productive. This is invaluable information: such tests have shown that one field in every five throughout the land is in need of at least 4 tonnes of lime per acre (about 10 tonnes per hectare) and that a similar proportion of our fields are deficient in phosphate and potash, two of the three main artificially compounded fertilisers.

The landowner must also keep an eye on the level of trace elements present in the soil. Indeed, not enough farmers realise this, resulting in a loss of thrive by the animals who eat the grass grown on the land, or loss of yield from the crops. These trace elements need to be renewed every now and then because the plants use it up quickly in modern intensive farming, and they include elements that you would think would be more appropriate in a science laboratory – copper, zinc, molybdenum, manganese, cobalt. These and many more (not all of them beneficial) are present naturally in all soils. The trick is to have soil tests done so that you know fairly precisely what elements need to be dusted onto the land or fed (or, indeed, injected) into farm animals. Precision of knowledge is necessary because toxic levels can be present or carelessly reached. From a public health point of view, for instance, farmers in one area of County Limerick were warned some years ago that toxic levels of the elements selenium and molybdenum had been discovered naturally in their soil. The public health issue arose because excessive intake of

selenium by humans has been associated with a higher than normal incidence of dental caries (bad teeth).

Drainage

Something else we can't see from where we are standing is whether the field has been artificially drained or not. There is a very strong likelihood that it has been, because nearly one-third of the land in the Republic has artificial drains running through it. This is basically because we get too much rain in this country. You knew this, of course, didn't you! But did you also know that grass needs only 400mm of rainfall each year to thrive, while we get twice that much in the driest parts of the country and four times that much in the wettest (the west, where else)?

I should not give a wrong impression here. Those figures are annual measurements averaged out over a number of years, and we do need the rain – but only at the right time of year and in the right place. An abiding memory of mine is standing in a field with a farmer friend and listening to him explaining why he desperately needed rain in the field we were in, but didn't want a drop of rain to fall on the next field.

Between 40 and 45 per cent of the annual total falls during the April-to-September period, so there is generally a fairly even distribution throughout the growing season. However, this rainfall, coupled with the shallow topsoil depth of many of our impermeable soils, gives rise to serious farming problems. If the soils are not drained, major difficulties arise for both animals and machinery. Also, the farmer may miss a critical week in the year for doing some important task, simply because the land is too wet to work on. For example, the first cut of silage should be made in the second-last week in May – not the week after or indeed the week before – for a whole variety of reasons tied in with fertilising, growth and other things. In this general context, it is said that the difference between a good farmer and a bad farmer is a fortnight!

Wet, undrained land means that the farmer finds it difficult to get out early enough in the spring with the first nitrogen application (for silage cut in May). During wet summers the land can be impassable for harvesting forage.

In addition, grazing animals often 'poach' (the farmer's term for churning up the land) the soil surface and trample a lot of the valuable grass into the mud.

So drainage is essential. In fact, responsibility for the biggest single contribution to change in the Irish countryside must be given to drainage. Without it, a substantial amount of land would be permanently fallow, there would be fewer animals on the land (good land can

support and feed an adult cow at a stocking rate of one acre (0.4ha) per animal per annum) and far fewer crops.

In the absence of any real opportunities to reclaim land from the sea, drainage of wet land is the only method we have of 'creating' land and, as such, has been used by the authorities since as far back as before the time of the Famine. In the hundred years from 1840 to 1940, the state drained about 450,000 acres through arterial (river)

Above
Oil-seed rape adds vivid colour
to this modern farm landscape
in Co. Carlow.

Opposite
In recent years there has been a
resurgence of interest in sheep
as a lucrative farm enterprise:
between 1983 and 1987 there
were 8000 new entrants to
sheep farming.

Right
Ireland is a landscape of fields,
separated each from the other
by an elaborate network of
walls and hedgerows. The
creation of the Irish fieldscape
began 5000 years ago, when the
earliest farmers began to tame
the wilderness.

drainage, equal to 4 per cent of farmland. Serious arterial drainage began in 1948, and since then just over 600,000 acres have been influenced by this work.

Not everybody is in favour of arterial drainage. It changes the landscape to such an extent that it can often evoke a generalised sense of loss in some people. Memories of picnics, walks and childhood adventures frequently centre on the nearby river which, after drainage, looks more like a geometric canal than a natural watercourse with undisturbed vegetation and associated trees, shrubbery and verges. This is not merely an Irish problem; recognition of this led the US government, for instance, to give statutory protection to what it called 'wild and scenic rivers', which cannot be modified except in exceptional circumstances.

However, arterial drainage is essential for the proper functioning of vast tracts of farmland and it is therefore no wonder that scarcely an election takes place in this country without mention being made of the really big one – the drainage of the Shannon. This would directly improve 250,000 acres (100,000ha) and would be more than twice as big as any previous scheme.

The state was much slower to get involved in field drainage. Progress was slow after the first grants were introduced in 1931, and twenty years later only 140,000 acres (56,700ha) had benefited. However, things picked up after the second world war when opportunities increased because of the start of arterial work. (There was little point in draining individual fields if the surplus water had nowhere to drain to, since the level of the nearest river was probably higher than the outfalls of the field drainage.) Better machinery also became available at this time and work took on a new lease of life, so much
190

so that between 1949 and the present, about 3.5 million acres (1.4 million ha) have been improved through land drainage, although it is reckoned that a further 3 million acres (1.2 million ha) could do with drainage.

Stock

Isn't it just amazing how long you can dally at a farm gate! So much to see and think about. And we have hardly even mentioned farm animals yet. In their own way, they have contributed to the changing colours of the countryside. In addition to the stark blacks, whites and patchy browns of the Friesian, Aberdeen Angus, Hereford and shorthorn, we now have more subtle colourings to watch out for. The pale brown-and-white of the Simmental arrived from central Europe in the early 1970s, around the same time as the deeper reddish brown of the Limousin from France. Before that, in the early 1960s, the pale, blond Charolais was introduced as a major beef breed, also from France; ten years later came the equally blond but not so pale blond d'Aquitaine, from France too.

Not so obvious has been the comparatively recent arrival of the Canadian Holstein, impossible to tell apart from its identical black-and-white cousin, the Friesian. There, though, the similarity ends because, although the Holstein is an outstanding dairy breed, its beef characteristics are almost nil and it cannot hold a candle to.the dual purpose (dairy and beef) attributes of the Friesian.

So, there you have it – a multitude of changes. Only some of them threaten our environment and, indeed, there are parts of Ireland where you would hardly know that farming is being practised at all, such is the absence of even one farm building behind the bungalow at a turn on a narrow road. But where it is being

practised intensively, greater awareness and care is called for in the future. An urban Irish society won't settle for less.

In the meantime, take advantage of our unspoilt countryside, keep your eyes open – and be sure and close that gate behind you.

PADDY SMITH is a journalist who was born in Trim, County Meath, where he has lived all his life. He commutes the thirty miles daily to Dublin, where he is editor of *The Practical Farmer*, a monthly magazine for intensive farmers, and editor of *Build*, a monthly magazine for the construction and building design industry. He is a contributor on agribusiness affairs to the weekly magazine, *Business and Finance*. Previously he was the first agricultural correspondent with RTE and he still broadcasts regularly on farming matters on *Morning Call*, RTE Radio 1. He has also worked with *The Drogheda Independent* (a weekly newspaper) and the *Irish Press* group, and is a former editor of *The Provincial Farmer*. Aged forty-four, he is married to Mary and they have three children, Barry, Elaine and Jane.

FORESTRY IN NORTHERN IRELAND

Janet Wilson

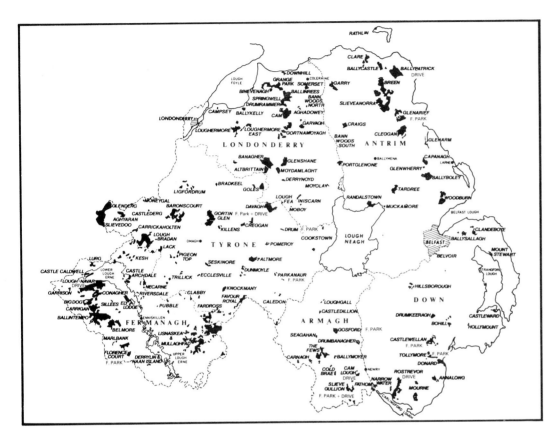

The forests of Northern Ireland

Trees are a valuable source of raw materials: coal and oil reserves, once used, are gone forever, but forests can be replaced and so represent one of the world's greatest renewable resources. They also have an important role to play in regulating the climate, and trees in the landscape are vital for the general well-being of society. Within a generation, however, most of the great natural forests of the world will be felled to meet increasing world demand for timber, and the long-term environmental consequences of this are as yet unknown. Enlightened governments now recognise the need to produce timber, for environmental as well as economic reasons, and as a result comprehensive state forestry programmes have evolved, and Northern Ireland is no exception.

State forestry in Ireland dates back to 1903, with the establishment of a Forestry Branch of the Department of Agriculture and Technical Instruction which acquired the Avondale estate in County Wicklow in 1904 and set up a forestry centre and training school. The first state forest in the north was acquired in 1910 at Ballykelly, County Londonderry. The destruction of forests during the first world war emphasised the need for home-grown timber, and in 1919 the

Forestry Commission was established and took control of forestry in Great Britain and Ireland. Following the partition of Ireland in 1921 management of Northern Ireland forestry was transferred to the Forestry Division of the Ministry of Agriculture, now the Forest Service of the Department of Agriculture. When we consider that less than 5 per cent of Northern Ireland is under woodland, compared with a European average of 21 per cent, itself rather low, and indeed that the next least-wooded country is Iceland, we begin to realise the very real need for a state forestry programme.

Forestry has certainly changed the landscape. When trees are planted one habitat is replaced by another, but with careful planning and sympathetic management, this change does not necessarily mean a loss to the environment and may bring about a range of positive benefits for people and wildlife. Indeed, as pressures on the natural environment increase, with more people seeking to use less available space, forests may well become the last major areas of countryside where public access is not restricted and where wildlife has an opportunity to flourish.

The lands controlled by the Forest Service are as varied as the province itself, ranging from the upland regions of the Sperrins and Mourne mountains to the Glens of Antrim and the Fermanagh lakelands. Several of the early acquisitions were developed around old stately homes, such as Tollymore and Castlewellan Forests in County Down, and have the added advantage of mature broad-

Timber production

The Forest Service aims to establish 120,000 hectares of state and private forestry by the end of the century. This goal could be achieved from the 340,000 hectares of marginal land in Northern Ireland. Half of this could probably be planted without detriment to agricultural production. Agriculture and the land are embedded deep in the social life of the Ulster community, however, and there is an inherent reluctance to sell land, so acquisition of new land for planting is a problem. In an attempt to attract private investment, which has an important role to play, the Forest Service provide free technical advice and have extended the planting grant scheme to encourage broadleaf planting in addition to conifers.

Most of the land that becomes available to the Forest Service is on upland peat, land of low agricultural potential. Species selected for these upland areas are limited to those able to withstand the inclement conditions and it is the sitka spruce, a tall conical tree with sharp, blue-green needles, that occupies over 60 per cent of planted areas. Other species include lodgepole and scots pine, Norway spruce, larches and firs. Within some of the upland areas there is generally a portion of land too poor to support any trees, but those areas have a value for conservation or recreation and help to diversify the forest.

Low-lying, more fertile areas and those selected specifically for amenity purposes have a higher proportion of hardwood species. Although these varieties take considerably longer to mature; over one hundred years compared with forty to fifty years for conifers; they help to diversify the environment and encourage wildlife.

Timber production generates employment in the community, from nursery to harvest,

leaved woodlands and the trappings of estate life. Others are completely artificial, such as Gortin Glen in County Tyrone, but sympathetic use of natural features in these areas has enabled them to be developed so that today they are much more than vast blocks of trees, but blend into the landscape with a fair degree of compatibility. Just as the individual character of the forests varies enormously, so too does their potential for secondary uses, and today a policy of multiple use is practised at each state forest, co-ordinating the principal aim of timber production with conservation, recreation and education.

and has spin-off in local industry. Roads are laid, areas ploughed and fertilised, young trees planted and their growth and development continually monitored. From about twenty years, forest blocks are thinned to enable the best trees to attain optimum size. Clear-felling at the end of the cycle removes all the trees from the area and so the crop rotation begins again. Just as the initial planting of areas sometimes provokes public criticism, the practice of clear-felling is also often regarded with great disdain. Undoubtedly it can have a dramatic visual impact, but modern felling policy is designed to enable cleared areas to blend into the

surroundings without the harsh, geometric edges characteristic of former days. Furthermore, felled areas are quickly re-established. Young trees are planted among the stumps of the old crop to give shelter, and nature very quickly heals the scars on the landscape.

Conservation

In the forest estates, there are at present fifty-three areas designated as nature reserves. These areas represent or protect habitats and flora or fauna unusual in the country that are of conservation or education value. The Forest Service is now committed to a policy of active conservation at all stages. All new plantings, replantings and felling areas will make provision for landscape amenity. By planning the management of forest rides, road verges and forest edges a greater variety of vegetation can be maintained, which will attract a more diverse range of wildlife. In order that stands of trees may be retained as examples of particular species of forest culture, 'heritage stands' of between one and two hectares are to be identified in each district. Gosford Forest near Markethill in County Armagh has many fine specimens of broad-leaved and coniferous trees up to two hundred years old and is being developed as a special conservation forest.

In the early days of forestry, planting schemes characterised by blanket planting of single species in solid blocks was rightly criticised for creating unnatural landscapes. Commencing in 1987, Forest Service policy will be that 5 per cent of all trees used will consist of broad-leaved species. More sensitive landscaping and greater use of hardwoods will benefit conservation and amenity interests alike.

The speed with which conifers grow means that there is a rapid change in the habitats they provide and the wildlife they attract. The rough grass that grows after fencing excludes sheep and rabbits, attracts a range of small mammals, birds and insects. These in turn are prey for a variety of predators which find plentiful food supplies and nesting sites until the canopy closes over. The population of the hen harrier, which thrives on young plantations, has significantly increased with the development of forestry in Northern Ireland. Partly as a result of moorland afforestation, the red grouse is a declining species in Ireland but, for example, management of Slieveanorra Moor in north Antrim is aimed at increasing the grouse population locally. This forest nature reserve is an unplanted upland moor surrounded by an extensive coniferous forest.

As the trees grow taller and the canopy closes the species preferring more open habitats retire. True, the conifer plantations are less well endowed with flora and fauna than mixed woodland, but they are by no means sterile. Wildlife abounds in the canopy in the form of caterpillars and moths, and squirrels and crossbills occupy the branches in search of seeds in spruce or pine cones. In autumn, the layer of needles that carpets the forest floor burst into colour with the appearance of a variety of fungi.

The seclusion of the mature conifer plantations is attractive to deer, which graze quietly on the forest rides and verges. It is assumed that deer will colonise almost all forests and suitable provision will be made to control them in the form of glades and lawns which will be integrated with new planting design. Deer can be seen by the public at a number of forests: sika deer in Gortin Glen and white fallow deer at Parkanaur, for instance.

Water is a great asset for conservation, and where lakes or ponds exist care is taken to maintain and develop them for people and wildlife. Randalstown Forest on the shore of Lough Neagh combines old natural woodland and coniferous plantations to produce a wide range of habitats supporting deer, red squirrels, pine martens, badgers and bats. The insect life along the shore attracts a great variety of birds and two lagoons support large numbers of wildfowl.

Seskinore Forest in County Tyrone is the Forest Service's game farm, rearing some twenty thousand game birds and wildfowl for release or forestry shoots annually. To many people, shooting and conservation seem to have little in common, but shooting provides a major incentive to retain both woodland and game species. If the corncrake, whose numbers have sadly declined in Northern Ireland, flew like a grouse and tasted like a pheasant, there would be many more of them because the shooting man would regard them as a priority for conservation!

Clearly, all the forests in Northern Ireland have a role to play in nature conservation. The range of sites means that somewhere in the forest estate are to be found most species of Irish land mammals and a great variety of birds. Implementation of the new conservation policy will ensure that as state forestry matures the long-term objective of conservation will benefit enormously.

Recreation

In the early 1960s a leisure boom erupted, as more money, greater mobility and vastly increased leisure time awakened public awareness of the countryside. As a contrast to the pressures of daily life, ever-increasing numbers of the urban-based population seek to visit the countryside, but because more people want to use less available space they threaten the very resource they seek. Forests have a positive contribution to make. They have a remarkable ability to absorb large numbers of recreational visitors without detriment to the environment. Trees absorb noise easily and help to screen people and activities, and so create a sense of solitude.

The idea that forests may have as much significance for their secondary uses as for their timber harvest began to be recognised by the Forest Service in the 1950s. The new concept of forest recreation was launched in 1955 with the opening of Tollymore Forest Park in County Down. Nestling at the foot of the beautiful Mourne mountains near Newcastle, Tollymore combines many attractive features of an old estate with the recent developments of the Forest Service. Basic facilities include carparks, toilets and picnic areas and whether one chooses the soft, earthy environs of the old broad-leaved woods or the sharp resinous atmosphere of the conifer plantations, a number of well-planned walks take the visitor along the Shimna river or up into the mountains. Camping and caravan sites are available for the long-stay visitor, a facility increasingly in demand.

Today there are nine forest parks in Northern Ireland. Many more small recreation areas have been developed and today no town in Northern Ireland is more than 10 miles (16km) from a forest area, although the degree of recreational development varies from place to place. Many people require no more than a place to park the car, to walk undisturbed and have a picnic, and a great number of modest sites fulfil these requirements. For those unable to participate in more active pursuits, forest drives scattered from north Antrim (Ballypatrick) to Fermanagh (Lough Navar) afford spectacular views over some of the most geologically interesting countryside. Drum Manor Forest Park near Cookstown, which has special features including a butterfly garden, has recently developed a disabled trail — a new venture for people formerly precluded from the enjoyment of these places because of difficult terrain.

Where old buildings exist care has been exercised to maintain them in harmony with the environment. Equally, where modern

A young deer safe in its bed of furze in the forest.

facilities are required, development has attempted to be sensitive to the surroundings.

Education

Forests provide an ideal setting for education: they have something to say about history, geography, art, the sciences and technology. The Forest Service actively encourages the educational use of forests and in accordance with increasing demand, has developed a number of educational facilities. These include educational trails, forest exhibits and lecture rooms with visual aids. Specialised forest guides are now available at a number of centres, their task being to identify the interests and needs of the groups or individuals with whom they are dealing and to provide material and information accordingly. An extensive range of free information leaflets is also available to schools and the general public.

A purpose-built forest education centre was opened at Belvoir Park Forest in the early 1980s. Although in extent the forest is fairly modest, situated on the south bank of the River Lagan within the Greater Belfast region, it is unique in its location on the doorstep of so many schools. A history of habitation dating from the fifth century provides many points of interest, and indeed much of the historical evolution of the region can be traced through human activity at Belvoir. The economic activities of forestry can be seen in the new plantations while a section of the forest has been set aside as a conservation area, a feature of importance not only to Belvoir but to the city as a whole. It is also the headquarters of the Royal Society for the Protection of Birds in Northern Ireland and of the Lagan Valley Regional Park. It draws together a wide spectrum of interest of benefit to schoolchildren and public alike.

The success of Belvoir prompted the Forest Service to adopt similar schemes elsewhere and today a number of forests offer educational facilities.

For the first several thousand years of human history on this island, natural forest was a part of everyday experience. The wildwood no longer survives, but the coniferous woodlands which now dominate forest landscapes in Ireland, such as here in Gortin Glen, give our children an opportunity to recapture some small spark of the atmosphere.

Larch is a native of the mountains of central Europe, and is frequently planted in forests and parks in Ireland. Unlike the other common conifers it is deciduous, and its delicate tufts of vivid-green leaves usually appear in spring long before those of broad-leaved trees.

JANET M. WILSON BA comes from a farming background and maintains a close interest in agriculture and the countryside. She undertook research at Queen's University Belfast on forest recreation in Northern Ireland and later became a forest guide with the Forest Education Centre at Belvoir Forest Park. She is particularly interested in the production of biomass as an alternative and renewable energy source.

INLAND WATERWAYS
Ruth Heard

Lining up for the Offaly Rally in 1983

Not many years ago Ireland's inland waterways lay neglected, unused and forgotten, but today, with people enjoying more leisure time, the waterways are entering on a new era. The Grand Canal, the Royal Canal and the Barrow navigation have recently been taken over by the Office of Public Works, and now almost all the waterways in the Republic are under one authority. The Commissioners of Public Works have set up a waterways division and they intend to develop the waterways not just as navigations but as 'linear parks' for all sorts of water activities and as pleasant places to walk and enjoy the natural habitat which these ribbons of water have encouraged.

The move to maintain and develop the waterways came just in time to save some of them from permanent abandonment. Sadly, two branch canals of the Grand Canal are gone beyond recall, but most of our waterways in the Republic can still be rescued. In Northern Ireland things are not so good, and the task of restoring many of the canals as navigations would be almost impossible. Even so, they are still well worth seeking out to walk along their routes.

Even if you do not have a boat, walking along the waterways is a lovely way to spend an afternoon. Canals must seek out level

ground, and so towpaths make for easy walking, cutting a quiet highway through the country, away from the noise and exhaust fumes of the roads. As part of the landscape for about two hundred years they have become a valuable habitat for all sorts of birds, wildlife and flora which need the proximity of water, and for the industrial archaeologist the canal works of the early engineers are of immense interest: the locks, attractive hump-backed bridges, aqueducts and warehouses are all worth looking at and have stood the test of time well.

The story of the canals

Why do we in Ireland have such a rich heritage of waterways? It all goes back to the 1750s. At that time the canal age was just beginning in these islands, and in England canals were being built to carry raw materials to the factories and the finished products of the Industrial Revolution to the centres of business and the ports. These canals were a good investment, yielding substantial profits for people who bought shares in them. However, it was a different story in Ireland. The Industrial Revolution failed to cross the Irish Sea. An early attempt to make the River Liffey navigable in the 1720s ended in financial failure, and it was left to the government to try to establish waterways using public funds. Commissioners of Inland Navigation were set up with funds raised by duties imposed on a wide range of luxury goods, and they set about making a canal from Lough Neagh to the sea at Newry, so that coal from the Tyrone coalfields could be transported more cheaply to Dublin.

Early attempts to make navigations had concentrated on improving the natural navigation provided by the larger rivers, cutting short canals to by-pass shallows, but

the Newry Canal was the first successful attempt in these islands to construct a watershed canal – a stillwater canal linking two river catchment areas by a series of locks which climbed up out of one basin and dropped down into the other.

With their limited funds the commissioners were not going to be able to proceed very rapidly with the establishment of a waterway network, but they did begin work on a second navigation from Lough Neagh towards the Tyrone coalfields, and they carried out surveys based on a grand concept of linking up the major rivers, the Boyne, the Barrow and the Shannon. Some work was carried out on the River Boyne and surveys were made of the Shannon. The Liffey proved unsuitable as a navigation, and a line for a canal from Dublin to the Shannon was surveyed.

At this point, in the mid-1750s, the Irish parliament found that it had surplus revenue. Because of the relationship between Ireland and Britain at the time, this surplus had to be handed over to the king across the water. The crown would probably have ploughed back this money into Ireland, but some members of the Irish parliament resented the fact that the money had to be handed over, and so they resolved that they would not have a surplus in the first place. They would absorb it by allocating money to public works and manufacturing enterprises. Making canals was a good way to use up the money, and so the Commissioners of Inland Navigation received greatly increased funds. Naturally, with all this extra cash at their disposal, they started work on a number of schemes throughout the country. There were

Opposite
Typical stone bridge over the
Grand Canal in Co. Kildare

Above
Lock gates at Naas, Co. Kildare

accusations of 'jobbing' (what we would call 'jobs for the boys' today) and the financial bonanza did not last very long. Once begun, however, most of the navigations were eventually carried through to completion one way or another in the years that followed. And so Ireland gained a waterway network, built largely with public money, far in excess of what was warranted by the amount of trade in the country at the time.

The people who were in favour of navigation works had looked on the establishment of an efficient transport system as a vital element in encouraging industrial development, but it did not work out that way. There was a great deal of political unrest in the country, investment in industries was not forthcoming and the principal commodities carried on the waterways continued to be agricultural produce.

Just when the waterways were beginning to make some small profits, the railway age arrived. The faster transport they offered quickly killed the passenger services on the waterways and a war of rates began for the commercial trade. The abandonment of the passenger boats brought to an end the colourful era of the canal hotels and the flyboats, which had travelled the canals at astonishing speeds towed by a team of galloping horses. Riding up on their own bow waves, these boats averaged 8 miles an hour (over 12km an hour), including the time taken to pass through the locks. Whatever chance the waterways had to compete with the railways for the heavier cargoes, there was little hope of coping with the added competition of road transport which emerged strongly after the second world war, and it was between the late 1940s and 1960s that the fate of many of the navigations was sealed. Fortunately, revived interest in the waterways as leisure and tourist amenities has come just in time to save most of them, and today we are still able to enjoy the heritage of our waterway system.

Following the Grand Canal

The Grand Canal starts at Ringsend basin and circles Dublin, its tree-lined banks and ribbon of water providing a welcome breathing space for the city. You have probably looked across at the old canal hotel at Portobello as you sat in a traffic jam. Recently refurbished and now an office block, it dates back to 1807 when this was open country and was the terminus for the passenger boats. It was said that 'the beauty and salubrity of the situation enlivened by the daily arrival and departure of the canal boats, render it a truly delightful residence'. But not so many people have followed the canal after it disappears towards the west at the Naas Road at Inchicore. If you would like to do this it is a good idea to get a copy of the *Guide to the Grand Canal*, published by the Inland Waterways Association with the assistance of Irish Shell. This provides maps of the canal showing the road approaches and whether the towpath is drivable or walkable. The Grand Canal was the most successful of all the waterways and the main line has remained open to navigation ever since it opened back in 1804.

Speeding along the new Naas by-pass, you may have noticed that you pass over a canal beside a mill complex. This is the Naas Canal, a branch of the Grand Canal, which was closed to navigation in 1961. Its five locks have now been restored, with new gates made by apprentices financed by AnCO, and it has been reopened. It is a most attractive stretch of canal and you can drive along it most of the way from near Sallins to the harbour at Naas; a further five miles of canal from Naas to Corbally is obstructed by a low bridge near Naas but the towpath is walkable, and the new Newbridge by-pass will soon reveal part of it to the passing motorist. Just west of Sallins you can drive along the main line of the Grand Canal for a number of miles, crossing the River Liffey by the fine Leinster aqueduct, designed by Richard Evans in the 1780s. Further west the canalside village of Robertstown in County Kildare is well worth a visit. Here is another of the old canal hotels and a walk along the towpath to the nineteenth lock at Lowtown will reveal a world of boats of all shapes and sizes. This is the summit level of the canal, 85m above sea-level, and above the nineteenth lock the main supply of crystal clear water from Pollardstown Fen enters the system. Below
200

the nineteenth lock, the Barrow line swings away to the south to join the Barrow navigation at Athy, 44km away, while the main line continues on westwards to the Shannon.

Dropping down from the eighteenth level, the canal crosses the great Bog of Allen, a remarkable piece of engineering which took ten years to accomplish; this is best viewed from the Blundell aqueduct near Edenderry. At Tullamore in County Offaly there is a fine harbour, and this is the central engineering depot for the canal. Look out for The Thatch at Rahan, west of Tullamore. A drink at this very old canalside pub can be combined with a visit to the nearby ancient churches of Rahan. Shannon Harbour, near Banagher, where the canal eventually meets the Shannon, is a popular mooring place for many boats. There is a strong atmosphere of the past, with the old buildings and ruined hotel, from the steps of which Father Mathew once administered the pledge to the assembled emigrants as they waited to board the passage boat to set out in search of a new future away from their famine-torn land.

Following the Royal Canal

It is easier to follow the eastern end of the Royal Canal, which runs close to the N4 main

Opposite
The Huband Bridge, over the Grand Canal in Dublin. The Grand Canal was the most successful of all the waterways. The main line has been open to navigation since 1804.

Milford lock as it was in 1971.

road all the way from Dublin to Mullingar in County Westmeath, but a copy of the *Guide to the Royal Canal* will again be a help. You have probably watched the canal for mile after mile if you have travelled by train from Dublin to Athlone. The Midland Great Western Railway Company purchased the entire canal back in 1845 in order to gain a convenient route for the railway to the west, a move which was to hasten the demise of this waterway. However, if you have made this journey over the years you will have noticed great things happening along the canal in recent years. It was closed to navigation in 1961 but was rescued from oblivion by a campaign launched in 1974 by the Royal Canal Amenity Group (RCAG), which was set up to revive interest in this disused waterway. Sections of it are now navigable again for small boats, and the location of new slips for launching are shown in the guide. There are quite a number of places where the motorist can seek out interesting locks, bridges, aqueducts and canalside buildings.

The Dublin end of the canal has undergone a transformation in recent years, with levels refilled, locks restored and towpaths tidied. Using funds provided principally by Dublin Corporation and Dublin County Council, materials to make the lockgates were purchased by the RCAG, and a lockgate building programme was inaugurated with the assistance of AnCO. There is an attractive walk along the towpath from Blanchardstown, on the outskirts of Dublin, to Clonsilla through the Deep Sinking; two miles of canal cut through solid rock, where the towpath in places is carried some ten metres above the canal. Travelling west along the N4 it is worth stopping off to look at the great embankment which carries the canal over the Ryewater near Leixlip, and again to inspect the restoration work at Maynooth, Kilcock and Enfield. West of Enfield, you must make a detour off the N4 to look for the

Boyne aqueduct, where the canal crosses the river by one of the finest aqueducts in Ireland. From Thomastown the canal passes up through a flight of locks to the summit level, which circles around the town of Mullingar. Westmeath County Council is restoring these locks with the co-operation of AnCO and has made the canal around Mullingar into an attractive feature.

West of Mullingar both the N4 and the railway go their different ways and it is more difficult to follow the canal, which passes out of County Westmeath in a north-westerly direction and through County Longford to join the River Shannon. At the western end of the summit level is another flight of ten locks, all of which will need to be restored, down to Ballynacargy harbour. This harbour and the thirty-sixth level have been re-watered, providing a good local amenity. The level from the thirty-eighth lock through Abbeyshrule has also been re-watered, and it is worth looking at the canal here. It crosses the River Inny near the village by another fine aqueduct, but in the village, beside the harbour, the canal is obstructed by a culverted bridge. The last 32km of the canal from the thirty-ninth lock to the Shannon present rather a gloomy picture. The canal bed is dry and overgrown and there are five more culverted bridges. There is an interesting stretch just west of Ballymahon where the canal is carried along a rocky escarpment, following the contours around Mullawornia Hill, with the ground falling away sharply on the west side and Lough Ree visible in the distance a few miles away. The towpath is just about walkable along this stretch, but it is not for the poorly shod or the faint-hearted. The Royal Canal finally meets the Shannon at Termonbarry, and there is a fine harbour here, Richmond Harbour, with

some attractive nineteenth-century buildings. The harbour was re-watered in 1972 to enable boats from the Shannon navigation to lock up into it.

The Shannon navigation

Unlike the Barrow navigation, the Shannon navigation never had towpaths; before the days of steam, the boats had to be poled or sailed up and down the river and across the lakes. For this reason it is not so easy to follow the navigation by road, but at most of the river crossings, like Termonbarry, it is worth stopping to look at the large locks which were constructed in the 1840s to accommodate the steamers on the river. These navigation works had scarcely been completed before the spread of the railway network brought severe competition. It is possible to drive down to the shore at various places around the larger lakes, and Athlone is another place where extensive navigation works were carried out: a large lock, a weir controlled by sluices and quay walls were built.

The Ballinamore and Ballyconnell navigation

Near the northern limit of the Shannon navigation is the village of Leitrim and it is here that the Ballinamore and Ballyconnell navigation started, which linked the Shannon and Erne systems. This navigation, which was never completed to its full depth, had a short working life in the 1860s during which eight boats passed through paying a grand total of £18 in tolls, a poor return for the expenditure of nearly a quarter of a million pounds of public money. After that the navigation was allowed to deteriorate and it is only in recent years that attention has once again been focused upon it. With the rapid development of pleasure traffic on both

the Shannon and the Erne, there is now a strong case for restoring this previously unwanted waterway as a joint cross-border undertaking. It is possible to follow its route by road as it rises up from Leitrim to its summit level at Lough Scur and then passes down through a series of small lakes and the Woodford river into Upper Lough Erne, near Belturbet.

The Erne navigation

The Erne navigation is principally made up of two large lakes which can be seen from the roads around them and the shores can be visited at a number of places. Upper and Lower Lough Erne are connected by the River Erne, through Enniskillen, from where there are boat trips up to the nearby Devenish island with its fascinating monastic settlement. At the southern end of Upper Lough Erne (which is the lower lake on the map!) the border passes through the navigation and the final stretch up the River Erne to Belturbet is in the southern jurisdiction.

Northern Irish canals

The Ulster Canal formerly linked Lough Erne and Lough Neagh. This canal, which is now completely derelict, can be traced here and there along its route through counties Monaghan and Armagh. It had a troubled history and was never profitable. John Macneill, the well-known railway engineer, remarked in 1861, 'The only plan. . . by which any return at all can be obtained from the undertaking. . . is to take off all the lockgates, drain the canal and convert its bed and slopes into grassland which may be let for grazing.' These were to prove prophetic words: the last boat passed through in 1929, the canal was officially abandoned two years

Ireland's Inland Waterways

Open navigations ——
Closed navigations - - - - -

Harbour Trust, which went into liquidation in 1974, and efforts are now being made to vest ownership of the canal in the local authorities of counties Down and Armagh. When this has been achieved, it is hoped that it may be possible to restore the canal, initially as a linear park and ultimately as a navigation.

The Tyrone navigation, the extension of the Newry Canal to the Tyrone coalfields, was another canal to be abandoned in the 1950s. It ran to Coalisland and, from there, efforts were made to extend the waterway right up to the collieries by using inclined planes, or 'dry hurries' as they were called locally. The boats were hauled up these slopes on rails to avoid climbing up through conventional locks. It was the first attempt to use an inclined plane in these islands, but it did not succeed. (This system was later used successfully in a number of places in England.) Some remains of these dry hurries, abandoned back in the 1780s, can still be seen today near Coalisland.

There were formerly three outlets to the sea from Lough Neagh: the Newry navigation, the Lower Bann navigation, which enters the sea through Coleraine and is still in operation today, and the Lagan navigation, part of which, sadly, is now the M1 motorway. There are moves to develop the lower end of the Lagan at Belfast and once more the irretrievable loss of part of this navigation so recently must be a source of dismay to the authorities. The old ship canal from the River

later, and parts of it were sold off to local farmers. The Ulster Canal entered Lough Neagh via the Ulster Blackwater, and the lower reaches of this river, together with the Upper Bann as far as the derelict Newry Canal and Lough Neagh itself are now much used for pleasure-boating.

The Northern Ireland authorities must be regretting the decisions made in earlier years to abandon the Ulster waterways. Parts of the Newry Canal will be familiar to anyone who has travelled by rail between Dublin and Belfast. It was that same railway which gradually deprived the canal of its trade; the last boat passed through in 1936. The canal was administered by the Newry Port and

Lock 43 of the Royal Canal

Foyle to Strabane also succumbed as long ago as the 1930s, but a ship canal from Newry to Carlingford Lough was not closed until 1966.

Southwards again

Turning south, as William of immortal memory did so many years ago, the Boyne navigation, which passes the famous field of battle, is being restored in places as a linear park and makes pleasant walking for much of its length between Drogheda and Navan. Its restoration to full navigation presents many problems but, who knows, maybe once again it will be possible to make a trip along it to visit the historic site of Newgrange.

For the enthusiast there are one or two other derelict navigations to be sought out. Efforts were made back in the mid-1700s to make the Nore navigable near Kilkenny and the Blackwater near Mallow in County Cork; neither scheme ever came to anything, but they have left their mark on the landscape. There is the Eglinton canal, which linked Lough Corrib with the sea at Galway, now spanned by a series of low bridges, and the Cong canal, which was destined to link Lough Corrib and Lough Mask but which was never completed. In between is the beautiful Lough Corrib, which today has once again come alive with boating enthusiasts. Further south, at Tralee in County Kerry, there are moves to try to restore the lock and seaward end of the old ship canal to provide a haven for the increasing number of pleasure craft visiting the area.

So, as you journey through the countryside, keep an eye out for the waterways, stop and look at them and enjoy their world of peace and tranquillity. They are a part of our heritage that we very nearly lost.

DOROTHY RUTH HEARD MLitt HDipEd (née Healy) became interested in the history of waterways when she completed a book that her first husband Vincent Delany, one of the founder members of the Inland Waterways Association, had been working on when he died. That book was *The Canals and Waterways of the South of Ireland* (David and Charles 1966), and she subsequently wrote *The Grand Canal of Ireland* (David and Charles 1973), *Ireland's Inland Waterways* (Appletree Press 1986) and *By Shannon Shores* (Gill & Macmillan 1987). She is co-author of IWAI guides to the Grand and Royal Canals, the Barrow navigation and the River Shannon. She was formerly president of the IWAI and editor of *IWAI News*. She is also interested in sailing and has cruised extensively offshore.

WOODLANDS IN NORTHERN IRELAND
Roy Tomlinson

The Beech Wood, Mourne
Park, Co. Down

How much woodland is there?

Woodlands are scarce in the northern counties of Ireland. Though no systematic survey has been done on a county basis, studies in the Mourne and Antrim areas of outstanding natural beauty (AONB) show that only 4 per cent of land that is low enough for trees to grow on is wooded. This is a very low percentage in comparison with Great Britain, which, with 8 per cent, is itself low by European standards, and in comparison with France and Germany, which have 20 per cent. (State forests which occupied 3.9 per cent of the total land area (1980) are not included; but parklands, estates and large gardens are.)

Woods ancient and modern

We had more woodland in Tudor times than now, but there were then large areas without woodland too. Most of the uplands were then, as now, unwooded, but this was not always so; peat cuttings in blanket bogs reveal many tree stumps, often of pine and birch. The pollen content of layers from the peat bogs record changes in the climate, especially towards increased wetness, which have played some part in the decline of tree cover in the uplands, but it is man who has removed most of the trees. After wooded areas were cleared in the lowlands, 'secondary forest' could establish itself, but in the uplands clearance was permanent. Once trees had been felled and agriculture practised, soils were soon acidified and eventually turned to blanket peat. Trees found it difficult to colonise boggy areas, especially once bog mosses had become established and waterlogged conditions prevailed.

Radiocarbon dating tells us that two major periods of change from mineral soil to

205

blanket peat occurred: one around 1700 to 2000 BC and the other within one or two centuries of 700 BC. The earlier period coincides with a marked agricultural expansion at the beginning of the Bronze Age, and the later is associated with renewed agricultural developments by people of the 'Dowris' period of the Bronze Age. However, there were climatic changes at the same time, so it was probably a combination of natural and human forces that led to change from woodland to peatland in the mountains and plateaux.

Secondary regrowth of woods in the lowlands ended with the English and Scottish settlements from the mid-sixteenth century onward. The land was divided into enclosed fields and farms, and woods remained only in the more inaccessible parts, on steep slopes and in incised river valleys, such as in the Glens of Antrim, the steep-sided rivers of the south-west Mournes or of the Sperrins. However, the influences of landowners were not entirely negative: towards the end of the eighteenth century, and especially in the nineteenth, when wealth from industry and commerce could be used to purchase and plant parks and estates, woods were established. General farmlands were cleared, especially when fuel could not be imported, as in the world wars, and the parks and estates now account for a high proportion of the woodlands. For example, in the Mourne AONB 54 per cent of woodlands (excluding state forests) are in parks or estate woods or around other large houses. Sadly, the twentieth century has seen very little private planting and where it has taken place it has most often been of coniferous species, particularly of spruces: thus 29 per cent of woodland outside state forests in the Mourne AONB is in coniferous plantation. Relatively

206

little, only 12 per cent, is in more 'natural' situations; half of this in 'carr' woodland (ie marshy areas of willow and alder) and the remainder along the steep-sided slopes of the incised rivers.

In the Antrim AONB relief is more marked: steep-sided slopes are more extensive and flat or gently undulating agricultural land is less common. Along the east coast in particular there are the deeply cut glens. Consequently, 47 per cent of woodland outside state forest in this AONB is found in the more 'natural' situations, with 25–30 per cent of the total woodland on hillsides and 14 per cent alongside the rivers. However, many of these more 'natural' situations have been landscaped, with specimen and ornamental trees planted by key points. Parks and estate woods constitute about 40 per cent of the woodland.

Types of tree

These parks and estates have different sorts of species, depending to some extent on the local climatic conditions: thus in the older parts of an estate in north Antrim the environment is harsher and woodlands are more exposed to westerly and north-westerly airstreams than those in south Down and nineteenth-century estates were planted largely with 'native' species, with exotics restricted mainly to the hardier conifers. In south Down, with sheltered, mild conditions, the urge to collect specimen trees from various parts of the world and to establish arboreta, had a freer rein.

Beech and elm were the most frequently planted species in north Antrim, but sessile and pedunculate oaks were widespread, and other species were used to give highlights and changes of colours and shapes to the woods – thus scots pine, silver fir, Douglas fir,

Corsican pine, larches, horse chestnuts, occasional limes, Spanish oak and Japanese cedar – most of them eighteenth- and nineteenth-century introductions – can be found. Most of these species are quite hardy and able to survive the conditions of this northern, coastal area: the relatively tender are generally found deeper into the wooded areas, where some protection is afforded by the surrounding trees.

Today, these parkland woods are no longer dominated by the species listed above, but by sycamore and ash. These must have been planted originally, but these highly successful colonisers have invaded all areas except the conifer patches and represent 16–30 per cent of the trees found in the various areas. Some parts of the older areas have been infilled also with sitka spruce and these, like the ash and sycamore, detract from the graceful lines of the original plantings.

Other estates of the north coast may be seen at Clare Park, Whitehall, Runkerry House and Magherintemple: at these beech, elm, oak and sycamore provide the main parkland trees whilst coniferous exotics are similar to those described above although Monterey pine also was found.

In the estates of south Down the plantings of native and exotic conifers were similar, but in many the range of species was extended. For example, around one large, late-nineteenth-century house in Rostrevor the grounds have a parkland appearance with beeches, oaks, elms and Spanish chestnut, but upslope a somewhat overgrown arboretum is found which contains cork oak, Oregon myrtle (Californian laurel), sweet bay, *Pittosporum*, red oak, atlas cedar, oval-leaved southern beech and Spanish fir. Many of these species are mid-to-late-nineteenth-century introductions to the

The Minnowburn Beeches, just south of Belfast, has a fine stand of beech trees, some dating from the first half of the nineteenth century.

British Isles and were clearly adopted as part of the planning of the house and grounds. In a similar fashion a park further east along the north shore of Carlingford Lough is a reflection of its time. This house too is a late-nineteenth-century structure: to the north side an eighteenth-century parkland of open pastures and groups of beeches, elms and ash is found, but to the west, where rocky knolls outcrop in the grassland, a Victorian 'highland' was created with abundant use of scots pine. To the south of the house, leading down to the shore, formal gardens are interplanted and fringed with a wide range of exotics. Amongst coniferous species found are west Himalayan spruce, monkey puzzle, wellingtonia, white cedar, Algerian fir, coast redwood and the deodar, whilst other trees include the orange-barked myrtle, sweet bay, blue gum and chusan palm.

Other woodlands

Variations in local climates have favoured or limited the species planted in estates, but other features such as rock and soil types affect the woodlands of the more 'natural' locations. In the northern counties rock types vary from the calcareous limestone and chalk through to acid, igneous rocks and sands and gravels of glacial origin and these affect soils. Soils vary also in drainage so that wet, inter-drumlin hollows and lake margins may be occupied by carr woodland, whereas the slopes, particularly in areas of limestone or chalk, will be well drained.

Ash woods

Ash is common in woodlands throughout the north of Ireland; it is an invasive species and is becoming more plentiful. This widespread occurrence and expansion originates from the hedgerow plantings of nineteenth-century field enclosure. In the Carboniferous limestone area of Fermanagh, steep-sided valleys and slopes beneath cliffs and around the larger sinkholes are occupied by ash woodland. Two sites have been given national nature reserve status – Hanging Rock and Marble Arch – and both have good stands of ash. In the latter case, 'landscapers' have been active and have introduced beech, oak and conifers, but substantial areas of dominant ash remain. Accompanying species include birch, willow, wych-elm, alder and rowan, while hazel is a common undershrub, together with some hawthorn. Ground flora is dominated by umbellifers, including wild angelica and pignut, but bluebell and meadowsweet are common.

Hazel woods

Hazel woods are dominant on the steep chalk slopes of the Antrim glens, although hazel is a common undershrub in many woodlands elsewhere. Examples of well-grown hazel woods include those of Straidkilly, the eastern Garron slopes and Glenariff. In Glenariff the most extensive stretch of dense hillside woodland occurs on the western slopes between Glasmullen and Kilmore townlands: this is typical hazel woodland on steep, till-covered, chalk slopes beneath the basalt cliffs, although even this has not avoided the individual occurrence of planted species – though in some cases the trees are possibly 'escapes'. Over 50 per cent of trees in this area are hazel, with ash as the next most abundant species and the most common

standard tree: indeed silver birch is the only other common standard. Other species include sycamore, goat willow, mountain ash and individuals of wych-elm, European larch, beech and holly.

The ground flora is extremely rich, containing many spring-flowering species which add to the attractions of the woodland at that season. Primroses, violets and bluebell are common, but there are extensive areas of wood garlic, barren and wild strawberry, wood anemone, wood sorrel and herb robert amongst others. Ferns are also plentiful, including lady fern, male fern and hard fern while woodrush, wood sedge and ground ivy are common.

Oakwoods

Oakwoods can be found in relatively inaccessible areas throughout the north of Ireland; some have been presumed to be natural successors to original woodland as, for example, the Rostrevor National Nature Reserve in County Down or Breen NNR in County Antrim. Other oakwoods have been planted as part of landscaping, but even so may occupy sites which have always been wooded, for instance, in the valleys of the Low Mournes; in yet other cases, such as around Craignamaddy in County Tyrone the history of the woodland is unknown, although they are shown on maps dating from 1813.

Breen oakwood has been surveyed and its ecological history examined: there were two clearances, followed by recolonisation by the trees, which may suggest that not all the treed areas were removed, perhaps because the

Opposite
Plantation perched on rolling
open countryside

Right
Oakwood, Breen National
Nature Reserve, Co. Antrim

woodland occupies very steeply sloping glacial spillways and intervening ridges. Clearance of the steepest valley sides would have been extremely difficult, so trees surviving here could recolonise the cleared areas. Today 35 per cent of the trees are of sessile oak and 5 per cent pedunculate oak: 32 per cent are birch which have a clear distribution – they predominate on the flat ridge-tops between the spillways where drainage is relatively poor, and for similar reasons on the upper, moorland slopes towards the edge of the wood. Mountain ash, hazel, willow, alder and some sitka spruce are found, and there are scattered individuals of scots pine – the latter two species indicating that people have been active in recent times. In recent years seedlings of oaks have been planted in an attempt to conserve the wood, since many of the existing oak trees are post-mature or reaching that state. The shrub layer at Breen is not well developed, with fairly isolated individuals of holly, hawthorn, hazel and mountain ash. Most of the oak trees are multiple-stemmed and this may indicate a coppice history, and may also be a reason for the poorly developed shrub layer. Ground flora is likewise poor, but this results from the removal of grazing from most of the reserve, so that woodrush has now taken over.

The oak woodland at Ballyberidagh North, in Glenshesk in Antrim, is almost certainly planted: nearly 40 per cent of the trees are hybrid oaks and a further 28 per cent sessile oaks; ash is the only other abundant tree, though hazel forms a good shrub layer in

209

more open parts: a few larch and birch also occur. This woodland, which so emphasises the sweep of the incised tributary river, is only a part of extensive landscaping which has taken place in Glenshesk.

Riverine woodland in Glenshesk has no one dominant species but is a true mixed woodland of ash, hazel, sessile oak, alder, sycamore and birch with lesser quantities of willows, mountain ash and, a most attractive spring feature, bird cherry. The grouping and distribution of many of these species and additional specimen trees indicate that though the riverine woodland may occupy native woodland sites it has been much modified. Nowhere is this better seen than from Glenshesk Bridge, where the variations in tones, textures, shapes and forms may be appreciated: here the woodlands act as frames through which distant views of the glen may be glimpsed – the romanticism of the painter brought to life in the work of some nineteenth-century landscape architect.

Woodlands in the landscape

Woodlands play a major part in making particular landscapes attractive and it is vitally important that their role is understood if the countryside is to be conserved for future generations. Nor is such conservation merely to please a small lobby: even in these troubled times in Ireland, tourism produces considerable benefits to the economy – both to the governments and people as a whole, and to residents of the attractive areas.

Perhaps the most important quality of any landscape is that of unity; the view can be appreciated without any jarring intrusions. Such unity exists in all aspects of the physical and cultural environment – the grain of landforms, which includes the trend of the hills and their constituent rocks; landforms
210

themselves, their shape and slopes; the skies, including the prevailing cloud forms; the division of the land into fields, their shape and the nature of their boundaries; farms, houses and settlements and the materials from which they are constructed; the crops and natural vegetation. Unique combinations of form and shape, colour and tones and textures create the distinctive landscapes found in the north of Ireland as the following examples demonstrate.

The High Mournes have landforms which rise to spectacular peaks, though they are not towering sharp 'horns' as in the Alps. Even the faulted, glaciated valleys with their steep slopes, for example the Rostrevor valley, are not harsh; but if there is anywhere in the Mourne AONB where coniferous plantations can be established without damage to the landscape, and indeed where they will be in unity with the landforms, then it is here. This has been appreciated by both nineteenth-century planters and the present-day Forest Service, but the two types of plantation offer a differing appreciation of landscape unity: the Batt estate of the last century has species arranged in a less regular manner, with a lower density and a greater irregularity of shape; the Forest Service plantations, on the other hand, are regular, dense and geometric in outline. Whereas the Batt plantations complement the grain of the landforms and their constituent rocks, the more recent plantations blanket the slopes – unity in diversity has been replaced by uniformity.

Form and shape relate not only to trees *en masse*, but to individual trees and to the species. Coniferous plantations have a serrated outline because of the conical, layered growth form of individual trees. Whereas the sky and light may be seen through, for example, the ash tree in a

random, irregular fashion, this is not the case with a spruce, where foliage is solid except between the annual whorls of branches. Not all conifers, however, have the same growth form; the scots pine is less regular in branching habit and larch less dense in foliage, and these species do not therefore have the same harshness of outline. This is another reason for the attractiveness of the Batt estate – the tree forms, as well as the plantation forms, are in harmony with the landforms.

The colours and tones of a landscape are a product of the rocks, soils and plants and vegetation growing on them. A hillside may have a number of colours: on the western slopes of Altataggart mountain the greys of rock outcrops mix with reddish soils in some areas and dark grey-green in others. Vegetation varies from the yellow-greens of the boggy areas to the brownish greens of the moors. However, vegetation changes colour seasonally; in spring bracken and purple moor grass are bright, light greens but in autumn the former has turned golden brown and the moor grass is a pale oatmeal. If unity is to be maintained, then the trees in these landscapes must complement the colours: blocks of spruce are a solid blue-green colour not found in these landscapes at any season. A mix of scots pine and larch, scattered less regularly across the hillside of Altataggart, in the Batt estate, does complement the colours and tones of that hillside.

The mixture of species in a woodland not only creates tonal variation but also textural patterns. Individual species have differing branching habits, crown shapes, leaf sizes and shapes and they attain different heights and crown widths. All these factors create an uneven surface, a varied texture. If woodlands are to maintain the unity of a landscape they must have a texture which complements the landforms: on the slopes of Altataggart there is a linear texture to the rock and landforms, and the broken, linear texture of the woodland therefore complements the slopes.

Glendun in County Antrim contains some of the most splendid woodlands found in the north of Ireland; the jewel must be Craigagh Wood – its position on a spur at the narrow opening to the upper glen is like a pendant; just as the large necklace jewel attracts the eye leading it to other parts of interest, so too does Craigagh Wood. On the north side of the valley it receives sunlight which brings out the warm tones and as the woodland bends round the hill so the trees cast shadows or attract shafts of light and, particularly in autumn, behave like some roughly cut ruby. Here is a prime example of how woodland can not only be in unity with its surroundings but can embellish the scene. Mourne Park is another such example, and in particular Beech Wood on the south-facing slopes of Knockchree on the northern edge of the park. Here trees curve around the hillside in a broad band which gradually thins to moorland upslope: their form, textures and colours blending with those of the land and yet also drawing the eye even when viewed from considerable distances.

Hillside woodland is essential to the landscape of Glenariff occurring in a discontinuous band between the pasture below and craggy cliffs of basalt above. The rounded billowy forms of ash and horizontal canopy of hazel complement the harsh, angular lines of the basalt sheets – one softening the lines and the other echoing them though in a gentler form. The colours and tones of the wood carry the green pastures through to the brown-grey of the basalt and

the wood prevents a sharp dividing line between living pasture and sterile basalt. How such unity contrasts with areas of modern planting! Could anything be more eloquent than the example to be seen at Robin Young's Hill where plantations are perched on rolling, open countryside?

Conservation

Woodlands are a vital part of the countryside of the north of Ireland, both from the points of view of nature conservation and countryside conservation, and yet many threats hang over them. A high proportion of the woodland is in parks and estates where trees are vulnerable to the high costs of replacement and financial difficulties of estate upkeep. Such areas are not open to the public, but through their contribution to the panorama, are of direct importance to the general public: so should public monies be spent to aid the upkeep of these areas? Equally, many of the more 'natural' locations have been landscaped in the past; as these trees reach post-maturity how are they to be replaced? Should the taxpayers replace the private benefactor and if so should a programme of education be launched not only to convince them that their money should be so spent but also that they should refrain from using woodlands? Here the two arms of conservation come together – nature conservation and scenery; for example, can farmers be persuaded to fence off woodlands to allow species to regenerate naturally and can they be educated not to use them for firewood or hedge-fillers? If species can regenerate not only is the composition of the woodlands saved but also their appearance.

Composition and appearance depend also on other factors of management; there is some suggestion that hazel woodland needs

to be coppiced if it is to retain its vigour and if it is not to be converted into high 'forest' with a dense canopy. Such a conversion would result in the loss of highly varied ground flora. Coppicing needs to be done correctly, under a strict rotation and keeping the coppiced area free from grazing, otherwise regeneration will be hindered. How is this to be organised, superintended and paid for? Coppicing is not pretty – how is it to be done and yet maintain the landscape value?

Sycamore and ash pose other problems: their invasive nature not only leads to a reduction in species variety but in landscape value, for tonal, textural and morphological interest is lost when they dominate. Ring-barking and other forms of removal have been done in isolated areas but it is a general problem – again who organises and who pays? If species variety is to be maintained, and species are not regenerating naturally, then planting of saplings needs to be done – but by whom?

DR ROY TOMLINSON is a lecturer in Geography at Queen's University Belfast and he formerly lectured at the University of Rhodesia. His research interests include peatlands, woodlands, remote sensing and the geography of the USSR. He has published over forty papers and articles on varied topics.

CULTIVATING THE COUNTRYSIDE
Farming Landscapes in Northern Ireland
James Armstrong

Agriculture employs some 9 per cent of the workforce of Northern Ireland and farmers are probably the largest group of self-employed persons. Dairy and beef cattle are of prime importance in the farming system, with farmyard enterprises – mainly pigs and poultry – playing a secondary, but useful role in supplementing farm income. As a result, the farming landscape is dominated by grassland. Yet there are very distinctive farming landscapes too, and more variety than you might think. Here we will take a look at only a selection of Northern Ireland's farming landscapes.

The crops being grown, the livestock present in the landscape, the size and shape of fields and the architecture of farm dwellings and outbuildings tell the story of settlement of the land and the way of life of farming people. Over the centuries, there have been many changes in the crops grown and livestock produced, methods of husbandry, levels of mechanisation and numbers employed. The pace of change has been particularly rapid since the second world war and the rural way of life has changed dramatically, though the farming landscape still retains evidence of the old way of life that is part of the heritage of perhaps the majority of families in Northern Ireland. Now in the mid-1980s there is a heightened awareness of yet further dramatic changes to come as the role of farmers and farming in an urbanised society is being reviewed.

To the town dweller, the use of taxes to grant-aid land and farm improvements which are sometimes harmful to the environment and to increase the output of products which are already being stockpiled at great cost is nothing short of a public scandal. This situation has existed for the past twenty years, but price subsidies have protected the

farming industry from the consequences. There is the political will to change all this, but the farming community has been protected for so long that it is now particularly vulnerable, and the process of adjustment to a new role over the next few decades is going to be all the more difficult.

Fruit and vegetables in Down and Armagh

Although horticulture accounts for only a small part of total farm output, its spatial concentration into a few areas gives rise to some very distinctive landscapes. The two best known are the Comber area of north

Down and the orchard country of north Armagh.

Around the end of June or early July the Comber growers produce the first local potatoes of the new season and consumers breathe a sigh of relief because thereafter the price usually begins to fall. The scene in the photograph (see page 212) includes a crop of potatoes which is being harvested. The tractor is probably being used to operate a potato spinner which throws the new potatoes out of the drill so that they can be easily seen and lifted by the team of gatherers. This area also produces a wide variety of field vegetables – carrots, parsnips, cabbage, brussels sprouts – and in the foreground there is a healthy crop of cauliflower. Market gardening is well suited to the alluvial soils on the flat or gently sloping land on the northern shores of Strangford Lough. The higher ground rising to the well-known landmark of Scrabo Tower, is devoted to cereals, which are just beginning to ripen, potatoes and grass. Climate, soil and proximity to Belfast explain the location of the market gardening, but there is also a strong sense of tradition in the area, with farming families having produced more or less the same range of crops over several generations. Most farms are large enough to maintain a comfortable standard of living and their neat appearance reflects careful husbandry and a pride in the job which insists that every crop drill is absolutely straight. An expanding market for the vegetables they produce probably means that dramatic change in this way of life is very unlikely.

Bramley seedling apples from the drumlin country of north Armagh, some of which are being harvested in the photograph on page 216, are respected throughout Britain and Ireland for their culinary qualities. Orchards are mainly concentrated in an area which surrounds the village of Loughgall, up to a radius of about 9–16km. Although climate and soil conditions are favourable, they are not exclusive to this area and the importance of apple-growing must also be attributed to the enthusiasm of the English settlers who compelled their tenants to plant orchards from the middle of the seventeenth century.

Planting an orchard is a long-term investment and many of them are over sixty years old. Traditional husbandry systems favoured the use of large, umbrella-shaped trees, which produce an almost complete canopy at about 4m. Modern systems use a

Left
A midsummer scene on the northern shores of Strangford Lough. Field production of vegetables, particularly early potatoes, is the dominant farming activity in the area.

Right
The Myroe Polderland, Co. Londonderry. Much of this land is below sea-level. It was reclaimed from the sea in the middle of the nineteenth century by building a wall to retain the sea and pumping the drainage water from the ditches and lagoons immediately behind the wall.

Hill-farming in the Sperrin mountains. Here at the physical margin of agricultural production, the human imprint on the landscape is much less assertive, and there is an attractive blend of artificial and natural features.

smaller tree, such as those in the photograph, which fruit earlier and are easier to spray and pick. The apple-growing area is particularly worth a visit at blossom time in May, but those who prefer fruit should wait until late September or early October. Apple-picking provides a useful source of seasonal employment for local people, and although the season is very short, a good picker can make a useful wage while it lasts. The development of local processing, storage and marketing facilities in the last fifteen to twenty years has almost eliminated reliance on the fickle prices offered by English buyers.

214

This, along with expansion of the market in the EEC, will probably ensure that the only landscape changes in this area will be those reflecting further changes in husbandry or marketing techniques. News of these new techniques does not have to travel far, because most of the field trials are carried out at the horticultural research centre in Loughgall.

Cash crops around Lough Foyle

The farming landscape of north Derry or Londonderry is quite distinctive for a number of reasons. Cash-cropping is an important

enterprise and some farms have no livestock of any kind, while many concentrate on winter feeding rather than summer grazing. Farms are larger than the Northern Ireland average and much of the land is renowned for its high yielding capacity. The wealth accrued from farming large acreages of good land is reflected in the scale of the outbuildings and size and style of the farmhouses.

Examples of this type of farming can be found almost anywhere in the valleys of the Strule, Foyle or Roe, but it reaches its purest form on the Myroe polderland. This large area of almost completely flat land was reclaimed from the shores of the Foyle estuary by the London companies in the nineteenth century. Much of it is below sea-level and successful farming depends on pumps which drain large ditches which run parallel to the sea dykes. Individual fields of 30–50 acres (12–20ha, the equivalent of the average Northern Ireland farm) are quite common. The farmhouses, many built in red brick, imitate the style of prosperous English farmhouses. Cricket is a very popular sport and the association of well-kept greens, roadside pubs, red-brick houses and large fields of cereals creates an atmosphere which is perhaps more English than Irish.

Farming practices and the social structure of this area have changed greatly in the last two decades. The acreage devoted to cereals, particularly winter wheat and barley, has increased since entry to the EEC in 1973. The substitution of machinery for labour has reduced employment and in the last inter-censual period the electoral ward containing this area suffered one of the highest rates of population decline in Northern Ireland. Larger combines, tractors and seed drills require larger fields to work economically and many hedgerows have been removed to accommodate them. Those that remain are trimmed back to the minimum size. The result is that this farming landscape may be pleasant to look at but its natural habitats and wildlife are scarce.

This farming system is under pressure, since wheat, beef and milk are the products most in surplus in the EEC, while competition from Dutch producers in particular is reducing the profitability of both seed and food potato production. In order to maintain profit margins, farmers have already begun to diversify by including oil-seed rape, peas and beans in their cropping system. The oil-seed rape adds vivid colour to the landscape in May but an obnoxious odour during desiccation in August. There is no doubt that this north Derry area will continue to support prosperous farming into the foreseeable future, but in this progressive farming community farming practices will continue to change rapidly.

Small-holdings on the Kilkeel plain

Around the town of Kilkeel, the Mourne mountains do not run down to the sea. Between the two there is a relatively flat area known as the Mourne or Kilkeel plain. High and carefully built stone walls are the most distinctive feature of this landscape, particularly where the fields are small. Farms are also small, but they are very carefully farmed and the farmers are noted for their thrift. Neatly built and well-maintained walls, farmhouses and outbuildings all reflect this.

The slightly acidic but well-drained soils are particularly well suited to seed potato production and this cash-crop has been an important source of income for the small farms, but prices are declining as Northern Ireland struggles to retain its share of the export market. Sheep are an important livestock enterprise and flocks have expanded considerably since the introduction of the EEC sheepmeat marketing regime in 1979. However, larger farms would be required to produce a reasonable family income. When land does become available for either renting or purchase there is a lot of competition between local farmers to acquire it. The result is that the cost of farm enlargement becomes very high and particularly when interest rates increase, the viability of the whole holding can be threatened.

Most families would be very reluctant to give up their land and home, but they may be forced to look outside the farm for employment and income. If the time available or their enthusiasm for farming declines, maintenance of the walls, gates, buildings and lanes, which is crucial to the preservation of amenity in the landscape, can also decline.

Less favoured areas

Some 75 per cent of the land in Northern Ireland has been defined as 'less favoured' according to the terms of an EEC directive which makes provision for the payment of extra state aid to farmers in areas so designated. In general terms, less favoured areas are described as those liable to rural depopulation, but the specific criteria on which they are designated are poor land, low population density, a heavy dependence on farming and low farm incomes. Two quite different types of physical environment are included in Northern Ireland: the poorly drained lowlands of Fermanagh and west Tyrone and the hill lands of the Mournes, the Sperrins and the Antrim plateau.

In Fermanagh the poor drainage can be attributed to the high rainfall and an impervious boulder clay moulded into drumlins by retreating ice. The inter-drumlin hollows collect water which has no outlet and on the slopes of the drumlins the clay retains large quantities of moisture. The widespread wet soil conditions are more amenable to rush than grass growth and despite the use of chemicals to eradicate these rushes, they readily reinvade the pasture, particularly if it has been cut up by grazing livestock. Generally in Fermanagh the problem has increased over the last two decades as tillage has almost completely disappeared, tractors and higher stocking densities have caused greater soil compaction and disturbance and the old hand-built stone drains, made in the days when labour was both plentiful and cheap, have collapsed. Not only do rush-infested fields have a low grazing capacity, but for most of the year their dun colour and dishevelled appearance produce a strong atmosphere of dereliction in the landscape.

The higher ground is mostly covered in a scrub in which hazel is the main species, and it represents quite a different natural environment. The western edge of County Fermanagh is dominated by a limestone upland, similar to the Burren in Clare but unique in Northern Ireland. Very thin soils and many rock outcrops have discouraged the use of fertilisers and cutting for hay and silage. Natural species have therefore been allowed to survive and some of these plant communities are being designated as areas of scientific interest.

Sheep graze these uplands but the poorly drained lowlands, including most of the farms, are only suitable for cattle grazing. The production of beef-type calves from suckler cows is the main type of farming. In the less favoured areas each grazing ewe and suckler cow entitles its owner to claim an annual payment to compensate for the higher costs of farming in this difficult environment. In some years many farms will depend on these allowances for their incomes and they are at least partly responsible for the increase in stocking density that has taken place since entry into the EEC. During particularly wet seasons, such as the summers of 1985 and 1986, these cattle roam the soft pastures in search of scarce grass and the result is widespread destruction of the grass sward and soil structure which takes years to repair.

Farmers in the less favoured areas are also eligible for higher rates of grant for farm

216

Apple-picking in Co. Armagh

improvements. Following the release of additional funds for this purpose in 1981 the level of grant aid for some improvements reached 70 per cent of the total cost. On this wet land cattle must be wintered indoors, and a large proportion of farms have erected a modern range of buildings, clad in shining corrugated iron. A particularly high rate of grant was available for the improvement of farm roads and many lanes leading to farmhouses, and other less useful destinations, were relaid in concrete. On exposed positions in upland areas they appear as white scars on the landscape. On the upland limestone areas scrub clearance has destroyed both valuable natural habitats and grazing capacity by denuding much of the area of its thinly distributed soil. Investment in these schemes may provide a temporary boost to local employment, but their impact on farm output and incomes is often questionable.

However, a new era in farm policy is just beginning. In the last few years the level of grant aid has declined considerably and it is now being proposed that grants for farm improvements should not be available if the

objective is to increase the output of milk, beef or wheat. The hill livestock compensatory amounts are unlikely to increase. The future for the small-scale livestock farmer in the less favoured areas is therefore particularly bleak and unless some alternative source of employment and income can be found on the farm then these family farms may soon disappear.

Hill-farming in the Sperrins

The landscape of the upper reaches of the Glenelly valley in the Sperrin mountains in many ways is representative of hill-farming areas throughout Northern Ireland. The physical margin of agricultural production is marked by the transition of the enclosed and improved grassland into open rough grazing on the higher ground. The gentle slopes of the summit are covered in blanket peat and the rush-infested fields in the top left of the photograph on page 214 also indicate poor drainage. However, on the steeper slopes to the right and in the foreground, where drainage is better, a bracken-covered hill merges into clean pasture at lower altitudes. An irregularly shaped field on the left still retains the evidence of hand-dug potato beds, possibly dating from the nineteenth century and surviving because the irregular shape and terrain in that field has inhibited mechanised cultivation subsequently.

The glen in the middle of the scene which contains both natural deciduous trees and planted conifers, the irregular field patterns and the gradual transition from improved land to open hill, create an attractive blend of artificial and natural features which is typical of areas near to the physical margin of agricultural production.

There is also evidence that the grip of human beings on this environment has been slipping. The abandoned potato beds, the encroachment of the hill back onto previously improved fields and the derelict farmhouse are all signs of a retreat which may have started in the nineteenth century. As in Fermanagh, the small mixed livestock farms have been heavily dependent on hill livestock compensatory payments and other sources of state aid for agriculture in the less favoured areas. Particularly since the second world war subsidies have acted as a brake on the rate of retreat from hill-farming, without ever providing a comfortable lifestyle for the small farm family. If the support for farming declines, then these rural communities may simply disappear. It would seem to be widely accepted that the social, cultural, economic and environmental repercussions would be undesirable. However, a rural development policy which reconciles the need for physical and economic development (better housing and more jobs) with soundly based conservation objectives (preservation of landscape amenity and areas of scientific interest) still has to be developed. At the same time, alternative strategies for economic development must recognise the existing and future role of multiple job-holding in a marginal area where farming, forestry and tourism are coexisting land uses.

Farming practice and changing landscapes

There are few landscapes in Northern Ireland which are totally unaffected by farming practice. The different combinations of fields, boundaries, roads, buildings, crops and livestock frequently enhance landscape amenity. In other cases, for example the orchard country of north Armagh, the landscape is entirely dominated by the features of the farming system. At the same time, recent additions to the farming landscape can destroy amenities while some husbandry techniques can reduce both the extent and diversity of natural habitats.

The details of the farming landscape often give a glimpse of the past, while allowing a consideration of the state of farming today and some speculation on how that landscape might respond to clearly defined forces of change, such as the reduction in the level of state support for types of farming whose products are already in surplus. Dairy farming, which is the dominant activity in most lowland areas, has already had to respond to measures aimed at reducing output. The ability of these farms to produce large quantities of good-quality grass and high levels of management generally will provide them with enough room for manoeuvre, and it is likely that the dominance of grassland and dairy cows in Northern Ireland's farming landscapes will continue. Arable farmers are being encouraged to diversify into new crops. The introduction of some of these, for example oil-seed rape, can have a very vivid impact on the landscape, while others such as peas and beans might bring about a welcome reduction in the dependence on artificial fertilisers. However, the whole future of farming in the less favoured areas is under threat. As joint custodians of the countryside, these farmers make an important contribution to the maintenance of amenity and the environment. If further dereliction and decay are to be avoided, then there is a need for an alternative rural development strategy which will maintain the existing population.

JAMES ARMSTRONG is a graduate of the Department of Geography at Queen's University Belfast. He has taught at the University of Exeter and at Queen's.

NATIONAL PARKS IN THE REPUBLIC

Alan Craig

Left
The Colleen Bawn caves at Killarney are made of limestone which has been honeycombed by the erosive action of the acid water at a time of higher lake level.

Opposite
The Connemara National Park is renowned for the great diversity and interest of its flora, which includes those rare plants of North American or Mediterranean origin which so fascinate botanists, and for the extraordinary quality of its ever-changing light and colour.

There have been parks in state ownership in Ireland for a long time, but it is only in recent years that the concept of national parks, in the internationally accepted sense of the term, has been applied here. The International Union for the Conservation of Nature criteria for national parks and equivalent reserves include the presence of outstanding natural features, extensive size, effective protection by a central government authority, and admission of visitors.

The two fundamental purposes of national parks are conserving natural features, while providing for public enjoyment of them. Reconciling these dual purposes if they conflict is the basic dilemma of national park management.

Irish parks

The first park entrusted to the care of the Commissioners of Public Works was Phoenix Park, Dublin, which has been their responsibility since 1860. Although it is of national significance, it is not a national park

in the sense described above. It is now regarded, on the basis of its historic landscape character, as one of a separate, distinct category of national historic parks.

In 1932 the Bourn Vincent Memorial Park, County Kerry, formerly known as the Muckross estate, was given to the Irish nation by Mr and Mrs A.W.B. Bourn and Senator Arthur Vincent. The Commissioners of Public Works were charged with the responsibility to 'maintain and manage the park as a national park for the general purpose of the recreation and enjoyment of the public'. This park, over 4000 hectares in extent, had the potential to be a national park in the full modern sense of the term. However, few changes took place in the early years of the park's existence. Although the park was open to the public, it was managed primarily as an extensive farm, as it had been when in private ownership. Tourism had not then assumed its present importance in the national economy, and ecology and conservation of the natural heritage were the

concern of only a few scientists and amateur naturalists. It was not until the 1960s, when several changes were proposed, that the future management of the park became a matter of public concern.

In 1969 the various parts of the Office of Public Works concerned with conservation of aspects of the national heritage were brought together as the National Parks and Monuments Branch. The branch was authorised to pursue a development policy in relation to national parks. The approach to national parks in other countries, particularly the USA, having been studied and considered, the international concept of a national park already described was adopted as the right one for Ireland. Development of a network of national parks was further stimulated by subsequent events including European Conservation Year 1970, the Stockholm Conference on the Human Environment and the Second World Conference on National Parks, both in 1972. As a result of the development policy, Ireland now has three

national parks and the nucleus of a fourth.

The Killarney district, where the Bourn Vincent Memorial Park is situated, is internationally renowned for its scenic beauty, and its ecological interest is equally great. In recent years further lands and waters have been acquired and added to the park. Killarney National Park comprises the mountains and woods surrounding the lakes of Killarney, as well as the three lakes themselves. The Killarney oakwoods, most of which are within the park, form the largest remaining area of the oakwoods that once covered much of Ireland. Their oceanic character is reflected in an abundance of mosses, liverworts and lichens growing on the trees and on the ground, and of evergreen trees and shrubs, particularly holly. The yew woods of Muckross, with trees rooted in crevices in almost bare limestone, have few parallels elsewhere. The extensive bogs of the uplands, though not unique in Ireland, are quite rare on an international scale. Red deer roaming the uplands are the only wild herd of large mammals of native origin left in the country. Also of great interest is the occurrence of arbutus (strawberry tree) and other plants usually found in southern and south-western Europe.

Glenveagh National Park in north-west Donegal, officially opened to the public in 1986, was formerly an enormous private estate almost 10,000 hectares in extent. Like Killarney, it has beautiful lakes set in impressive mountain scenery, but the character of the landscape is quite different. There are ecological similarities too, in the form of natural woodlands, mainly of oak and birch, though these are less extensive than in Killarney; larger tracts of bog and moorland; and red deer, differing from those of Killarney in that they are not of native Irish stock. No roads run through the heart of the park, and many square miles of glen and mountain show no direct signs of human activity. This wilderness character, with the sense of remoteness and solitude that it conveys to the visitor, is perhaps the outstanding feature of Glenveagh.

Connemara National Park in west Galway, open to the public since 1980, stretches from sea-level at Letterfrack up to some of the peaks of the Twelve Bens mountains. Its rugged hills and mountain slopes of quartzite and schist are mainly covered by blanket bog and wet heath vegetation, with varied wildlife. There are plans to establish a second section of this park in the contrasting rocky lake-strewn landscape to the south, near Roundstone, where expanses of blanket bog support several rare heathers.

The grey limestone hills of the Burren in County Clare appear from a distance to be devoid of vegetation. Actually they support a profusion of colourful wild flowers, often growing in narrow fissures on the limestone terraces. Many of these flowers are rare elsewhere, and the combination of plants usually found in Arctic regions or on high mountains with others from southern Europe is remarkable. There is little surface water in the Burren, but turloughs (temporary lakes) are a feature of the eastern edge of the region, where the nucleus of a future national park has been acquired.

Conservation

While the emphasis in the national parks is on nature conservation, they all contribute to conserving features of our cultural heritage also. Both Killarney and Glenveagh National Parks include former stately homes: Muckross House – now housing a folk museum – and Glenveagh Castle respectively, together with outstanding gardens with fine plant collections. Muckross Abbey, Ross Castle and other monuments are within the park at Killarney, while Connemara National

Part of the recently acquired Glenveagh National Park

Park contains remains of two neolithic court tombs, as well as many other features associated with centuries of agricultural land use.

Conservation of national park features cannot always be achieved just by leaving them alone. Often active management is necessary, which must be based on careful scientific research. One problem which has been the subject of study in Irish national parks is the spread of rhododendron. This vigorous shrub was introduced to Ireland in the nineteenth century by private landowners, partly because of its attractive flowers. It now spreads actively on acid soils, and threatens to destroy oakwoods in Killarney and Glenveagh. No easy solution to this problem has yet been found but clearance work is proceeding well. Research has also been carried out on deer and their management. In the past, deer populations may have been controlled by natural predators such as wolves, but these no longer exist in Ireland. Park managers have to intervene to maintain deer populations at satisfactory levels by humane means, and so prevent damage to their habitat by overgrazing. Understanding the natural regeneration of woodland is a related problem. Unless suitable conditions exist for young trees to grow naturally from seed and replace old ones when they fall, the long-term survival of the woods as natural features of the parks cannot be ensured.

Visitors

The function of national parks in relation to visitors is to provide a special experience that cannot be obtained in areas of lesser interest or beauty, rather than just to be available for any form of outdoor recreation. By careful planning this can be achieved. In the case of Glenveagh National Park it meant keeping the park closed to the public while its resources were studied and facilities were planned instead of admitting visitors as soon as the lands were acquired. As a result visitors are now able to appreciate and benefit from the natural features and wilderness character of the park, without harming the very features they come to enjoy. It is also sometimes necessary to restrict or prevent particular activities within the parks. For example, to many people national parks seem like ideal camping sites. But experience in other countries has shown that camping in a park can lead to gradual deterioration of the distinctive character of the park. Irish national parks are small enough for people to be able to visit all parts of them without staying overnight within their boundaries, so this is not permitted.

Interpretation is the key to providing a special experience for visitors. This consists of much more than just conveying information and involves helping visitors to observe the features of the park themselves and revealing the meanings and relationships behind the objects seen and facts communicated. For each national park there is an introductory audio-visual presentation, shown in a comfortable auditorium. Wall displays explain various aspects of the parks in detail. The most elaborate of these displays, accompanied by models and objects of interest, are in the new visitor centre at Glenveagh National Park. Self-guiding nature trails enable visitors to find out more about the parks at their own pace. Guided nature walks are also offered during the summer, and two of the parks have regular series of illustrated talks. All these services are backed up by publications, from basic leaflets with maps to longer guidebooks and booklets on special topics.

National parks have a key role to play in nature conservation in Ireland, and in awakening greater understanding of the Irish heritage and environment. With wider public recognition in the years ahead should come greater public support for their existence and for their management to the highest standards. Such public concern is necessary to ensure that the resources of national parks really are conserved for future generations as well as our present population to enjoy. Public interest may also lead to extension of the network of national parks as has happened in other countries. They will never cover more than a small fraction of the country but it is possible to envisage a small number of other areas of great national interest and beauty being set aside in this way, apart from the four national parks already existing or planned.

Ross Castle, in Killarney National Park.

ALAN CRAIG is Chief Parks Superintendent with the National Parks and Monuments Service of the Office of Public Works.

HUMAN IMPRINTS ON THE COUNTRYSIDE

Frank Mitchell

The rocks, the soils, the weather patterns are so variable in Ireland that it is impossible to arrange any of them in a neat hierarchical order. Most of the inhabitants are also allergic to order or to being ordered. Not long before the time of the birth of Christ the Celts with their language and their way of life were widely distributed across Europe, and I believe they reached Ireland in sufficient strength to establish their language and their way of life here. The Romans then came to power in western Europe (including Britain), and they proceeded to impose their language and their way of life throughout their empire. And the keystone of their empire was order, order in law, order in language, order in thought. Inhabitants of the Roman Empire had to accept discipline.

The Romans never conquered Ireland, and the Celtic way of life continued. The plantations of the sixteenth and seventeenth centuries were the latest serious attempt to move new people into Ireland, and it was only in the north-east that a cohesive group of newcomers became established. They brought their inherited sense of discipline with them. In the rest of the country it was the Celtic traits that were inherited, most closely in the Irish language where the thought structure behind the words was very different to that in English; discipline remained unknown. Today in many areas individualist lack of thought for the common good leads to action that is not only damaging for the general population and for the countryside, but in the long run for the doer too.

The new technologies now available have enormous power to alter the countryside. Immense efforts must be made to bring the Irish people to realise that the planner is not an enemy to be thwarted but one who, if given the right support, can make the Irish countryside a better place for ourselves and our children.

History in the Landscape
Stone Walls
Mills and Houses
Dyes from the Countryside
Bridges
Potteries
Folk Tradition and the Rural Environment
Graveyards and Gravestones
Pollution

HISTORY IN THE LANDSCAPE

Michael Ryan

The Stone Age

Some of the evidence for human influence on the environment is obvious – many monuments of prehistoric and later times are easily visible. Some of them, the neolithic stone tombs or the so-called ringforts (raths) of the Iron Age and early medieval period, are very prominent and, in some parts of the country, quite common. Others are less obvious and known mainly from characteristic scatters of artifacts in the plough-soil or detectable by means of aerial photography. Some areas – the Dingle peninsula or the Burren of County Clare – are exceptionally fortunate in the degree to which standing monuments survive. Recent authoritative estimates suggest that as many as 140,000 archaeological sites may be identified in Ireland. This represents an extraordinary cultural asset, but it is a wasting one as development – road building, quarrying, town growth on agricultural areas – devours the ancient landscape. Recent calculations suggest that roughly a third of our monuments have been obliterated since the first Ordnance Survey maps were published in the nineteenth century and, in some areas, the rate of destruction is far in excess of that. Nevertheless, a great deal survives and it is possible to read much of the history of Ireland in the countryside. It is vitally important that what is left is cherished and protected against unnecessary interference.

The mesolithic period

The earliest evidence for the interaction of humans and the environment in Ireland belongs to what is known in Europe as the mesolithic period or Middle Stone Age. After the retreat of the glaciers of the last Ice Age, the area habitable by animals and the bands of hunters who preyed on them expanded.

Forests gradually spread northwards as the climate improved and people in Europe adapted to hunting the smaller herds of woodland animals. Human communities, too, became smaller and more scattered, and pronounced regional differences grew up. Ireland was connected to Britain and hence to Europe by a land-bridge – perhaps not a continuous stretch of dry land, but a series of islands, sandbanks and narrow and shallow waters – in what is now the north Irish Sea. These were overwhelmed by 8000 BC and Ireland was fully separated from Britain by the rising waters of the postglacial ocean. There is no evidence that people had arrived

by then. Our earliest sites – at Mount Sandel in County Derry and at Broughal, Lough Boora, County Offaly – belong to the period after 7000 BC. The evidence of these two excavations shows an economy dependent on food-gathering, fishing, hunting and fowling. Pig was commonly eaten: at Boora, eels were caught in substantial numbers and caches of hazelnuts were found. At Mount Sandel there was an oval hut which was renewed on a number of occasions. Flint tools, including axes, small blades and microliths (tiny slivers of flint worked so as to be hafted on stone or bone shafts) were made on site. At Boora similar tools of chert were found together under peat far out in the bed of the modern Lough Boora. The excavations showed beyond a shadow of a doubt that our great midland bogs – or what is left of them – seal an ancient landscape of lakes and forests over which the earliest inhabitants hunted and gathered food.

Larnian way of life

Gradually, from about 6000 BC onwards, there was a great change in the kind of tools used. Briefly, the tradition of small delicately wrought microliths and blades gave way to a range of heavier implements often simply struck from a core with little or no further working. This material was first identified in the nineteenth century at Larne in County Antrim and is often referred to as *Larnian*. The coastal finds are often heavily worn as they were deposited in the raised beaches left by the sea at its maximum height in the postglacial period. It was thought that the artifacts were produced by communities dependent in the main on shellfish collecting and related beachcombing activities but in recent years material of this kind has been widely recognised on midland lake shores such as Loughs Derravaragh, Kinale, Iron and Gara. We badly need excavated sites with faunal remains to shed light on the way of life of these later mesolithic food-gatherers. Some later mesolithic coastal sites, such as Sutton and Dalkey Island, both in County Dublin, were occupied at a time when farming economies were being established in Ireland.

It seems that the mesolithic peoples were passive exploiters of their environment, rather than active cultivators. Nevertheless, a viable population was able to subsist in Ireland for 3000 years and to spread widely throughout the country. As an established

Opposite
Mount Sandel, Co. Londonderry, the site of a mesolithic hut excavated by Professor Peter Woodman. The hut, which was renewed a number of times, dates to shortly after *c.* 7000 BC and is thus the oldest known man-made structure in Ireland.

Right
The bed of Lough Boora, Co. Offaly. Protruding through the peat is the ancient shoreline on which mesolithic man camped *c.* 6500 BC. The shore was laid down in early postglacial times, later covered in peat and eventually by the waters of Lough Boora.

with axes ground from long pebbles.

Mount Sandel was on bluff overlooking the Lower Bann and the Boora encampment was on the shore of a lake. In many ways, Boora documents the dramatic changes which have taken place in the landscape over the last 8000 years. The beach on which mesolithic people camped had been thrown up by a lake many times larger than the modern Lough Boora. This had gradually become choked with the growth of reeds and eventually a peat bog formed. Peat covered much of the bed of the old lake and the high peat banks which developed in the area impounded the waters at a higher level than the original lake. Thus it was that the mesolithic site was found sealed

population, they would have been in a position to contribute to later developments and we may be seeing in some of the uniquely Irish features of our neolithic culture the influence of the earlier population.

The neolithic period

Around 4000 BC a major change was under way in Ireland – the shift from *food collecting* to *food production* by the cultivation of domesticated plants and the breeding of domesticated animals. It was profoundly significant because it afforded people greater security of subsistence and offered the possibility of surpluses, which in turn permitted specialisation, because some members of the community were freed from the work of providing food to a greater extent than in most mesolithic cultures. The appearance of farming among the neolithic or New Stone Age people in Ireland marks the beginning of active management of the physical environment by humans, the effects of which are still with us today.

The arrival of agriculture

Farming as we know it in Europe originated in the Near East and spread rapidly throughout the region. Its dispersal throughout Europe was very rapid, in some cases due no doubt to actual movements of groups of people, in others to more complicated processes involving the adoption of the new skills by existing peoples.

With the exception of the pig, none of the plants and animals which formed the basis of the neolithic economy is native to Ireland. It is necessary, therefore, to assume that they were brought to the island by sea voyages together with the skills necessary to grow the crops, breed the animals and cull the surplus young systematically without damaging the

breeding stock. Here we enter an area of speculation. Is it necessary to propose the arrival in significant numbers of new people to account for this great change? What constitutes 'significant' numbers in the context of the thinly spread mesolithic population? From where did the first Irish farmers come?

It is theoretically possible that the native mesolithic population adopted agriculture and stock-breeding through contact with other peoples, but there is as yet no evidence for this. It is much more likely that a group or groups of people, however small, came, bringing with them not only the seed and animals but also the organisation and discipline necessary to establish a viable agricultural economy. Where they may have come from is unknown. One respected writer, Professor Frank Mitchell, believes that the

shortest sea-crossing – ie from Britain – was the most probable route, when you consider the logistical problems of transfer of a new way of life to an island. Others, arguing from quite different grounds (the assumed ancestry and significance of certain kinds of stone tombs to which we will return below) have proposed a series of neolithic colonisations of Ireland directly from north-western France. Confusingly, still others, using the same evidence, have opted for a British origin and the shorter routes! None of these theories can be proved. Given the preparation necessary for the transfer of food supplies and livestock and the contacts which one assumes must have preceded such a move, it is on balance likelier that Britain was the immediate place of origin of Irish agriculture, but the alternative view can by no means be ruled out.

Opposite
The neolithic chipped stone axeheads from Rathlin Island, Co. Antrim. Top, Ballygill Middle and, bottom, Ushet Lough. The Ushet Lough axehead is partly polished. Experiments have shown that stone axeheads are efficient tools for clearing forest. They are amongst the commonest prehistoric finds in Ireland.

Right
Passage tomb cairn, Carrowkeel, Co. Sligo

Pollen analysis

It is still generally accepted – although with some reservations – that the best evidence for the first appearance of the neolithic way of life in Ireland is to be found in the effect that the new economy had on the landscape. For illustrations of this, we must turn to *pollen analysis*. The pollen produced by plants can survive in fossil form, sealed in bogs, for centuries and give us a picture of the vegetation of ages past. Many years ago scholars in Scandinavia studying fossil pollen identified phases when there was a marked decline in the pollen of trees and a corresponding increase in those of grasses and other plants associated with clearings. Cereal pollens often occurred in the same deposits as the decline of tree pollen and also, sometimes, weeds of cultivation. Especially clear was a dramatic decline in the pollen of

the elm. Such episodes were christened *landnam* or land-taking (settlement) phases. So dramatic and widespread in Europe was the decline in elm pollen found to be that it was taken as an especial marker of early neolithic land clearance. It was suggested that the elm leaves and bark were favoured as fodder by neolithic farmers and that the trees were therefore marked for special attack. However, elms are susceptible to epidemic disease of the type that happened in Europe and America during the 1970s and the elm decline may have been caused by natural agencies and not have anything to do with farming. What is important is not the precise significance of the decline in the representation of elm in the pollen deposited in bogs, but the clear evidence of cycles of forest clearance followed by regeneration of woodlands and further clearances. Some

early attacks on woodland are now known to precede the decline in elm.

A good example of a *landnam* phase was identified in a bog at Fallahogy, County Derry. Because of the use of radiocarbon dating (here given in years BC), we can see vividly how the landscape was changing as a result of human interference. About the beginning of the fourth millennium BC the representation of the pollen of elm began to fall, while at about the same period there was an increase in the pollens of mixed deciduous forest, followed by a rapid decline in woodland. This was matched by an increase in the presence of the pollens of grasses, nettles and ribwort plantain. These in their turn declined, to be followed by a general rise in tree pollens (including elm), as forest re-established itself. About a thousand years later, a similar cycle was detected. Looking at

227

the pollen record and the radiocarbon dates, there are obvious ambiguities in the evidence – the record of the rise in some pollens does not exactly match the decline in others, the radiocarbon dates do not themselves form a neat sequence but overlap. These are insignificant factors – the trend of the evidence is unequivocal and the radiocarbon dates agree remarkably well in placing the first *landnam* phase around 4000 BC or slightly later. Evidence for early interference with woodlands by people is fairly widespread – for example, at Red Bog, County Louth. At Ballynagilly, County Tyrone, there had been active destruction of forests by about 4000 BC. Other, perhaps later, instances have been noted at various sites in the south-west in counties Cork and Kerry. An early clearance at Cashelkeety in Kerry was associated with the occurrence of cereal pollen.

In general, the earliest radiocarbon dates for *landnam* phases in the pollens preserved in bogs are earlier than any so far obtained for neolithic monuments such as tombs or houses. There are two exceptions – a rectangular house excavated at Ballynagilly was dated by the radiocarbon method to what should be shortly after 4000 BC in calendar years, and a similar date is possible, but not proved, for a simple megalithic tomb at Carrowmore, County Sligo. A court tomb at Ballymacaldrack in County Antrim may also have been in use at about the same time.

We are faced therefore with a number of problems. Firstly, it is simply not possible at present to link a particular group as defined by their monuments and characteristic artifacts with the earliest clearances. It is, in fact, well-nigh impossible to identify even those responsible for later clearances except

in the most general terms. Are we to see the establishment of the farming economy as a process which had begun some centuries before the monuments which we have been taught to identify as typical of the Irish neolithic became widespread? Or is it merely that we have not found the necessary links?

Part of our difficulty lies in the fact that large areas of the countryside have been covered with blanket bog since neolithic times, thus effectively concealing habitation sites in the areas in which many pollen studies have been carried out. The regeneration of forest even before the growth of bog may well have obliterated the more obvious traces of

such sites.

Behy-Glenulra

One extremely hopeful research project in recent years has been the investigation of field fences buried by bog in the west of Ireland, especially in County Mayo. There, Dr Séamus Caulfield has been revealing a remarkably vivid picture of the ancient landscape and the organisation of early agricultural communities. Important results have come from two sites in north Mayo. At Behy-Glenulra, a large system of stone-walled fields was recorded. Long strips defined by parallel stone walls were subdivided into substantial

228

Opposite
The Carrowkeel passage tomb cemetery on the Bricklieve mountains, Co. Sligo. The hill-top siting of these clusters of tombs is typical.

Above right
Aerial view of the reconstructed neolithic houses at Lough Gur, Co. Limerick. The buildings are based on those found in the excavations of this neolithic and Early Bronze Age settlement.

fields of up to 7 hectares in extent. Small enclosures, some in the middle of fields, one attached to a boundary wall, may indicate the sites of settlements. One of them, in Glenulra townland, was excavated and produced neolithic pottery, scrapers, stone axeheads and a leaf-shaped arrowhead. A radiocarbon date suggests the site was occupied shortly before 3000 BC. Dates for the growth of peat which later covered the area suggest that the bog was established by about 2500 BC. The excavator is convinced that the region had already been extensively cleared of forest before the fields were laid out – he regards the planning of the regular system as a single operation.

There can be little doubt that the Behy-Glenulra field system and its associated settlement is a work of a mature phase of the Irish neolithic period. It is the product of an organised community capable of mobilising labour for large works of group effort. The community had clearly achieved consent for improving land management, especially by controlling grazing areas for stock. Who can doubt that behind the practical uses of fencing lies a complex web of legal obligations and social relationships? In the corner of one of the fields at Behy is a well-known court tomb. Robbed of cairnstones

Ballymacdermott court tomb, Co. Armagh. The characteristic forecourt occurs at the broader end of the denuded cairn.

for a second, later phase of wall-building there is no absolute evidence that the tomb belonged to the earlier, neolithic inhabitants, but the close relationship of the finds from the tomb and the settlement makes this very likely.

Belderg Beg

Seven kilometres west of Behy-Glenulra is the site of Belderg Beg where two phases of enclosure activity were found. The later phase was evidently built after the bog had begun to grow, because one of the boundary walls was built partly on peat. Radiocarbon dating and finds of neolithic pottery, flints and a polished stone axehead suggest that the first phase belonged to the neolithic, not far removed in time from the Behy-Glenulra complex. Direct evidence of cultivation in the form of plough marks and ridges (at one point the ridges overlay plough marks) was found at Belderg Beg. This imaginative programme of work has shown the immense potential of settlement studies for social and economic reconstruction when conditions of preservation are good.

Houses and tools

Elsewhere, rectangular houses of the early farmers have been found not only at Ballynagilly but also at Ballyglass in Mayo (under a megalithic tomb) and at Lough Gur in County Limerick. The Ballynagilly house was built of massive radially split oak planks. Less substantial structures were found under tombs and cairns at Townley Hall in County Louth and Moneen in County Cork. Coastal sites are well known in the north-east and east

230

of the country.

Artifacts typical of the neolithic – leaf-shaped and lozenge-shaped flint points for arrows and spears and a variety of scrapers for preparing hides or woodwork – are widely found in Ireland but the most widespread is the polished stone axehead. Many of these may well have been manufactured with whatever materials lay to hand, but at Tievebulliagh mountain and Rathlin Island, County Antrim, a suitable fine-grained rock, porcellanite, was exploited in the regular, quasi-industrial manufacture of axeheads. Finished and unfinished examples were widely traded. Trade in flint was also likely because the sources in Ireland are confined in the main to the north-east and especially to County Antrim. The range of artifacts of the neolithic is much richer than that of the mesolithic: pottery – including domestic and funerary wares – beads of stone, bone pins and even fragments of

baskets have been found.

Megalithic tombs

The most striking memorials of the neolithic inhabitants are the great stone (megalithic) tombs of which large numbers survive in Ireland. They are now largely denuded of the cairns or mounds which covered them. The Irish megalithic tombs belong to a great family of structures found in Atlantic Europe from southern Spain to southern Scandinavia. Argument about their purpose, relationships and significance has been intense, but excavation shows that the vast majority were used for burial – in Ireland mostly cremations – accompanied by the characteristic pottery and flints of the time. Using comparisons with surviving societies, some archaeologists suggest that they acted as a focus for social identification, places of assembly and trade or exchange of goods between groups. There is reason to believe that some of these tombs fulfilled a variety of such roles. The manner in which examples like Newgrange figured in later mythology shows that they could transcend their primary purpose as graves.

Elaborate classifications of tombs exist and have been argued about for years. Broadly speaking two categories occur in Ireland – those which are set in long cairns or mounds and those which are covered by round tumuli. Those in long mounds are what used to be called *gallery graves*, that is long, stone-built galleries, often divided into chambers, along the whole length of which burials might be placed. Those in round tumuli consist of distinct burial chambers, which are generally entered by passages leading from the edge of the tumulus and are referred to as *passage tombs*.

These simplified distinctions are still useful for descriptive purposes, but they need more elaboration. In Ireland, gallery graves can be divided into two broad types, court tombs and wedge tombs. The *court tombs* are the monuments *par excellence* of early neolithic culture. About 330 are known and they are found mainly in the northern third of the country. They occur singly, frequently on lighter upland soils and have been taken to reflect the pattern of settlement of the early agriculturalists. Court tombs are so called because they have at the broader ends of their characteristic trapeze-shaped cairns crescent-shaped, stone-built, unroofed forecourts. In some cases, the court is completely enclosed in the body of the cairn and the burial gallery opens off it. In some elaborate examples more than one gallery occurs. The galleries are divided by jambs and sills into chambers and they are roofed by means of corbelling.

Especially elaborate court tombs are to be seen in counties Mayo and Sligo where they are very common. However, the most spectacular derivatives of the court tomb are the *portal tombs* or *portal dolmens*. These are normally single-chambered, composed of massive capstones placed on three substantial upright stones. The capstone is generally pitched high over two paired, tall stones which together with a sillstone, form the characteristic portal. In the case of Browne's Hill, County Carlow, the capstone is estimated to weigh over one hundred tonnes. Such dolmens were also set within long cairns and are usually seen now in an eroded state. They are often sited on the slopes of river valleys. These situations may have been chosen to make it easier to raise the capstone into position by rolling it downslope on ramps of earth. Like the court tombs, portal dolmens represent a considerable outlay of effort by the communities which built them and they imply a good deal of organisation to achieve. Sadly, we know very little as yet about the dwellings of these people and so inferences about their society tend to be drawn from the structures and their siting and the contents of the tombs. Portal tombs are normally also found singly rather than in groups. They are distributed more widely than court tombs and in the east and south-east many imposing examples may be seen.

The *wedge tomb* is so called because it tapers from front to back both in plan and in cross section. These tombs are normally single-chambered and built on the lintelling principle. They are set generally in long cairns, some of them an elongated D-shape in plan. Wedges are the most numerous and widespread of megaliths in Ireland – over four hundred are known with massive concentrations in the Burren in Clare and very substantial numbers in Cork and Kerry. Like the court tombs, they occur individually in the landscape. Excavation leaves no doubt that they were built and used in the earlier Bronze Age, but it is likely that they were also in use during at least the later part of the neolithic period.

Passage tombs make a vivid contrast. Their burial chambers, set in round cairns or mounds, are often very elaborate in their planning and building. The walls of many tombs, especially in the Boyne Valley and Loughcrew in Meath, are covered with a variety of incised motifs including spirals, zig-zags and concentric circles, the meanings of which are unknown. In the Boyne Valley and Loughcrew and at Carrowkeel and Carrowmore in County Sligo there are major clusters or 'cemeteries' of passage tombs and smaller concentrations occur elsewhere. Hill-top sitings – often commanding panoramic views of our now treeless landscape – are favoured. Not all tombs of this class are elaborate – very simple versions of dolmen construction but quite distinct from the portal tombs are common at Carrowmore and occur widely in County Antrim.

Because of their ambitious architecture and scale some passage tombs have excited a good deal of theorising, much of it ill-founded. Monuments like Newgrange, Knowth and Dowth in the Boyne Valley are massive and obviously absorbed enormous quantities of resources. One archaeologist has even suggested that the Boyne Valley cemetery served a quasi-urban settlement. There is no evidence for this nor for many of the other contemporary myths about these tombs. Even the amount of labour involved in their construction is overestimated, because the builders could have had draught animals at their disposal. What is more interesting is that the great mounds of Newgrange and Knowth contained vast amounts of turves in their

231

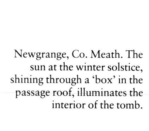

Carrowmore passage tomb cemetery, Co. Sligo. In the foreground a small passage tomb of simple construction, in the background Maeve's Cairn on Knocknarea mountain.

Newgrange, Co. Meath. The sun at the winter solstice, shining through a 'box' in the passage roof, illuminates the interior of the tomb.

make-up, proving that a great deal of clearance of forest had taken place in the area, allowing grassland to form before the tombs were built.

Newgrange is planned so that at the winter solstice the early morning sun shines down the passage to light up the furthermost recess. Once local sunrise at the solstice had been observed and marked, it was a relatively simple task to lay out the proposed construction with poles. Newgrange was not built to show the time of the year, but was achieved because the people who built it already had a good working knowledge of astronomy and engineering, but, above all, the social organisation to plan and execute a great work and the economy to support it. We may guess that this social order was hierarchical, but we have as yet no idea of

232

how it was organised and little knowledge of the settlements in which the people lived.

Origins of the tombs

Passage tombs are clearly related to similar monuments in Brittany and the Irish examples are almost certainly derived from there: it is highly likely that a group of settlers introduced the tomb type to Ireland. The great passage tombs of Knowth and Newgrange were being built before 3000 BC.

Various authorities have sought the origin of the court tomb in the early neolithic of southern Britain, where similar monuments are known, and in north-western France. No entirely satisfactory conclusion has been reached but the recent discovery at Donegore in County Antrim of a type of enclosure typical of southern Britain strengthens the

links with that area. The court tombs and portal tombs were in use earlier, and the latter continued to be used after 3000 BC. Around 3000 BC other variants of megalithic burial traditions – especially in the southern half of the country – are identifiable as well as simple burial in pits.

The neolithic period in Ireland may have lasted for some 2000 years and our knowledge of it is very patchy. In some parts of the south there are few, if any, recognised neolithic monuments and a great deal of work is needed before we can be confident that we understand all the variations of the neolithic way of life in Ireland.

The Bronze Age

Gold disc, one of a pair, Earlier Bronze Age, Tedavnet, Co. Monaghan. Of thin beaten gold, the disc was made to be attached to a backing, perhaps textile. These so-called 'sun-discs' are amongst the earliest gold ornaments to have been made in Ireland.

The date and processes by which metal technology was introduced to Ireland are difficult to understand. Imported metal objects, perhaps copper trinkets or small tools, were probably in circulation in the later neolithic period as a result of trade and other contact. There is no evidence for an initial period of experimentation with metal, so it is likely that the technology was introduced in a developed form into the country.

The Earlier Bronze Age (c. 2500–1200 BC)

The earliest phases of metalworking in Ireland were based on the use of copper cast simply in open moulds. Bronze, an alloy of copper and tin, came into use later. Two broad traditions may be identified: one in the southern part of the country typified by thick-butted copper axeheads cannot be clearly associated with known burial customs; another, perhaps slightly later group,

characterised in a general way by axeheads with curved sides and thin butts, found rarely with simple knives, may have been linked to the users of 'Beaker' pottery – a distinctive vessel-style which occurs widely in western and central Europe at about the time that metallurgy first became widespread. There was, however, no single source for early Irish metallurgy, but influences from central as well as from Atlantic Europe have been

Left
Crouched skeleton buried with a food vessel at Clonickilvant, Co. Westmeath, Earlier Bronze Age. Such cist-burials are common at this period.

Opposite
Stone circle ('the piper's stones'), Athgreany, Co. Wicklow

detected. Some have argued that the wedge tombs represent, in the south-west, the graves of early groups of prospectors and miners.

The economy of the early metal-using age in Ireland was complex and probably varied from region to region. There can be little doubt that there was strong continuity with neolithic times in agriculture, more particularly in stock-raising. The study of animal bones from a Beaker habitation at Newgrange, revealed the continued dependence on oxen, pigs and sheep with a much smaller reliance on hunting wild animals. Agriculture is attested also. The pollen record for the whole of the Bronze Age indicates phases of expansion and contraction of forest perhaps partly to be explained by clearance and abandonment but also, in part, the effect of climatic variations. Flint and other stone remained important raw materials for tool-making in this period.

The introduction of metalworking ushered in new economic developments. There is evidence that mining, smelting, fabrication and distribution of metal products were highly organised. A number of ancient copper mines are known – a well-preserved series on Mount Gabriel near Schull, County Cork, is particularly noteworthy. It has been estimated that the recorded copper mines of prehistoric Ireland could have provided sufficient metal to support the native industry throughout the Bronze Age as well as a substantial surplus for export. Moulds of stone for casting implements have been found, but not normally in the areas in which copper was mined – this suggests that centres of manufacture imported metal from mining areas and that there was a sophisticated system of exchange of goods at the time. Recent studies have shown that the products of individual moulds were widely traded

throughout the island. Trade with western Europe is attested also. It is probable, for example, that most, if not all, of the tin used in Irish bronze was imported from overseas.

At a point when metalworking was firmly established in Ireland, about 2000 BC, the first gold objects appear. They are all made of sheet gold of which the best known are the so-called 'sun-discs', that is circular plates of gold made to be sewn to a textile or, perhaps, leather backing. Lunulae – 'little moons' – are crescent-shaped neck ornaments also of sheet gold, which were very common in the Earlier Bronze Age of Ireland. The earliest ornaments seem to have been made of Irish metal, but there is some disputed evidence that later in the Bronze Age gold was imported.

Evidence from burials
The history of Ireland in this period depends to a large extent on two very different types of

pot now contains the bones, the body having been cremated. There is a tendency to place the urns in pits or tiny polygonal cists in cemeteries rather than in rectangular cists. But there are many combinations of fashion and the Food Vessel tradition overlaps heavily with the urns in many respects.

Cist and pit graves of the Early Bronze Age are often grouped in flat cemeteries, specially constructed cemetery mounds or cairns and, occasionally, inserted into the tumuli of earlier megalithic tombs. The absence of good correlations between burials and metalwork makes it very difficult to document the history of these burial practices, but it is impossible, in the light of present knowledge, to demonstrate the survival of urn-burial beyond c. 1400 BC, Food Vessels having gone out of fashion a century or so earlier.

Metalwork

The other major form of evidence from the Bronze Age – the metalwork – is reasonably well known in outline. Our understanding is that there were two progressions: firstly an increasing competence in working metal – the change from simple open moulds to complex ones and even, perhaps, sand-casting, improvements in alloying and so on – and secondly the gradual modification of implements to function more efficiently. These developments should not be seen as isolated: change was frequently initiated by adopting fashions from outside Ireland. At the beginning of the Earlier Bronze Age, simple flat axeheads and knives cast in open stone moulds predominate. By the sixteenth century BC true closed-mould casting had been firmly established and socketed spearheads cast in complex matrices – often still of stone – became common. Axeheads showed radical developments throughout the period: at first

evidence: the material from burials and that from hoards and other finds of metalwork, and it has proved extremely difficult to link the two. In burial traditions there is some variety: at the opening of the metal-using period, megalithic tombs were still widely used. The mounds and chambers of court tombs and passage tombs contain evidence of later burials, sometimes intruding upon those of the earlier rite, while wedge tombs were also being purpose-built for burial. Single burials and burials other than in megalithic tombs were known in the neolithic and became common in the Earlier Bronze Age. This is not fully explained but some new influx of people may partly account for the trend. In the eastern half of the country, single and limited multiple burials are especially frequent in the Earlier Bronze Age. These commonly take the form of 'cist-graves', box-like constructions of stone slabs set in pits. In

these, both unburned and cremated remains were placed, sometimes accompanied by elaborately decorated funerary pots called 'Food Vessels'. Other grave goods, rarely of metal, are occasionally noted. A particularly common form of burial is that of the single crouched skeleton, lying on its side with the Food Vessel placed at the head. It is a close approximation to the rite of Beaker burials in Britain and is especially frequent in the east and the midlands. Many of our round mounds and cairns may date to this time, but without excavation it is impossible to say in any given case.

There can be little doubt of the strong contacts between Ireland and parts of Britain at this time. Contacts which are apparent in Food Vessel burials are renewed at a slightly later period by the appearance of forms of burial urn which had developed in Britain. These bring with them a change in rite – the

Left
A cauldron made from riveted sheets of bronze, Castlederg, Co. Tyrone, *c.* 700 BC. Produced towards the end of the Bronze Age, the cauldron displays the mastery of technique achieved as well as the wealth of the period.

Opposite
Urn-burial, Glassymullin, Calary, Co. Wicklow. The urn was placed in a pit and the small stone slab acted as a cover for the grave: Earlier Bronze Age.

they were simple and mounted in holes in wooden handles like stone axeheads, gradually stop-ridges and side flanges were added as the fashion of hafting changed from a straight to an inverted L-shaped handle. At first plain, later axeheads are frequently elaborately decorated. Knives and daggers, too, became gradually transformed and by the end of the period, elaborate long-bladed thrusting weapons – 'dirks' and 'rapiers' – had become common. In the earlier part of this period, caches of tools ('hoards' in archaeological terminology) are frequently found.

Monuments

Habitations of the Earlier Bronze Age are not well known. Some of the houses at Lough Gur, County Limerick, may well have been built and occupied in that period. Coastal sites frequently yield generalised evidence of Food Vessel and urn-using peoples. A small hut associated with Beaker pottery was excavated at Monknewtown in Meath, and may be one of the earliest habitations of the Earlier Bronze Age. The area in front of the entrance to the great passage tomb, at Newgrange, was occupied for a time by the same people.

One intriguing field monument which seems to belong largely but not exclusively to the Earlier Bronze Age is the stone circle. Ranging in size from a matter of five or so small monoliths to very imposing circles many metres in diameter, they have been variously interpreted as ritual sites and astronomical calendars. Whatever their original function, we know that they are to be found mostly in the south-west, in counties Cork and Kerry, in the north – especially in County Tyrone – and only sporadically elsewhere. Much more work needs to be done to establish their function and precise cultural associations and their links with stone circles elsewhere. Associated with them, and also found more widely, are 'gallauns' or standing stones, near some of which Bronze Age

burials have been found. Occasionally rows of standing stones are found. Radiocarbon evidence suggests that some stone circles and alignments may have been built as late as the early first millennium BC.

Also in the Earlier Bronze Age, in Beaker times, the practice of making great circular ritual enclosures – in British terminology, 'henges' – appeared. One, at Monknewtown, County Meath, near Newgrange was excavated recently and evidence for a Beaker association was found. A number of burials turned up, including one of cremated bone in a neolithic pot of the kind found in passage tombs. Much Early Bronze Age settlement may have been in areas now covered by bog,

and it is difficult today to see in the countryside as clearly as in parts of Britain the signs of the settlement of this period. Many finds of metal objects have come from the midlands and typical burials of the period are known from the gravel ridges of the region. The great raised bogs may mask settlement features comparable with those of regions of mountain bog in the west.

The Later Bronze Age (c. 1200–300 BC)

The Bishopsland phase

Some time around 1200 BC Ireland began to feel the effects of great social and economic changes which were taking place throughout Europe. While in the Mediterranean world

great civilisations were falling, the changes which archaeology reveals in Ireland must by comparison appear muted; nevertheless botanical studies suggest that there was a renewal of forest clearance combined with a rise in agricultural activity at about that time. Hoards, lacking in the final centuries of the Earlier Bronze Age, began to be deposited again and these now yield evidence for the appearance of new tools and new technologies in Ireland. Socketed axeheads and sickles appear. Casting in clay moulds is attested for the first time. New weapon types, including a form of sword, appear towards the end of the phase, side by side with surviving native traditions of spearhead and rapier. The hoard from Bishopsland, County Kildare, after which the phase (1200–1000 BC) is named, contained the novel axe and sickle, together with bronze hammers, gravers, a chisel, an anvil, a clamp and a saw.

Hoards of ornaments of gold reappear in this phase, together with impressive numbers of stray finds. Ribbed bracelets – such as those from Derrinboy, County Offaly or finer grooved examples from St John's, County Kildare – occur. The commonest and most impressive objects are, however, those made of twisted metal – the torcs.

The evidence of artifacts suggests that during the Bishopsland phase Ireland enjoyed contacts with south and south-west England, northern France and with north Germany and Jutland. There can be little doubt of the prosperity of the period – the renewed interest in gold strongly suggests this – but the other changes which took place are difficult to gauge. Burials of the Bishopsland phase are not known and habitation sites are almost unknown – there is one lakeside palisaded settlement at Cullyhanna, County Armagh, which is dated on independent grounds to

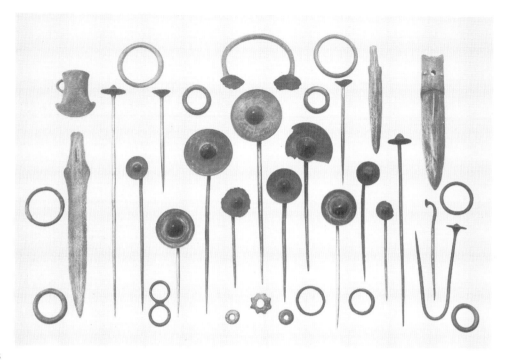

about the beginning of the period, but its contents shed very little light on the society and material culture of the time. The resumption of the practice of depositing hoards may be significant but the possible reasons for concealing valuables are so many that this approach must be treated with caution.

The period after about 1000 BC is not very well understood. It is highly likely that the basis of the Bishopsland reorganisation, with its strong indigenous element, continued, and that some new additions to the range of tools and weapons appeared. Neither settlements nor burials of this phase have been found in Ireland and the hoard record is scanty. Nor is botanical evidence of much help. Suggestions of expansion of farming at this period are difficult to sustain, and the appearance of advance and destruction of woodlands in some pollen studies may only indicate highly localised patterns of agriculture.

Whatever the form of material culture was in Ireland at this time, by the end of the period the scene is set for a dramatic reorientation of foreign contacts, for the emergence of powerful and wealthy regional groups and for a brilliant flowering of the arts of the metalworker.

The Dowris phase

During the eighth century BC new types of ornaments, tools, weapons and other objects began to appear in Ireland. There was substantial technological development which allowed larger and more ambitious and complex objects to be made. Sheet-bronze working was introduced with the adoption of central European style buckets – one of a range of influences from this area. Cauldrons of riveted sheets of bronze and ceremonial bronze shields appeared, both perhaps based

238

on Mediterranean prototypes. Elaborate horns of cast-bronze were fabricated, representing a highly sophisticated development of the techniques of casting on a clay core in a two-piece mould.

It is in gold ornaments that the full flowering of the arts of the metalworker can be most readily seen and the wealth and sophistication of the patrons glimpsed. One especially wealthy group seems to have been centred on the area of the lower Shannon and in this region a great variety of personal ornaments of gold have been found. Three great hoards are known to have been discovered there – two of them from Askeaton, County Limerick, and the Bog of Cullen, County Tipperary, contained many pieces but are now lost. The great Clare hoard, from Mooghaun North, is known from a few surviving objects and casts of the remainder which were melted down shortly after discovery. Add to this the numbers of stray finds and smaller hoards and the impression of a concentration of wealth is inescapable. Some of the gold ornaments

betray influences from the region of Jutland or north Germany, and others may show continuity with the preceding phase, while still others lack satisfactory prototypes and may be new local inventions. The insular craftsmen, while borrowing types, motifs and techniques from abroad as in other periods, gave to them an essentially Irish character by adapting exotic influences to local tastes and traditions. Amber beads, probably imported from the Baltic, are fairly common in the Later Bronze Age in Ireland and remind us that not all personal ornaments were made of gold and that trade must have played a part in the concentration of wealth which this great tradition of metalworking implies.

Analysis has shown that the gold of which the Dowris phase objects were made had a high silver content and a modest naturally occurring copper component as well as deliberately added copper. Strong resemblances in the composition of the gold with material of contemporary date in Jutland and contemporary and earlier times in central Europe raise very interesting

Opposite
A hoard of bronze ornaments and implements, Later Bronze Age, Derryhale, Co. Armagh

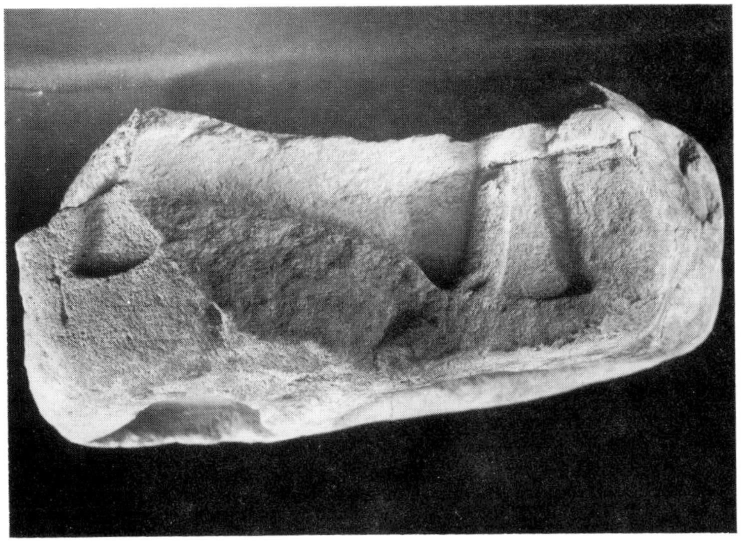

Right
Stone with a number of matrices (moulds) for casting bronze axeheads, from Ballygusheen, Co. Carlow. Simple open moulds were used early in the Bronze Age, and later, as technology improved, more elaborate two-piece moulds capable of producing hollow, socketed forms were used.

questions about the use of gold as a medium of exchange or as an object of trade in its own right. The source or sources of the gold cannot be chemically identified beyond question, but the great accumulation in Ireland indicates considerable wealth, even if the precious metal was obtained elsewhere.

Settlements, burials and pottery can once again be identified. A number of lakeside habitations, some on artificially built-up platforms have been found, the forerunners of the crannogs of the Iron Age and later periods. One of them at Lough Eskeragh, County Tyrone, was evidently a metalworker's smithy, as fragments of clay moulds for casting tools and weapons were found. There is evidence also for hill-top settlements. One of exceptional importance is at Rathgall in Wicklow, which produced many hundreds of clay mould fragments. At Rathgall, a coarse bucket-shaped pot containing cremated human bones was found and there is some evidence to suggest that similar pottery accompanied burials within embanked and ditched mounds – 'ring barrows' – for example, at Mullaghmore, County Down.

The chief characteristic of this period is the great number of hoards of ornaments, tools and weapons, including some broken and worn objects perhaps assembled for melting and reuse. A number of explanations for deposition or concealment suggest themselves. Some may have been hidden by their owners because of danger, others may have been cached for storage purposes quite unrelated to hypothetical danger. It is difficult to escape the conclusion that some were votive deposits ritually cast into lakes and bogs. The great find at Dowris near Birr, County Offaly, after which the period is named, may have been such a series of offerings rather than a single cache. The fact that it contains a representative range of bronzes, including types with marked regional distributions, may be significant. Some have also seen a ritual purpose in the bronze horns. Musically they are severely limited when played according to the modern conventions. A recent study suggests that they were used instead to amplify complex rhythms produced by mouth to accompany singing and chanting in the manner in which the *dijeridu* is used by contemporary Australian aborigines. Such a use may well have been ritual also.

It may be that we can see in this period the emergence of chieftaincies and of centres of power and influence which presage the developments of the succeeding period. Certainly there is strong evidence for concentration of wealth and hence, perhaps, political authority. The achievements of the Dowris phase in metalwork testify to a time of confidence and vigorous industrialisation together with a finely developed aesthetic sense. It is probable that this society entered a decline around the end of the seventh century BC, about the time when certain bronze swords and a few other novel objects derived from the Early Iron Age Hallstatt culture of central and western Europe reached Ireland. It would be most unwise, on the basis of so few highly portable objects, to postulate a major upheaval such as an invasion as the cause of change, if major change there was at that time. It may be that the final Bronze Age society of Ireland survived for several centuries in relative isolation, gradually adopting the use of iron following renewed foreign contacts in the third century BC. It is not necessary to think that the adoption of iron as the normal material for implements and weapons entailed wholesale disruption of the existing order; indeed the absence of evidence for dramatic change in itself argues for continuity.

From the Iron Age to recent times

A great deal of uncertainty surrounds the period when iron first became a regular material for the manufacture of tools. In the past, simple equations were made between the beginning of the 'Iron Age' and the 'arrival' of Celtic-speaking peoples. This arrival was often, on flimsy evidence, placed at about 350 BC. Certainly, one object decorated in the art style known as La Tène, which is associated with Celtic peoples on the continent, was imported into Ireland during the third century BC. It is a gold collar from near Clonmacnois in County Offaly and, of its nature, something which might have been traded over long distances. It is not until we begin to get evidence for the regular manufacture of objects in Ireland – a series of beautiful scabbard plates from Lisnacrogher crannog in Antrim, for example, in the third century BC, and the carving of immovable monuments like the Turoe Stone, County Galway, in the first century BC – that we can say that aspects of continental Celtic culture were firmly rooted here. Such a notion sheds no light whatever on questions such as when a Celtic language was first spoken in Ireland or when Celtic peoples first arrived in Ireland. These are issues which cannot be settled by archaeology, because artistic and technological ideas can be transmitted without major population movements. There are severe limits to the questions that archaeology can answer.

Forts of the Iron Age

Many of the sites which were important in early Irish history produce evidence of activity in the Later Bronze Age. Some of these, Emain Macha and Downpatrick for example, were enclosed to become hill-forts and retained their prominence in Iron Age and later times. Emain Macha (Navan Fort),

County Armagh, was the capital of the kingdom of the Ulaidh (Ulster) celebrated in ancient sagas.

Few Irish hill-forts have been excavated, and most are presumed to belong to the Iron Age. In broad terms, those in the eastern part of the country have single ramparts, while many in the west are provided with more than one bank and ditch. The banks follow the contours of the hills. Irish hill-forts are generally small – a few acres are enclosed by the biggest – and are dwarfed by many of those in Britain and the continent. Some like Emain have heroic associations. Tara, County Meath, lies at the heart of a complex of myths and traditions and the kingship of Tara enjoyed a particular status in early history because of the sacral origins of the office.

Promontory forts – that is forts made by

Opposite
Lisleitrim, Co. Armagh. Aerial view showing, on left, lake with crannog and, on right, large ringfort.

Right
Large, typical ringfort, Rough Fort, Co. Down

throwing banks and ditches across the necks of headlands – appeared also in the Iron Age. Some of them, like Drumanagh, Loughshinney, County Dublin, enclose large areas, but many are much smaller. Roman-style pottery was found at Loughshinney – it may have been a trading station in the early centuries AD. Other promontory forts are in bleak and inhospitable situations. Many are small and may have functioned more as

refuges than as places of permanent dwelling. They are very common on the west and south coasts where suitable promontories are numerous. The fort of Larrybane, County Antrim, was shown by excavation to have been occupied in early medieval times.

It was during the Iron Age that a type of enclosed dwelling – the rath or ringfort – became prominent. It is conceivable that some of the earliest were low irregularly

round walls or embankments surrounding houses such as those excavated at Carrigilihy, County Cork and Aughinish Island, County Limerick. Circular enclosures became the norm, with one or more banks and ditches or, in stony areas, stone-built walls. When built of stone, ringforts are often called 'cashels'. Raths, ringforts and cashels comprise the most numerous type of field monument in Ireland today. It has been calculated that

about 30,000 of them survived in the nineteenth century, although nowadays they are increasingly under attack and many have been wantonly destroyed in recent years. These ringforts are almost certainly the dwellings of the well-to-do farmers of the period. The majority date to the early medieval period and produce the typical domestic debris of the time. A number of examples in counties Antrim and Down were found to have been occupied for long periods and through a combination of rebuilding of the dwellings, bringing in earth for levelling

242

the area and the accumulation of refuse and industrial waste, the central areas have become high platforms as a consequence. A small number have proved to be of Iron Age date, for example Feewore, County Galway and Cush, County Limerick. The Rath of the Synods at Tara, an especially imposing earthwork, was occupied during the first centuries AD. The great heroic centre of Connacht, Cruachan (Rathcroghan, County Roscommon), unlike the hill-forts of Emain Macha and Tara, is essentially a cluster of earthworks including many of ringfort type.

We do not yet understand the significance of this. It has been argued that the ringfort is in origin the monument of an Iron Age culture, which has nothing to do with the La Tène cultural elements of the north and midlands. This is almost certainly untenable. By the dawn of history, the ringfort was widespread in Ireland, north and south, and represents the principal source of evidence for settlement in Ireland at that time.

Excavation shows that these sites were essentially domestic in nature, not defensive or military, although some examples like

Cahercommaun, County Clare, and Caherballykinvarga, also in Clare, may have had a quasi-military purpose. (Caherbally-kinvarga, like Dún Aonghasa on Inishmore, is surrounded by a *chevaux-de-frise* or obstruction of spiky stones.) Magnificent cashels like Staigue Fort in Kerry and Grianán Aileach in Donegal are likewise clearly in a different category from simple domestic dwellings.

Crannogs, too, are known in the Iron Age – Lisnacrogher, County Antrim, is famous as the source of some of the finest metalwork of

the period. Excavations at Lough Gara produced evidence of extensive Iron Age occupation. Crannogs enjoyed a long life and indeed remained in use in Ulster until the seventeenth century. Essentially, like ringforts, they were domestic in nature and the practice on them of crafts compares with our experience of ringforts. A recent tendency to regard them primarily as craft workshops is grossly overstated and, in some instances, manifestly absurd.

The great bog trackway recently discovered at Corlea, County Longford, dates to the middle of the second century BC and is undoubtedly the result of impressive social co-operation and also a reminder that bog growth was continuing apace in the midlands, rendering more and more land unfit for agriculture and hampering communications. At Carrownaglogh, County Mayo, an upsurge in agricultural activity was noted at about the beginning of the Christian era and similar phases were detected in Littleton Bog, County Tipperary. How widespread these were, is difficult to assess.

In the first century AD the Romans invaded Britain and very quickly conquered most of the island. They set up a flourishing colony with all the apparatus of Roman government – towns, markets, roads, military garrisons and so on. The Irish traded with Britain and, as the empire declined, were one of the peoples who raided the Roman colony and eventually established settlements there. One of the effects of this contact was the introduction of Christianity to Ireland, and with it the art of writing. Some centuries later, when native legends and sagas were written down, a remarkable insight into late prehistoric society was preserved. It was hierarchical, aristocratic and warlike. There

were no towns and cattle-raising – and raiding – was important. Some overseas trade was carried on. Roman coins and trinkets found at Newgrange have been interpreted as offerings by foreign merchants to a local deity. An archaic form of Irish – recorded on numerous ogham stones – was spoken everywhere. Changes were taking place: the old tribal centres were in decline as powerful new overkingdoms emerged to disrupt a more ancient polity.

The early medieval period

In AD 431 Pope Celestine dispatched Palladius as first bishop to the Irish 'believing in Christ' and, some time later, Patrick began his successful mission in the northern half of Ireland. After an initial period of consolidation the church became firmly rooted and, by the end of the sixth century, strongly monastic in character. This was a logical development in a society which was entirely rural.

Monasteries
Notionally, most land belonged to clearly defined kin groups and it was not open to individuals to alienate it. To give land to the church posed problems. Thus it was that many monasteries remained in the control of the founder's family, the office of abbot being termed 'comarb' or heir, and monasteries fitted neatly into the scheme of things.

The earliest monasteries may have been formed by pious devotees clustering around the hermitage or tomb of a recluse saint. Many foundations were established in inhospitable locations – deserts, the 'dysart' of some place-names. The stereotyped view is formed by the stone-built monasteries of the western seaboard, often miraculously preserved on islands like Sceilg Mhichíl,

243

County Kerry, or Inismurray, County Sligo. Many, however, were founded in the fastnesses of the midland bogs – Clonard, Clonfert, Clonmacnois, Gallen, Rahan, Lorrha, Terryglass, Derrynaflan – the list is long. Pollen evidence suggests a significant increase in agricultural activity in the midlands at this time, and there can be little doubt that the monasteries were in the forefront of these developments, as the monks or monastic tenants brought new areas of marginal land into cultivation. Large, eroded enclosures, often detectable only from the air, are all that remain of many of these monasteries. Sometimes the remains of a church or some carved stones survive. A modern graveyard may occupy part of the site. It is important, however, to make the effort of imagination to see them as they originally were – places of learning to which foreign students flocked in the seventh and eighth centuries, centres of production commanding the resources and labour of large estates for wooden and stone buildings, for provisions and raw materials, for craftsmen and acting as trading centres. The term *manac*, 'monk' in Old Irish, may have signified monastic tenant more than a full member of a religious community. By the eighth century the wealthy monasteries had become an important factor in Irish politics and abbots had become powerful figures in secular life. Many of them were, in effect, lay lords and participated in the affairs of the time, even to the extent of taking part in warfare.

Nevertheless, it was from such houses that missionaries first set forth to contribute to the revival of Christianity in Europe and to the conversion of the Anglo-Saxons of Britain. Later a steady stream of Irish scholars went to work in the church in Europe and many

achieved prominence there. The contacts of the missionary period contributed to the blossoming of the arts in Ireland in the seventh and eighth centuries. In metalwork pieces made for the church such as the Ardagh Chalice and Derrynaflan Paten and in manuscripts the Books of Durrow and Kells testify to the wealth and cosmopolitanism of the monastic church. Stone carving began with simple cross-inscribed slabs in early monastic sites. At Reask in Kerry slightly more elaborate examples occur, including one with simple scrollwork and another with birds flanking a cross, a common theme on Christian sarcophagi in Gaul. Later cross-slabs become much more elaborate and incorporate much of the ornament of contemporary manuscripts and metalwork. By the early ninth century many monasteries were commissioning imposing high crosses of carved stone, some decorated with scenes from the scriptures, and erecting substantial

stone churches and, slightly later, belfries – the round towers that are so striking a feature of the Irish landscape.

The first Viking raids from AD 795 onwards came as a shock to the monastic chroniclers of Ireland. Monasteries became the favoured targets of attack mainly because they were centres of wealth and sources of foodstuffs and other perishable goods, although it must have seemed at the time like a systematic campaign by the ungodly against religion. Many monasteries suffered repeated plunderings, demonstrating clearly that they could replenish their stocks and therefore that the economic and social system remained fundamentally in working order. In short, the system was being milked by the pirates not destroyed. In the mid-ninth century the Scandinavians, many from Norway, began to establish winter encampments – Dublin in AD 842 – and gradually changed from seasonal raiding to overwintering and

244

Opposite
The Rock of Dunamase, Co. Laois. An Anglo-Norman castle was built here in the thirteenth century on an early Irish site. It was greatly modified during the later medieval period and destroyed in the wars of the mid-seventeenth century.

Right
The *Lavabo* (wash-house), Mellifont Abbey, Co. Louth. The earliest (twelfth century) buildings of this abbey, on the regular continental pattern, contrasted markedly with traditional Irish monastic layout.

Baltic are just some of the surviving relics of a vast trade, which included perishable goods of all kinds. It was a Norse–Irish king, Sitric, who struck the first Irish coinage in AD 997. By that stage, however, Irish kings had been systematically milking the profits of Dublin by exacting tribute and, after the Battle of Clontarf in 1014, the coastal towns came more and more under the control of native rulers.

Because of the remarkable conditions of preservation, the Dublin excavations have shown vividly how the town relied heavily on the countryside. There was a huge demand for flexible osiers (lengths of willow) for wicker and poles for building houses and fences, oak for heavier timbers – doorposts, log pathways and drains. Large amounts of bedding (bracken) and sod for roofing, wood for domestic fuel and for quasi-industrial craft-working all were required. Wild fruits, shed antler (for comb-making), pigs and cattle for meat, hides for leather-working, all were gathered in from the countryside. Fishing and the collection of edible molluscs contributed to the diet.

In the eleventh and twelfth centuries, partly no doubt as a result of the opening up of Irish society through the contacts of towns, Irish kings began to behave more and more like their counterparts in Europe. Several tried, without success, to establish a genuine overlordship of the whole island. The church, too, began to change. A movement to reform it and bring it into line with continental organisation and practice gained strength and in the early twelfth century a series of synods was held which led to the establishment of territorial dioceses ruled over by bishops. The reformers also encouraged the introduction of regular monastic orders, and thus the Cistercians founded their first Irish house at

permanent settlement. Thus the first towns in Ireland were a contribution of the Vikings. With these settlements came new trade and the Viking-age graves of the Kilmainham–Islandbridge cemetery revealed the warrior–trader ambivalence of the Scandinavians clearly. The Scandinavians left their mark in place-names: Arklow, Wicklow, Wexford and Waterford were major settlements. Cork and Limerick, although bearing Irish names, were also successful Scandinavian ports.

Others, less enduring, included Annagassan and Carlingford in Louth.

Modern scholarship discounts the devastation recorded in the ancient sources, but there is no doubt that the Vikings *were* a major disruption, and it took some time before native leaders came to grips with them. On the credit side, the trading ports opened up new trade routes and helped to generate wealth in which rural Ireland shared. Silks and silver from Asia and trinkets from the

Mellifont in AD 1141 which eclipsed the nearby native monastery of Monasterboice. The religious orders laid the foundations of the wealth of Ireland in the following century, but with their new organisation and taste they gradually supplanted the patrons on whom the native craftsmen depended, and so, indirectly, led to the rapid decline in the indigenous arts of Ireland. The process of change was accelerated by the Anglo-Norman invasion of AD 1169.

Later medieval developments

The Anglo-Norman invasion was triggered by internal Irish events, but its consequences for Ireland were dramatic and far-reaching. The invaders were spectacularly successful against the ill-prepared Irish. The adventurers who began the conquest were rapidly brought to acknowledge the authority of the crown of England even if they frequently chafed at restraint. Seizure of new territories was the constant imperative of the barons of the conquest who required land to reward their followers and large estates to support their households and maintain their prestige. The crown required an administration to dispense justice, raise revenues and enforce the royal will. The lords of the conquest held their new territories with castles. These were often of motte-and-bailey type – that is earthen mounds (mottes) with small enclosures (baileys) attached. In the immediate conquest phase, the mottes were often crowned with prefabricated castles of wood hung with hides as a precaution against fire. At a slightly later period, stone keeps were built on the mottes for example at Shanid, County Limerick. In the later twelfth century and in the thirteenth, royal castles were built at Dublin, Athlone and Limerick. The largest and finest castle to be built in the early thirteenth century was at
246

Trim, County Meath.

Architecture underwent a dramatic change with large cathedrals and other churches in the Gothic style being built in Dublin and elsewhere. The regular religious orders enjoyed the support of the conquerors, and abbeys like Jerpoint in County Kilkenny and Holycross in County Tipperary became very wealthy, as did the colony in general in the thirteenth century. Settlement in Ireland was encouraged, and attempts were made to entice settlers to rural areas by granting them burgess privileges. Many early settlements, the so-called deserted medieval villages, failed to survive. New resources were created, mines such as the Silvermines, County Tipperary, were exploited with imported expertise, and wool became an important part of monastic economies. In the thirteenth century, the Irish colony played a major part in victualling and shipping royal armies campaigning in France. The Dublin

Derryhiveny Castle, Co. Galway: tower house with fortified enclosure (bawn). Probably the last of the tower houses to be built, it was erected by Donal O'Madden in 1643.

excavations show a massive reorientation in foreign contact in this period. The finds are dominated by pottery from England, northern and south-western France, the latter almost certainly associated with the wine trade.

During the fourteenth century the colony went into decline – the revival of the Irish and the devastation of the 'black death' in mid-century, together with economic difficulties created problems for the royal administration. Many of the great Anglo-Norman families intermarried with the Irish, began to adopt native practices and identify more and more with Gaelic Ireland. The effect of this was that royal authority, apart from in a few walled towns, was effectively confined to an enclave on the east coast, the 'pale'. In the fifteenth century, architecture revived but with more modest buildings. The castles erected at this period tended to be small towers, sometimes with a defined, walled 'bawn' sometimes without, the so-called 'tower houses'. These, often very elegant fortified residences, remained popular until the seventeenth century because the rugged terrain and poor communications of Ireland inhibited the use of artillery. Church building was likewise more simple. Powerful Gaelic lords in the west, however, founded numerous religious houses with a distinctive local character.

In the sixteenth century, the Tudor monarchs of England set about the reconquest of Ireland. The process was slow and difficult because Gaelic Ireland lacked a centralised authority, so each lordship had to be subdued either by conquest or by the wooing of its ruler. In late medieval times, Ireland was still heavily forested, and there were great unhealthy tracts of undrained bog and so the terrain made campaigning

difficult. One important instrument of the conquest was *plantation* – the importation of new English or Scottish proprietors to occupy the lands of dispossessed Irish and Anglo-Irish and to provide, at a stroke, a loyal population or, at least, a landed class, who would form the basis of stable government in the crown's interest. Modern counties Laois and Offaly (formerly Queen's County and King's County) were planted under Philip and Mary, and Munster, after the rebellion of the Earl of Desmond somewhat later. The most enduring was the Ulster plantation of the early seventeenth century which followed the collapse of the last independent Gaelic lordships of Ulster.

The seventeenth century may well be noteworthy for its many and depressing military and civil events. For the student of the landscape it is the period of the final destruction of the forests which had been developing in Ireland since the end of the last Ice Age. Trees were felled for export for ship-building, for pike-staves for the wars of religion, for cooperage, for fuel for the smelting of iron in the countless small bloomeries of the time. Ireland gradually became a treeless landscape, dominated by the stone walls and hedgerows of later enclosure. The loss of trees increased the dependence on peat for fuel and so intensified the exploitation of bogland. The attack on the bogs was continued by improving landlords in the eighteenth century and by government-sponsored drainage schemes in the nineteenth. Today, the bogs themselves, with their unique flora and their precious record of environmental history and man's place in it, are threatened with extinction. We shall all lose a great deal if it happens.

DR MICHAEL RYAN is Keeper of Irish Antiquities at the National Museum of Ireland. He has travelled widely in Europe and America, working in museums and lecturing on Irish topics. Author of numerous articles on Irish archaeology, Dr Ryan has edited a number of books including *Treasures of Ireland* (National Museum of Ireland/Royal Irish Academy 1984) and *Ireland and Insular Art* (Royal Irish Academy 1986). He is chairman of the National Committee for Archaeology of the Royal Irish Academy and a member of the National Monuments Advisory Council and of the Historic Monuments Council.

STONE WALLS

John Feehan

White stonecrop is one of a group of plants very particularly associated with stone walls. Their fleshy leaves store water and act as storage coolers.

The earliest Irish fields were enclosed by massive dry-stone walls, but most of the straight field walls of today were built in the eighteenth and nineteenth centuries.

Right
A dilapidated early field wall showing traces of primitive rock-carving. Apart from passage tomb art, early rock carving is very rare in Ireland.

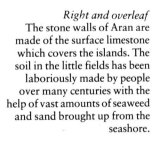

Right and overleaf
The stone walls of Aran are made of the surface limestone which covers the islands. The soil in the little fields has been laboriously made by people over many centuries with the help of vast amounts of seaweed and sand brought up from the seashore.

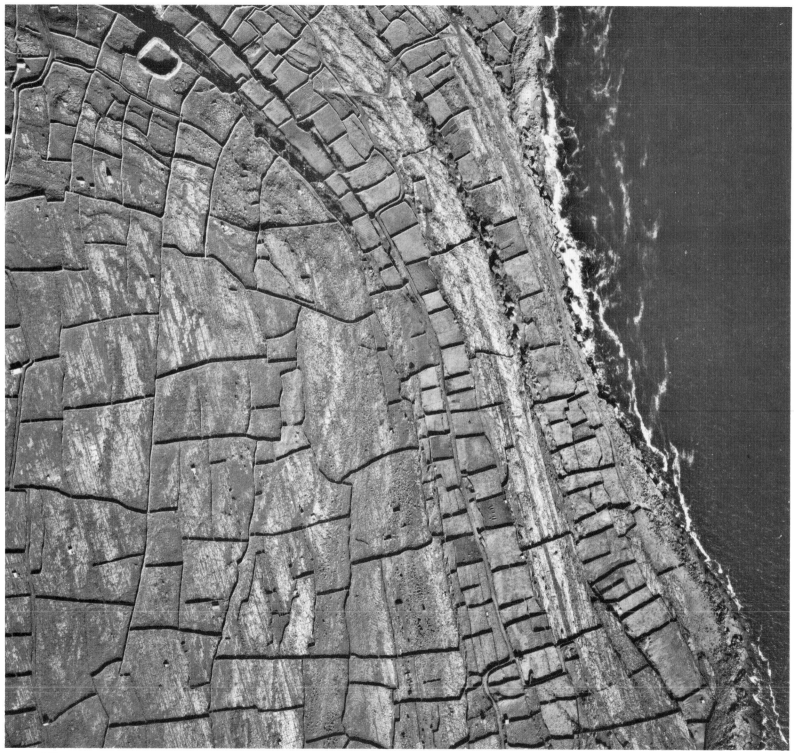

MILLS AND HOUSES
Drawings by Michael Craig

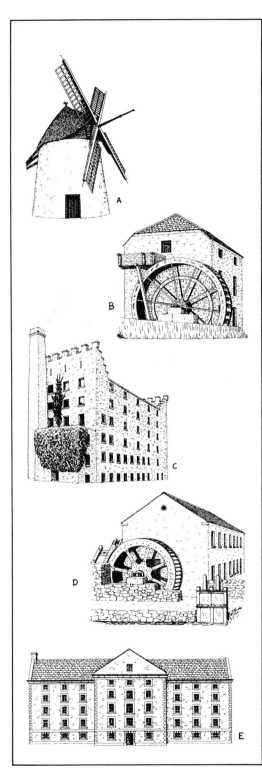

Mill buildings are the most widespread monuments of industrial archaeology in the countryside, and many are fine buildings with excellent stonework. Mill-wheels and machinery have seldom survived, but where they have they are an important part of the industrial past which should be preserved.

A Tacumshin, Co. Wexford
B Armytage's grist mill, near Nenagh, Co. Tipperary
C New Haggard Mills, near Trim, Co. Meath
D Wellbrook, Co. Tyrone
E Slane Mill, Co. Meath, 1766

The pattern of settlement in the countryside today is essentially that which began to develop from the late seventeenth century, and very few earlier houses survive. In the three centuries since then two broad trends in house-building can be identified: one following the classical tradition of Britain and Europe, generally identified with the wealthier groups in society and often showing little real regard for the existing natural character of the landscape, and in many cases eventually coming to dominate it; the other, following an earlier vernacular tradition in building, was often more in harmony with the surroundings.

A Mount Ivers, Co. Clare, built in the 1730s
B Corbally, Co. Kildare
C Luogh, Co. Clare
D Glencullen, Co. Wicklow
E Cloonagher, Co. Longford
F Alwories, Co. Tyrone

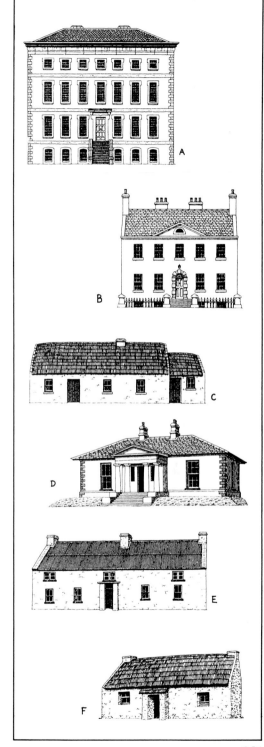

DYES FROM THE COUNTRYSIDE

Mairéad Dunlevy

Traditional dyes were used on the west coast of Ireland even after the development of chemical dyes. Today, the Guild of Spinners, Weavers and Dyers does much to promote interest in natural dyes.

The importance of colour in early Ireland is suggested by the Annals of the Four Masters which said that it was Tighearmas, king of Ireland, who first ordered clothes to be dyed purple, blue and green: colours which were then the most difficult and expensive to produce. Eight years later – by their reckoning about 1530 BC – his successor Eochaidh Eadghadach (Eochaidh the cloth designer) ordered that colours of clothes should denote a person's rank: different colours for the slave, soldier, lord, ollav (scholar), king and queen. Such a hierarchical approach to colour was not uniquely Irish. Considering this and the abundant references to colourful mantles in the first millennium AD as well as to brightly coloured clothing in the medieval period, it is surprising how little is known about the actual dyes used.

Obviously native vegetation – roots, bark, leaves and berries – was used. There is mention, for example, of a woman who had:

a vessel into which the juice of berries drips;
in that juice her black shawl was washed.

Moreover, Françoise Henry's excavation of a hut site on Inishkea North, off the Mayo coast, uncovered a late-seventh-century factory for making purple dye from *Purpura* shells. On the other hand Richard Warner's work on a crannog at Teesham, County Antrim, suggests that as early as the seventh or eighth century AD madder (a red dye) was imported. There is documentary evidence too for the importation of woad (a blue dye) in the thirteenth century.

Throughout much of the historic period it would seem that people – possibly according to their wealth – used native or imported dyes. Some of the latter became so popular

252

that attempts were made to grow them in Ireland. Such was the case with saffron which may have been grown at Castle Saffron, County Cork, if not elsewhere. The cultivation of madder, a colour commonly used into this century, was promoted in 1567. Although grown in Ireland then it would seem that the crop was not considered significant. In 1691 Sir William Petty – who pointed out that women remained as cloth dyers in rural areas, while men were in charge of industrial centres – recorded that:

Madder, Allum and Indico are import'd but the other dying stuffs they find nearer home, a certain mud taken out of the Bogs serving them for Copperas, the Rind [Bark] of Several Trees, and Saw-dust for Galls; as for wild and green weeds; they find enough, as also of Rhamus-Berries.

This would seem to have been the situation even in the eighteenth century when the Dublin Society (now the Royal Dublin Society) offered premiums to encourage the growth of certain popular dyes which were then imported. On the other hand, John Angel showed that in 1781, whatever about imported dyes, people commonly relied on indigenous plants. He listed those used in south County Dublin as hazel crottle which gave an orange colour; horehound, a deep lichen black; 'cup moss', a purple; elder juice, a peach; wormwood, a brown; 'blackberry alder', a yellow; and the bark of a barberry bush, a 'more beautiful' yellow. Angel said that south Dubliners also used sheep's sorrel with copper to get an olive dye.

Although chemical dyes were developed in the mid-nineteenth century the basic, traditional dyes remained in use on parts of the west coast – lichen, also known as crottle, being a particular favourite. Others included heather, bracken, blackberry, furze, fuchsia, onion and the edible seaweed called dulse. An interest in vegetable dyes which was encouraged by William Morris in England, was promoted by Evelyn Gleeson and her Dun Emer Guild here in the first decade of the twentieth century. The colours produced with vegetable dyes by the Wynne sisters at Avoca from 1927 are legendary. In our own time Lillias Mitchel has done much to encourage an interest in natural dyes, as has the Guild of Spinners, Weavers and Dyers, which she founded.

BRIDGES

Michael Barry

At practically every twist and turn of even the most minor country road in Ireland there is a bridge, even if it is no bigger than a culvert. Indeed, we have over 30,000 bridges altogether. Most people cross bridges every day, but rarely give them a second glance. Perhaps it is a tribute to how well our bridges blend and integrate into the scenery that they are hardly noticed. But they are there, not only adding grace and elegance to the environment, but carrying people, vehicles, trains and goods over the natural obstructions of river, sea and valley.

Bridges in ancient times

The first bridge was probably a tree blown by the wind which happened to fall across a stream and so came to be used by ancient peoples as a convenient passageway. In time, people learned to build bridges for themselves. Timber is an easy material to work and wooden bridges were apparently in use in Ireland from earliest times, though naturally nothing remains of these structures, as wood rots with time.

The Clapper Bridge at Louisburgh in Mayo is similar to a prehistoric type of bridge where simple stone slabs were used, and other bridges like this were built at Buttevant and Gougane Barra in County Cork.

The use of the arch in buildings goes back as far as the Sumerians in 4000 BC, and the Romans developed stone arch bridges and built them after their great conquest of Europe. The arch was used in early Christian Ireland in church buildings, but there is no evidence of masonry arch bridges from this period.

The Middle Ages

The monks, who were highly organised, were probably among the first stone bridge builders in the Anglo-Norman period. Monk's Bridge at Abbeyleix was built by the Cistercians. This old masonry arch bridge spans the River Nore and is located in the De Vesci estate in County Laois. With a narrow carriageway and small arches the bridge appears to be of an ancient form of construction. The stone in the arch soffits is built in a random manner. The cutwaters on one side appear to be of a later style, using

The Clapper Bridge, Louisburgh, Co. Mayo

dressed stone. It is believed to have been built in the thirteenth century by the Cistercian monks who founded a monastery here. It may even be older, possibly dating from the twelfth century, which would make it the oldest known surviving example in Ireland.

As the first stone bridge across the Thames was being completed, King John ordered the construction of stone bridges across the Liffey at Dublin and the Shannon at Limerick. At the beginning of the fourteenth century, an ecclesiastical builder, Canon Jakis, built Leighlinbridge. Although heavily modified on one side, this bridge is still in service.

Bridges of the fifteenth century include the

bridges at Newtown, near Trim in Meath and Glanworth in County Cork. The strategic needs of expansion of English rule led to the continuing development of roads and bridges from the sixteenth century onwards.

Recent times

Although we have some early bridges still in existence, not many very old bridges survive, because the poor foundations of old bridges tended to give way in flooding and so the bridges were destroyed. In the eighteenth century, however, bridge-building became more sophisticated, and George Semple, in his classic book *The Art*

of Building in Water described how he rebuilt the former Essex Bridge in Dublin in 1751–5, developing a cofferdam to construct sound foundations.

With the introduction of the canals and turnpike roads came a great period of bridge building, and much of the building work was supervised by expatriate engineers.

In the late eighteenth century an American, Lemuel Cox, built a great bridge of American oak at Derry, followed by others at Waterford, Ferrycarrig, Wexford, New Ross and Portumna.

Nimmo, Griffith and Bald, among

254

Opposite
Monk's Bridge, Abbeyleix. The monks were probably the first stone bridge builders in the Anglo-Norman period, and Monk's Bridge was built by the Cistercians in the twelfth or thirteenth century.

Right
The Spectacle Bridge, Lisdoonvarna, Co. Clare, spans the River Aille and carries a road across a deep gorge. A very unusual masonry bridge, it is thought to have been built in the period 1875–80.

location over the centre of the arch. This opening reduces weight on the structure below and would provide an easier passage for water if the river flooded to a high level.

The metal footbridge over the Liffey, known as the Ha'penny Bridge, was constructed in 1816. It is one of the earliest cast iron bridges. Another excellent example of cast iron construction is the graceful suspension bridge at Balleevy, County Down. It was built in 1845 to a design by James Dredge of Bath. The deck is suspended from wrought iron links, which rest on cast iron columns at each end of the bridge. Dredge built several other bridges in England, with varying degrees of success. Two of his bridges were at Caledon, County Tyrone, one of which still survives.

The Balleevy bridge is still in service, although load restricted. It carries a minor road over the Upper Bann. This is the sole remaining suspension bridge in the country which carries public road traffic.

Once again, the advanced technology of the age was used in a far-flung part of Ireland, using pre-cast concrete in a skilled way. The two arched ribs were pre-cast in sections on site. Using wire ropes as a temporary support they were built out from the abutments. The remainder of the bridge was cast *in situ*, suspended from the completed arch ribs. Despite poor access and unfavourable weather, the bridge was completed in 1910. With a span of 52m it was then the longest span reinforced concrete arch in these islands. In the grandeur of its setting, it is arguably the most resplendent bridge in Ireland.

A backward glance and a forward look

Many of the engineers of the eighteenth

others, were engaged in building roads and bridges in the remoter areas of Ireland during the early part of the nineteenth century. In France, Jean-Rodolphe Perronet had developed a method of design of bridges by calculation rather than by the old empirical methods. Alexander Nimmo emulated Perronet's masterpiece at Neuilly near Paris with his Wellesley Bridge at Limerick, completed in 1835. Now renamed Sarsfield Bridge, it is considered to be one of the finest masonry bridges in Ireland.

The Spectacle Bridge over the River Aille, about a kilometre south-west of the spa town of Lisdoonvarna in County Clare is one of the most unusual masonry bridges in the country. The bridge carries a road across a deep gorge and is thought to have been built in the period 1875–80.

The lower part of the bridge is a conventional semi-circular arch built over the river. Over this is built a circular opening of the same diameter as the arch below. Cylindrical openings were first incorporated in a bridge at Pontypridd in Wales, built in 1756, and became something of a style for bridges thereafter. The Spectacle Bridge, however, is unique in the large size of the opening and its

and nineteenth centuries, men like Brownrigg, Trail, Vallancey, Nimmo, Bald, Griffith, Benson, Macneill, made a great contribution to this country, but are scarcely heard of now. Engineers were the Renaissance men of that era and in Ireland they have left us with a legacy of magnificent bridges, which are not only functional enough to take today's traffic and loads, but are beautiful and elegant as well. In an ideal world these engineers would be commemorated in the same way as their contemporaries in Irish literature, art, and politics.

We are fortunate to have such a wealth of beautiful bridges, but many have been demolished and others have been abandoned. If we are not aware of the need to care for this legacy of our past we are in danger of losing it. Let us hope also that our bridge designers of the future will continue an older tradition and design bridges that are an ornament to their surroundings.

The coming of the railways

From about 1830 onwards, the introducion of the railways marked another great stride in bridge-building. Great viaducts were constructed and long distances spanned. The Craigmore Viaduct is one of the larger masonry railway bridges. It curves gracefully across the deep Camlough river valley. With eighteen semicircular masonry arches, each of 18m span, the bridge reaches a height of 43m over the valley. Situated about three kilometres north-west of Newry, County Down, it carries the Dublin–Belfast main line. The former electric tramway which ran from Newry to Bessbrook once passed under a central span of this bridge.

The viaduct was built in 1851–2 by William Dargan for the Dublin and Belfast Junction Railway Company at a cost in the region of £50,000. One of the larger engineering works of the mid-nineteenth century, it was designed by the eminent Victorian engineer, Sir John Macneill, who also prepared the original design of the

Boyne Viaduct.

The Boyne Viaduct is one of the premier bridges in Ireland. It carries the Dublin–Belfast main line over the River Boyne at Drogheda. It is 536m long with twelve masonry arches on the south and three on the north side of the river. Finally opened in 1855, it dominates the Drogheda

skyline. Most of the masonry came from quarries opened at the site of the viaduct. The lighter coloured stone used for fine detailing came from quarries at Ardbraccan and Milverton.

It was conceived by Sir John Macneill. James Barton, chief engineer of the Dublin and Belfast Junction Railway, designed and constructed it. Three spans, the centre one 81m long, arch over the waterway, with a clearance of 27m above high water. Originally, the wrought iron centre spans carried double tracks. Because of increasing axle loads and extensive corrosion, it was decided in the 1920s to renew the centre spans. Designed by G.B. Howden, chief

engineer of the Great Northern Railway, a new steel centre portion was completed in 1932 by the Motherwell Bridge and Engineering Company of Scotland. Before being removed, the old wrought iron lattice girders were used as support during the construction of the new structure. Double tracks at each end converge to interlaced tracks over the centre part of the viaduct.

Modern bridges

The railways led to innovations in bridge-building, a tradition which continues today. The reinforced concrete overbridge at Rosslare (1907) was among the earliest examples of 'ferro-concrete'. CIE built the

first pre-stressed concrete overbridge in 1952, the first all-welded steel bridge in 1958 and the first steel and concrete composite bridge at Tivoli, Cork, in 1969.

It is perhaps symbolic that a road bridge over the River Foyle became the longest bridge in Ireland in 1984, surpassing the 650m Barrow railway bridge. Just as the canals declined with the onset of the railways, the railway system has contracted as the road system has improved.

Recently in the Republic, earlier in Northern Ireland, there has been a great expansion in road building. As a result, there is a large number of new concrete bridges. While structurally efficient, few have the same aesthetic appeal as the older bridges. The opening of the toll bridge across the Liffey in 1984 marks a return to an older method of financing bridges.

The bridge at Mizen Head is one of the finest twentieth-century structures in the country. It is located in a rugged part of west Cork known locally as 'the nearest parish to America'. At a height of 45m over the sea below, this footbridge spans a chasm, giving access to the Irish Lights station at Mizen Head.

Opposite
Mizen Head, one of the finest twentieth-century bridges in Ireland.

Right
The Boyne Viaduct was opened in 1855 and carries the Dublin–Belfast railway line over the River Boyne at Drogheda.

MICHAEL BARRY was born in 1949 and is a native of Ballydehob in west Cork. He was educated in Waterford and Bristol and graduated from Trinity College Dublin in 1971. A chartered civil engineer, he has worked in Zambia and Bahrain. He is now employed by Irish Rail as Assistant Divisional Engineer, based in Dublin, and is currently involved in the maintenance of bridges and trackwork. He is the author of *Across Deep Waters – Bridges of Ireland* (Frankfort Press 1985). Michael Barry lives in Dublin and is married with two children.

POTTERIES

Mairéad Dunlevy

Archaeology shows that pottery was made in Ireland by the earliest farmers about 4000 BC, yet by the early Christian period, only an inefficiently fired plain ware was produced here, and potters had a position amongst the lowliest of inartistic craft-workers. The introduction of the potter's wheel and new-style kilns to urban areas in the thirteenth century brought a new type of potter, however, one who was conscious of the guild system and who worked close to the market. Following that example, the traditional potter in rural areas began to make wheel-turned wares. The greatest deterrent to the development of a wide variety of decorative wares in Ireland in the medieval period would seem to have been the absence of an enthusiastic buying public: as late as 1570 John Derricke noted that Irish people preferred to use turned wood or leather vessels. Excavations prove that the reasonably wealthy in cities and castles gave insufficient support to the local potter, being happier to spend their wealth on colourful ware imported from the continent and from Britain.

Growth in the seventeenth century

It would seem that potteries were transformed in the second half of the seventeenth century, a time of great general change in Ireland. The native population was adapting to a new lifestyle: one in which table manners (and therefore tableware) became more refined, as the kitchen was separated from the eating area in the homes of the wealthy. The transformation was prompted also by waves of immigrants who were used to ceramics in their homeland. There were other influences too: the quick acceptance of Sir Walter Raleigh's tobacco-smoking habit may be judged by the establishment in the seventeenth century of centres for pipe manufacture in areas convenient to a source of white clay.

Country potteries

'Country potteries', built close to red clay sources, were established by potters who were usually part-time farmers, many of whom seem to have been immigrants from Devonshire and Cornwall. A typical example is Carley's Bridge near Enniscorthy in County Wexford, which is now one of the oldest of these potteries surviving. It was established about 1654 by the two Kerley (Carley) brothers. They sited it beside a good red clay source and on the banks of the River Urrin. For generations the family have owned the pottery and a farm. For generations too the principal potters at Carley's Bridge were members of the Brickley family, immigrant potters who had worked initially in a pottery in nearby Davidstown. A direct descendant, Paddy Murphy, has established his own pottery near Carley's Bridge now and works it in the traditional manner.

The style of building at Carley's Bridge is similar to those of long-abandoned country potteries in the same county. The work area allotted to the potter is small, considering that there he will cut the worked clay into required weights, throw it on the wheel and then place the thrown and shaped pieces on a plank for carriage to the drying shed. Nowadays the

Samuel Brickley and his sons in the brickfields at Carley's Bridge, Enniscorthy, Co. Wexford, *c.* 1890

potter's wheel is worked electrically, but in the past that energy was supplied by the muscles of an assistant who sat in a pit and turned a crank wheel. In contrast the drying shed is long, narrow and airy so that the pots can dry slowly on the wooden shelves. The kiln at Carley's Bridge is built in the lee of the buildings. This method of protecting the kiln fires from the wind may have been considered adequate in an under-capitalised industry in bygone days. This probably explains why we do not have today the remnants of many bottle kilns, which might have added interest to the landscape.

Ware produced in these country potteries would seem to have been well-fired red-bodied tableware, together with pails or crocks with a glazed interior, particularly useful in the dairy. Their markets would have been confined to the immediate districts, possibly directly from potter to purchaser.

Bricks and pipes

Other traditional pottery areas in which the abundance of clay is clearly obvious when you visit them today are Coalisland, County Tyrone, and Youghal, County Cork. Many such potteries also made bricks. Indeed the number of 'brickfields' as place-names are testimony to the extent of this local industry. The photograph of Samuel Brickley and his sons working in the brickfield at Carley's Bridge shows the style of manufacture, a method which remained unaltered since the introduction of brick-manufacture to this

country in the seventeenth century. The wet clay was thrown into a wooden mould, which was then placed on the ground to dry. When leather-hard, the bricks were stacked and dried further in the sheds before firing. With the expansion of the building industry in the nineteenth century, factories were established to make bricks mechanically. Some of those bricks were stamped with the name of the pottery. The quality of the machine- and hand-finished terracotta bricks made may be seen in some fine period buildings throughout the country. The outstanding quality of the Kingscourt, County Cavan, bricks – an area in which bricks are still made – is particularly noticeable.

Although clay pipes were imported particularly from Bristol, they were also made in Waterford by the 1640s. In due course tobacco pipes were made in centres such as Carrickfergus, Derry, Newry, Belfast, Dublin, Cork, Limerick, Waterford and Knockcroghery, County Roscommon. Each

period brought its own style of clay pipe, the bowl size being not unrelated to the tobacco price at the time.

Fresh growth in the nineteenth century

The nineteenth century saw a growing demand for a change of attitudes in Ireland. Patriots and idealists such as William Smith O'Brien advocated that people should 'rely on themselves, exert natural energies more and depend less on chances of Government patronage'. Sir Robert Kane illustrated that high quality ceramics – with white or red bodies – could be made in Ireland, and indicated sources of clay which would be suitable for different types of wares.

Such zeal and encouragement bore fruit: the older country potteries were injected with a new vitality and other potteries were established. There was, for example, an increase in the number of potteries making drainage pipes, tiles for roofing and flooring, hollow bricks and fire bricks. These existed as

Rolling shapes for clay pipes at Hamilton's of Belfast in the 1920s. Hamilton's began making pipes in 1812, but like many other factories went out of business with the introduction of cigarettes.

Classical ewer of burnished red clay made at Florence Court, Co. Fermanagh about 1860.

aware of the development of art pottery elsewhere in the late nineteenth to early twentieth century and so a number ventured into an artistic range. The pioneer of this in Ireland may have been the third Earl of Enniskillen who, because of destitution in his district caused by the Great Famine, and because there were local clay deposits, started a brick and tile factory in Florence Court, County Fermanagh, in the 1840s. About twenty years later his pottery made a superbly proportioned classical-style ewer of burnished red clay. Similarly Samuel Murland of the Castle Espie works near Comber in County Down complemented the regular slip, sgraffito and agate-style products of his factory with a remarkable *jardinière* (garden pot) which used an Egyptian sphinx motif.

Belleek

The most successful project of this mid-nineteenth-century industrial drive was the Belleek pottery. Like practically all of the Irish potteries mentioned, it was sited convenient to sources of clay (porcelain clays and fire-clay for saggers) to turf banks and to fast running water (the River Erne). Belleek pottery is remarkable in many ways. A sophisticated pottery was built in a rural area which was remote from Staffordshire (the centre of pottery in Britain) and which was desolated by famine. It is also surprising how quickly people who were used to working on the land and who continued to farm 'after hours' adapted to the discipline of long hours of industrial labour. They readily adopted the traditional attitudes of Staffordshire potters, including a superb pride in their products. With great vision, the planners built a private track to transport clay to the works long

far apart as Tipperary, Dungannon, Enniskillen, Limerick, Dublin, Larne, Youghal and Cork. Success was assured as their products were in demand in the second half of the nineteenth century; the raw

material was available locally and little capital or skill was required.

Art pottery

The proprietors of those manufactories were

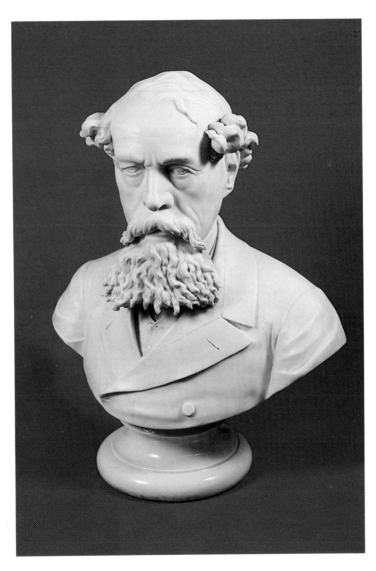

Bust of Charles Dickens by William Gallimore, Belleek, *c.* 1865

washed rough-stone walls and winding stone stairs with a narrow iron hand-rail. Down these stairs long planks laden with ware have been carried for over a century.

A surviving tradition

Many Irish art potteries today use imported clay, but it is comforting to see the survival of tradition and watch the potters of Enniscorthy, Youghal and Shanagarry digging, working and throwing local clays. The most exciting new development, though, must be that at Kiltrea Bridge, near Enniscorthy, where Michael Roche not only makes beautiful pots in red clay but prepares and sells various Irish clays, challenging and enabling potters throughout the country to take a pride in their own tradition.

MAIRÉAD DUNLEVY MA is assistant keeper in charge of glass, ceramics, textiles and philatelic collections in the art and industrial division of the National Museum of Ireland. She has published articles in various journals on ceramics, lace, glass, postal history and aspects of the decorative arts and two books under the name of Mairéad Reynolds: *A History of the Irish Post Office* (MacDonnell Whyte 1983) and *Some Irish Fashions and Fabrics* (National Museum of Ireland 1984).

before the Great Northern Railway was extended to Belleek. Until 1866 fragile porcelain was packed in willow crates and transported by donkey, or horse and cart, to the port of Ballyshannon or the nearest railway station at Enniskillen.

The building at Belleek is remarkable. It was built of local granite about 1858/9 for a reputed £10,000. The management still preserves the original interior of white-

FOLK TRADITION AND THE RURAL ENVIRONMENT

Séamas Mac Philib

Ireland has a folk tradition that is specially rich in comparison with that of other European countries. This rich folk-culture evolved partly because Ireland is geographically isolated. Most people had to look to their own personal resources and to the natural resources that lay to hand around them in order to meet their physical and artistic needs.

Vernacular houses

Local materials and the influence of the prevailing environment can clearly be seen in vernacular houses (houses built according to the folk tradition). These houses were formerly the majority house type throughout the country but are rapidly becoming relatively rare.

From a visual point of view, the use of local building materials meant that the traditional house formed almost a natural part of the landscape. The tradition dictated simplicity of style and proportion, in contrast to the vernacular styles of some other cultures. Traditional Irish houses are typically rectangular in plan, one room deep, with a sloped, thatched roof. Thatch has now been replaced by slate and tiles or corrugated iron in many cases. Walls are typically of stone or clay, white-washed on the exterior, and windows and doors are usually in the side walls rather than at the ends. The hearth lies on the long axis of the house and traditionally is at floor-level.

The traditional house is relatively narrow, partly because long lengths of timber to form wide roof-beams were not available, as the country had been almost denuded of forests by the end of the seventeenth century. Some vernacular houses of the seventeenth and early eighteenth centuries, when suitable timber was available, had larger roof-spans however. From this time on, fossil timber buried in bogs was used increasingly for roof-beams. On top of these, twigs or laths would be arranged to support a layer of sod taken from a closely grazed sward and having a thick mat of grass-roots. This layer served both as an insulation and as a base for the subsequent layers of thatch.

Thatch was most commonly of wheat straw, which is now becoming scarce as modern strains of wheat developed for the combine harvester leave a short straw which is not suitable for thatching. Rye straw and, in the north, flax, were among the alternatives. Reeds, which were used in parts of Munster

An original vernacular house now used for tourist accommodation in Connemara, Co. Galway. Newly built 'traditional' houses for holiday rental do not always conform with strict local building tradition.

and around Lough Neagh, are becoming increasingly popular as a thatching material, as it is relatively long-lasting and perhaps because of imported British and continental traditions of thatching.

The most common method of securing the thatch to the roof was by means of 'scollops' – bent, sharpened rods, which held bundles of thatch in place and were concealed by subsequent bundles placed above them. This form of thatching might last over ten years, but it will not stand up to gale-force winds for long. Consequently, all along the exposed seaboard from Antrim westwards to Cork, the thatch was commonly secured by a network of ropes, kept taut by tying weights to their ends where they overhang the eaves or fastened to pegs driven into the outer walls of the house. Roped thatch is less waterproof than scollop thatch, however, as the criss-cross of ropes breaks the flow of rainwater. Consequently, it is necessary to renew this type of thatch every two years or so. Often chicken-wire or an old fishing net is used to supplement the rope-network. Apart from these common methods of thatching, in parts of north Leinster thatch was sewn directly with cords onto the roof timbers and in County Down, 'stapple' thatching, whereby straw bundles were embedded in mud laid on the roofing rods, has been encountered.

House-walls were largely built of local materials, local stone and mortar being the most common material. The mortar might be made from burnt limestone or sea-shells or from subsoil clay. Clay was sometimes also used to make the walls of houses when stones were not plentiful. It was prepared by digging in a pit, and adding water, straw and rushes or other materials for binding. It was built up in layers to form the walls, rarely using shuttering. Windows and doors were cut out using a spade. Houses of this type were often regarded as warmer than houses constructed of other materials, though they need to be kept well roofed and plastered. When such houses are de-roofed, the action of the elements breaks down the walls within a short space of time.

There are two fundamental types of roof-form on the traditional house. North and west of a line drawn from approximately Drogheda in the east to Carraroe in the west, and in west Clare, Kerry and west Cork, the majority of houses have high, triangular gable-end walls, which leave a roof of two sloping sides. Elsewhere a 'hip' roof-type predominates. This is more rounded in shape, having four sloping sides. There is evidence to suggest that the hip-type predominated in areas where the gable-type now does, and in Ulster this transformation appears to have come with the influx of English and Scottish settlers during the seventeenth century.

The hip-roofed house is characterised by a hearth located in the centre of the house, while a gable-roof also permits location of the hearth in a gable-wall. On the western seaboard and in the northern half of the country where the gable-type predominates, houses are typified by an entrance which opens directly into the living space and is situated well away from the hearth. Often a rear-door lies directly opposite the front-door. This feature is associated with a tradition of byre-dwelling, in which several cows were accommodated in the same living space as the human occupants. The opposite doors permitted easy entrance and exit of the animals. This type of house survived in north-west Connacht and north-west Ulster until the end of the last century and in a few cases into this century, after which time the space for animals was generally converted into an additional bedroom. The combined human-byre dwelling has also been recorded in parts of Britain and western France.

Another distinctive feature of many northern and north-western Irish vernacular houses is the 'outshot' or bed-alcove, which is a small recess in the rear wall beside the hearth, and took the form of a small projection on the outside rear wall. This alcove usually contained a bed for an old member of the household as one of the Irish names for it, *cailleach* (hag), indicates. The feature has been recorded in many of the same districts in Britain and France where byre-dwellings are also found.

Distinct from the direct-entry house is the 'hearth-lobby' type, where the entrance door leads directly onto the hearth area, but is separated from it by a screen or 'jamb' wall which forms a lobby immediately inside the entrance. This wall is usually fitted with a small 'spy' window, which allows light into the hearth area, and also gives a person sitting at the hearth a view out the door when open. This type of house plan is ubiquitous, apart from the extreme north and the western seaboard. It is almost unknown in Scotland, but occurs in north-east and north-west England. Its distribution in Ireland in the areas of greatest English settlement points to an English origin, which documentary evidence for its introduction in Derry in the early seventeenth century bears out.

The jamb-wall made it more or less impossible to bring cows into the house and had the effect too of emphasising the distinction between the area outside the house and that which lay within. It created a reception area which separated a caller to the house from the family living space. Increasingly with rising living standards, the breakup of communal villages and with other

263

Left
Vernacular house at
Ballyconneely Bay, Co. Galway.
The thatch is secured by ropes.
Houses with high gable walls
and the entrance away from the
hearth predominated on the
western seaboard and in the
northern half of the country.

Opposite
St Bridget's holy well,
Clondalkin, Co. Dublin.
Religious objects, but also rags,
coins or other metal objects
were often attached to the trees
found alongside holy wells.

social changes, the creation of reception areas became a feature of traditional houses. This, and other changes, such as the provision of separate bedrooms, reflected an increased concern with individualism and privacy. From the latter half of the nineteenth century increasing numbers of vernacular houses would be of two storeys and there would be less reliance on local materials in their construction. Such houses still retained the basic vernacular character, however.

Little of the housing erected in rural Ireland in recent decades retains this character. Designs are mostly derived from standard design-books, reflecting urban/suburban values or the fashions of other countries. Demolition of vernacular houses is also taking place at a great rate. For instance, of twenty-nine traditional thatched houses recorded in Rush, in north County Dublin in 1980, only fifteen now remain. Relatively

little refurbishment of such houses to accord with contemporary needs takes place. A grant structure for preservation of these dwellings, coupled with extension of home-improvement grants to assist re-thatching, would go some way to stem the tide of destruction, otherwise one can only hope for an increase in appreciation of the folk-heritage alongside that which seems to exist in larger measure for the formal cultural heritage.

Traditional skills and crafts

Formerly, apart from the materials used in house construction, the average country person was skilled in exploiting a great range of materials from the surrounding environment to other practical effect. Some skills using local materials were of course primarily practised by specialists, such as pottery, 'fancy' basket-work and carpentry. However, the average person was adept at

fashioning a variety of materials for all kinds of useful purposes.

Use of straw in particular reveals the ingenuity and skill of people in fashioning a wide range of items from a simple local material. Rope-making from straw (and also from hay, animal hair and even fibres of bog-deal) was a common skill. Apart from the normal use which a rope might be put to, straw rope or *súgán* was formed into mats, baskets, screens, bee-skeps, armchairs, hens' nests, harness, mattresses, pads for carrying loads on the head and as the seats of *súgán* chairs. In parts of Cork and Kerry, an outdoor granary known as a *fóir* or *síogóg* was made from thick coils of straw rope built up around an internal filling of grain. When thatched the granary looked like a haystack.

Other grasses were pressed into a variety of uses also. Rushes were fashioned into baskets and into a range of toys such as butterfly

cages, rattles, nets for catching small fish, and whips. Peeled rushes dipped in oils were widely used in the pre-electric age for lighting. Tied bundles of dried rushes were used as swimming aids. A unique raft in north-European terms made from reed is preserved in the folklife collection of the National Museum of Ireland. These craft were in use up to about sixty years ago on the River Suck in south Roscommon, particularly for negotiating floods which were common in the area, as well as for fishing and hunting fowl.

Plant-lore

Plants were exploited in a variety of ways. Apart from their use in making dyes, they had particular value in the treatment of sickness. Many hundreds of varieties were used, especially dock, elder, ivy, garlic, nettle, sorrel, coltsfoot, crowsfoot and dandelion. Most herbs were used to make poultices or liquid medicine for common ailments such as cuts, swellings, warts, ringworm and stomach-ache. Many of the herbs undoubtedly did contain curative properties: foxglove was known as a cure for a bad heart and in modern medicine also, the extract from its leaves, digitalis, is used to treat heart and kidney ailments.

Certain plants and growths were believed to have magical properties too. Houseleek growing on the gable or roof of a house was believed to protect it from fire and lightning. It was believed that pimpernel gave second sight to a person who carried a sprig. Yarrow was supposed to ward off evil and if placed under one's foot in the shoe, gave temporary fluency of speech. Similarly, various types of wood supposedly had extra-normal properties. A piece of rowan or mountain ash in the collar of a hound was supposed to increase its speed. A band of rowan twigs might be tied around the churn when the butter failed to come, as it was believed that butter could be 'taken' by magical means. Hazel was also believed to be powerful in warding off malevolent fairies.

The supernatural

Sacred trees

Certain trees had a para-normal significance. The distribution of the Irish word for a sacred tree, *bile*, in place-names, indicates that the cult of the sacred tree was relatively widespread. These trees were often associated with ecclesiastical and inauguration rites, and where the memory of them survived in modern folk tradition it was believed that great misfortune would befall anyone who interfered with them. Sacred trees feature in many cultures internationally and in antiquity.

In more modern folk tradition, the lone whitethorn bush is attributed a supernatural significance and the earlier tradition of the *bile* may have been transferred to it. The lone whitethorn is believed to be under the care of the fairies and woe betide anyone who interferes with it. This belief still holds a degree of sway all over Ireland and indeed in recent years, the destruction of a lone bush in the course of the construction of the De Lorean motor-car plant in Belfast was believed by some to have caused the collapse of that enterprise.

Holy wells

Sacred trees were also commonly found alongside that ubiquitous feature of the Irish countryside, the holy well. It is estimated that there are some 3000 of these throughout the country. They are generally dedicated to a saint and were traditionally visited – and many still are – on the feast day of the saint or on some major religious feast day. 'Rounds' are usually performed and prayers are recited and often religious objects such as medals and rosary beads but also pins, nails, buttons, coins or rags may be attached to the tree at the well. Holy wells were generally held to have curative qualities in their waters. Some wells had specialised powers, particularly for eye ailments. At several of these wells, the healing power is attributed to St Bridget, who according to legend had plucked out her eyes to dissuade an unwanted suitor, but had her sight restored again by the water of the well.

Many, if not most, wells are of pre-Christian origin. In France sacred wells have been shown to go back as far as the neolithic era. Christianity came to embrace the cult eventually, but during the Middle Ages attempts were made to stamp it out in Europe. Despite their association with Christianity, the belief that a curse could be placed on someone by performing an anti-clockwise round of the well survived into relatively recent times. Similarly, cursing stones, where they occur, were often located beside or near to a holy well as at St Bridget's Well, near Blacklion, County Cavan; Tobar Mhuire on Caher Island, County Mayo; St Colmcille's Well on Tory Island; Tobar na Seacht nIníon at Rinville, County Galway; St Bridget's Well, Faughart, County Louth; St Molaise's Well on Inismurray, County Sligo; St MacDara's Island, County Galway. The stones are usually on an altar-like structure and these may have been used in the pre-Christian as well as in the Christian era.

The fairies

There was a complex and all-pervasive corpus of beliefs, traces of which are still encountered, about the fairies. Not unsurprisingly, these supposedly ubiquitous

supernatural beings left their mark on the countryside. Their supposed dwelling places abounded and were believed to be in mounds and certain specific hills and mountains such as Knockma in Galway, Slievenamon in Tipperary, Cnoc Áine in Donegal, Knockfierna in Limerick and Knocknarea in Sligo. There are parallels for such traditions in early Irish mythology. When the *Tuatha Dé Danann* (the peoples of the goddess Danu) were defeated by the invading Gaels, they are described as having retreated underground and each of their chiefs as having been assigned a mound or *sídh*. The *Tuatha Dé* were gods of pre-Christian Ireland and traditions about them bear many similarities to traditions about the fairies of later folk tradition. The reluctance of people

to interfere with forts for fear of provoking the wrath of the fairies is one of the reasons why so many forts have survived. Feelings were so strong on this matter that in one instance in County Mayo in 1959 and reported in the *Daily Mail*, when construction of a new road would have meant encroaching on a fort, the Land Commission labourers involved went on strike rather than proceed with the road.

People who were believed to have been kidnapped by the fairies – which was a way to explain inexplicable death, illness or oddness of behaviour – were supposedly imprisoned in the forts and might be rescued from the fairy host within by using holy water or a black-handled knife. Such beliefs could motivate individuals to the 'appropriate'

Left
A raft made from reeds with a wooden superstructure. Used on the River Suck, Co. Roscommon. There is little evidence for such craft elsewhere in northern Europe.

Opposite
A swimming aid made from rushes of a type used on Upper Lough Erne. Locally called a *currach*. This is not to full size which normally had a diameter of a car-tube, approximately. Now preserved in the Ulster Folk and Transport Museum.

266

action. Bridget Cleary, a housewife of twenty-six years of age, was tormented and burnt to death by her husband and several neighbours in the district of Ballyvadlea, near Mullinahone in County Tipperary in 1894 in the belief that she was a fairy-changeling. (Her possible mental ill-health and childlessness were probably the cause of this belief.) In the celebrated trial which followed the murder, one witness reported that he saw the husband in possession of a big table-knife. He said apparently that it was his intention to go to the fort where his real wife would be riding a grey horse and where he would cut the ropes that were tying her to the saddle with the knife. He was subsequently convicted of manslaughter and sentenced to twenty years penal servitude.

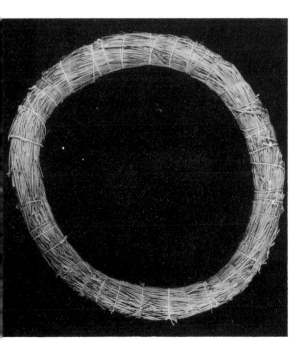

Apart from their dwelling places, which might be recognised by the human eye, the fairies were believed to have numerous paths and roads which, if blocked or interfered with, could invoke their wrath. Consequently, when a site for a house was being selected, great care was taken in ensuring that a safe site was chosen. An old two-shilling piece, bearing a cross on the obverse side, might be tossed in the air on the site and if it came down cross upwards all was deemed well. Otherwise, small piles of stones, cut bushes, or rods might be placed in the four corners of the site and left overnight. If they remained undisturbed in the morning it could be assumed that there was no objection. Similarly a shallow trench might be dug and left overnight for inspection on the following day. The concern of these practices with the supernatural may also mirror a concern not to interfere with the paths and places of nocturnal and wild animals generally.

Some forts, mounds and hills were reputed to have other occupants within apart from the fairies. A relatively common legend in Ireland was the 'Arthurian' legend told in many other European countries of a sleeping hero and his army waiting somewhere for the opportune time to free their people from bondage. This legend most commonly attaches to Gearóid Iarla (Earl Gerald) and seems to be based on the real historical personages of Garret Fitzgerald, the third Earl of Desmond (1338–98) who was chief justice of Ireland from 1367 to 1369 and a noted Gaelic poet, and also Garret Fitzgerald the eleventh Earl of Kildare (1525–80), a stepbrother of the rebel, Silken Thomas. The legend also attaches to Balldearg (Red Spot) O'Donnell (1650–1703), who fought on both sides during the Williamite wars. It was believed that an Earl of Tyrconnell marked with a red

spot would free his country. Balldearg is said to sleep with his men in Killargue mountain in Leitrim. Red Hugh O'Neill (1599–1649) and Red Hugh O'Donnell (1571–1607) are supposed to await the time in the Grianán of Aileach in Donegal and Finn MacCool and the Fianna in the hill of Sheamore in Leitrim.

Forts were often the burial places of stillborn children or children who died unbaptised, and could not therefore enter heaven, according to Roman Catholic doctrine. Other places which were believed to be somehow in contact with the supernatural world were often chosen as burial places such as crossroads, lone bushes and holy wells. Apart from such places, unconsecrated burial grounds for the unbaptised and also suicide victims, strangers or bodies washed ashore abound all over the country.

It was also believed that if one stepped on a place where an unbaptised child had been buried one might be overcome by an uncontrollable hunger – such a place was known as the 'hungry grass' or *féar gortach*. One might also become totally disorientated in that even the most familiar location became totally unrecognisable – the 'stray sod' or *fóidín mearbhaill*. These spots on the landscape were also believed to have been places where famine victims died or where a dead baby had touched the ground.

High places such as hills and mountains often have supernatural associations. This is the case internationally and probably derives from the nearness of mountains to the sky, which is believed to belong to superhuman powers and beings. In pre-Christian Ireland, it appears that offerings of corn were made to the god *Lugh* from hill and mountain tops on the festival of Lughnasa at the beginning of harvest.

In modern times this festival was celebrated

Making a mat from *súgán* or straw rope. Baskets, bee-skeps, armchairs, mattresses, harness, chair seats and other articles were made from straw rope.

mostly on the last Sunday in July or the first Sunday in August and usually took the form of an excursion to a hilltop, or to some sites beside certain lakes and rivers. Sports, dancing, drinking and feasting and sometimes faction fighting were indulged in. Some sites became pilgrimage venues such as Croagh Patrick in Mayo, to which thousands still come on the last Sunday in July, Mount Brandon in Kerry, Slieve Donard in the Mournes, Church mountain in Wicklow and Mám Éan in the Maumturks, Galway.

Apart from the traditions common to many localities outlined here, every locality had its own unique traditions about the surrounding environment arising from particular local events and circumstances. Every locality has traditions attaching to its place-names for

example and the apportioning of place-names could often be very detailed. In one Irish-speaking townland, Kilgalligan in north-west Mayo comprising only 852 acres, over 800 place-names have been recorded in recent years. The use and retention of many place-names is declining with succeeding generations as are many of the types of traditions outlined here, however.

In many and diverse ways the countryside formerly had a use value and a significance which has changed. For many rural people until relatively recent times, the relationship with the countryside could often be very close by virtue of material necessity and strength of association of tradition. The countryside for many was imbued with an emotional complexity which is now perhaps difficult to

appreciate. While traditions and practices of a former way of life have largely passed on, a knowledge and awareness of them provides us with a deeper appreciation of the countryside around us and with a deeper appreciation of the peoples who have inhabited the countryside from earliest times to the present day.

SÉAMAS Mac PHILIB studied folk tradition at University College Dublin, in Finland and at the Ulster Folk and Transport Museum. He is currently pursuing a doctoral degree at UCD on the impact of the landlord system on folk tradition in Ireland. He works in the Department of Finance in Dublin.

GRAVEYARDS AND GRAVESTONES

Richard Clarke

Glendalough, in a wooded valley in Co. Wicklow, showing the round tower, ruins of the cathedral and surrounding graveyard.

Old graveyards with weathered stone gables, perhaps a round tower, and scattered lichen-covered gravestones are among the most evocative features of the Irish countryside. They have a peaceful air, and the grass grows up and dies from season to season with little interference.

Early Christian graveyards

In remote rural areas you can sometimes find a type of graveyard that has passed out of general use: a burial ground for special groups. The best known of these are killeens or plots for the burial of unbaptised children. There were similar special plots for suicides, shipwrecked sailors or men killed in battle, none of whom would have received the last rites. There are even some special burial grounds for women, of which there are examples at Inismurray, County Sligo, and Relignaman (which means 'the women's graveyard') in County Tyrone. The reason for the separate burial of women is not clear, but it is presumably related to chastity and the practice of separate worship, as in the Nuns' Church at Clonmacnois.

A notable feature of medieval burial grounds is that they are raised above the surrounding countryside. This is particularly apparent when there is a ruined church which appears to have sunk into the ground. Constant disturbance of the soil over many generations and the accumulation of organic matter help to raise the level steadily and indeed gravestones also sink. Sometimes also the graveyard was established on a natural hill as at Killeen Cormac, County Kildare, or Slanes, County Down, and excavation at Kilnasaggart, County Armagh, showed that the graveyard area had been artificially heightened to create a greater depth for burials.

Many of the old churchyards are circular, and this may be because an old rath or ringfort was donated by an Irish chieftain as a

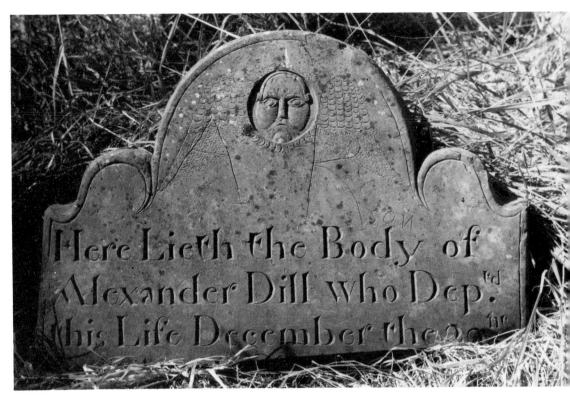

site of the new Christian church. Sometimes the ancient circular centre is visible in a larger graveyard, as at Maghera, County Down, with later burials spilling out beyond. Circular graveyards occur also in western Britain, and the explanation is not fully understood.

The settings of the Celtic monasteries are particularly beautiful, even among the general run of old graveyards. Part of their attraction arises from the proximity to water, whether they are on the banks of the River Shannon as at Clonmacnois, high above Strangford Lough as at Nendrum, County Down, or on an island in Lough Erne as at Devenish. All were pillaged by the Vikings many times, but since then they have become places of pilgrimage and burial (apart from Nendrum which was forgotten until it was rediscovered by Bishop Reeves in about 1840). Devenish has been spared the tasteless modern memorials with 'stones' which are mixtures of cement, perspex insets and ceramic flowers which have appeared even on medieval sites.

The earliest Christian memorials to individuals are the cross-inscribed slabs of the eighth to twelfth centuries, and a particularly large group is to be seen at Clonmacnois. However, only a few stones of this type name the person concerned. Clonmacnois has a slab from *c.* AD 900 reading 'Or do Feidlimid qui occisus est sine causa'. The 'Or do' formula (meaning 'a prayer for') appears in many old graveyards, and there are similar slabs in Movilla, County Down, with 'Or do Dertrend' and in Kells, County Meath, with 'Or do Riag. . .'. Unfortunately in most cases nothing further is known of the individual, and they cannot be tied in with the names in the Irish Annals. The high crosses scattered through the older graveyards were not, of

course, personal memorials at all. In fact, the term 'scripture crosses' indicates their main function, which was to illustrate important episodes from the Old and New Testaments. These can be found in relatively obscure graveyards, such as Donaghmore, only a mile from the Newry–Banbridge road, but much less famous than Kells and Monasterboice.

Gravestones down the centuries

The Norman conquest brought a new and distinctive type of grave monument. They are coffin-shaped slabs with bevelled edges and a carved cross occupying the whole length of the stone, and they would have lain horizontally over the grave. The arms of the cross usually terminate in a stylised flower or sometimes in a crescent. The shaft rises from a stepped base and may have drooping leaves at the sides. Such slabs are to be found in the areas of Norman occupation, east Ulster, Leinster and Munster, with the highest

concentration in east Down where about fifty have been identified. In this northern group the sex is usually indicated by the representation of a sword (for a man) on the left side of the cross-shaft, or by shears (for a woman) on the right side. There are also more steps at the base and a characteristic cross-bar at the top of the shaft in the slabs of County Down. The largest single collection of these thirteenth-to-fifteenth-century slabs is in the graveyard at Movilla, Newtownards, but they are found in very many country graveyards.

Sixteenth-century slabs are usually rectangular and the cross no longer dominates the design. The MacSweeney family stone of this period in Castle Doe churchyard, County Donegal, preserves the older style, but adds various animals beside the cross-shaft and an inscription in middle English. Another late slab, at Clonca in north Donegal, has a design which includes a hurley

Opposite
Fragment of Dill headstone
with primitive carving of face
and angel's wings.

Right
The Celtic monastic site on
Devenish Island with its
complete round tower (twelfth
century). It was founded by St
Molaise in the sixth century,
raided by Vikings in 837,
burned in 1157, but still
flourished later as an
Augustinian priory and parish
church.

stick and ball and an inscription in Scottish
Gaelic. However, these inscriptions are
unusual and the principal language on
memorials before 1600 was Latin. Another
late medieval development is the depiction of
a corpse or skeleton, often with a shroud, as
at Castledermot, County Kildare.
Throughout the period 1200–1600 there
were also slabs with incised effigies of knights
and ecclesiastics as well as the more elaborate
sculpted figures, but all of these are more
usually features of churches rather than
graveyards.

The rectangular slabs of the seventeenth
century continue to have an inscription in
raised lettering round the edge or across the
centre, but figures or a coat of arms appear
instead of a cross. The lettering during this
period was usually in roman capitals and
raised rather than cut, so that it has survived
the effects of weathering particularly well.
Latin and English are both found, but later
English became the norm except for clerics.

The eighteenth century saw the first
appearance of headstones or large vertical
stones at the head end of the grave. At about
the same time more elegant styles of lettering

developed, though capitals continued to be used. Inscriptions from this period have often survived well. However, in the last hundred years cutting has become shallower and this, along with the practice of using lead insets, has contributed to the poor quality of relatively modern inscriptions.

Survival of an inscription often depends as much on the type of stone used as on the lettering. Slate is undoubtedly the best and that from Bangor in north Wales has been imported into the east coast ports at least since the eighteenth century. Its fine grain prevents the entry of water which in other stones swells with freezing and causes flaking. In addition, the texture permits very sharp cutting of letters and has encouraged the addition of elaborate art-work, both religious and geometric. Sometimes a local shale was substituted for slate and the inscription has gradually flaked off with the years. Where granite was available, as in the Mourne mountains, it was used in its rough state and weathering has almost obliterated any inscription. In modern times a polished granite has been introduced, and though it does not weather away, it can be very hard to read in bad light. Weathering is also a major problem of the soft sandstone of County Down. In the last hundred years also economy has led to the use of a soft, easily-carved limestone but unfortunately it soon dissolves in our polluted atmosphere. On the other hand, the old Carboniferous limestone, which may be blue or pink and has numerous fossils, can last some hundreds of years.

The information on gravestones

Older inscriptions usually contain much more information than our modern stones, and this is because they were regarded as a person's most enduring memorial. Stones may give many generations of a family with dates and ages, and no other type of record has this continuity. Maiden names were commonly indicated: 'Ann Quinn alias Duffy' or 'Nancy Fitzsimons otherwise Ward', '. . . William Farrell. . . Also his wife Mary Courtney' or simply 'Mary Courtney Farrell'. The adults buried in a grave were usually listed on the headstone, but with the high infant mortality children might be recorded simply as 'Also three children who died in infancy'.

In the days when the vast majority of the population were farmers, occupation was usually recorded for the special few who were not. Many long departed trades have a special interest now, including cutlers, glovers, whitesmiths and a 'sugar baker', as well as others which were more common than now, such as the innkeeper, carpenter, tanner and seedsman. Many of these have the tools of

Left
Stone of red Castle Espie limestone dating from 1715, in Comber, Co. Down. This stone is full of fossils and was popular for fireplaces.

Opposite
The graveyard at Clonmacnois, beautifully situated on the banks of the River Shannon, contains a large number of cross-inscribed grave-slabs dating from the eighth to twelfth centuries.

their trade illustrated alongside.

The cause of death was not usually recorded on a gravestone in the past, any more than it is now, though there are isolated references to consumption, scarlatina and yellow fever (the victim died in South America) and one inscription reads: 'Thomas Simpson of Moira, surgeon, who fell a victim to malignant cholera on the 29th of December 1832 aged 32 years'. In this year there was one of the great epidemics of the century, which led to the creation of a 'cholera ground' for mass burials in several urban graveyards. Another who died for his flock, this time during the Great Famine was

'the Revd. Patrick McEvoy, P.P. of Kilbroney, Rosstrevor, who after a mission of 25 years in said parish, 16 of which being P.P., caught malignant typhus fever in the discharge of his sacerdotal functions, and after an illness of 9 days, departed this life on the 16th of October 1847.'

The commonest recorded cause of death is probably drowning and this one is typical of many all round the Irish coast: 'Here lieth the bodies of Killaly William Musgrave aged 19 years; and Aron Bellingham aged 27 years, mate, son and son-in-law to the late William Musgrave, Civil Engineer to the Port and Harbour of the City of Waterford, together with the Captain and the rest of the crew of that ill-fated vessel the Menapia of Waterford, which was lost on the rocks at St. John's Point on the night of the 13th December 1836, not one surviving to tell the melancholy tale.'

The most often quoted gravestone inscriptions are usually unverifiable, but there is the mysterious

> Lavery's Place.
> A singular man you were it's true
> Which made me chuse this place for you.

Perhaps the nearest to humour comes in the verse 'To the Memory of Denis McCabe, Fidler, who fell out of the St. Patrick's Barge belonging to Sr James Caldwell Bart and Count of Milan & was drown'd off this Point Agust ye 13th 1770.

> Beware ye Fidlers of ye Fidler's fate
> Nor tempt ye deep lest ye repent too late
> You ever have been deem'd to water foes
> Then shun ye lake till it with whisk'y flows
> On firm land only exercise your skill
> There you may play and safely drink yr fill.'

This stone is, in fact, the size and shape of a double-bass fiddle.

Much more common is the moralising type of inscription:

> Go home dear friends and cease from tears
> We must lie here till Christ appears
> Prepare for death while time you have
> There is no repentance in the grave.

It is a common practice in copying stones to ignore such passages as of no factual value, but they certainly help to paint in the background of the family.

The great events of Irish history are, of course, commemorated on gravestones, at least from the 1641 rising, and perhaps those of 1798 can now be quoted without bitterness. Comber church in County Down contains a memorial to three English soldiers killed at the battle of Saintfield, the only battle in the north in which the insurgents were victorious. Two of the latter are buried in Saintfield First Presbyterian churchyard, which actually includes part of the battlefield. Greyabbey has the grave of the Reverend James Porter, who was hanged outside his meeting house for giving general support to the United Irishmen, as indeed did most of his congregation. Particularly moving are the dialect verses to Archibel Wilson who was hanged at Bangor on 26 June 1798 after conviction for taking part in the rising:

> Morn not, deer friends, tho I'm no more
> Tho I was martred your eys before
> I am not dead but do sleep hear
> And yet once more I will apeer.
>
> That is when time will be no more
> When thel be judged who falsly sore
> And them that judged will judged be
> Whither just or on just, then thel see.

Slate gravestone to John Gaw
with well-carved lettering and
masonic symbols.

Particularly elaborate scenes on headstones are found in the south-east of Ireland, roughly from Wexford to Louth. They were probably derived from designs known as the 'Heraldry of Christ' in the seventeenth century and in their simplest form consist of a crucifixion surrounded by emblems of the passion, such as a hammer, nails, cock, robe, flail, spear, ladder. However, one in Glendalough in Wicklow has the three figures of the crucifixion, the centurion on his horse, the soldier thrusting his spear into the side of Christ, King David and his harp, the Virgin of the Rosary and a church with cross. The best of these are signed by Dennis Cullen, stonecutter, of Monaseed near Gorey, who flourished from 1760 to 1790. He even produced a design including a magnificent church and eighteenth-century carriage in a rural setting for the Protestant family of White in Hacketstown. Cullen's work spreads over several counties and presumably the more crude variants were executed by assistants or indeed followers into the next century. Most stones are unsigned, but the names of Miles Brien or O'Brien, James Byrne, Martin Kenny and David Doyle are all found in the Wicklow–Wexford area. Apart from the crucifixion, popular scenes include the nativity, the elevation of the cross and Christ in glory.

In Protestant areas the commonest type of

Purpere, deer friends, for that grate day
When death dis sumance you away
I will await ayoul with due care
In heven with joy to meet you there.

Gravestone art

The floreated crosses of Anglo-Norman coffin-lids were followed by coats of arms. These were plain representations but by the eighteenth century the helmet and mantling were used as an excuse for artistic flights of fancy. Such arms did not necessarily imply high pretensions, for they were often the arms of a whole named family rather than specific to an individual as is heraldically correct. The other common decorative features over the centuries have been symbols of mortality, such as a skull and crossbones, a bell, an angel in a wide variety of styles, or a weeping willow.

symbolism is the masonic compass and square, but this was frequently elaborated to include the sun, moon, stars and theorem of Pythagoras, with similar groupings for the memorial to prominent Orangemen. Alas, decorative art has almost entirely gone, but I have seen a modern rural stone with a tractor and plough and the text 'He ploughed a straight furow through land and through life.'

The conservation of graveyards

This has become an increasing problem over the past thirty years, particularly where money is available for tidying or job-creation schemes. In the past the old graveyard was either left untended or perhaps a man was paid to cut the grass with a scythe once or twice a year. Now, however, a strong lobby feels that it is unseemly to leave the graveyard as it is, though the labour costs of keeping the grass short and tidy round the stones are often too high. As a result, a movement has come about to level graveyards so that a mechanical mower can be used, and also to remove a proportion of gravestones and bushes to facilitate this.

The result, particularly in Northern Ireland, has been wholesale destruction of gravestones, so that the graveyard becomes more like a public park and loses both its character and its value as a record of local history. One of the worst examples is the old Shankill graveyard in Belfast where, out of approximately 1300 gravestones, 1000 were destroyed and most of the remainder were arranged round the walls. It must be said that this operation took place in 1960 and city councils might be less destructive now. However, every few years similar examples have occurred on a smaller scale, usually carried out by the Church of Ireland rector. The most recent example was the demolition

CHURCHES have a very special place in the Irish countryside as the focal points for the beliefs and aspirations of the various traditions within the community. Although distinctive styles of ecclesiastical architecture can be identified for different periods and in the different traditions, there is also a clear local character in church-building which results from the variety of materials used and the individual character of the relationship between church and landscape.

A Temple Benen, Inis Mór, Aran Islands: an early Christian single-chambered church built of large stone blocks.
B Taghmon, Co. Westmeath: this medieval church, 'beyond the Pale', felt the need of a fortified tower at one end to protect the clergy.
C Presbyterian church, Corboy, Co. Longford: mid-eighteenth-century church with paired entrances, allowing for the division of the sexes.
D An example of a standard 'Board of First Fruits' church, hundreds of which were built throughout Ireland in the early nineteenth century.
E Finny, Co. Galway: this Roman Catholic church of the early nineteenth century was built in a truly vernacular style which was typical of the period.
F Glenbrien, Enniscorthy, Co. Wexford: a fine example of a T-plan Roman Catholic barn-church.

Vault at Knockbreda churchyard, Co. Down, one of a classical group decorated with urns and pillars and erected in the late eighteenth century. It was demolished in 1986.

of a vault in Knockbreda graveyard near Belfast, the climax of a year of removal of all grassy mounds and railings, and the addition of concrete paths.

It should be possible to convince people that it is not necessary for everything to be neat and tidy to be beautiful. The charm of old graveyards lies in the blend of grey stones, church walls and an irregular landscape of trees and bushes. If the grass can be kept short, so much the better, but this can often be

done by voluntary labour if someone gives the lead. Certainly gravestones are the oldest written records of many of the inhabitants of Ireland. We must give their preservation top priority, and, as an additional consideration, we should preserve the character of the old graveyard as a place in which to wander about, contemplate our latter end, and learn about the past inhabitants of our particular area.

RICHARD SAMUEL JESSOP CLARKE was born in Belfast in 1929. He is Professor of Clinical Anaesthetics at Queen's University Belfast and Consultant Anaesthetist at the Royal Victoria Hospital. He has been interested in his family history since childhood and claims roots in most counties of Ireland. He took up copying gravestones in 1962 to develop a broader interest in local history and to get into the fresh air. The Ulster Historical Foundation, of which he is a trustee, has published twenty-five of his books on gravestone inscriptions.

POLLUTION
Roger Goodwillie

Pollution is the addition of anything to water or air that changes its natural qualities adversely. The concept therefore has a subjective dimension – what is pollution to a person wanting to drink some water is bounty and goodness to a waterweed growing in it. Talk of a 'dead' river or a 'dead' lake is usually highly inaccurate. Unless chemical poisons are involved, there will be abundant life present in polluted water, in the form of bacteria or fungi if nothing else.

Pollution eats up the oxygen supply

Water pollution is the result of waste material reaching a river or lake. In Ireland it is usually waste organic matter, that is biological material like sewage, silage effluent or whey. Everything organic eventually decays: there are fungi or bacteria that will grow on it and break it down to the simplest of chemicals.

Therefore the quantity of a material entering water is critical. Rivers and streams are subjected to leaf-fall every year in the autumn and they can cope with this form of 'natural' pollution. The leaves are slow to break down and many reach the sea before they have been fully colonised by fungi. Simpler substances may be much more significant, as they provide an immediate food source for millions of bacteria. The liquor that seeps out

277

of a new silage heap is particularly lethal. It is immediately seized on by bacteria which multiply enormously. They require oxygen for growth and they may use up all the oxygen that is dissolved in the water, causing the death of other organisms, especially fish. A fish kill results for this reason, not because silage effluent itself is particularly poisonous.

Bacteria as they grow release simple chemicals into the water like nitrates and phosphates and these are also contained in sewage and animal slurries. Water plants are literally fertilised by such chemicals and grow numerous. Algae are the quickest to react and the water may turn green with their floating cells or the bottom may be blanketed by their green strands. Plants produce oxygen during the day but at night they consume it. Therefore they too may cause the oxygen level to fall so low as to kill fish. Measurements are taken just before dawn to record how bad a river is.

Organic pollution can, then, be tolerated by a river if it comes in small enough quantities or as material that takes some time to decay. But this is far from the case. The inputs to our rivers today are becoming more concentrated and larger. Farms are growing bigger and more intensive, manure is handled as a slurry which can drain into natural watercourses, and large numbers of animals kept together may produce as much sewage as a small town.

Industrial pollution

Food-handling industries like creameries grow larger as do our inland towns. The major waste introduced into our rivers is from industrial sources. Effluent from the larger plants is now often handled in treatment works but these have the effect in all but a few cases of releasing nutrients back

into the water, which may cause significant algal blooms.

Looked at in general terms it seems that about 80 per cent of our rivers can be thought of as unpolluted, about 15 per cent are moderately polluted and 5 per cent seriously so. The last figure has tended to drop in recent years, as trouble spots are eliminated, but the middle figure has correspondingly risen. Practically all lakes in populated regions have become enriched and their fauna of aquatic organisms changed.

The incidence of chemical pollution is relatively low because of our low level of industrial development. Mining wastes occur in a few locations and since many metals are highly toxic this can be a serious problem in such rivers as the Avoca and the Kilmastullagh.

Pesticides and herbicides

Pollution by agricultural chemicals is always present but nowadays the chemicals themselves are less harmful than in the past.

The very stable organochlorine pesticides were the most serious, for they can build up in the soil and in wild animals exposed to them. Such chemicals as DDT and dieldrin caused large population declines in game birds and in predatory birds like the peregrine falcon. This is because the predators accumulated many small doses from their prey which built up to adversely affect their mechanism for making shell. Their eggs were broken frequently, therefore, and no young birds reared. Insecticides now are of shorter-lived but no less lethal chemicals, which must destroy a lot of non-target animals. Herbicides too have done away with many weeds to the advantage of arable crops, but to the disadvantage of wildlife: the partridge is a well-known case, its chicks being dependent on insects living on various weeds.

Air pollution

Air pollution consists of two parts, the visible smoke made of soot particles derived from oil, coal or turf and the invisible gases like

sulphur and nitrogen oxides which have more serious or certainly less obvious effects. Smoke particles clog up plants – and lungs – preventing proper gas exchange. Sulphur dioxide by contrast affects cell processes directly by killing cells.

In the study of air pollution and indeed many other sorts, 'indicator organisms' have been most useful. These are animals or plants that respond in a consistent way to pollution. Lichens and leaf yeasts are particularly useful in examining air pollution. Leaf yeasts are tiny wild yeasts that normally inhabit leaf surfaces. They are killed off rapidly by pollution incidents also but can reinvade the leaves. Lichens respond more slowly and each species differs in its susceptibility to sulphur dioxide. They can thus be used for mapping the severity of air pollution from the worst areas which are effectively lichen deserts to the best, where large leafy species still survive.

Lichens as well as mechanical air samplers have shown quite severe pollution in Dublin on occasions and significant levels also in most other cities. Cold frosty weather traps smoke-filled air at ground level and blankets the city.

When sulphur and nitrogen oxides escape from this blanket or are released at high levels by tall chimneys they may be carried many miles in the atmosphere before being brought down again in rainfall as acid rain. Rainfall in Ireland as well as throughout the northern hemisphere has become significantly more acidic in the last forty years and has begun to affect the environment. It is particularly harmful on naturally acid soils where it adds to the leaching effect and washes chemicals, both nutrients and aluminium, from the soil. The released aluminium is toxic to fish as well as to plant roots and this in turn affects forest trees. It works in conjunction with the leaf-damaging ozone, produced largely by vehicles. Acid rain falls in Ireland, particularly when east winds bring continental air in our direction, but so far toxic effects have not been shown. We are very fortunate in having a low level of industrialisation, relatively few vehicles, predominantly westerly winds and a lot of limestone country, but it is without doubt a problem that needs to be watched.

INDEX

ACKNOWLEDGEMENTS

The publishers wish to thank the following organisations and individuals for their assistance in the preparation of this book, for photographs and other illustrations and/or for advice with regard to the text:

Michael Barry; Liam Blake; Bord Fáilte; R.A. Browne; Gwen Buchanan; Jim Busby; Bill Carter; Central Fisheries Board; Richard Clarke; Wm Collins Sons and Co. Ltd; Moira Concannon; Michael Craig; Margaret Cruickshank; Cahal Dallat; Department of Folklore, UCD; Department of Geography, QUB; P. Ditch; Declan Doogue; Dermott Dunbar; Wendy Dunbar; Terry Dunne; ERA, Dublin; John Feehan; Tim Fogg; Forest Service NI; Alan Gailey; Michael Gibbons; Geological Survey, Dublin; Ruth Heard; Michael Herity; Historic Monuments and Buildings Branch, Department of the Environment NI; Linen Hall Library, Belfast; Nigel McDowell; Kenneth McNally; John McSorley; MAPTEC, Dublin; Meteorological Service, Dublin; Richard T. Mills; N.C. Mitchel; Frank Mitchell; Professor Paul Mohr, Department of Geology, UCG; Richard Nairn; National Museum, Dublin; National Trust in Northern Ireland; Northern Ireland Tourist Board; Office of Public Works, Dublin; Ordnance Survey, Dublin; Norah Owens; Rex Roberts; Tim Robinson; Royal Irish Academy; Slide File; Roy Tomlinson; Ulster Folk and Transport Museum; Ulster Museum; University of Cambridge; Tony Waltham; Janet Wilson.

The illustrations on pages 172 and 173 are reproduced from *Field Guide to the Animals of Britain* and on pages 175, 176 and 177 from *Field Guide to the Butterflies and Other Insects of Britain*, both published by Reader's Digest Ltd, London.

The opinions expressed are strictly those of the authors and are not attributable to any institution or organisation to which they may be attached.